Managing Serials

FOUNDATIONS IN LIBRARY AND INFORMATION SCIENCE, Volume 35

Editors: Thomas W. Leonhardt, *Director of Library Technical Services, Bizzell Memorial Library, University of Oklahoma*

Murray S. Martin, *University Librarian and Professor of Library Science Emeritus, Tufts University*

Foundations in Library and Information Science

Edited by **Thomas W. Leonhardt**, *Director of Library Technical Services, Bizzell Memorial Library, University of Oklahoma* and **Murray S. Martin,** *University Librarian and Professor of Library Science Emeritus, Tufts University*

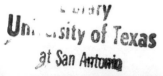

Managing Serials

by: MARCIA TUTTLE
Head, Serials Department
University of North Carolina
at Chapel Hill Library

With Chapters by: LUKE SWINDLER
Social Science Bibliographer
University of North Carolina
at Chapel Hill Library

FRIEDA B. ROSENBERG
Head, Serials Cataloging
University of North Carolina
at Chapel Hill Library

 JAI PRESS INC.

Greenwich, Connecticut   *London, England*

Library of Congress Cataloging-in-Publication Data
Tuttle, Marcia.
  Managing serials / with chapters by Luke Swindler,
Frieda B. Rosenberg.
    p.   cm. — (Foundations in library and information science;
v. 35)
  Includes bibliographical references and index.
  ISBN 0-7623-0100-7
  1. Serials control systems—United States.   2. Newspaper and
periodical libraries—United States.   I. Swindler, Luke.
II. Rosenberg, Frieda B.   III. Title.   IV. Series.
Z692.S5T88   1996
025.1'732—dc20   96-24349
                                                             CIP

Copyright © 1996 JAI PRESS INC.
55 Old Post Road No. 2
Greenwich, Connecticut 06836

JAI PRESS LTD.
38 Tavistock Street
Covent Garden
London, WC2E 7PB
England

ISBN: 0-7623-0100-7
Library of Congress Catalog Number: 96-24349

Manufactured in the United States of America

CONTENTS

LIST OF FIGURES

LIST OF TABLES

LIST OF APPENDIXES

Chapter 6

PREFACE

HISTORY OF THE BOOK

This book originated in the mid-1970s in the Library School Education Committee of the Serials Section, Resources and Technical Services Division, American Library Association. Each committee member was to write one chapter. The purpose was to provide a text for library school courses on serials management, as an encouragement to library science faculty and administrators to include a serials course in their curricula. The committee itself had been created in response to practicing serials librarians' feelings that their formal professional education had not prepared them adequately for responsibilities in serials librarianship.

Because ALA work is volunteer work and because committee membership changes, the serials management book was never written. However, JAI Press had promised to produce it, had advertised it, and had orders in hand. Thus, other authors took on the project and *Introduction to Serials Management* appeared in January 1983. Since that time serials management has changed significantly, thanks in large part to automation of serials functions, the increased significance of serial literature, pressures resulting from rising subscription prices, and expanding communication among librarians, publishers, and serials vendors.

This book, based on *Introduction to Serials Management* (JAI Press), is written from the perspective of the librarian who works entirely or largely with serially-published literature. Its primary audience is other serials librarians, especially those with little experience with serials. Although not specifically a text, the book can be used as such or as supplementary reading in library science courses. The authors have kept in mind the secondary audience of subscription agents and publishers of serials for the library market who want to learn about library serials management.

ARRANGEMENT OF THE BOOK

Not only has serials management changed since 1983, but the authors have also changed in that they are several years older and have broadened their knowledge and experience in serials management. They have added several new chapters to the book reflecting this experience and the increased awareness of serials managers of the necessity of working intelligently with their suppliers. Management, automation, and standards are given their own chapters in *Managing Serials*. The former acquisitions chapter has been divided into two chapters. Finally, serials publishing is treated in three new chapters, covering serial publications, serials pricing, and publisher/vendor/librarian relationships.

AUTHORS' BIAS

There is an unavoidable academic library bias in this book, because the authors are employed by a university library and because research libraries are most likely to have serials departments and staff members working exclusively with serials and serials related services. Yet, each author has made an effort to remember that librarians other than those in academic libraries work with serials and to consider differences that may occur.

PHILOSOPHY OF AUTOMATED VS. MANUAL

In 1983 serials automation was just beginning to appear. A few library administrators felt able to take risks in this area, and vendors of commercial automated systems were tackling serials functions. Thus, *Introduction to Serials Management* mentioned automated processing but, except for cataloging, it concentrated on manual operations. Today many more libraries are at least partly automated with respect to serials; consequently this book emphasizes online serials management over the manual variety.

BIBLIOGRAPHY

A companion volume to *Managing Serials* will be an extensive annotated bibliography of articles, books, and reports on serials and serials work, as well as the primary tools used by serials librarians. With 649 items listed in the Annotated Bibliography included in *Introduction to Serials Management* and nearly that many in a supplement published in volume one of *Advances in Serials Management* (JAI Press, 1986), together with the vastly increased volume of writing on all the topics within the scope of this book, the bibliography has to be issued separately. It supersedes the two compilations noted above and will add materials published through the end of 1996.

ACKNOWLEDGEMENTS

The authors thank all their co-workers at the University of North Carolina at Chapel Hill Library, 1968-1995, for their support and patience, and also for reviewing manuscripts and answering questions. Thanks go also to families and colleagues elsewhere who have reviewed chapters and continued to ask: "When will the book be out?"

Marcia Tuttle
Luke Swindler
Frieda B. Rosenberg
October 18, 1995

Chapter 1

THE NATURE OF SERIALS

WHAT IS A SERIAL?

What is a serial? To set the scene, here is what one serials librarian said in 1974:

> Almost all books are published by sophisticated, experienced, well-financed professionals who understand their self-interest in as well as their customers' need for bibliographic consistency. Problems abound, but the standard is well-defined and usually adhered to. On the other hand, any knucklehead with a typewriter and access to an offset press can publish a serial.[1]

Substitute "microcomputer" for "typewriter" and replace "offset press" with "laser printer," and the statement is as true today as when David Taylor wrote it. Using the Internet, one can publish a serial with very little effort and perhaps no capital expenditure, just the value of one's time.

To most librarians and library science students the word *serial* evokes a definite positive or negative feeling; few responses are neutral. Experience, personality characteristics, and hearsay all influence the nature of one's attitude toward serials and serials management. Serials work is full of problems, because the serial itself is often a problem. It is the problems, though, that make working with serial publications challenging and rewarding. While one resolves a series of disguised title changes or manages to reinstate a subscription to an English professor's favorite literary magazine, patrons are bringing apparently meaningless citations for identification and location, another subscription has stopped coming, and a periodical suddenly appears in a variety of formats unsuitable for binding. The work is not seasonal, it does not end, and it is never dull.

Why is a serial likely to be a problem? Is it because the library orders once and issues or volumes continue to arrive? Is it because journals appear in pieces and someone must gather and bind them? This chapter introduces serial publications, defines them, and looks at some of their unique qualities.

1

DEFINITION OF A SERIAL

The first step in developing an understanding of serials and serials management is defining the concept of the serial. This is not a simple matter! Through the years, as this section illustrates, no standard definition has evolved. Davinson captures the essence of the problem:

> It would be pleasant to be able to supply a short, neat, all-embracing, universally-accepted definition. It is not possible to do so. To dip even the most tentative of toes into the definitional water is to risk drowning in a sea of conflicting interpretations and variations in terminology.[2]

Nevertheless, it is necessary to make an effort to define *serial* and related terms, because it is only by agreeing upon the meaning of these words that discussion is possible. For example, when the government or a professional association asks for the number of serial orders, the responding librarian must know exactly what the organization means by *serial*. To get optimum benefit from and maintain the integrity of a union list of periodicals, the compiler and the users must define *periodical* in the same way.

There have been many written definitions of *serial*. Clara Brown said that serials "contain two ingredients: they are numbered; they intend to continue for an indefinite period."[3] In contrast, in his standard work, *Serial Publications*, Andrew Osborn had a twenty-one page chapter entitled "Definition of a Serial."[4] A succession of written statements over the years has attempted to define serials and related terms for general purposes. Lynn S. Smith reproduced several of them in *A Practical Approach to Serials Cataloging*.[5] There are also many definitions for special purposes: a union list, a catalog code, or an annual compilation of statistics. However frustrating it is to encounter multiple definitions, it is worse when a union list or a statistics form provides no definition at all, for then there is no way to determine the scope of the list, and its validity is questionable.

Here is Osborn's own practical definition:

> The elements which, by and large, constitute a serial publication are (1) a name and (2) either periodical or serial numbering of the successive parts of a work which appear under the original name or a later name. The qualification "by and large" is significant because at times one element—even both—can be lacking.[6]

Likewise, he says, both elements can be present and the title may still be treated as a book. At the other extreme, the National Agricultural Library once defined *serial* as: "Any title issued in parts, which is incomplete in the library collection."[7] A serials acquisitions librarian might define a serial as anything that is ordered once and keeps coming.

In North America, *serial* has traditionally been the term encompassing all types of continuing publications except those having a planned conclusion, such as an author's complete works. In the United Kingdom, until recently *serial* was a specific term, comparable to what Americans know as *periodical*. British librarians used *periodical* as the broad term. Davinson comments on the confusion:

> In the principal British discussion of definitional problems, David Grenfell elects for the term periodical.* The term "serial" is becoming unpopular and a more comprehensive interpretation is being given to the term "periodical."
>
> It should be noted that Grenfell carefully covers himself by entitling his book *Periodicals and Serials*!
>
> *David Grenfell, *Periodicals and Serials: Their Treatment in Special Libraries*. (London: ASLIB, 2nd ed., 1965).[8]

Thus, the scope of titles included in the *British Union Catalogue of Periodicals* is virtually the same as the *Union List of Serials in Libraries of the United States and Canada*. Publication of the second edition of the *Anglo-American Cataloguing Rules* (AACR2) in 1978 may have resolved the longstanding controversy. AACR2 uses *serial* for all continuing publications and has dropped the word *periodical*.

No standard definition of *serial* exists, but the following statement from AACR2R is close to a standard definition for English-speaking librarians:

> A publication in any medium issued in successive parts bearing numerical or chronological designations and intended to be continued indefinitely. Serials include periodicals; newspapers; annuals (reports, yearbooks, etc.); the journals, memoirs, proceedings, transactions, etc., of societies; and numbered monographic series.[9]

Giving credit in 1980 to the AACR2 wording as "easily the best library definition of a serial that has yet been devised," Osborn adds, "It is still not scientifically sound in the sense that it can be applied to settle all doubtful cases." He then lists eleven qualifications that need to be added. Briefly, these are:

1. The intention to continue indefinitely cannot always be known or determined in the first instance, particularly when a publication originates in a foreign country....
2. With the coming of first-issue cataloging the problem of intention has become somewhat more problematic....
3. Multiple authorship is held by some librarians to be an essential characteristic of a serial (it is not mentioned in the AACR2 definition, however)....

4. Author series, that is, successions of works by one author but held together by a serial name and numbering, are generally not treated in libraries as serials but as collections of an author's works. The expression "author series" does not occur in AACR2.
5. There are genuine periodicals, written by one or two authors...which may reappear in simple book form....[T]hey are usually treated as books....
6. Single issues of a newspaper or periodical, even a whole periodical, may be republished in simple monographic format....
7. Some publications which are not intrinsically serials are "held together" by artificial numbering schemes....
8. Certain nonserials...have all the earmarks of serials while they are current....
9. There is a gray area for proceedings of recurrent and international conferences which may be treated as monographs or serials....
10. Continuations, provisional serials, and pseudoserials...may or may not fit in with the AACR2 definition....
11. The most experienced serial librarians cannot always tell whether an item is a serial or a nonserial when it first appears....[10]

The AACR2R definition of *serial* is an expansion of Charles A. Cutter's 1904 statement that a serial is "a publication issued in successive parts, usually at regular intervals and continued indefinitely."[11] During the intervening years the qualities of a serial were sharpened to include "under a distinctive title"[12] and "a publication not issued by a government agency,"[13] to suit the purposes of the definer. The latter qualification limited the scope of the 1927 *Union List of Serials in Libraries of the United States and Canada* and is not generally accepted.

The thread running through all the definitions is the continuing nature of the publication, the quality that gives serials the tendency to cause problems, to change, to haunt. The ongoing nature of serials also makes them a fascinating format to work with.

Types of Serials

Serials are divisible, based on intended frequency of publication, into periodicals and nonperiodical serials. *Periodicals* are magazines, journals and newspapers; all other serials—annuals, conference proceedings, monographic series—are *nonperiodical serials*. As with the term *serial* itself, there is not general agreement about the qualities of types of serials. All the same, Table 1 separates the various terms and gives their definitions as used in this book.

A *periodical*, also called journal or magazine, is intended to appear regularly and more often than once a year (although the U.S. Postal Service stipulates

Table 1.1. Types of Serials

Type	Definition
Serial	Publication issued in successive parts intended to be continued indefinitely
Periodical	Numbered serial intended to appear regularly in parts and more often than once a year; usually collection of articles by several persons; usually paid annually, in advance
Journal	Scholarly periodical
Magazine	Nonscholarly or popular periodical
Newspaper	Daily or weekly periodical concentrating on current events, either in general or on a specific topic
Nonperiodical Serial	Usually appears in complete bibliographic volumes; issued either less often than once a year or irregularly; usually not paid in advance
Annual	Issued once a year; not paid in advance; not issued in parts; may be collection of articles
Monographic Series	Each volume is complete work with own author/title; may or may not be numbered
Provisional Serial	Nonserial base publication with serially issued updating volumes
Pseudoserial	Frequently reissued and revised monograph
Continuation	Issued in parts, but has planned conclusion

that a periodical must appear at least three times a year to qualify for second class postage rates). Many definitions stop after categorizing by frequency, but others go on to specify one or more of the following characteristics:

1. A periodical carries numbering, usually of primary and secondary order (e.g., volume 7, number 4), so that the collected parts comprise a whole.
2. A periodical is a collection of articles by several persons.
3. A periodical is paid once a year, in advance.

Thus, this book uses *periodical* to define certain types of serials: journals, magazines, and newspapers. These three terms have their own definitions. In brief, a *journal* is a scholarly periodical; a *magazine* is a popular periodical; and a *newspaper* is a daily or weekly periodical concentrating on current events (either generally or on a specific topic). All three, however, are both periodicals and serials.

Nonperiodical serials appear either less often than twice a year or irregularly, usually in complete bibliographic volumes. These serials may or may not be numbered, and they typically are not paid before publication. Nonperiodical serials include annuals, conference proceedings, occasional publications, and monographic series; in short, any title intended to continue indefinitely that is not a periodical.

Some definitions of the term "periodical" include *annual serials*. From an acquisitions standpoint this makes sense because annuals are paid once a year, as are journals and newspapers. However, although they often are collections of articles, annuals are not issues to be collected into a bound volume, nor are they usually paid in advance. One may make a practical distinction between periodicals and nonperiodical serials based on predictability of publication and of annual price. It is rather easy to predict the cost of journals, newspapers, and annuals, because they are invoiced once a year. One cannot always predict the annual cost of nonperiodical serials that are irregular in publication, for the number of pieces appearing in a year can vary widely. Some nonperiodical serials have a regular frequency of one volume every three to five years, so the librarian cannot account for their costs on a yearly basis. *Annuals* overlap the two major divisions of serials; this book treats them as nonperiodical serials.

One type of serial, the *monographic series* (in which each volume is a complete work with its own author and title), could be considered simply a group of monographs, especially if the publisher does not number the series. The librarian has several options for acquiring and cataloging monographs in series. Choices are often determined by whether one wishes to acquire all volumes in the series or just those of particular relevance to the collection. Whether these works are considered a series composed of monographs or a group of monographs that happen to have a covering series title, catalogers need to treat both aspects of the publication—monographic and serial— because citations are sure to appear in the literature in both forms, and patrons will request these volumes both by author/title and by series.

Some continuing publications are not serials and do not fit the AACR2 definition. However, librarians often treat them as serials, because serials processing is the most efficient means of handling them. Osborn names these publications "near-serials" and describes three types: (1) *provisional serials*, a nonserial base publication with serially issued updating volumes (encyclopedias having annual supplements); (2) *pseudoserials*, "A frequently-reissued and revised publication which quite properly may be, and on first publication generally is, considered to be a monograph" (*World Almanac*); and (3) *continuations*, works issued in parts, but having a planned conclusion (foreign dictionaries published in fascicles).[14] Although these materials are not true serials, serial acquisition and, perhaps, cataloging treatment simplifies their processing. Thus, many libraries acquire and process them through the serials unit.

SIGNIFICANCE OF SERIALS IN
THE DISSEMINATION OF INFORMATION

Periodicals are expensive to buy, difficult to store, awkward to use, and not particularly efficient as vehicles for transmitting information. The patterns of bibliographic control for periodicals are uneven from country to country and from subject to subject. Despite this they continue to be perhaps the most significant element in the pattern of recorded knowledge other than books itself— and even that proposition would be debatable in certain circumstances....The fact of massive numbers of periodicals existing (and it does not seem possible to be specific about how many do eixst [sic]) tends to hide an undoubted fact that relatively few of those which do exist are of real significance.[15]

This gloomy assessment notwithstanding, the role of serial publications in disseminating information for research or for pleasure has grown in recent decades. In many disciplines, especially the sciences, serials have long been the primary means of communication because of the relative speed with which human beings must and can share information. Scientific researchers have preferred to publish in serials both to advance knowledge and to be the first investigator to document specific research. Scholars in the social sciences and the humanities have come to rely increasingly on serials to convey the results of their endeavors. Serial publication is timely; the information appears far more rapidly than in a monograph. Further, it is easier to write and publish a journal article than a monograph; the process is less complicated, less risky.

Thus, one communicates more rapidly through serials, particularly periodicals, than through monographs. Newsmagazines and newspapers are the only feasible way to transmit current events in print. Annual reviews are an appropriate way to summarize yearly events in general or in a specific field of knowledge. Magazines are just as significant a means of discussing developments about hobbies and other interests; the devotee keeps informed regularly by the publication. A serial may be worthwhile even when the library does not retain it. For example, the photocopied or otherwise rapidly-produced newsletter is perhaps the fastest means of printed communication among persons having a common interest.

Producing a journal issue is not ordinarily so complicated a project as publishing a monograph, because the journal is geared to regular publication of article-length contributions. Journals have long been the vehicles for scholars to disseminate information to their colleagues before it became obsolete, just as newsmagazines aim to inform readers about current events while the events are still current. Especially good for rapid distribution of scientific information have been publications limited to "letters" and "communications"—brief notices or announcements of hypotheses and results of experiments, about which a scholar may request criticism and/or supporting evidence. However, with so many scholars, so much pressure to publish, and so high a cost of periodical publishing, even for "communications" there is often a backlog of papers at highly regarded journals. An author may have to wait more than two years after acceptance by the editor to have work published. This situation leads both to launching new journals (both print and electronic) to take care of the overflow and to charging fees to authors. The best journals are refereed; that is, anonymous submissions by authors' colleagues (perhaps editorial board members) evaluate anonymous submissions and may accept, reject, or return them for more work and polish before publication. This practice, known as "peer review," upholds the high quality of these journals and bestows extra prestige on work they publish; however, it means even more delay in communicating scholarly work to others in the field.

Today producers and readers are questioning the appropriateness of the traditional journal as a rapid means of communication. Electronic communication, usually available at no charge to the individual in educational and research institutions, is replacing the letter and the telephone. Why, some say, should it not replace the scholarly journal? As electronic technology has accelerated the scholar's research, so it has spread the results of this research, as well as news about current events or any other topic, so rapidly that the printed journal or magazine now seems quite slow. Within the world of scholarship electronic bulletin boards, electronic newsletters, and increasingly, electronic refereed journals are becoming commonplace as the means of communicating research results and research in progress. Scholars in some disciplines use the printed journal only to authenticate their research. Most recently, large commercial publishers (often in partnership with universities) have begun to experiment with the distribution of their printed journals in electronic format. The electronic medium continues to mature, and its long-term impact on printed serials remains to be seen.

COMPLEX QUALITIES OF SERIALS

In the late 1970s, during heated discussion of the proposed second edition of the *Anglo-American Cataloging Rules*, Dorothy Glasby of the Library of Congress asserted that "Serials are different!" That straightforward statement about a complex form of communication contains the essence of serials librarianship. Serials differ from other library resources in several ways that make them particularly challenging for librarians and readers.

Change

It is said that the only constant of serials is change. Serials change title, change size, change format, change publisher, and of course, change price.

Their frequency changes, their scope changes; they merge or split; they suspend publication for varying lengths of time. Retired serials librarian Clara Brown lists eighteen such things that can happen to serial titles,[16] and her list is probably not exhaustive. While change of publisher and size are sometimes simply nuisances to librarians, a change in title or format creates a new publication and requires the closing of old records and the creating of new ones. Thus, change is expensive to the library and confusing to the library staff and patrons.

The most obvious and expensive change is a title change. For several years *Title Varies*, a serials librarianship newsletter of the 1970s, awarded its "Worst Title Change of the Year" prizes at the American Library Association annual meeting. "Winners" included publishers Williams and Wilkins, which changed *International Journal of Obstetrics and Gynecology* to *International Journal of Gynecology and Obstetrics* and a multiple winner, the Economic Intelligence Unit, Ltd., which changed about one hundred related titles beginning *Quarterly Economic Review: [Country]* to *QER: [Country]*, then to *Quarterly Economic Review of [Country]*, and then to *Country Report [Country]*. These actions by publishers appear frivolous, but they also reflect the publisher's ignorance of (or disregard for) organization and access in libraries.

To a cataloger a title change means altering records. With automation the changes are not so many as with manual files, but still the work is expensive. In serial acquisitions, one must update the receipt record to reflect the new title; in public service, someone must change the shelf label and move current issues to the new location. In a manual serials department filled with single-purpose files, someone must change other records: binding specifications, current receipts lists, vendor file, and so on. Automation helps, but it does not eliminate the problem. Implementation of an integrated automated system also raises the question of which staff member will be responsible for changing library records.

Besides the expense of changing serial records, there is a high risk of losing early issues of the new title, because publishers do not always mention the old title or the title change on the cover, where check-in assistants look. Issues of the new title may seem to be unsolicited gifts; serials personnel may route them to selectors for consideration for purchase, or they may even discard them. Unnoticed title changes may exact a public relations cost, by denying patrons access if issues are missing, if records become obsolete, or if no staff member has noticed the title change.

A title change in itself is bad enough, but a title change can be a symptom of other changes. Several years ago the *British Journal of Marketing* changed title to *European Journal of Marketing*. Then in 1973, the publisher changed the title again to *Journal of General Management* and appointed a new editor, sending the following memorandum to subscribers:

Dear Sir,

As a subscriber to European Journal of Marketing, you will be interested in our future plans for the journal.

Today, virtually all established institutions are in the process of being reorganised. In industry, too, extensive reorganisation is taking place. Generally speaking, these changes, as they affect top executives, involve a "total" approach to management.

To meet this broader approach, readers will be better served by a new journal that we shall be publishing, the Journal of General Management. This will incorporate the European Journal of Marketing. Your existing subscription to the European Journal of Marketing will be transferred to the new journal, the first issue of which will be published in November.

You may rest assured that the Journal of General Management will still contain articles on marketing of the same high standard as before. In addition, we think that you will find it of more practical use to you with articles on finance, policy making, production, and other subjects that must be included in the long-term strategy of any company.

Yours faithfully,

The former editor selected a new publisher and continued *European Journal of Marketing*. Subscribers received the following announcement dated November 24, 1973 on the new publisher's letterhead:

Gordon Wills v Mercury House Publications Limited
(1973 W.No. 3270)

You may have heard recently that *European Journal of Marketing* is to be incorporated by its present publishers in their new magazine JGM and that your subscription is to be transferred to that magazine.

I am now writing to inform you that the *European Journal of Marketing* is *also* to continue publishing in its present form under my direction although through different publishers. If you would be interested in taking out a subscription to this magazine we should be pleased to arrange this if you write to me at the above address.

Yours sincerely,

Professor Gordon Wills

The text of this letter is as mutually agreed by counsel for the Defendants and the Plaintiff November 6th 1973.

Thus, each journal claimed to be the successor of the original periodical and solicited renewal orders. Most libraries probably took the easy course and subscribed to both journals. Both titles have survived, but one wonders what happened that caused the unfriendly divorce.

Several other types of serials change can disrupt library processing and patron access. These changes also add to the expense of acquiring and retaining serials. A journal may change size. In the late 1970s, some publishers reduced the size of journal pages, trying to hold subscription prices for a year or so longer. Librarians had to change their binding specifications. The subscriber may receive less for the price paid if there is a frequency or size reduction, so it is well to notice any such change in material received and alert appropriate selectors. On occasion, a publisher has issued a journal, usually a literary magazine, in a variety of sizes and creative formats. In some of these instances it is impossible to bind the title, and issues require special treatment and storage in a box or portfolio, increasing the risk of loss or theft.

At times a journal moves from one publisher to another. This change creates the possibility of subscriber records being discarded or misplaced, resulting in the library's having to claim or try to purchase missing issues, which may not be available. As with other changes, a change of publisher has implications for the library. It is not unusual for a journal's price to increase when a new publisher takes over. The content and the editorial philosophy of the journal may be different with the new publisher. For these reasons library serials personnel are necessarily participants in collection development, as they identify and make known changes in journals.

A library's commitment to a serial lasts, as long as the publication continues, until someone acts to end it; in this continuing nature of the publication and the library purchase order there is much opportunity for change.

Ongoing, In Theory

By definition a serial is a publication that has no planned conclusion; it is intended to continue. The ongoing nature of serials carries significant implications for the library. Both journals that have appeared for decades under the same title and those that change title often have an impact on library operations and costs.

Placing a continuing serial order involves the library in a long-term commitment, while the acquisition of a monograph is a one-time transaction: the book is selected, searched and verified, ordered, received, paid, cataloged, and sent to the stacks. On the other hand, a subscription to a journal or a standing order for a nonperiodical serial arrives regularly until someone— librarian, subscription agent, or publisher—acts to end the relationship. A currently published serial is a living, growing, often multiplying, occasionally ailing, and sometimes dying publication.

The continuation of a serial depends upon many factors. It must have substantive matter; an editor to solicit, select, and organize its contents; a person or a company to produce it; subscribers to purchase it; and ideally, readers to use it. All these contributions occur not once, but again and again, indefinitely. In ordering a serial the library makes a financial commitment, a spatial commitment, a bibliographic commitment, and a public service commitment. One has to employ staff to process incoming serials, provide space to house the materials, and supply funds to bind them or purchase microform replacements. Trained staff members must be available to provide service to patrons seeking access to the contents of serials.

Most obviously, there is the financial commitment. By placing a continuing order, the library agrees to pay each year's subscription price (including surcharges for added pages and other price increases), unless it cancels the order. Likewise, the publisher agrees to supply the library with a product in exchange for the payment. Whatever the economic climate, subscription prices rarely decrease. On the contrary, most journals increase in price every year.

Subscription price is not the only financial commitment the library undertakes. Libraries usually retain serials either as bound volumes or in microform, both of which add to the cost of their acquisition. Just as subscription prices increase, so do binding and microform charges. Many journals, particularly scientific titles, are growing rapidly in size, leading not only to higher purchase price but also to more volumes to bind or more microform to buy. The economic and technological conditions are right for libraries to begin to acquire and/or retain serials in electronic format and to change from a policy of ownership alone to one of shared access.

Serials occupy shelf space, and as the bulk of a journal grows, so does its need for space. One may also view the space commitment as a financial commitment, for library space costs money.

Finally, there is the bibliographic commitment. Usually catalogers add serials to a database or a card catalog. These records occupy space. When the title changes, AACR2R directs that old records should be closed and new ones created. The cataloging process has its own associated costs.

Thus, the subscription price of the serial is only the first of several financial commitments a librarian must consider. Journal cancellation projects conducted in times of financial stringency might also count among the resulting savings these less apparent costs of owning serials.

Indirect Access

Access to cataloged books is direct; patrons locate monographs through the library's public catalog. They look up author, title, or subject; they write or print the call number; and they go to the shelf and find the book. Access to serial literature is indirect. Patrons often locate serial titles in the public catalog. If not, tasteful signs direct them to a book or microfiche catalog of serials. Many libraries, particularly small collections, do not classify journals, but shelve them alphabetically. However, locating the library's run of a periodical is not the point of the search. Bibliographic tools used to find books are rarely adequate for serials, although it is becoming feasible for a library to offer access to journal contents through its online public access catalog. In the great majority of libraries the patron seeking journal article information still must use an intermediate finding tool such as a periodical index or a separate online bibliographic database to identify the desired article. Only then is the patron ready to go to the public catalog and look up the journal's call number or go to an alphabetical periodicals section of the stacks.

Difficulty of Communication about Serials

From the foregoing discussion it is obvious that working with serial literature, whether as librarian, supplier, or user, can lead to difficulties in communication. Definitions of "serial" and of the various types of serials vary among librarians, publishers, vendors, and readers. Effective communication requires standard definitions and formal standards covering serial publications, their processing, and their use. Some standards do exist, although they are voluntary, and others are on the horizon.

Communication about serials suffers from a lack of specific formal education or training for serials librarianship. Few library schools include such a course in their curricula, preferring to let serials be treated in other courses such as cataloging and reference. By this action, serials are perceived—if not actually presented—as exceptions, as problems. This negative approach to serials librarianship does not attract graduates to it.

Parties involved with library serials have different objectives. Many publishers and all serials vendors are commercial operations, in business to make a profit. Libraries are typically service organizations and have tended until recently to consider service above cost. Scholars and most other authors of journal articles are not in business for financial gain, as are publishers and vendors. However, they want and need serials for research purposes and do not like to think about cost. These four parties come from different perspectives, and communication does not occur easily. The late 1980s and early 1990s have seen, however, the beginning of sincere efforts by all parties to learn, to teach, and to work together to provide serials in the best and most efficient manner.

PHILOSOPHY OF ACCESS VS. OWNERSHIP

Today's libraries do not attempt to collect everything their constituents might need; they cannot come close to filling every patron request from their own collections. Instead, librarians are increasingly using other libraries and commercial suppliers of information published in serial format for on-demand fulfillment of patron needs. In addition, they are providing patrons direct access to information suppliers, often used at the person's own expense.

Two phenomena of the late twentieth century have made this situation necessary: rising journal prices and the explosion in volume of scholarly information. The pricing story is in Chapter 7; the increase in amount of information available to researchers and other library users comes in Chapter 2. Today's library administrators are forced to admit that no library can stand alone; no library can be self-sufficient. It is fortunate that, at the same time, material is satisfactorily available from outside the library. The same technology that created the flood of scientific articles has made it possible for librarians to save time and money by acquiring these articles individually from elsewhere.

SERIALS *ARE* DIFFERENT!

Glasby was correct: serials ARE different. They continue and they change. They are ubiquitous and they are elusive. One who works with serials should not be surprised by anything that happens. Boredom is rarely a problem. After many years of feeling ignored and abandoned, librarians who work with serials are now in the spotlight in their profession, largely because of the expensive nature of these publications. What the future holds for serials librarianship is not certain, but it will feature change.

NOTES

1.   *Title Varies* 1 (1974): 29.
2.   Donald Davinson, *The Periodicals Collection*, rev. and enl. ed. (London: Andre Deutsch, 1978), 7.
3.   Clara D. Brown and Lynn S. Smith, *Serials: Past, Present and Future*, 2nd (rev.) ed. (Birmingham AL: EBSCO Industries, Inc., 1980), 17.
4.   Andrew Osborn, *Serial Publications: Their Place and Treatment in Libraries*, 3rd ed. (Chicago: American Library Association, 1980), 3-23.
5.   Lynn S. Smith, *A Practical Approach to Serials Cataloging* (Greenwich CT: JAI Press, Inc., 1978), 1-4.
6.   Osborn, *Serial Publications*, 3.
7.   Bella Schachtman, "Simplification of Serial Records Work," *Serial Slants* 3 (1952): 6.
8.   Davinson, *Periodicals Collection*, 9-10.
9.   *Anglo-American Cataloguing Rules*, 2nd ed. (Chicago: American Library Association; Ottawa: Canadian Library Association, 1978), 570.
10.   Osborn, *Serial Publications*, 10-13.
11.   Charles Ammi Cutter, *Rules for a Dictionary Catalog*, 4th ed. (Washington DC: Government Printing Office, 1904), 22.
12.   J. Harris Gable, *Manual of Serials Work* (Chicago: American Library Association, 1937), 28.
13.   *Union List of Serials in Libraries of the United States and Canada*, edited by Winifrid Gregory, 1st ed. (New York: H.W. Wilson Company, 1927), [iii].
14.   Osborn, *Serial Publications*, 16-18.
15.   Donald Davinson, *Bibliographic Control*, (London: Clive Bingley, 1981), 92.
16.   Brown and Smith, *Serials*, 23-24.

Chapter 2

SERIALS PUBLISHING TRENDS

Luke Swindler

INTRODUCTION

Constant growth has been the hallmark of serials: growth in numbers, growth in variety, growth in cost, and growth in importance. Such trends make the rational development of serials collections complex and challenging. Serial publications, which include a proliferating number of journal monographs and an exploding array of electronic services, typically represent the principal informational resource in libraries. They also often constitute the largest and most rapidly growing component of the materials budget, especially at institutions committed to supporting research.

UNIVERSE OF CURRENT SERIALS PUBLISHING

Increases in the number of active journals have been fairly constant over the last three centuries, with the total doubling every fifteen years.[1] Cumulatively, estimates of the total number of serials that have ever existed range from one to five million titles.[2] Interestingly enough, concern about over production of serials and the fear of being inundated by new titles has been expressed since at least the early eighteenth century.[3] Since World War II serials publishing has been marked by a growing number of titles from an expanding array of sources, an increasing specialization and concomitant audience fragmentation that has affected both popular and scholarly publishing, and most recently the appearance of electronic titles.

Although no general agreement exists on how many serials are being published, the figures available are astounding. The 1994/95 edition of *Ulrich's International Periodicals Directory*, for example, lists 147,000 active titles. Indeed, so many serials of value to the scholarly community are being published that subscriptions at the most comprehensive research libraries approach

Table 2.1

Year	Number of Titles Listed
1953	14,000
1963	20,000
1973/74	80,000
1983	102,000
1993/94	140,000

100,000 titles and amount to millions of dollars in annual costs.[4] In terms of the contents of just the research-oriented serials, according to John Naisbitt's *Megatrends*, between six and seven thousand scientific articles appear each day, while an annual growth rate of 13 percent guarantees that their number will double every 5.5 years.[5]

Equally staggering is the proliferation of new serials. A search of the *Ulrich's Plus* database indicates that during the 1990s approximately 3,000 serials were launched annually, while each triannual issue of *Ulrich's Update* lists approximately 2,000 new and newly-added titles. The escalating growth in the number of serial publications worldwide for the last generation can be charted by the listings in *Ulrich's International Periodicals Directory* and its former companion work *Irregular Serials and Annuals* (see Table 2.1).

One can get a geographical perspective on the pervasiveness of serials and how closely their growth is correlated with the relative economic performance of individual nations by comparing the 1988 and 1995 editions of *Ulrich's Plus* for the countries that produce the largest number of active serials (see Table 2.2)[6]

Table 2.2

Country	1988 Number	1995 Number	% Change
United States	36,534	50,364	38
United Kingdom	10,532	13,799	31
Germany	5,898	9,519	61
France	4,376	5,102	17
Italy	3,736	4,897	31
Australia	2,810	3,414	21
India	2,552	3,214	26
Netherlands	2,413	3,666	52
Japan	2,237	5,508	136
ex-USSR	1,351	1,121	-17
Switzerland	1,333	1,878	41
Spain	1,244	2,277	83
China (PRC)	211	2,285	983

Table 2.3

Circulation	1988 Number	1995 Number	% Change
Less than 100	711	509	-24
101-500	11,881	13,194	11
501-1000	12,145	18,246	50
1001-5000	17,636	27,976	59
5001-10,000	7,076	12,321	74
10,001-20,000	5,525	10,500	90
20,001-50,000	5,106	9,981	95
50,001-100,000	2,274	4,593	102
Over 100,000	2,782	5,310	91

Serials are not only omnipresent, but they are also read widely. A comparison of the 1988 and 1995 editions of *Ulrich's Plus* reveals circulation patterns as demonstrated by Table 2.3.

Insofar as these statistics are representative of the entire serials universe, they indicate that growth has been skewed toward the higher end of the circulation spectrum, with titles having the largest readerships being those that are proliferating the most rapidly.

WORLD OF SCHOLARLY AND SCIENTIFIC SERIALS

In addition to the trends cited above, the scholarly and scientific/technical/medical (STM) component of serials publishing has been marked by the growing dominance of English as the common language and the United States as the critical market. It has also been characterized by a proliferation of journals published by transnational—especially Dutch, German, and British—corporations, the creation of specialized titles that grow rapidly in size and cost, and a price revolution that threatens to undermine both libraries and the traditional system of scholarly communication.

The predominance of English initially went hand in hand with the growth in size and importance of the American scientific and scholarly community as both the major source of articles and their principal market.[7] As a consequence, in the 1950s and 1960s the leading German firms, which before the Second World War had been preeminent in the STM market, changed the language of publication of their principal periodicals to English.[8] More recently, transnational European firms have dramatically increased their U.S. holdings, because of its centrality in the economics of journal publishing.[9] The economic surge of Pacific Rim nations in the 1980s and 1990s—with their English-reading scientific and technical cadres along with their widespread use of English as the language of commerce and higher education—has reenforced this linguistic dominance.

During the last quarter century West European multinational corporations have become the dominant players in STM serials publishing, particularly in terms of producing specialized titles with high prices and high inflation. They also have continued to expand their output, even during this period of tight economic times for academic libraries.[10] As a consequence, by the late 1980s the three largest foreign commercial publishers—Elsevier, Pergamon, and Springer—together accounted for a quarter of periodicals budgets of major university libraries.[11]

As foreign commercial firms increased their dominance of journal publishing, the role of American scholarly, scientific, and professional societies and university presses declined dramatically. At the same time, the distinction between commercial and non-commercial publisher blurred as societies and associations increasingly viewed their publications as profit centers and contracted out their serials to the commercial sector. The fact that over 70 percent of the journals covered by *Science Citation Index* are now commercially published is clear evidence of the magnitude to this shift.[12]

The potential high profitability, coupled with the high costs of launching new journals, have been significant factors behind this trend. The lucrative nature of serials publishing and the attitude of its for-profit sector is exemplified by the following statement of the chairman of Elsevier, the world's leading producer of STM titles:

> During the last 20 years, the Company's consolidated profit has increased by an annual average of 21%....Seen as a graph, not corrected for inflation, the curve having started slowly, ascends sharply, and it may well be asked how high it will go. If, however, this is the beginning of the classic S curve, we shall have to try for as long as possible to prevent it from leveling out.[13]

This high level of profitability is not unique. By the 1990s commercial scientific journal publishing routinely averaged profits of 30 percent per annum.[14]

Robert Maxwell, the founder of Pergamon, has expressed the philosophy and ultimate goal of at least some of these commercial publishers most brazenly:

> I set up a perpetual financing machine through advance subscriptions....If Pergamon could win the trust of scientists it could establish the standard journal in each specialisation, and that would give it a series of publishing monopolies...scientists are not generally as price-conscious as other professionals, mainly because they are not spending their own money.[15]

For those librarians who hope for financial salvation through technological change without a restructuring of serials publishing and copyright, Maxwell went on to state that his company was moving into electronic publishing as quickly as possible, because he would be "able to recycle the same piece of information, selling it several times over, having either bought it outright or paying a royalty that is less than the price the company can obtain by reselling it."[16] And he concluded by contrasting electronic publishing with traditional print serials:

> In paper-based publishing, this process involves the additional cost of paper, printing, packaging, and transport, and in many sectors the market price is restrained by competition. None of those applies in electronic publishing, once a user has the equipment…that means that every additional sale can amount to pure profit—and every use is metered and charged for, unlike books when they are plucked off a shelf.[17]

Such statements increase librarians' concerns over the waves of acquisitions and mergers of the last decade. Elsevier's recent purchase of Pergamon has been particularly troubling, because their combined titles account for nearly a quarter of the Association of Research Libraries (ARL) institutions' expenditures on science journals and as much as 35-40 percent in some sub-disciplines.[18]

This emphasis on lucrative journal publishing is by no means limited to European-based transnational corporations. For example, the U.S.-based firm of John Wiley intends to focus its publishing efforts in the STM field and within that area to "emphasize subscription and continuity products, which generate predictable revenues and substantial cash flow."[19] Furthermore, the switch to commercial publishers and charging what the market will bear is spreading from the STM fields to the social sciences and humanities.[20] Not incidentally, the profitable nature of specialized serials publishing encourages the same publishers to move away from producing books.[21]

Because commercially produced specialized titles have both higher costs and higher inflation rates than other serials, the consequences have been disastrous for library budgets. In addition, pricing trends in the commercial sector have had a secondary effect of inflating the cost of journals produced by supposedly not-for-profit scholarly, scientific, and professional societies.[22] For example, the American Chemical Society justified one of its rounds of price increases by arguing that its journals had been priced lower than comparable titles by commercial firms—and were therefore "undervalued."[23]

As the number of journals has increased, their scope has narrowed. At the same time, attempts by publishers to counter this trend toward ever greater specialization with more broadly-based titles have not been successful.[24] Moreover, both the general and specialized periodicals have relentlessly increased the number of articles they publish in response to a research universe that rewards faculty and other researchers on the basis of the number of publications they produce. The growing number of articles has certainly contributed to the cost spiral and probably decreased the chances of any particular article actually being read.

Table 2.4

	Index			% Increase		
Year	CPI	HEPI	USPPI	CPI	HEPI	USPPI
1986	180.9	199.7	261.5	1.9	4.6	8.2
1987	187.5	207.9	288.3	3.7	4.2	10.3
1988	195.2	217.1	315.5	4.1	4.4	9.4
1989	204.6	229.9	341.3	4.8	5.9	8.2
1990	215.6	243.7	373.3	5.4	6.0	9.4
1991	227.5	256.1	414.5	5.5	5.1	11.1
1992	235.3	264.4	466.6	3.4	3.2	12.6
1993	238.4	273.2	494.5	1.3	3.3	6.0
1994	244.5	282.0	537.2	2.6	3.2	8.6
1995	N/A	N/A	588.2	N/A	N/A	9.5

Reader response to this phenomenon has been to read only the periodicals that they must and to rely increasingly on institutional rather than personal holdings.[25] As a consequence, most STM journals depend almost entirely upon library subscriptions for their survival. More recently, declining personal subscriptions to STM journals have been matched by declining institutional subscriptions.[26] Nevertheless, responses from publishers invariably involve continued production at current levels, more intensive marketing, and—particularly for commercial firms—launching new journals in order to maintain revenues.[27]

The growing dominance of serials publishing by commercial firms committed to the maximization of profit, the explosive growth of specialized periodical literature and concomitant fall in subscriptions to individual titles, and the increased cost of traditional publication[28] have led to massive price inflation, especially for STM titles. For American libraries the pricing crisis has been exacerbated by the economics of imperial decline and the resultant depreciation of the U.S. dollar coupled with a journal universe increasingly dominated by titles published abroad.

As a consequence, the cost of serial subscriptions has increased at a much higher clip than either the general inflation rate (as measured by the Consumer Price Index) or the inflation rate for the labor-intensive world of academe (as measured by the Higher Education Price Index). The annual U.S. Periodical Price Index (USPPI) provides graphic evidence of this trend (see Table 2.4).[29]

Such dramatic inflation has, in turn, created a severe financial squeeze on materials budgets, particularly for research and special libraries, because of their need to acquire expensive research periodicals. Between 1986 and 1994 serial expenditures in ARL institutions increased by 93% and serial unit prices by 115 percent, although they were buying 4 percent fewer subscriptions; monograph expenditures, on the other hand, grew by only 17 percent and unit prices by 55 percent.[30] Viewed globally, during the same period serials increased their share of the total materials budget by 9 percent—from 52 percent to 61 percent—while the portion spent on monographs declined by a corresponding percentage.[31] Yet, even these statistics underestimate the crisis, for the largest research institutions had to collectively cancel nearly one million dollars in subscriptions annually during the 1980s to keep their expenditures from going even higher.[32]

The serials crisis, then, is specifically a library funding crisis, but more generally it reflects the lack of financial resources to support the current system of scholarly communication. It is also fast becoming a publishers' crisis. Since the mid-1970s STM publishing has become increasingly a buyers market. As a consequence, publishers have put more emphasis on marketing, particularly in terms of vulnerable specialized titles.[33] They also have turned to automation to increase efficiency, although computerized handling of manuscripts has contributed more to publishers being able to get a journal issue into print more quickly than it has to lowering costs.[34]

In this financial environment collection development and serials librarians need to be on guard against publishers' attempts to force them to acquire new journals either indirectly via aggressive marketing techniques or directly through combination or "free" subscriptions. In the former case, the library is informed that it cannot continue to get a journal unless it adds subscriptions to other periodicals. In the latter instance, the library ends up paying for the "free" title through a surcharge on an existing subscription it has with a publisher or by eventually receiving an invoice.[35]

Despite these high pressure efforts by publishers, the time it takes a journal to achieve financial stability has lengthened. A large STM publisher such as Karger estimates that a fifth of its periodicals are to some degree experimental in the sense that they represent good ideas but may not prove valuable enough or find a large enough audience to be viable. In fact, in recent years it has even had to cease titles with Nobel Prize laureates on the editorial board.[36]

Because all authorities agree that these trends in serials cost will continue, collection development officers can expect to find themselves in a state of permanent financial siege, especially since most libraries cannot count on sustained increases in funding to cope with serials inflation.

NEW OPTIONS AND NEW CHALLENGES

In addition to managing an ever-expanding pool of increasingly expensive serial publications, librarians face a future of new and unprecedented options and ever-more complex choices. The universe of serials is increasingly characterized by a growing variety of formats that exist in rapidly-changing economic, politico-legal, and technological environments. Although the

Table 2.5

Year	# Databases	# Producers	# Online Services
1980	411	269	71
1985	2,247	1,316	414
1990	3,943	1,950	645
1995	5,342	2,220	828

traditional printed serial will maintain its ascendancy within the near future and may always dominate certain niches, electronic options and innovative pricing mechanisms, coupled with users' need for the most current information in the most convenient manner, have already resulted in a proliferation of transformations, supplementary services, and innovative products, together with novel means of delivering and paying for serial information.[37] Continued advances in telecommunications and computer technology promise even more startling options during the coming years.[38]

The proliferation of electronic subscriptions is particularly important and dramatic. The overall pattern of growth of this publishing segment is demonstrated by the statistics presented in Table 2.5.[39]

The 1994/95 edition of *Ulrich's* contains 4,115 online and 1,119 CD-ROM titles, increases of 7 percent and 27 percent, respectively, from the previous year. Similarly, a comparison of editions of the *Directory of Electronic Journals, Newsletters, and Academic Discussion Lists* indicates a sixfold growth between 1991 and 1995 and a two-thirds increase in the number of titles between just 1994 and 1995 (including a doubling of those that are refereed and a quadrupling of serials created solely for Web reading/distribution).

The first electronic products consisted primarily of reference and bibliographic periodicals, almost all of which paralleled pre-existing print titles. Through such ventures as the Adonis and TULIP projects and delivery mechanisms pioneered by STN and OCLC, major STM research and news periodicals began to appear in electronic versions, often without graphics. At about the same time free or inexpensive scholarly journals in the humanities, such as *Postmodern Culture*, and free bulletin boards and other information services available only electronically came into existence.[40]

Electronic serials will not only provide radical alternatives to traditional paper-bound publishing and raise critical questions about the ownership of and access to information but will also pose fundamental questions regarding the role of libraries in general and the use of acquisitions funds to provide access to these titles via computer terminals rather than to actually purchase physical entities in particular.[41] In addition, electronic titles constitute basic challenges not only to the very economics of serials publishing but also to the essential notions of ownership and access that have evolved over the centuries since the appearance of printing during the Renaissance. From the publisher's point of view the ease with which readers can capture and print out information from a database threatens to undermine copyright and the financial viability of journals, while the cost of both traditional and new products threatens to undermine the whole system of scholarly communication.[42]

At present it is not clear what changes in the nature of serials will occur or when and how they will happen—much less their ultimate implications. Moreover, the most significant influences on serials publishing and distribution will be at the macro-level, with librarians exerting minimal impact. These transformations will involve both national politics and priorities, such as fair use and information policy, and international contexts, such as the nature of copyright and publishing economics within a global market. Nevertheless, how librarians react to what promises to be a revolution in communication will be of critical importance not only in terms of effectively meeting user needs for serial information but also for redefining the very nature of libraries themselves.

NOTES

1. King Research, Inc., *The Journal in Scientific Communication: The Roles of Authors, Publishers, Libraries, and Readers in a Vital System* (Washington, DC: National Science Foundation, 1979), pp. 9 and 11.

2. Hazel Woodward and Stella Pilling, "The International Serials Industry: An Overview," in *The International Serials Industry*, eds. Hazel Woodward and Stella Pilling (Brookfield, VT: Gower, 1993), p. 3.

3. Andrew D. Osborn, *Serial Publications: Their Place and Treatment in Libraries*, 3rd ed. (Chicago: American Library Association, 1980), p. 35.

4. Within the universe of university libraries, Harvard has the greatest number of current subscriptions (96,291) and pays the most money for them ($6,098,550). *ARL Statistics* 1993/94, pp. 49 and 59.

5. Cited in Woodward and Pilling, "International," p. 3. This may be a conservative figure. According to a 1995 brochure of the Institute for Scientific Information Research Services Group, as many as 20,000 new research papers are published each day.

6. *Ulrich's* coverage of U.S. and West European production is much better than for other parts of globe; on the other hand, it is comprehensive enough to list 13 active titles from Antigua and 67 from Zaire.

7. A survey of British STM serial publishers, for example, showed that in 1991 the United States and Canada accounted for 33 percent of all subscriptions, with the United Kingdom taking an additional 27 percent. By way of contrast, continental Europe accounted for only 21 percent, Japan for 9 percent, and the rest of the world just 10 percent. Priscilla Oakeshott, *Trends in Journal Subscriptions 1990 & 1991: A Survey of Members of the Publishers Association Serials Publishers Group and the Association of Learned & Professional Society Publishers* (London: Publishers Association, 1993), p. 20.

8. Harold M. Schmeck, Jr., *Karger, Turning Medical Progress into Print: A Mirror of a Century of Medical and Scientific Publishing* (Basel: Karger, 1990), p. 85. Karger had earlier been one of the first medical publishers to accept articles in the three major languages of science: English, French, and German. p. 84.

9. For example, a key element of Elsevier's growth strategy involves such acquisitions: "Whenever possible, we will look for these acquisitions in the United States, a country which, for publishers in particular, is attractive because it is a large and affluent single language market, with a high level of education. Since many expansion-minded (European) publishers are pushing for corporate growth in the United States, the prices for American publishing companies have risen considerably." Its *Annual Report* (official English translation of the Dutch-language annual report) 1986, p. 9. For a fuller discussion of these trends, see Gayle Feldman's article on Elsevier and Wolters Kluwer, "Going Dutch," *Publishers Weekly* 238, no. 27 (21 June 1991), p. 19-26.

10. Oakeshott's survey of British STM serial publishers revealed that the net number of journals they produced increased by 19 percent during the period 1989-1991, with the ratio of new launches to cessations being nearly 4:1. *Trends*, p. 3-5.

11. Woodward and Pilling, "International," p. 8.

12. Woodward and Pilling, "International," p. 9.

13. Elsevier, *Annual Report* 1986, p. 8.

14. Woodward and Pilling, "International," p. 8-9.

15. Cited in James C. Thompson, "Journal Costs: Perception and Reality in the Dialogue," *College & Research Libraries* 49 (1988), p. 481.

16. Thompson, "Journal," p. 481.

17. Thompson, "Journal," p. 481-482.

18. Feldman, "Going," p. 25.

19. John Wiley & Sons, Inc., *Annual Report* 1993, p. 1. The report goes on to refer to its STM journal business as "a jewel in Wiley's corporate portfolio" whose products "entail virtually no risk in inventories or accounts receivable," p. 3.

20. This was the view of a representative from the National Endowment for the Humanities at the 1989 Modern Language Association Convention. See Patricia Buck Dominguez, "ALA Librarians, Faculty, and Scholarly Organizations," *College & Research Libraries News* 51 (1990), p. 396.

21. Publisher representatives freely admit their companies make larger profits from serial rather than book operations, with the latter sometimes barely breaking even. Indeed, during the past decade Elsevier has either terminated or reduced its trade books subsidiaries and its scholarly monographs operations. See its *Annual Report* 1986, p. 8. More recently, Reed Elsevier put its entire consumer book, magazine, and newspaper operations on the market in order to concentrate on the more lucrative STM and professional publishing sectors. *The Bookseller* no. 4674 (21 July 1995), p. 7.

22. Librarians interested in monitoring this situation should subscribe to the *Newsletter on Serials Pricing Issues*. To get this electronic journal, send a message to listproc@unc.edu saying "subscribe prices" followed by your name. Back issues are available at http://sunsite.unc.edu/reference/prices/prices.html.

23. Thomas Weyr, "Professional Association Publishing," *Publishers Weekly* 235, no. 24 (16 June 1989), p. 38. The author goes on to note that this "point of view is widely shared in association circles," p. 38.

24. Schmeck, *Karger*, p. 130. Moreover, Oakeshott's survey indicated that there may also be a long-term though slow decline in the number of subscriptions to long-established general science titles. Oakeshott, *Trends*, p. 28.

25. In his discussion of the impact of the proliferation of publications on the academy, Bruce Wilshire contends that not only are journals so numerous that few researchers can keep up with what is published, but the huge number of articles they contain threaten to overwhelm the entire system of scholarly communication and "make the quality of many of the journals and their editors suspect." *The Moral Collapse of the University: Professionalism, Purity, and Alienation* (Albany, NY: State University of New York Press, 1990), p. 74.

26. Oakeshott reported that British STM serial publishers experienced a 4 percent drop in the average number of subscriptions between 1989 and 1991, on top of a 6 percent decline between 1988 and 1989. When only full-rate—that is, library—subscriptions are considered the drop for the 1989-1991 period increases to 10 percent. *Trends*, p. 11. In fact, the decline in subscription bases has been so extensive that even Elsevier's largest and most respected journals experienced a 28 percent cumulative reduction during the period 1976-1992. Janice E. Kuta, "AAP Seminar Explores Document Delivery," *Publishers Weekly* 239, no. 52 (30 November 1992), p. 20.

27. Oakeshott, *Trends*, pp. 27-28.

28. The direct costs of serials production—for example, typesetting, printing, binding, materials, and postage—have increased faster than the general inflation rate. In addition, the associated editorial costs also have risen sharply as academic institutions have reduced their support for publication activities. Woodward and Pilling, "International," p. 5.

29. This annual study has been produced for over thirty years and now appears in one of the spring issues of *American Libraries*. All figures cited are derived from "U.S. Periodical Price Index for 1995," *American Libraries* 26 (1995), p. 446-57. This index is complemented by the Periodical Price Survey, which appears in one of the spring issues of *Library Journal* and contains detailed price projections for the forthcoming year. The latter source includes foreign as well as U.S. periodicals and is based a on larger number of academic titles.

30. *ARL Statistics* 1993/94, p. 6.

31. Calculated from *ARL Statistics* 1992/93, p. 6, and 1993/94 p.32 and 38. This shift has, in turn, resulted in what Kendon Stubbs has called a "monographs crisis." By 1993 ARL institutions were buying 23 percent fewer books than in 1986 and, if present trends continue, by the year 2000 their monograph acquisitions will be down to half the 1986 figure. *ARL Statistics* 1992/93, p. 6. The same shift in spending prevails in the United Kingdom, where the percent of the budget university libraries spent on serials went from 49 percent in 1980/81 to 60% by 1990/91. Woodward and Pilling, "International," p. 7. For data on the widespread cumulative disappearance of monographic titles from research collections and the increasing homogeneity of library holdings, see Charles A. Schwartz, "Empirical Analysis of Literature Loss," *Library Resources & Technical Services* 38 (1994), pp. 133-38, and Anna A. Perrault, "The Changing Print Resource Base of Academic Libraries in the United States: A Comparison of Collection Patterns in Seventy-two ARL Academic Libraries on Non-serial Imprints for the Years 1985 and 1989," Dissertation, Florida State University, 1994.

32. Dominguez, "ALA," p. 396.

33. Schmeck, *Karger*, pp. 102-103.

34. Schmeck, *Karger*, p. 126.

35. Robin B. Devin, "Your Library's Not Buying Any New Serial Titles?" *Against the Grain* 2, no. 2 (April 1990), pp. 13 and 33. The author goes on to note that librarian protests against such publisher strategies are effective.

36. Schmeck, *Karger*, pp. 128-30. Schmeck further notes that Karger estimates a specialized medical title currently needs about 750 subscriptions to survive. Most subscribers are institutions, although a few of its journals do have a substantial number of individual subscribers. In such cases the title may have subscriber bases of 2,000 or more. p. 129.

37. For a good overview of some of the major current debates, see Ann Shumelda Okerson and James J. O'Donnell, eds., *Scholarly Journals at the Crossroads: A Subversive Proposal for Electronic Publishing: An Internet Discussion about Scientific and Scholarly Journals and Their Future* (Washington, DC: Association of Research Libraries, Office of Scientific & Academic Publishing, June 1995). In addition, whereas most of the voluminous literature on electronic journals focuses on the economic, legal, and technical issues, electronic journals will only truly supplant paper titles when they replicate the higher cognitive and communicative features of print. On this important subject, see Jan Olsen, *Electronic Journal Literature: Implications for Scholars*

(Westport, Conn.: Mecklermedia, 1994), especially chapter 4: "The Scholars' Requirements for an Electronic Journal System," pp. 29-61.

38.   One of the best means of keeping abreast of the impact of the electronic revolution on serials is to read the essays in the annual *Directory of Electronic Journals, Newsletters and Academic Discussion Lists*. In particular, each edition contains a bibliography on electronic publications and publishing. Subscribing to the VPIEJ-L listserv offers another way to keep up with developments related to the electronic publishing of scholarly serials. Its subscription addresses are listserv@vtvm1.cc.vt.edu [INTERNET] and listserv@vtm1 [BITNET].

39.   *Gale Directory of Databases* 1995, v. 1, p. x. For an overview of this industry's growth that includes many statistics, see Martha E. Williams, "The State of Databases Today: 1995," *Gale Directory of Databases* 1995, v. 2, pp. xvii-xxix.

40.   In fact, the shift to electronic-only publication may occur here rather than with the major STM journals, for small humanities journals have significantly reduced start-up costs and the failure would have less severe economic consequences. If so, it would be another example of Thomas Kuhn's thesis that paradigm shifts begin with change at the periphery. Dominguez, "ALA," p. 397.

41.   For information on how research libraries are handling electronic serials, see the two following reports from the Office of Management Services, Association of Research Libraries compiled by Elizabeth Parang and Laverna Saunders: *Electronic Journals in ARL Libraries: Issues and Trends*, SPEC Kit 202 (Washington, DC: OMS, ARL, 1994) and *Electronic Journals in ARL Libraries: Policies and Procedures*, SPEC Kit 201 (Washington, DC: OMS, ARL, 1994).

42.   As Schmeck notes, "It was not so much that users were deliberately flouting copyrights as it was that the extraction [from databases] was so quick and simple that the old rules simply fell apart." *Karger*, p. 101.

Chapter 3

MANAGING THE SERIALS COLLECTION

Serials management is a specialization found particularly in academic libraries. It has been said that good serials librarians seek and find positions as heads of technical services or directors of small libraries. Today's serials manager, however, works in a professional world that is different from that of even a few years ago. It is no longer necessary to go on to other specialties. Successful serials management is a continuing challenge because of four trends: constant change in serial publications; runaway proliferation of journals; rising subscription prices; and new technology applied to serials publishing, distributing, and processing. These developments have created an environment that requires knowledge and strong leadership from serials specialists.

Change, growth, and cost, the first three catalysts in the evolution of serials management are negative influences from the librarian's perspective. New technology, for the most part, has had a positive impact. Technology of the 1990s allows unprecedented control of serial literature and its contents. Comprehensive online serials management systems, hard discs replacing labor-intensive card files, and compact-disc and online periodical indexes are current examples.

With today's increasingly sophisticated automation systems, serials work has changed. Some aspects have become simpler and quicker; check-in of issues is an example. Other functions, such as claiming, have become more time-consuming. Still other aspects, such as management reporting, suddenly are possible when they were not previously. Experience with an online serials system is a desirable quality in selecting new staff members.

Serial publications are more complex today than ever; change is undoubtedly their most constant quality. To the aspect of change one may add David C. Taylor's concept of the "serials explosion:" "Since 1970, subscription prices for old standard journals have gone haywire—doubling, tripling, quadrupling and more. Meanwhile, new journals with important-sounding titles appear each week at unreasonable prices."[1] Growing specialization within academic disciplines has narrowed target audiences for scholarly journals. It has brought split titles, esoteric but nearly identical topics, and fiscal and processing challenges for serials managers. The domestic currency rises and falls against foreign currencies in a manner that makes budgeting little more than a guessing game.

The librarian who accepts responsibility for managing a serials collection may come to the position with experience in serials librarianship, with professional experience in another aspect of librarianship, or often directly from graduate school with no prior experience as a librarian. In each case, this person needs to arrive at a comfortable understanding of serials management, based upon a deepening knowledge of library serials, local library policies and conditions, and personal feelings about serials. The ideal serials manager develops abilities in three areas: (1) supervisory skills, in order to motivate staff members in the midst of constant chaos and exceptions to the rules; (2) accounting principles, to work within the allocated funds and obtain the best service for the lowest cost; and (3) communication skills, to facilitate the exchange of information with library personnel, patrons, publishers, vendors, and binders. The ideal serials manager can adjust to sudden crises, is curious and eager to investigate things that do not seem quite right, and maintains a sense of humor. Never underestimate the importance of a sense of humor and the ability to step back and take a look at the immediate crisis from a broader perspective.

The broader perspective includes not only the entire library, but also the universe of library serials operations. Sharing experiences with other serials librarians at state or regional meetings and workshops or at the American Library Association (ALA) or the North American Serials Interest Group (NASIG) conferences is a way to gain a feeling of community as well as practical advice. Electronic mail and serials-related electronic bulletin boards and discussion groups have made it increasingly possible for serials managers to become acquainted and communicate without leaving their workplaces. Electronic mail does not replace face-to-face discussion, but it permits these encounters to begin at an advanced level and to build on an existing relationship. Another librarian's solution to the problem one is facing, ideas generated during a brainstorming session around a dinner table, and electronic mail exchanges are all valuable experiences. The ability and the willingness to listen, to question, to share, and to speculate is perhaps the most desirable quality of the serials manager.

RESOURCES FOR SERIALS MANAGERS

Serials librarians who acquire, describe, preserve, and make serial publications accessible, often must rely on on-the-job training and continuing education opportunities to develop proficiency in their work. The person who sets out to learn will find resources available in books and journals and from professional associations. Before the 1980s, very few resources existed. Fortunately, a good number of valuable published materials have appeared in recent years. In addition, a growing number of professional organizations contribute to the education for serials librarianship. This section discusses the specific resources that are available.

Monographs

Several monographs on serials management are suitable as library science textbooks, as resources for librarians responsible for a serials collection, and as reference works for those who find serials occupying an increasing portion of their work day. The books appear here in reverse chronological order.

The newest monograph is *Serials Management: A Practical Guide*,[2] by Chiou-Sen Dora Chen, a 1995 ALA publication. Because of its practical nature, Chen's book complements this one. She describes in detail procedural matters such as bibliographic searching and acquisitions records but gives light treatment to collection development resources and serials cataloging.

Hazel Woodward and Stella Pilling, two outstanding British serials librarians have collected thirteen essays by industry leaders into their 1993 publication, *The International Serials Industry*.[3] Contributors include publishers and vendors, as well as librarians from throughout the world. Two chapters treat serials production, marketing, and use in developing countries. Gillian Page's essay updates in part her book *Journal Publishing*.

Serials Management: A Practical Handbook, is a collection of essays edited by two British librarians, Margaret Graham and Fiona Buettel.[4] Some of the discussions and conclusions do not apply to American library situations, but on the whole the work is valuable because of the quality of its content and its recent publication date. The book groups nine chapters by British specialists into three categories. "Collection Development" consists of selection/deselection, acquisitions, and financial control and budgeting; "Collection Management" consists of housekeeping routines, cataloging/classification, storage/preservation, and user services. "Automation" and "Standards" comprise one chapter each.

The classic American work on serials is Andrew Osborn's *Serial Publications*.[5] Its third edition came out in 1980. Osborn's comprehensive, scholarly monograph covered the history of developments and trends during the twentieth century and, at the same time, included such present-day issues as cooperation and reprography. Despite its age and the scant treatment of serials automation, Osborn remains a useful resource for serials managers because of its comprehensive scope, its historical perspective, and the principles imparted by the author. The chapter titled "Principles of Selection" is particularly useful.

Also published in 1980, the second edition of *Serials: Past, Present and Future*,[6] by Clara D. Brown and Lynn S. Smith, is an expanded version of Brown's procedures manual on serial acquisitions. This edition includes cataloging and other issues in serials management. The very practical treatment includes information, illustrations, and advice that are particularly useful to the new serials librarian. The procedures recommended are long outdated, but Brown and Smith's situational checklists are worth remembering. Examples include "Items to keep in mind when paying invoices," and "What may happen to mail." The book is also full of such nuggets as: "There is no use setting up a claiming project while there is unchecked material sitting around on the shelves."

Two older British works may occasionally be useful. *The Periodicals Collection*,[7] by Donald Davinson, published in London in a "revised and enlarged edition" in 1978, is particularly strong in collection development, acquisitions, and public service. It includes extensive references at the end of each chapter. David Grenfell's work, *Periodicals and Serials: Their Treatment in Special Libraries*,[8] was published in a second edition by Aslib in 1965. It takes a practical point of view and concentrates on acquisitions and public service.

Journals

Within the past twenty years several journals covering serials management have begun publication in the United States. Until the early 1970s only the journal of ALA's Association for Library Collections and Technical Services (ALCTS), *Library Resources and Technical Services*,[9] offered a likely source of articles on serials work. Until 1993 it published an annual review of serials librarianship, listing publications and discussing new developments. The annual reviews of cataloging, collection development, preservation, resources, and reprographics also covered serials.

The first of the journals devoted specifically to serials was *Serials Review*,[10] which began quarterly publication in 1975. Originally this title concentrated on actual reviews of serials, including an index of reviews in other publications. However, after a few years *Serials Review* changed to approximately half reviews of serials and half peer-reviewed articles about serials management. It features an array of regular columns on specific aspects of serials (e.g., Electronic Journal Forum, Tools of the Serials Trade), which have column editors. *Serials Review* is a good place to find conference reports.

In the following year *Serials Librarian*[11] published its first quarterly issue. From the beginning this journal has concentrated on both scholarly, theoretical articles and more practical contributions on all aspects of serials management. Each issue features sections on U.S. government document serials and on serials news. *Serials Librarian* has occasional supplements on current topics. These supplements are published and priced separately.

Advances in Serials Management[12] contains substantial articles on all aspects of serials management. It is not a journal, but has come out about every two years. Volumes 1-5 were not peer reviewed; the two editors invited and edited most articles. Volume 6 reflects a change in editorship and uses a call for papers. The papers will be refereed.

Serials[13] is the journal of the United Kingdom Serials Group and continues its *UKSG Newsletter* and the proceedings of its conferences. Published three times a year, *Serials* contains both conference presentations and other articles on the topic, along with news from libraries, publishers, and vendors.

The most recent journal devoted solely to serials is Haworth Press's *Australian and New Zealand Journal of Serials Librarianship.*[14] This quarterly publication concentrates on articles by Australians and New Zealanders and on subjects reflecting conditions in those countries.

The remaining journals do not limit their scope to serials, but to a specific function. *Library Acquisitions: Practice & Theory*[15] covers the selection, procurement, and management of library materials. Published quarterly since 1977, *LA:PT* has improved coverage of serials matters in recent years. It includes some edited conference proceedings.

Cataloging and Classification Quarterly[16] specializes in the bibliographic control of library materials. Its present editor, Ruth Carter, is a former serials cataloger, and articles on serials receive their full share of space. One topical issue featured the CONSER Project.

Technical Services Quarterly,[17] begun in 1983, treats all aspects of its topic. TSQ includes articles on serials management except for public service.

These journals are not the only ones carrying articles on serials management; they are merely the most likely ones. More general journals occasionally have articles on the subject. Among these are *Journal of Academic Librarianship, Small Computers in Libraries*, and *Information Technology and Libraries*. To find other articles on serials management, consult *Library Literature* or *Library and Information Science Abstracts*.

Online Publications and Discussion Groups

As more librarians begin to use electronic mail, more online resources appear for communication among serials managers. These are generally available at no charge to the subscriber through listserver software at an Internet node, usually a university computing center. Increasingly, one may access electronic journals on the World Wide Web.

The University of Michigan Press has mounted its *Journal of Electronic Publishing*[18] on the university's Web site. It is a new kind of journal, one that does not have numbering or issues, but is an electronic archive of articles on electronic publishing. Some articles were first published elsewhere (and the authors retained electronic publishing rights) and some are transcriptions of talks. Some articles provide hypertext links to other sites. This journal is both an example of a type of electronic publishing that will increase in availability in the next few years and a valuable resource for serials specialists.

SERIALST[19] is the oldest and most general online discussion group about library serials matters. Birdie MacLennan, a serials cataloger at the University of Vermont, started the list because she felt the need to talk to others about work-related matters. SERIALST is a moderated discussion group, covering all aspects of serials management. Messages are archived monthly. To subscribe, send a message to LISTSERV@UVMVM.UVM.EDU saying: subscribe SERIALST [your] [name]. There are perhaps ten to fifteen messages a week and more when a lively discussion crops up.

The North American Serials Interest Group (NASIG) works through the computer facilities of the American Mathematical Society to provide NASIGNET for its members. Members become subscribers automatically to the private discussion group NASIG-L by sending an electronic mail address to the membership directory. NASIG has also created a gopher for its proceedings and its newsletter, among other documents, as well as discussion groups for its committees to use.

Several electronic resources include serials topics within their scope, among them: the electronic version of the *ALCTS Newsletter*, the electronic newsletter of the Science and Technology Section of ALA's Association of College and Research Libraries, PACS-L/PACS-Review, AUTOCAT, and LIBADMIN. Charles Bailey maintains a list of library-related electronic publications and discussion groups and distributes it periodically on PACS-L from the University of Houston.

Continuing Education

For serials managers, continuing education opportunities were scarce until about ten years ago. Then—perhaps because of the notoriety of the journal pricing issue—there seemed to be almost too many opportunities. New conferences, institutes, and organizations appeared, and existing ones expanded their scope to include serials. Now there are far too many meetings for any person to attend, and one must make choices to stay within the budget.

Library Organizations and Their Publications. The Serials Section of ALCTS is the oldest organization specifically for serials librarians. For many years it was the only formal means of meeting one's colleagues and working together on relevant issues. The Serials Section is directed by an executive committee headed by a chair and has a full slate of committees reporting to the executive committee. The various groups meet at each ALA conference, twice a year. At every summer conference there is at least one program sponsored by the section. Around two thousand persons are members of the section, but active members number many fewer. Despite being a part of the massive ALA hierarchy, the Serials Section welcomes new librarians at its committee meetings and tries to find a place for anyone interested in becoming an active member.

Within ALCTS, other groups than the Serials Section are relevant to serials specialists. The Acquisitions Section and the Collection Management and Development Section are concerned with both monographs and serials, and they have committees treating both topics. The Cataloging and Classification Section includes the bibliographic control of serials in its activities. Some ALCTS divisional-level committees cover serials topics: the Publisher/ Vendor/Library Relations Committee, and the Automated Acquisitions Discussion Group, among others.

In addition to ALCTS, both North America and the United Kingdom have active, established associations devoted to serials. Since 1978, the United Kingdom Serials Group (UKSG) of Great Britain has carried out an ambitious program of conferences, publications, and workshops. Its members represent all facets of "the serials information chain"—publishers, subscription agents, librarians, binders, educators, and anyone else with an interest in serials. The annual conference, held on a university campus, attracts between 250 and 400 members from several countries. Each year through 1987 the UKSG published its conference proceedings, which were sent to members at no charge. Also through 1987 the *UKSG Newsletter*, issued twice a year, carried news and short articles. In 1988 the newsletter changed to a journal entitled *Serials*, published three times a year. Selected papers from the annual conference now appear in the journal. The UKSG has occasionally published other works on serials as well, including *The Year's Work in Serials 1985*, a collection of excellent bibliographic essays.

Modeled on the UKSG, the North American Serials Interest Group, or NASIG, was organized in 1985 and held its first annual conference in 1986. Its membership includes librarians, publishers, subscription agents, binders, library science students and faculty members, and others interested in library serials. NASIG holds its annual conference on a college or university campus, and the program consists of plenary sessions, workshops, discussion groups, and social events. The decision to use institutional facilities has kept the registration fee under $300.00 (including room and board), so many newer serials librarians are able to attend. A competitive student grant program enables prospective serials managers to participate. With over 1,000 members and conference attendance of over 600, NASIG is working to match the UKSG in its publication and continuing education programs. Proceedings of the conferences have been published as issues of *Serials Librarian*, as well as separately, by Haworth Press. The group retains electronic rights to the proceedings and makes them available on the NASIG gopher. The bimonthly *NASIG Newsletter* serves as a source of news items and reports on serials activities. It is also available electronically on the gopher. NASIG sponsors continuing education programs such as day-long workshops, preconferences before state and regional library meetings, and tours in connection with the annual conferences of the UK Serials Group.

Serials managers in other countries have also formed organizations. The groups in Australia and South Africa form part of their national library and information science associations. The serials group in The Netherlands is closely related to the European Serials Conference, held in that country or elsewhere in Europe about every two years. Other sponsors of the meeting are the UKSG and Swets Subscription Services. The European Serials Conference appears to be the most nearly international meeting, with participants and speakers from most areas of the world.

Other Continuing Education Opportunities. It is not only librarians' organizations that offer opportunities to broaden one's professional knowledge. Much of our growth comes from communication with the nonlibrarians we work with—publishers, subscription agents, and computer experts.

The Society for Scholarly Publishing was formed in 1978 for the purpose of drawing together persons involved in the process of scholarly communication. While most of its members are associated with university presses, societies, and commercial publishers, an increasing number of librarians, subscription agents, binders, and printers are becoming active. The organization sponsors an annual Top Management Roundtable, a full program of seminars, and an annual meeting that is attended by several hundred members. The society publishes a bimonthly newsletter, *Scholarly Publishing Today*. Participation in SSP's activities promotes communication among publishers, vendors, and librarians.

Each November the College of Charleston (SC) sponsors a conference on acquisitions and collection development. Serials play a role in the discussions and papers at this meeting. The conference tends to be informal and features social activities and gatherings of persons sharing an interest in some aspect of the subject. Papers from this conference were published for several years in *Library Acquisitions: Practice and Theory*.

An annual conference at the University of Oklahoma features serials among its major topics: aspects of acquisitions or collection development. Proceedings of these meetings are published by Haworth Press as issues of *Journal of Library Administration*.

The American Society for Information Science is of particular interest to those librarians with technical expertise. The society holds an annual meeting and publishes the highly regarded *Journal of the American Society for Information Science* (JASIS).

The International Federation of Library Associations and Institutions (IFLA), an international organization meeting once a year, has a Section on

Serial Publications. At the annual conferences the section has both closed committee meetings and open program meetings. While representation from any single country is limited, other librarians occasionally are invited to participate in the committee's activities. The IFLA Section on Serial Publications has recently been active in the areas of union lists, newspapers, and serials management for third world libraries.

Increasingly, a library organization or a publishing association will offer a conference or an institute on a serials topic. ALCTS has presented both a serials institute and an acquisitions institute (which included serials) at several locations.

One thing that will be obvious to every librarian participating in the activities covered in this section and reading the journals is that no two libraries are likely to organize serials functions in exactly the same way.

ORGANIZATION OF SERIALS FUNCTIONS

The place of serials functions in a library's formal organizational structure varies widely; there is no standard or "right" way to handle them. Library organization is influenced by several variables. Size of library is a factor; many libraries are not large enough to justify a separate serials unit. At times the administrative organization of the library is affected—even determined—by the structure housing the collection. Physical arrangement may be rigid, and administrative organization follows the physical arrangement. Quite often the philosophy of the library director determines organization. If serial literature is important to the director, it is likely to be treated well in the library. Finally, as libraries automate their processing and access to materials, traditional organizational structures must be examined to determine their suitability for the emerging technology. Staffing is expensive, and automation has created new possibilities for efficiency.

The serials manager may have an opportunity to organize the library's serials functions, but it is more likely that tradition and facilities have imposed a structure which one cannot easily rearrange. Traditionally, libraries organized by format of material group serials processes into one administrative unit (a serials department), often including a reading room and public service station. Libraries organized by function disperse serials processes, perhaps making them subsections of the acquisitions, cataloging, and reference units.

The concept of the "integrated serials department" gained in popularity for several decades after it was articulated by J. Harris Gable in 1935.[20] Based on the idea that serials are best treated and made available to patrons by persons familiar with serials' idiosyncracies, this organizational structure groups all library functions relating to serials in the same department administratively. The fully integrated serials department contains selection, acquisition, cataloging, preservation, and public service. However, many integrated departments include fewer functions; selection may be done by collection development personnel, cataloging by the catalog department, or public service by reference librarians. Serials are involved in so much of the library's activity that it may be unrealistic to attempt to restrict every contact with them to one department.

Hans Weber, writing before serials functions were automated, described and evaluated the range of organizational schemes for serials functions.[21] He joins Gable, Fred Rothman,[22] Beatrice Simon,[23] and Samuel Lazerow[24] in supporting general centralization of serials functions where possible. Weber qualifies his endorsement of the integrated serials department by submitting the level of 5,000 active orders as the minimum for this structure to be optimally efficient. Whatever the specific organization of serials functions, Weber sees the serial record handling receipt and claiming as the core of the unit. Cataloging, he writes, is the function most often missing from a centralized department, although it is of equal importance with the serial record in processing serials.[25]

Serials cataloging is quite different from monographic cataloging. It is so different that most libraries with several catalogers consider serials a specialty and segregate it. These libraries have one or more catalogers working exclusively with serials, whether they treat serials generally in an integrated or segregated fashion. There is some question as to whether it is cataloging or selection of serials which is most often missing from the integrated department. Bibliographers qualified to work with monographs are, more than monographic catalogers, qualified to work with serials. At the same time, in many libraries serials selection is done by a committee composed of librarians or of librarians and faculty members, because of the continuing commitment of funds. Often the serials librarian, as well as the bibliographer, has a significant role in the deliberations and decisions of the committee.

Since the advent of automated technical processing, and with the new widespread use of OCLC and other bibliographic utilities, the trend for organization of serials functions seems to have swung from centralization to decentralization. The reason librarians cite for the shift is efficient use of staff. Automation has blurred the lines between monographs and serials, causing library administrators to have serials functions absorbed by units processing monographs. Although automation has facilitated such a change, economic factors have also contributed. In times of mandatory staffing reductions, eliminating a department head position is an attractive move. Other libraries have reorganized into a single technical services department (giving the serials public service function to reference personnel) or decentralized processing into units organized by subject. Librarians will undoubtedly continue to search for ways to decrease costs while doing as little damage as possible to the service they offer.

Two articles applied specific management principles to serials librarianship, and both authors determined that an integrated serials department is likely to be more efficient than a decentralized administrative arrangement, even in an automated library. One article described Mitsuko Collver's application of James D. Thompson's principles of "grouping for coordination" to serials management. Thompson described three types of processing interdependence: (1) *pooled*, use of common resources or facilities (such as a public catalog); (2) *sequential*, a one-way flow of work (monographs moving from acquisitions to cataloging); and (3) *reciprocal*, repeated interaction among functions (the effect of serials cataloging on all serial records).[26] Collver showed that reciprocal interdependence, the most complex to coordinate, described the relationship among serials functions, because of the ongoing and changeable nature of serial publications:

> Work is done by interaction, and no function can continue for long without reactions from other activities. In this type of interdependence, the cost of coordination is highest, and it receives the highest priority as a criterion for grouping activities. Thus, according to Thompson's theory, all serials-related activities should be grouped into one [administrative] unit for the benefit of maximum coordination.[27]

Collver applied Thompson's principles to her own library at SUNY Stony Brook and reported that the new organization was successful and particularly appropriate for an automated situation.

Margaret McKinley responded to the trend toward serials administrative decentralization by examining, in the context of serials operations, informal communication across organizational lines and personal influence strategies. She explained that the library's formal organization chart does not necessarily express reality; it is only a description of "ideal work patterns, communication lines, and supervisory relationships."[28] The intricacies of serials processing demand constant problem solving by means of a communication network involving cooperation and experience—the reciprocal interdependence described by Collver. Where the organizational structure does not match communication needs, an informal communication system must develop. In libraries where functioning serials units have been abolished, the communication system flourishes underground. McKinley pointed out the advantages to serials specialists of working within the library's formal organizational structure: "efficiency of serials operations would be improved, staff morale would be higher, and a better end product could be delivered to the library's clientele."[29] When the formal administrative structure fails to coincide with natural communication channels, serials librarians "will inevitably develop and utilize informal communication systems, personal influence, persuasion and, perhaps, deceptive practices, in order to accomplish the library's objectives and the objectives of the serials network within it."[30]

STAFFING

In an ideal situation both middle management and support staff are able to contribute to staffing decisions. In reality, however, the number and classification of staff members involved in serials services usually result from policies determined by the current and/or previous library administration. The policy considerations include human resources priorities, the hierarchy of services offered, decisions made about housing the collection, and often the definition of the scope of employees' responsibilities. For example, a library that subscribes to periodical indexes on CD-ROM, and promotes use of the World Wide Web, will have provided the appropriate hardware and software and staff to support the use of these materials and equipment. Similarly, the library with closed stacks must have personnel to retrieve items for patrons.

An integrated serials department, including both technical processing and public service functions, is a natural situation for using staff members in both types of work, because each aspect of serials work depends heavily upon the other. Managers who use technical service personnel part time for public service responsibilities and vice versa have more staff members directly involved with patrons than those who limit personnel to one function. This attitude requires a greater time and financial investment in training, because each employee has broader responsibilities than he or she would have if restricted to a single function. The opportunity for cross training in serials work may be more difficult to implement in a library organized according to function because more than one administrative unit is involved.

However, in serials work the investment is sound, because it makes use of the expertise of acquisitions and cataloging personnel in giving service to patrons. An acquisitions assistant may not agree with the policy of recording specific notes on check-in records for troublesome journals until a patron asks this same staff member when the next issue of a quarterly is expected. In answering the question, the benefit of knowing any publication irregularity for the title makes the extra check-in effort meaningful to the one who records that information. Providing details such as unusual publication pattern on the serial record and issue-specific holdings statements on permanent records requires time and attention; these procedures demand much of a staff member. Any resentment at producing such records is likely to disappear when that person uses these detailed records to respond to a patron's question.

Likewise, the public service employee benefits from the knowledge gained by creating acquisition and cataloging records which contain the answers to patrons' questions. Creating records to be used in offering public service may well enable the staff member to discover useful information that he or she had never realized was there. This experience promotes conscientious service to the library patrons and gives department personnel a fuller appreciation of their work, which can lead to improved ways of performing tasks that have become routine. Even when some aspects of serials work are allocated to other departments, the investment in extra training is worth the time, expense, and effort. The staff member who knows the entire range of library serials functions is more valuable to the library than one who has a narrowly defined position. A broader view of library operations and the implied trust of the individual accompanying this opportunity often lead to an increased sense of responsibility and foster leadership capabilities among staff members. An extra benefit is a pool of employees to cover service points in emergencies.

THE THREE-WAY RESPONSIBILITY

The serials librarian manages personnel, financial and material resources, technology, and change, working regularly with persons and businesses outside the library. This discussion focuses on two crucial external relationships: that with the subscription agent and that with the journal publisher. The following section emphasizes the obligation of the serials manager to be an equal and respected participant in the process of acquiring information for the reader.

The Relationships

Philip E.M. Greene has written of the "three-way responsibility"—the business relationships among the serials librarian, the journal publisher, and the subscription agent—and the obligations of each partner to the others.[31] John B. Merriman referred to the "information chain," consisting of author, publisher, vendor, and librarian.[32] Each of these parties has a role in communicating information to the end user, and all participants depend on the other links of the chain.

Tension and hard feelings may arise between the serials manager and both the subscription agent and the journal publisher. The primary reason for this disrupted communication is the difference in philosophy each side espouses. Most librarians represent libraries funded by nonprofit, service-oriented institutions: schools, towns, or other parent bodies. They subscribe to the service ethic that demands acquisition of appropriate publications, prompt access through library records, and cheerful, accurate assistance in locating serials and identifying the information they contain. The subscription agent and the publisher, on the other hand, must make a financial profit to survive.

Relationship with the Subscription Agent. Thirty years ago the subscription agency was able to pass on to the library a share of journal publishers' discounts. The vendor was simply a middleman who saved librarians time by consolidating ordering and paying, to the financial benefit of both parties. Rising costs forced many publishers to reduce or abandon the discount and caused the agent to add a service charge to the library's invoice. Many serials librarians then perceived the subscription agent as an adversary. Shortly thereafter, vendors' trial and error use of computers appeared to victimize serials librarians with missed renewals, duplicate charges, and sluggish claiming activity.

Now, however, the subscription agencies are very much in control of their computers. They can provide significant assistance to their customers in terms of bibliographic and subscription information, fast and knowledgeable claiming service, and guidance in budget planning. Many vendors hire serials librarians for sales and management positions, an investment which pays off handsomely for both the companies and their library customers. The subscription agent's librarians and the purchasing institution's librarians communicate easily about serials and serials problems, and they enjoy talking shop and sharing professional news. The best agents work hard to maintain a balance between service and profit. They are in business to provide services to libraries, but they must make a profit in order to continue to give service. The subscription agents combat cost increases by reducing their expenses. Today it is easy for the serials manager to feel that the subscription agents' personnel are trusted allies in the struggle to provide crucial journal information to the patron.

However, because of this feeling of trust on the part of serials librarians, vendors sometimes entice them with short-term price breaks, online serials systems, and very low service charges. Such offers may be quite valid and worth a change of agent, but the serials manager must evaluate each one carefully. The librarian must know which questions to ask. It is not to the library's advantage to play one subscription agent against another for a short-term gain. Changing vendors may cost dearly in staff time and public relations.

Relationship with the Journal Publisher. Librarians often do not understand the business of serial publishing, nor do they usually communicate directly with the publisher. On the contrary, the serials manager may assume that publishers neither understand nor care about library problems caused by changes they make. Gordon Graham, formerly of Butterworth and Company, discussing the relationship between librarians and publishers, states that each party feels "a little precious about his identity, displaying the slight edge of insecurity of those who know inwardly that they are neither the original creators nor the ultimate consumers of the products they handle."[33]

Librarians have felt frustrated by journal publishers, because of apparently unnecessary title changes. These changes require costly recataloging and replacement of records. In the mid-1970s serials librarians' frustration erupted in a newsletter named *Title Varies*. This publication was a vent for the anger and amusement that resulted from such publisher actions as changing *Conditional Reflex* to *The Pavlovian Journal of Biological Science*, and changing *Commerce Today* to *Commerce America*, "in the spirit of the 1976 American Bicentennial."[34] The frustration gave rise to an organization known as "LUTFCSUSTC," Librarians United To Fight Costly Silly Unnecessary Serial Title Changes, that lives today in the ALA/ALCTS Serials Section's Worst Title Change of the Year Awards. Unfortunately, *Title Varies* spread the bad news only after the fact, and it reached all too few journal publishers. Perhaps the greatest contribution of the newsletter was the sense of community that developed when serials librarians learned that they did not have to fight their battles alone.

Mistrust often accompanies the librarian's frustration with journal publishers. This feeling erupted in the mid-1980s with the furor over discriminatory pricing of some British journals for the North American market.[35] Sometimes serials librarians accept the changes in publishers' policy, although these make their work more difficult. Two examples are the controversy formerly surrounding individual versus institutional pricing[36] and the use of automated subscription fulfillment centers by mass-circulation magazine publishers.[37] Librarians criticized publishers both verbally and in print for these practices; however, no changes were made. Eventually the clamor subsided. Some librarians came to agree with the publishers, some tired of the fight and gave up, and others did not care enough to pursue the issues.

Mutual Interdependence

The previous section has discussed the serials manager's perceived relationships with the subscription agent and the journal publisher. However, as Philip Greene[38] stated, the association is a three-way responsibility: the three partners rely on each other in a complicated business situation akin to a love/hate relationship. It is an example of Thompson's "mutual interdependence."

Serials Managers. Serials managers are sometimes naive and passive in their business relationships with vendors and publishers. Their livelihoods are not totally contingent upon efficiency and fiscal economy, although the current economic situation has called attention to stewardship of materials funds. Thus, an unscrupulous subscription agent or journal publisher may easily exploit the serials librarian. Today's publishers and subscription agents understand serials. They also invest time and money in learning their library market and in making their business transactions with the library easier and more profitable.

This effort benefits each party, but it is certain to benefit the commercial partner most. For example, one major publisher decided that it would no longer use a vendor in the distribution of its nonperiodical serials. It would take on that work itself, in order to improve service. Libraries placing standing orders would receive a five percent discount. This arrangement sounded fine until one realized that libraries formerly had received from the vendors not only satisfactory service, but also a discount several times greater than that offered by the publisher. The publisher gained financially, while the library and the vendor lost.

This discussion is not intended necessarily to portray the serials manager as a victim of the journal publisher. Nor does it suggest that the library bypass the agent and order its serials directly from the publishers. Even with today's automated serials systems the costs of processing separate invoices, writing separate checks, and even mailing separate envelopes are prohibitive. This may change as electronic ordering and paying become more prevalent.

Subscription Agents. Chapter 6 contains a full discussion of the librarian's relationship with the subscription agent. Briefly, the longstanding market of the journal subscription agent was saturated some time ago. The companies must, however, continue to show growth in revenue if they are to remain in business. Thus, placing orders and sending invoices has decreased as a share of large vendors' activity. Vendors are using their databases creatively to offer more services to customers. They also promote these services heavily. Subscription agencies create "needs" among their library customers, and they must market the new products and services successfully. They respond to their customers' perceived needs in order to retain library business.

In the continuing struggle to circumvent or abolish geographical price discrimination, the subscription agent works with librarians and publishers in a low-margin business. Competition among subscription agents can be fierce, and any discriminatory treatment by publishers is financially damaging to an agent. So long as no vendor receives special pricing consideration from the publisher, the agent is not primarily concerned with minimizing the cost of the journal to the library.

Journal Publishers. David Taylor describes the mutually dependent relationship between librarians and publishers:

> Libraries depend on publishers to produce information that has the authority of creative authorship balanced by the critical judgment of the editor. It is ludicrous to think of the library as publisher of original material. It is not organized for this complicated task. Likewise, a publisher is not set up to be a library. A publisher can save copies of its own publications, but it cannot duplicate the ability of even a small library to acquire, organize, preserve, and make accessible a wide variety of materials without organizing itself into a library-like organization. In other words, both institutions play essential roles in the dissemination of information. Each is dependent on the other for those functions.[39]

Taylor's comments are equally valid in the context of electronic publishing.

Subscription agents pressure journal publishers to extend discounts of ten percent or more. The agent argues that its intervention saves the publisher time and money by consolidating library orders, paying the correct amount well in advance, and screening library claims.[40] It has become common for the large agents to order and pay electronically and to maintain electronic communication between major journal publishers and the agents' title information databases. There is no doubt that the subscription agent provides a service to the publisher.

The publisher who does not give vendors a discount claims that the journal price is as low as it can be already and that giving a discount to the agent will just raise the price to the subscriber. This publisher is reluctant to admit that the agent performs a service for anyone besides the library.

Discount-giving publishers may elect in some years to reduce the vendor discount instead of raising the subscription price. This action deprives the agent of expected revenue and forces him to raise the library's service charge, in order to make the necessary (or desired) profit margin.

The Serials Manager's Responsibility

The serials manager's responsibility to the library and library users is to become a full and equal partner in relationships with the subscription agent and the journal publisher. Partnership requires that the serials manager invest in a career long program of education, communication, and action. Because the librarian, the journal publisher, and the subscription agent rely upon one another, the responsible serials librarian must participate in business dealings on a equal basis with the other parties. Knowledge of the serials publishing, marketing, and distributing industries creates equality. Serials managers gain this equality through formal and informal education, through communication with colleagues and representatives of library-related businesses, and through action supporting one's opinions and concerns. Schools of library and information science do not teach equality; it is up to the professional serials specialist to attain this status, and, if necessary, to create the continuing education opportunities that foster growth and confidence. Personnel from publishers and subscription agencies are available to share, to teach, and to learn. The serials manager needs to learn which questions to ask to earn the respect of agents and publishers. He or she can no longer accept the premise of service over cost. Serials managers must balance the two philosophies according to the objectives of the library and its parent body and according to their own informed judgment. The satisfaction of a job well done, enduring friendships, and the opportunity to have an impact on the profession will reward the one who makes this commitment.

Education. The first step toward becoming a responsible serials manager is education. Serials librarians report, almost unanimously, that their graduate courses in librarianship did not prepare them to work with serials, and that they had to learn serials work on the job. Despite the efforts of the ALA/

ALCTS Serials Section, few formal curricula or courses specifically in serials librarianship exist in schools of library and information science. Where such a unit is taught, often a practicing librarian or a graduate student is the teacher. That is not necessarily bad. However, in most instances, all contact with serials comes in other courses: cataloging, collection development, technical services, and possibly automation. Managing library serials remains a specialized career, one that is restricted mostly to academic and research libraries. Most public, school, and smaller institutional libraries lack a serials collection large and complex enough to require management by a serials specialist. However, staff members who perform serials functions benefit from exposure to serials management in library school. Professional groups have urged that serials courses be taught and have even developed course outlines,[41] but few schools have adopted this recommendation. In the absence of a formal course on serials, a student may be able to serve as a graduate assistant or part-time employee in the serials unit of a local library. Another learning opportunity is the preparation of the masters paper and/or fulfillment of a field work requirement under the direction of a local serials librarian.

Most new library and information science students do not arrive at school with an interest in serials; those who do must make their own opportunities to learn about serials. To a serials librarian this seems unfortunate, because serials play a part in nearly every aspect of academic and research librarianship, whether one be primarily a public service or a technical service librarian. One has only to look at the serials pricing issue and the involvement of librarians from the bottom to the top of the professional hierarchy to see the desirability of education for serials work.

Schools of library and information science generally do not teach courses in serials publishing and acquisitions; thus the serials manager must learn through formal business courses, continuing education programs, or informal study. In order to understand the process of serial acquisitions, one must understand the business of journal publishing, including marketing and economics. Gillian Page, Robert Campbell, and A.J. Meadows, two British publishers and a British librarian, have published a book that should be required reading for every serials manager, *Journal Publishing: Principles and Practice*.[42] The authors addressed the work to both publishers and librarians, because they recognize the interrelationship.

The economics of journal publishing is a fascinating topic. It involves creating a budget for new journals; the determination of the financial break-even point for a periodical, and the action to be taken if the goals appear to be in jeopardy; and financial terms that are negotiable among the publisher, subscription agent, and librarian. Library science may offer courses in publishing, but these courses are likely to concentrate on book publishing and need to be supplemented by further reading and by discussion with journal publishers.

Communication. Communication is the second step toward becoming a responsible serials manager. As noted earlier, several channels for communication exist, among them meetings and workshops, users' groups, and field visits. In addition, there is the network of serials managers that has developed from contact at professional meetings and electronic discussion groups. The response to one publisher's attempt to charge libraries for permissible photocopying provides an example of this group in action. Telephone calls, electronic messages, and letters alerted librarians and subscription agents and publicized measures taken to resist the charge.

Opportunities for professional communication exist in the context of various users' groups, sponsored by subscription agents and automated system vendors. An additional opportunity is the interaction between the serials manager and the sales and service representatives of these companies. Subscription agents occasionally bring several librarians together for a thorough and concentrated discussion of common problems. The producers of bibliographic utilities and online serials systems have regular user meetings, sometimes in conjunction with ALA. Journal publishers have librarian advisory boards to recommend policy and practice. During all of these meetings the communication grows not only between the host and the guests, but also among librarians attending the sessions.

A further incentive to communication is a grant or fellowship that can be used for an internship with a journal publisher, a subscription agency, or possibly a fulfillment center. Further sources of support may include one's own library or parent institution, the Council on Library Resources, and ALA's Association of College and Research Libraries' Samuel Lazerow Fellowship. Many libraries have a grants specialist on the staff who can assist in writing the proposal.

Informed Action. The final component in enhancing the three-way relationship is informed action. One must not only learn and communicate, but one must also act. The responsible serials manager questions what is taught, what is communicated, and what he or she does not agree with or understand. Action in the form of reading and questioning contributes to learning and to the development of confidence. Action by means of writing for publication is a way both to teach and to learn. Imparting one's understanding to others helps a writer clarify his or her own thinking as much as it instructs the reader. If one is fortunate enough to receive response to an article, the resulting interchange of ideas is beneficial and exciting.

Supported by education and communication, the serials manager negotiates with business and professional colleagues outside the library. The informed serials manager who is willing to act is in an excellent position to get results. In the case of an alleged injustice by a journal publisher, the active serials manager works with other librarians within the local library and perhaps with institutional legal counsel. The network of serials specialists is available for information exchange, for the collective evaluation of the implications of library action, and for creating the impact of concerted action. If a publisher or vendor engages in a practice that appears to be unfair, serials managers may force either the rescission of the practice or an acceptable compromise.

Beyond this network is ALA's professional clout. The Serials Section has a channel to the very top level of the association—the executive director and ALA Council—whose responsibility is to serve the needs and protect the interests of the profession. Additionally, there are relationships with commercial and other business-related groups and individuals, perhaps developed in the context of NASIG or perhaps coming through members of one's own institutional community. For example, a faculty member may edit one of an offending publisher's journals. Acting in informed concert can be very effective, and it is an essential role for the responsible serials manager. Even without the public backing of colleagues, an individual can negotiate favorable terms by coming to the discussion well informed and by asking the right questions. This kind of activity is the serials manager's obligation.

NOTES

1.   David C. Taylor, *Managing the Serials Explosion* (White Plains N.Y.: Knowledge Industry Publications, 1982), p. 1.

2.   Chiou-Sen Dora Chen, *Serials Management: A Practical Guide*. (Chicago: American Library Association, 1995). (Frontiers of Access to Library Materials 3).

3.   Hazel Woodward and Stella Pilling, eds. *The International Serials Industry*. (Aldershot, England: Gower Publishing, 1993).

4.   Margaret Graham and Fiona Buettel, *Serials Management: A Practical Handbook* (London: Aslib, 1990).

5.   Andrew Osborn, *Serial Publications: Their Place and Treatment in Libraries*, 3rd ed. (Chicago: American Library Association, 1980).

6.   Clara D. Brown and Lynn S. Smith, *Serials: Past, Present and Future*, 2nd (rev.) ed. (Birmingham, AL: EBSCO Industries, Inc., 1980).

7.   Donald Davinson, *The Periodicals Collection*, rev. and enl. ed. (London: Andre Deutsch, 1978).

8.   David Grenfell, *Periodicals and Serials: Their Treatment in Special Libraries*, 2nd ed. (London: ASLIB, 1965).

9.   *Library Resources and Technical Services*, 1- 1957- (Chicago: American Library Association), ISSN: 0024-2527.

10.   *Serials Review*, 1- 1975- . (Ann Arbor, MI: Pierian Press) ISSN: 0098-7913.

11.   *Serials Librarian* 1- Fall 1976- (New York: Haworth Press), ISSN: 0361-526X.

12.   *Advances in Serials Management*, 1- 1986- (Greenwich CT: JAI Press, Inc.), ISSN: 1040-4384.

13.   *Serials: The Journal of the United Kingdom Serials Group*, 1- 1988- (Bradford, England: United Kingdom Serials Group), ISSN: 0953-0460.

14.   *Australian and New Zealand Journal of Serials Librarianship*, 1- 1990- (Binghamton, NY: Haworth Press), ISSN: 0898-3283.

15. *Library Acquisitions: Practice & Theory*, 1- 1977- (Oxford, England: Pergamon Press), ISSN: 0364-6408.

16. *Cataloging and Classification Quarterly*, 1- 1980- (New York: Haworth Press). ISSN: 0163-9374.

17. *Technical Services Quarterly*, 1- 1983- (New York: Haworth Press), ISSN: 0731-7131.

18. *Journal of Electronic Publishing.* (Ann Arbor, MI: University of Michigan Press). ISSN: 1081-2711. URL: http://www.press.umich.edu/jep.

19. SERIALST. 1990- (Burlington, VT: University of Vermont Library).

20. J. Harris Gable, "The New Serials Department," *Library Journal* 60 (1935): 867-870.

21. Hans H. Weber, "Serials Administration," *Serials Librarian* 4 (1979): 144-149.

22. Fred B. Rothman, "Pooh-Bah of the Serials Division," *Library Journal* 62 (1937): 457-459.

23. Beatrice V. Simon, "Cataloging of Periodicals," *Ontario Library Review* 33 (1949): 237-245.

24. Samuel Lazerow, "Serial Records: A Mechanism for Control," in *Serial Publications in Large Libraries*, ed. Walter C. Allen, 108-119. (Urbana, IL: University of Illinois Graduate School of Library Science, 1970).

25. Weber, "Serials Administration," p. 146.

26. Mitsuko Collver, "Organization of Serials Work for Manual and Automated Systems," *Library Resources and Technical Services* 24 (1980): 307-316.

27. Collver, "Organization," p. 310.

28. Margaret M. McKinley, "Serials Departments: Doomed to Extinction?" *Serials Librarian* 5 (Winter 1980): 18.

29. McKinley, "Serials Departments," p. 23.

30. McKinley, "Serials Departments," p. 23.

31. Philip E.M. Greene, III, "The Three-Way Responsibility: Dealer—Publisher—Library," in *Management Problems in Serials Work*, edited by Peter Spyers-Duran and Daniel Gore, 89-103. (Westport, CT: Greenwood Press, 1974).

32. John B. Merriman, "The Serials Information Chain: Working Together Toward a Common Goal," in *Library Serials Standards*, edited by Nancy Jean Melin, 125-130. (Westport, CT: Meckler Publishing, 1984).

33. Gordon Graham, "Adversaries or Allies?" *Scholarly Publishing* 14 (1984): 291.

34. *Title Varies* 3 (1976): 24.

35. For a full account of this issue, see Charles Hamaker and Deana Astle, "Recent Pricing Patterns in British Journal Publishing," *Library Acquisitions: Practice & Theory* 8 (1984): 225-232; Marcia Tuttle, "The Pricing of British Journals for the North American Market," *Library Resources & Technical Services* 30 (1986): 72-78; Deana Astle and Charles Hamaker, "Pricing by Geography: British Journal Pricing 1986, Including Developments in Other Countries," *Library Acquisitions: Practice & Theory* 10 (1986): 165-181.

36. For a full discussion of this issue, see Patrick Joyce and Thomas E. Merz, "Price Discrimination in Academic Journals," *Library Quarterly* 55 (1985): 273-283.

37. For a full discussion of this issue, see Marcia Tuttle, "Magazine Fulfillment Centers: What They Are, How They Operate, and What We Can Do About Them." *Library Acquisitions: Practice & Theory* 9 (1985): 41-49.

38. Greene, "The Three-Way Responsibility," p. 89.

39. Taylor, "The Love-Hate Relationship," p. 30.

40. John B. Merriman, "A Subscription Agent's View," in *Learned Journals Pricing and Buying Round*, ed. Bernard Dunkley, 28-29. (Letchworth, Eng.: Epsilon Press, 1985).

41. Association of Library Collections and Technical Services. Serials Section, "Syllabus for Serials Cataloging Unit," *ALCTS Newsletter* 3 (1992): 89-91; "Syllabus for Serials Collection Development and Acquisition Unit," *ALCTS Newsletter* 3 (1992): 106-107; "Syllabus for Serials

Collection Management, Records Systems, and Preservation Unit," *ALCTS Newsletter* 4 (1993): 8-9.

42. Gillian Page, Robert Campbell, and A.J. Meadows, *Journal Publishing: Principles and Practice*. (London: Butterworth, 1987).

Chapter 4

SERIALS STANDARDS

Standards are documented agreements containing technical specifications or other precise criteria to be used consistently as rules, guidelines, or definitions of characteristics, to ensure that materials, products, processes and services are fit for their purpose.[1]

Everyone needs standards. Consider the seamless passage of a telephone call from one system to another. Think of the risk and expense in building or buying a home without the requirements of a building code. Relax in the realization that you can refill the car's gas tank from any brand's service station, using your credit card anywhere in the world. Standards enable people to talk to each other. They ensure that we get what we pay for, that we know what we are paying for, and that we can pay as little for it as possible.

Communication among librarians and between librarians and patrons or publishers is possible only when each party understands what the other is saying. For communication to occur, the sender and the receiver of the message must define their terms identically. Between two libraries within a city or institutional system, understanding is not often a great problem, particularly when interaction by telephone is feasible. However, nationwide or international communication through printed or online union catalogs requires that each person involved enter and interpret data in the same way. To ensure uniformity, standards are created. The CONSER project, for example, adheres to cataloging standards so that its records will carry the same meaning to all who use them. It is difficult to establish standards when old procedures are entrenched and when standardization sometimes causes the loss of what is special and unusual.

For far too long standards-making organizations seemed to lack interest in developing standards for serials. Within the past twenty years, however, organizations and individuals have recognized the need for serials standards and have worked to increase awareness of this need. They have created one standard after another. This chapter discusses the need for serials standards and standards-making organizations. It also covers the process of creating a standard, serials standards that already exist, those that are in process of becoming adopted, and those which need to exist.

WHY SERIALS STANDARDS ARE NEEDED

The lack of standards promoted a wide range of ways for publishers to design and identify serials. Also, librarians used different forms and descriptive terms in their work. Serial numbering is fertile ground for confusion and frustration. Some publishers name issues for the seasons, skip the number for an issue or volume not published, combine issues, or use two numbering systems. The use of a season to identify one issue of a quarterly journal is not always ambiguous: Summer 1957, for example, seems acceptable, but what is Winter 1978? Does it appear before Spring 1978, or after Fall 1978 and before Spring 1979? What if the title is published in New Zealand? Sometimes producing a combined issue is an effective means for editors and publishers to get a slow journal back on schedule, but there are acceptable and unacceptable ways to combine. Issues 1 and 2 or any other consecutive numbers within one volume may be combined without problem, but the following letter from one publisher created visions of a nightmare for librarians who received it:

> Dear Subscriber:
> In October we will publish a special double issue, combining our *spring/summer* and *fall/winter* issues; this will be *volume 14, no. 2/volume 15, no. 1.*
> These two issues will be bound together, and for this reason, we cannot mail one without the other. Your subscription will lapse after 14, no. 2, the first half of this double issue. We are therefore requesting that you renew early so that we may keep you on our mailing list for the double issue.
> A year's renewal at this time will cover the second half of this double issue, 15, no. 1, and the next single issue, 15, no. 2 (which we expect to publish early in 1978).
> Thank you in advance for your attention.
> Sincerely,
> PERSPECTIVES OF NEW MUSIC
> P.S. If you do not wish to renew at this time, we will send you our next single issue, vol. 15, no. 2, instead of 14, no. 2.[2]

An even worse combined publication was that devised by *Booklegger Magazine* and *Emergency Librarian*. In 1976 the two library science journals produced a joint issue on library education and called it "*Booklegger Magazine*, vol. XIII #3 and *Emergency Librarian*, vol. III #3." Try to bind that one!

To add to the complexity of serial literature, many serials have identical titles. There is a limited number of "generic" titles (Bulletin, Journal, Proceedings, etc.); even nongeneric titles may be popular and belong to a number of serials, as in the case of *Africa*. Readers and librarians need standards to distinguish among these serials.

Librarians have been as guilty of lack of standardization as publishers, for they use customized order forms, claiming forms, and invoicing stipulations, and they often ask their suppliers to make insignificant changes in the library's mailing address. In fairness, some of this variety is unavoidable because of the need to fulfill requirements imposed by the parent institution, but much of it is unnecessary, and attention to the problem can improve the situation. National and international library groups are working with publishers, vendors, and others to resolve these problems of inconsistency by creating and publicizing standards.

Librarians, publishers, vendors, and users all need serials standards for a number of reasons. Standards enable two or more parties to communicate and feel confident that they are talking about or working on the same thing. This need is illustrated by the problems caused by the lack of a standard definition of "serial." In order to avoid confusion, anyone taking counts of serials or compiling lists of serials must define the scope of each project. A standard definition of "serial" would make many people's working lives less complicated.

Standards help to identify—to verify—serials. The best example of the identification function of serials standards is the International Standard Serial Number (ISSN), discussed fully later in this chapter. Standards also help to clarify communication between two parties. Standard communication formats, known as Electronic Data Interchange (EDI), enable subscription agents and journal publishers to exchange data electronically and correctly.

At the same time, a standard may be defined as a goal to attain. Library standards are voluntary, usually an unfortunate circumstance. However, it takes time to bring all records and all communications into conformance with a new standard. This type of standard, for example, the standard for serials holdings statements, is an objective to aim for.

HOW STANDARDS DEVELOP

A new standard does not just happen, it is developed in response to a need. The identification of this need for standardization may come from within the standards-making body, from its members, from another organization, or even from an individual. Once the organization's directors recognize the need for a standard, they appoint a committee composed of persons with diverse expertise in the discipline and in the specific area of the proposed standard. These persons draft a preliminary standard, based on their experience, and submit it to the parent body. Perhaps they might circulate a draft-in-progress to other interested groups and individuals. The parent group follows its own procedures for adopting or rejecting the standard. The procedures may consist of an executive body's discussing the proposal, submitting the draft standard to membership for a vote, or simply declaring that the standard is in effect. Recognized national organizations such as the National Information Standards Organization (NISO) in the United States have the most weight in the process of developing standards within a given country. National standards may be submitted to the International Organization for Standardization (ISO) for adoption or revision as international standards.

STANDARDS-MAKING ORGANIZATIONS

There are multiple sources of the standards used in serials work. The National Information Standards Organization is the chief standards-developing group in the United States. Library of Congress cataloging (including cataloging rule interpretations) is generally accepted as standard in the United States, and certain divisions of ALA have authority to create standards in their areas. Other countries have national standards-making bodies (for example, the British Standards Institution), and, at the highest level, sits the International Organization for Standardization. This discussion focuses on the American standards-setting body and on its work with national and international groups to develop the International Standard Serial Number, the standard most visible to serials librarians.

National Information Standards Organization (NISO)

According to its online Fact Sheet, NISO is:

> a non-profit association which develops technical standards used in a wide range of information services and products....NISO is accredited by the American National Standards Institute (ANSI), the coordinator of the voluntary standards development system in the United States.[3]

NISO has authority to develop and promote library and information services and publishing standards and serves here as an example of a national standards-making organization.

American business has long recognized the need for mass produced goods conforming to specific industry standards so that these products may be offered at the lowest cost to consumers. Following this line of thought, four American library associations petitioned the American Standards Association (now American National Standards Institute, or ANSI) in 1939 to form a committee on library standards. The resulting committee, Z39, was responsible for setting standards pertaining to library, information science, and related publishing practices.

ANSI is a nonprofit organization embracing over 160 technical, professional, and trade organizations representing some 1,000 companies. As the national clearinghouse for voluntary standards agencies in the United States and through membership in the ISO, ANSI participates in preparing standards at the international level.

In 1984 Committee Z39 changed its name to National Information Standards Organization (Z39) and requested "ANSI accreditation as an independent standards developing organization."[4] Later, NISO merged with ANSI's Committee Z85, Library Supplies and Equipment. NISO defines its current mission as:

1. Identifying areas in which standards are needed
2. Developing, writing and maintaining voluntary technical standards
3. Reviewing and improving existing standards
4. Representing U.S. interests in international standards development
5. Coordinating NISO standards with other national and international standards developers.

The more than sixty organizational (i.e., voting) members of NISO represent libraries; professional, technical, and educational associations; abstracting and indexing services; publishers; government agencies; and commercial and industrial organizations. Its executive council is composed of a chair, vice-chair/chair-elect, and nine councilors, three from each of the three major areas of concern—libraries, information science, and publishing. This group sets goals and priorities for standards development activities. Each of the 55 member organizations appoints a representative to work, comment, and vote on proposed standards. Briefly, the standards-setting procedure is as follows:

NISO procedures for developing and approving American National Standards for libraries, information science and publishing practices conform to guidelines and procedures set by ANSI. These procedures ensure that all interested stakeholders have an opportunity to participate in the standards making process.

A NISO standards committee composed of professionals with expertise in a particular area—such as software, micropublishing, technical reports, indexing, or transliteration—is appointed to develop a draft standard. The entire NISO membership and other interested persons and organizations receive the draft for comment. Every attempt is made to resolve conflicting opinions before the draft standard goes to the NISO membership for a formal vote. The draft standard is also publicly announced in ANSI's biweekly publication *Standards Action* for wider comment.

After NISO approves the draft, it is reviewed by the ANSI Board of Standards Review and published. NISO reviews published standards every five years for continued applicability, in a process that retraces the steps followed for new standards development.[5]

NISO publishes a quarterly journal, *Information Standards Quarterly* (ISSN: 1041-0031), which includes reports, brief news notes, and updates on the work of its subcommittees, as well as articles. NISO maintains a listserver to provide online information about its activities: new standards, newly published standards, availability of draft standards, standards committee activities, general news about standards, and how to order NISO standards. To subscribe, send an electronic mail message to listserv@nervm.nerdc.ufl.edu. The message reads: subscribe niso-l [Your] [Name].

NISO has issued more than fifty technical standards; many relate to serials, including "International Standard Serial Numbering (ISSN)" (1992), "Serial Item and Contribution Identifier (SICI)" (1991), "Serials Holdings Statements" (1986), and "Abbreviation of Titles of Publications" (1985, being revised, 1995). Unfortunately, some NISO standards were never adopted by the library and publishing world and have gone out of print. These include "Claims for Missing Issues of Serials" (1983) and "Periodicals: Format and Arrangement" (1977).

By devising and publishing its national standards, NISO performs an essential service for librarians and others working with serials. However, adherence to these standards is voluntary, and their impact depends upon familiarity with the standards and recognition of their value by librarians, publishers, vendors, and others. The work of the National Serials Data Program, the ISSN center in the United States, in promoting use of the International Standard Serial Number, illustrates the effort that is required after publication of a standard to ensure that it actually resolves the problems for which it was created. The cooperation of representatives from all sectors of the information industry works for the benefit of all.

ISSN International Centre (ISSN-IC)

The ISSN International Centre, formerly the International Serials Data System (ISDS) originated in 1971 within the UNESCO/UNISIST program as an intergovernmental organization based in France. Its charge then was to create an international register of scientific periodicals to facilitate standardization of citations to science and technology journal articles. The concept of Universal Bibliographic Control and the development of new automation technologies made it possible to develop a standard that would meet the need for worldwide bibliographic control of serial literature.[6] The overall objective of ISDS was expanded "to provide a reliable registry of world serial publications covering the full range of recorded knowledge and containing essential information for the identification and bibliographic control of serials."[7] The product was to be a machine-readable register "identifying serials uniquely and unequivocally by means of ISSN and key titles."[8] ISDS published *Guidelines* to describe its governance, policies, and procedures. However, what is particularly important in the context of standards is the ISSN-IC responsibility for managing the International Standard Serial Number program, in conjunction with the network of national and regional centers of responsibility. These national centers and the ISSN International Centre in Paris form a two-tier structure:

- On the one hand, each National Centre contributes its bibliographic expertise and knowledge of the serials published within its territory. It keeps in close contact with the users and publishers and also acts as focal point for national and regional networks.
- On the other hand, coordination and file building on the international level ensure common policies, uniform operational procedures, coherence and constant maintenance of ISDS standards, rules and formats.[9]

The National Serials Data Program at the Library of Congress is the national center of responsibility for ISSN in the United States; ISSN/Canada, at the National Library of Canada, is the center for that country. In the United Kingdom the UK National Serials Data Centre at the British Library Bibliographic Services Division fills this role. In 1995 the network includes 64 operational centers (a few new ones are not yet in operation) covering most of the world's serial publications.[10] The ISSN International Centre in Paris assigns ISSN for serials published in countries without national centers. In December 1994 operational centers had assigned more than 710,000 ISSN, and the number increases at about 50,000 ISSN a year.[11]

The ISSN-IC machine readable file generates several products. One is the *ISSN Register*, the ISSN authority file, which the international centre updates continually. It is a quarterly publication available by subscription on magnetic tape or microfiche. *ISSN Compact* is the same file on CD-ROM and includes in addition the *List of Serial Title Word Abbreviations*, maintained and published by ISSN-IC. This list is also available in print and on floppy disc. It contains more than 45,000 words (in about fifty languages) from serial titles processed by the ISSN network and their abbreviations. Words are abbreviated according to the ISO 4 standard, maintained by the ISSN-IC.

In 1975, ISDS, with UNESCO and the International Council of Scientific Unions Abstracting Board, issued *Guidelines for the Coded Bibliographic Strip for Serial Publications*.[12] The designation includes ISSN and/or CODEN to be used as a title code, volume and issue identification, pagination and nominal date of publication. A similar system appears in *American National Standard for Periodicals: Format and Arrangement* (NISO Z39.1-1977; now out of print). The *Guidelines* includes the procedures for calculating check characters for CODEN and ISSN. Guidelines and national level standards often evolve into international standards that reconcile slight national differences and carry added authority.

Suzanne Santiago, Director of the ISSN International Centre, summarizes the role of ISSN-IC in standards activities: "ISDS being a truly international partnership, it is a good forum to evaluate needs and suggest solutions, in the fields of language codes, country codes, data exchange... and of course any issues relating to serials at national and international levels."[13]

National Serials Data Program (NSDP)

The National Serials Data Program (NSDP), housed at the Library of Congress in its Serial Records Division, illustrates the activities of a national center of the ISSN system. Created in 1972 as the U.S. representative to ISDS, NSDP is supported by the three national libraries: LC, the National Agricultural Library, and the National Library of Medicine. NSDP registers and numbers all serials published in the United States and obtains ISSN, upon request by institutions in the United States, for foreign titles. In addition, NSDP promotes ISSN use and fills requests for the standard numbers. The office has also played a crucial role in the CONSER project. This section concentrates on NSDP's role as an ISSN national center.

In order to identify serials needing ISSN, NSDP receives documentation from a variety of sources: the three national libraries, serials publishers, abstracting and indexing services, the U.S. Postal Service, and other ISSN centers, among others. Of these, the requests from publishers and the USPS take priority.[14] By the early 1980s NSDP had begun to notify publishers when it assigned an ISSN from sources other than those from the publisher and to encourage the publisher to display and publicize the ISSN.[15]

As an ISSN national center, NSDP is one component in a worldwide system and has stated responsibilities to the international program. It cannot delegate its responsibilities to any other agency, domestic or foreign, because there needs to be a known source of information about the serials within its scope. It must work constantly to keep up with new technology that would enhance its ability to register and retrieve data, because of the need to communicate rapidly and accurately with ISSN-IC. It is committed to the rules and standards of the parent body.

International Organization for Standardization (ISO)

The International Organization for Standardization, or ISO, is a federation of about 100 national standards bodies throughout the world. ISO is a non-governmental organization whose mission is

> to promote the development of standardization and related activities in the world with a view to facilitating the international exchange of goods and services, and to developing cooperation in the spheres of intellectual, scientific, technological and economic activity.[18]

The work of ISO's member bodies and committees, subcommittees, and working groups leads to international agreements which are published as international standards. A full description of and justification for the International Organization for Standardization appears on The Faxon Company's World Wide Web site at http://www.faxon.com.

Serials Industry Systems Advisory Committee (SISAC)

The Serials Industry Systems Advisory Committee, better known by its acronym SISAC, formed in 1982 as a committee of the Book Industry Study Group, Inc. to develop standardized computer-to-computer formats for the serials industry. According to SISAC promotional literature, members include publishers, database producers, librarians, manufacturers, subscription agents, document delivery vendors, system vendors, and other information specialists. These persons communicate through meetings and *SISAC News*, the committee's newsletter. From this communication come proposals for standards transmitted to NISO and ANSI-Accredited Standards Committee (ASC) X12. SISAC currently concentrates its work in three areas:

> Standardization of formats to facilitate computer-to-computer transmission of all business transactions for the serials industry (this is commonly referred to as EDI—Electronic Data Interchange). SISAC is actively involved in the development of ASC X12 formats specifically for the serials industry. Five subcommittees established by SISAC are developing ASC X12 subsets for orders, order acknowledgements, claims, cancellations, and invoices. All subcommittee work is reviewed and commented on by the entire SISAC membership.
>
> Automation of serials check-in and serials control in libraries through standardized machine-readable coding to identify specific issues of serials. Formulating the data string to represent unique serial information is addressed in the Serial Item and Contribution Identifier (SICI) standard—ANSI/NISO Z39.56 (1991)....
>
> Standardized coding of contributions within serials to facilitate identification and retrieval of an article in document delivery and bibliographic databases and to expedite payment of royalties—represented by the SICI.[16]

The most visible product from SISAC is the Serial Item and Contribution Identifier (SICI), mentioned above. Now a NISO standard, the SICI "is a string of letters and/or numbers which uniquely identify a particular issue and article of a serial."[17] Equivalent to an ISSN for articles, the SICI begins with the ISSN and continues with numerical data representing the issue date, volume, and issue. The NISO standard (Z39.56-1991) adds location number and title data (generally the first letter of the first four significant words) plus a standard version number and record validation character. Table 4.1 illustrates the SICI.

Among the uses of the SICI are document delivery applications, payment of royalties, identification of articles at the prepublication stage, verification of electronic journals, electronic reserves, reprint inventory, Electronic Data Interchange (EDI), hypertext links between holdings and citations, and interlibrary loan.

Table 4.1. Example of a SICI

Citation: "SISAC Announces Release of Time-Saving Diskette"
SISAC News, v. 7, no. 1 (Spring/Summer 1992), p. 4.

SICI: 0885-3959(199221/22)7:1L.4:SART;1

Associated with the SICI is the SISAC Bar Code Symbol, a machine-scannable representation of the SICI at the issue level. This code could greatly expedite the check-in process if journal publishers printed it on the covers of their issues and if library system vendors developed interfaces for it. As with all standards, use of the SICI is voluntary. Those in the commercial sector must anticipate a financial advantage before they will adopt the standard. Its immediate adoption by several major journal publishers should motivate others to print the code on their serials. If librarians will demand the necessary interface in their automated systems, the vendors will provide it.

INTERNATIONAL COMMITTEE ON ELECTRONIC DATA INTERCHANGE FOR SERIALS (ICEDIS)

The newest group involved in serials standards is the International Committee on Electronic Data Interchange, or ICEDIS. Members of ICEDIS include large subscription agencies and leading scientific, technical, and medical publishers. Its mission is to develop cooperatively EDI standards for the serials industry, and members work closely with SISAC and other organizations in this effort. The ICEDIS page on Faxon's World Wide Web site explains:

> A company cannot implement EDI in isolation but must do so in conjunction with its trading partners. The trading partners must then agree which EDI standards and transaction sets will be used and how the EDI codes will be arranged. For this reason the members of ICEDIS are working together to define industry standards for EDI for use by journal publishers and subscription agents....[19]

At this time ICEDIS uses standards promulgated by ANSI Accredited Standards Committee X12. The standards currently used or being tested permit EDI for claims and claim responses, journal dispatch data, subscription rates, and subscription cancellation. Much of the ICEDIS members' effort goes into promoting the use of the X12 standards by all parties within the serials industry. The Faxon Company has available on its World Wide Web site a full discussion of EDI, including a bibliography and a list of standards.

INTERNATIONAL STANDARD SERIAL NUMBER (ISSN)

The International Standard Serial Number (ISSN) is without doubt the most significant standard in serials librarianship, and its development is one of the top two or three most crucial events in the world of serials. The ISSN is an eight-digit number, two groups of four numbers separated by a hyphen and preceded by the letters "ISSN." For example, the ISSN for *Special Libraries* is ISSN: 0038-6723. The ISSN is used worldwide as an unambiguous code to identify a specific serial publication. The last digit of the ISSN is a check digit, effective in detecting transposition errors, and so the number cannot be broken down into meaningful digits, as can the International Standard Book Number.

The need for a unique serial identifier had long been recognized by the time of the development of the ISBN. ANSC Z39 had in draft form a standard entitled "Identification Numbers for Serial Publications," which it had submitted to both the British Standards Institution and the ISO's Technical Committee 46—Documentation, for consideration as an international standard. In 1974, the latter group issued for ratification a draft standard for International Standard Serial Numbers; it was accepted by members and published in 1975.

Even before final approval of the ISSN, the R.R. Bowker Company was authorized to assign the standard numbers to both its own database of serial titles and to titles being included in its publication of the 1950-1970 cumulation of *New Serial Titles*. Bowker completed the mammoth project with relatively few difficulties. There were instances of one title being assigned two ISSN or one ISSN being attached to more than one title, which led to all the numbers being considered provisional until they had been validated by NSDP or another ISDS national center. On the whole, however, the fact that numbers had been assigned to titles prior to adoption of the standard encouraged use of ISSN from the beginning.

The national centers are responsible for promoting use of ISSN, because its success depends upon consistent worldwide use by publishers, librarians, subscription agents, and scholars. To that end, NSDP provides publishers a brochure packed with information about the significance and proper use of ISSN, including an application form for the publishers to return for the free-of-charge assignment of an ISSN. Included in the brochure for publishers is a list of eight advantages of ISSN use:

1. ISSN provides a useful and economical method of communication between publishers and suppliers, making trade distribution systems faster and more efficient.
2. The ISSN results in accurate citing of serials by scholars, researchers, abstracters, and librarians.

3. As a standard numeric identification code, the ISSN is eminently suitable for computer use in fulfilling the need for file update and linkage, retrieval, and transmittal of data.
4. ISSN is used in libraries for identifying titles, ordering and checking in, and claiming serials.
5. ISSN simplifies interlibrary loan systems and union catalog reporting and listing.
6. The U.S. Postal Service uses the ISSN to regulate certain publications mailed at second-class and controlled circulation rates.
7. The ISSN is an integral component of the journal article citation used to monitor payments to the Copyright Clearance Center, Inc.
8. All ISSN registrations are maintained in an international data base and are made available in the ISDS Register.[20]

Thus, the ISSN benefits those who produce serials, those who process them, and those who read them. NSDP refers to the ISSN as "the 'social security number' of the serials world."[21] Serials librarians were probably the group of ISSN users most pleased by the standard, because it brought specific identification of titles to every area of their work.

The success of the ISSN was virtually assured in the late 1970s: at the urging of the National Federation of Abstracting and Indexing (now Information) Services, the Association of Research Libraries, and other groups, the U.S. Postal Service (USPS) began to require that most serial publications adopt and display the ISSN as USPS's official registration number, as qualification for second-class postage rates. NSDP set up a branch office in the main Washington DC post office and, with the assistance of CONSER participants and the support of a grant from the Council on Library Resources, identified and registered the serials involved.[22]

Associated with the ISSN and inseparably linked to it in the files of ISSN-IC is a corresponding "key title." This title is "based upon the title as it appears on an issue or volume, with the addition of an author statement if the title consists of a generic term [and] qualifying information [if necessary] to create a unique citation."[23] If the key title of a serial changes according to rules stated in *Guidelines to ISDS*, a new ISSN is assigned. The earlier ISSN remains as the unique identifier of the serial under the former title. Many key titles were assigned before the implementation of AACR2 and would be different if they were assigned today.

In resource sharing efforts and particularly in union lists of serials the ISSN eliminated problems created by use of more than one cataloging code. This unique serial identifier minimizes errors in transmission of bibliographic data from a local cataloger to a union list editor or from one collection development officer to another. Interlibrary loan requests carrying an ISSN no longer go unfilled as a result of garbled references. Finally, the ISSN is a much more satisfactory means of accessing a database than truncated title or other access point, because it retrieves a single serial title. With the proliferation of serial publications and the frequent revision of cataloging codes, it is now difficult to imagine working with serials that lack the International Standard Serial Number.

In the early years of its existence librarians and others used the ISSN primarily to counteract the different forms of entry for a single title. AACR reduced that need by permitting title entry for most serials. As time has passed, all parties have replaced most catalog and acquisition records that used the old cataloging rules. At the same time, automation of serials processes has become the norm for librarians, journal publishers and subscription agents. Serials specialists use the ISSN today more as a means of access to automated files than to resolve problems of entry.

USE OF SERIALS STANDARDS

The information science profession develops standards in response to specific needs. Its members use and amend or abandon them as required, and they create new standards to fill new communication needs. The acceptance of international standards represents a positive response to the need for worldwide sharing of resources. The national standards organizations have a significant dual role in the international scene: they identify where standards are needed and develop preliminary ones which then are tested and revised, and they promote existing international standards. Their success depends upon the degree of acceptance and use by persons and agencies concerned.

This acceptance comes only after a struggle, as illustrated by the ISSN story. In 1988, after NISO had approved several standards related to serials, the Serials Section Committee to Study Serials Standards of ALA's then-RTSD conducted a survey to determine the use of serials standards in libraries.[24] With 94 responses out of 300 questionnaires sent, the committee members found astonishing absence not only of use of serials standards, but also of knowledge about them. The reasons given were not surprising: no time to learn about standards, no money to implement standards, had to automate quickly with no time to implement standards, library administration did not want adherence to standards, local standards work fine, and so on. The committee report concluded with this thought: "But the most disheartening fact about serials standards work is that most technical services librarians don't seem to know about them, don't have anything to say about them, and haven't really considered them." [25] Attached to the report are five recommendations:

1. Members of the ALA RTSD SS Committee to Study Serials Standards recommend that there be more programs, workshops, and seminars on

serials standards. There is a need for more education concerning the existence of standards, the content of these standards, and the advantages of using standards.

2. We recommend that there be a trial period for any new draft standards. Participating libraries should encompass all types of libraries so as to receive sufficient feedback and input before a draft becomes an official standard. Therefore libraries do not have to tailor them for local use at a later date.

3. We recommend that librarians strongly consider choosing and requesting systems that meet the standards as the prerequisite for long-range library planning efforts.

4. We recommend that programmers adhere to national standards and that there be a continuing effort to modify and make plans for modification of local or present systems to conform to national standards or to handle changes and revisions in available standards.

5. We recommend widespread adoption of standards for better communication, information exchange and sharing, data transfer from one system to another, union listing, and so forth.

This committee deserves congratulation! The ignorance and apathy toward standards expressed by questionnaire respondence was embarrassing, and the committee report made excellent recommendations. To date, however, there seems to have been little movement toward general adoption of serials standards.

NOTES

1. "Introduction to ISO," from The Faxon Company's World Wide Web site (http://www.faxon.com).

2. *Title Varies* 4 (1977): 11.

3. "National Information Standards Organization, NISO Fact Sheet," from The Faxon Company's World Wide Web site (http://www.faxon.com). Much of this section comes from this fact sheet and from National Information Standards Organization. "What You Need to Know about Technical Standards for Information Services, Libraries, and Publishing." Bethesda, MD: National Information Standards Organization, 1993.

4. Sandra K. Paul, "Chairperson's Annual Report." *Voice of Z39* 6 (September 1984): 1.

5. "NISO: Making the Information Profession More Productive," brochure issued by NISO and sent to the author in November 1993.

6. Suzanne Santiago, "International Serials Data System," *Serials* 6 (March 1993): 41.

7. UNISIST, *ISDS Guidelines* (Paris: 1973), p. 1.

8. A.A. Mullis, "The International Serials Data System (ISDS)," *United Kingdom Serials Group Newsletter* 6 (June 1984): 12.

9. *ISDS Publications and Services*, 1980.

10. "National Centres of the ISSN Network," ISSN International Centre World Wide Web page (http://www.well.com:80/www/issnic). A list of the national centers appears in this article.

11. "1995 Statistics of the ISSN Register," ISSN International Centre World Wide Web page (http://www.well.com:80/www/issnic).

12. *Guidelines for the Coded Bibliographic Strip for Serial Publications* (Paris: United Nations Educational, Scientific and Cultural Organization; International Council of Scientific Unions Abstracting Board; International Serials Data System, 1975).

13. Santiago, International, 45.

14. Linda K.Bartley, "ISSN and NSDP: A Guide for the Initiated," in *The Management of Serials Automation*, ed. by Peter Gellatly, 171. (New York: Haworth Press, 1982).

15. Bartley, "ISSN and NSOP," p. 171.

16. "Serials Industry Systems Advisory Committee," from The Faxon Company's World Wide Web site (http://www.faxon.com).

17. "Serials Industry."

18. "Introduction to ISO."

19. "ICEDIS," on The Faxon Company's World Wide Web site (http://www.faxon.com).

20. *ISSN Is for Serials* (Washington DC: National Serials Data Program, 1979; also available on LC MARVEL).

21. "ISSN Numbers: An Introduction," available on The Faxon Company's World Wide Web site (http://www.faxon.com).

22. Detailed discussions of the plan to register these serials appear in Linda K. Bartley, "The International Standard Serial Number (ISSN) and its Use by the United States Postal Service." *Unesco Journal of Information Science, Librarianship and Archives Administration* 2 (1980): 245-51 and *CONSER* 1 (1978): 1-2.

23. Mary Sauer, "National Serials Data Program," *Drexel Library Quarterly* 11 (June 1975): 46.

24. Sally C. Tseng, et al, "Serials Standards Work: The Next Frontier." *Library Resources and Technical Services* 34 (1990): 139.

25. Tseng et al., "Serials Standards," p. 154.

Chapter 5

SERIALS COLLECTION DEVELOPMENT

Luke Swindler

INTRODUCTION

In all libraries serial publications—including books that are regularly updated and best acquired on subscription—form the core of reference and general information collections. In terms of supporting research, serials not only constitute the principal intellectual components but are more heavily used than monographs. Only a few humanities disciplines still present an exception to this trend—and even here the typical researcher reviews several journals each week on a regular basis.[1] At the same time, mounting pressures brought by the dynamics of serials growth, rising user needs and expectations, changes in the economic and technological environment, and concomitant demands for greater library accountability, efficiency, and effectiveness make it imperative that all librarians involved in managing serials become more knowledgeable and proactive than in the past.

This chapter examines the major issues and methodologies relevant to serials collection development. The first section discusses key philosophical and strategic considerations involved in effectively meeting the serials needs of users. The second and longest part discusses how one finds out what serials are available, concentrating on systematic identification and essential tools. A segment on selection follows, and the chapter concludes with a section on evaluation.

The perspective is that of a librarian with collection development responsibilities rather than someone working in a serials unit or a library administrator. Although the latter two need to comprehend the collection development process, it is the former who is charged with understanding serials as intellectual and informational resources and represents the crucial link between users and library collections. It is also the collection development librarian—either alone or in conjunction with other library staff and users— who makes the actual decisions regarding what specific serials will be provided and how. This chapter also emphasizes the situation in academic and research libraries, because their users typically have the greatest need for serials and, as a consequence, such institutions have the most extensive, expensive, and complex collection development programs for serial resources.

PHILOSOPHY AND STRATEGY

There is no such animal as serials collection development *per se*. Rather, the fundamental challenge is how to manage all relevant informational and intellectual resources in a wholistic context, within which serials are but one component and local ownership but one option. A library not only acquires or otherwise provides serial information in relation to books and other resources, but it must do so in terms of institutional missions and specific programs, if it is to be truly effective. By extension, the widespread inability to create cost-effective serials collections within an environment of limited financial resources and rapid technological transformation is largely explained by the failure of librarians to match materials spending closely with actual user and programmatic needs in general and to budget for serials in a wholistic and flexible manner specifically.

Contributing to this situation and the resultant "serials crisis" is the traditional emphasis on quantity rather than quality and ownership rather than access. As Paul H. Mosher observed:

> The literature of librarianship does not even agree on the meaning of the term *good* with regard to collections, to say nothing of providing us with ready techniques for analyzing or evaluating their quality. Often we are told in response to the question how *good*, how *many*, in the rather naive belief that quantity and quality are necessarily equivalent terms when applied to library materials.[2]

Librarians have considered the larger hoards to be the better collections, with completeness the ultimate goal. As a result, almost all types of institutions try to amass the largest accumulations possible.[3] The triumph of this ideology of massive acquisition as a substitute for careful selection reached its climax during the affluent 1960s.

Economic conditions in the 1990s, coupled with serials publishing and pricing patterns, have made these traditional collection development ideologies and budgetary patterns fiscally irresponsible. At the very least, the resulting runaway subscription expenditures have created collections of print titles that cannot be sustained, especially in scientific and technological fields. More fundamentally, they have caused many libraries to lose effective programmatic control of their budgets.

The typical American research institution acquires hundreds of thousands of articles annually that no one reads—and, at least in fields where knowledge rapidly dates, probably will never be read. At the same time these libraries are often barely acquiring enough books to meet student instructional needs, even though their materials budgets total millions of dollars. In fact, budgetary distortions have become so great in academe that even at the abstract level of program support, there often is no relationship between the relative levels of library spending on a subject and its quality and importance within the university.

This situation demands a more rational philosophy of serials collection development, emphasizing selectivity and quality and firmly based on meeting reasonable needs within an environment of limited resources.[4] Furthermore, quality can no longer be considered synonymous with quantity, but must be redefined in terms of the "utility or benefit of library collections to library patrons, their needs and work, and to institutional programs."[5]

In order to implement such a strategy, librarians must see themselves as providers rather than collectors, for even in the case of the most affluent institutions, serials collection development must essentially involve non-selection from an ever-growing universe of print and electronic subscription possibilities. Moreover, such an approach mandates a real commitment to cooperative collection development and the creation of efficient document delivery options for marginal, highly specialized, or low-use titles.[6]

The importance of selectivity and relevance as hallmarks of successful serials collection development cannot be stressed enough. Because the on-going nature of serial commitments translates into certain growth in cost, whereas sustained budgetary increases to cover these charges are at best problematic, a rational strategy demands that serials holdings be carefully controlled. Effective control, in turn, can be achieved only if librarians spend time systematically developing serials collections, monitoring relevance and use, and creating cooperative acquisitions programs that are coupled with non-traditional document delivery options.

A rational collection development philosophy begins with the realization that funds are allocated to libraries to support specific programs with the most appropriate configuration of resources—and not to purchase arbitrarily X dollars worth of materials in format A or Y dollars in format B. Within this context no one format is necessarily more important than any other. The tendency of librarians to budget by format, coupled with automatically transferring funds from the top of the budget to cover on-going subscriptions on a global basis, does not make sense in terms of supporting programs with the most appropriate configuration of resources or relating library spending to institutional priorities. Moreover, such an approach invariably impairs an institution's ability to meet needs equitably, given the differential rates of serials growth and inflation that exist.

Serials expenditures should be part of a consolidated budget allocation for the support of a particular program—and not viewed as privileged acquisitions to be taken off the top of the total budget. On a theoretical level this view demands that serials be fully integrated into overall collection development policies and programs. On a practical level this philosophy mandates that each subscription be regularly monitored, because it will inevitably increase in price and change in content.

Within this context a rational collection development program will be achieved only if selection consists of the most important titles that most clearly meet identifiable needs for a given price, particularly in terms of the core serials accounting for the vast majority of use.[7] Librarians not willing to give serials collection development the attention and scrutiny it deserves and budget for serials in a responsible manner will not only end up with poor holdings but will almost certainly come to financial grief.

IDENTIFICATION

Effective serials collection development begins with librarians specifically charged with the identification of titles on an on-going, systematic, and comprehensive basis. Because so many serials—particularly electronic titles— are non-trade publications and hence difficult to find out about, their identification should not depend upon chance. Moreover, collection development librarians can only fulfill this charge if they use a wide variety of tools.

Identification sources fall into three major groups: those for current serials, those for new titles, and those for retrospective acquisitions. Their corresponding identification tools allow a librarian to determine what serials are being published, what new serial publications have been launched, and what titles existed in the past and are readily available for acquisition. Ultimately, successful development of a serials collection depends more on a systematic view of identification than reliance on a single tool or set of tools, while the value of any one of the sources discussed below is determined primarily by individual needs and the particular combination of identification sources used.

Although nearly all the sources to be discussed have multiple uses, it is their value to a collection development librarian for purposes of identification that constitutes the basis for inclusion. As a consequence, this chapter ignores subscription agents' printed guides, such as *Faxon Guide to Serials* and EBSCO's *Librarian's Handbook* and their corresponding databases, such as DataLinx and EBSCONET. Although such vendor products provide the most up-to-date information on price and availability, these sources are aimed at staff working in a serials unit, while the online versions are typically neither user-friendly nor searchable in ways that are useful for collection development purposes. Furthermore, because this survey is selective, it concentrates on the tools of greatest potential utility in a general North American library. Finally, an attempt is made to indicate every format in which a source exists and to highlight significant differences between the print and various electronic versions.

Current Serials

A number of tools provide comprehensive coverage of the major classes of current serials, with the electronic versions typically providing greater currency, more powerful and sophisticated searching options, and a variety of data-capture and printout formats. Librarians should be prepared to consult more than one source, however, because each varies somewhat in scope, annotations, currency, and searching options.

General

Comprehensive Directories: International

Ulrich's-International Periodicals Directory. New Providence, NJ: Bowker, 1932-. Print version [0000-0175] is annual, with triannual supplement (entitled *Ulrich's Update* [0000-0174]) and toll-free *Ulrich's Hotline* [1-800-346-8110] available 9-5 EST every day at no cost to subscribers; also available in quarterly-updated microfiche (entitled *Ulrich's Microfiche*), quarterly-updated CD-ROM (entitled *Ulrich's Plus* [1068-0500]), online, and on magnetic tape.

Contains information on approximately 147,000 active titles from 70,000 publishers. Covers periodicals, annuals, and irregular serials published worldwide, with separate volume for 10,000 general U.S. and foreign daily and weekly newspapers. Titles that began within last three years have special indicator. Electronic versions list an additional 50,000 ceased titles.

U.S. daily and weekly newspapers are arranged geographically, while other titles are listed alphabetically under 967 topical categories, with a cross-index to subjects. Entries for any title can contain over 50 descriptive data elements, including subtitle; previous and alternate titles; brief description; Dewey Decimal and/or Library of Congress classification; indexing/abstracting coverage; country of publication; ISSN and CODEN; language note when the text is in a language other than that of the country of publication or is multi-lingual; year first published; frequency of publication; subscription price(s); publisher or distributor name, address, and fax and telephone numbers; special features such as book reviews and cumulative indexes; indexing and abstracting information; back issue, reprint, microform, and CD-ROM and online availability; document delivery availability and if registered with Copyright Clearance Center.

Has special listings for refereed, control circulation, CD-ROM, online, ceased, international organization titles as well as micropublishers/distributors, reprint services, CD-ROM producers, and online vendors. Has indexes by ISSN, title,

title change, and (for newspapers) geography. Electronic versions offer a wide array of searching and limiting options that constitute the most attractive feature of this database for purposes of collection development.

Although extremely useful, especially for North American and West European titles, *Ulrich's* coverage of titles from areas of the globe is incomplete, sometimes inaccurate, or often not up-to-date. Still, Bowker claims that a recent independent survey comparing *Ulrich's* to seven other tools found it to contain more entries and more accurate information, to be easier to use and read, and considered overall the best value for the money.

The Serials Directory: An International Reference Book. Birmingham, AL: EBSCO, 1986- . Print version [0886-4179] is annual with two cumulative updates and free serials research hotline for complex questions; also available on quarterly-updated CD-ROM (entitled *The Serials Directory: EBSCO CD-ROM* [1066-7490]).

Print version contains information on 151,000 serials (including newspapers, annuals, and irregular titles) from 87,000 publishers, while CD-ROM includes historical data for an additional 30,000 titles and provides access to *The Index and Abstract Directory: An International Guide to Services and Serials Coverage*, which contains information on over 1,300 indexing and abstracting services covering 56,000 titles.

Titles arranged under broad subject categories, and entry for any title can contain over 60 descriptive data elements, including subtitle, previous title, price, notations if began publication within last three years, editor's name, languages, frequency, circulation, and publisher's name, address, telephone and fax number, and E-mail and Internet addresses.

Has title and ISSN indexes, and special listings for titles accepting advertising or book reviews, peer reviewed serials, new titles, publications available on CD-ROM or online, titles available through the Copyright Clearance Center, and serials with a controlled circulation. CD-ROM version offers wide array of searching and limiting options plus expanded cross-reference and subject breakdown.

Comprehensive Directories: U.S./Canada

The Standard Periodical Directory. [0085-6630] New York: Oxbridge Communications. 1964- . Annual print edition [0085-6630] and a CD-ROM edition that is now annual and but will become quarterly in 1996; also available on magnetic tape and as customized extractions from the database.

Is the most comprehensive listing of U.S. and Canadian serials, providing information on nearly 85,000 titles appearing at least once every two years. Includes magazines, scholarly and trade journals, newsletters, house organs, directories, yearbooks, transactions and proceedings of learned societies and associations, some government publications, and serials issued by religious, ethnic, literary, political, and social groups.

Serials are divided into 265 subject categories and arranged alphabetically within each group (with a keyword index and guide to related categories). Entries include title (and previous titles); publisher's name, address and fax and telephone number; sponsoring group and editorial staff; description of editorial content and prime readership (along with selective ethnic group code); year established; frequency of issue; indexing/abstracting services coverage; single issue and subscription prices; circulation; advertising information; data on physical formats and average number of pages per issue; publication type; ISSN; and LC catalog number. Has cross index to subjects in the front and alphabetical title index and online index in the back.

Gale Directory of Publications and Broadcast Media: An Annual Guide to Publications and Broadcasting Stations. Detroit: Gale, 1990-. [1048-7972] Annual, which includes an interedition publication (entitled *Gale Directory of Publications and Broadcast Media Update* [with same ISSN]); also available on diskette/magnetic tape and online, with plans for a CD-ROM version being developed. Formerly: *Gale Directory of Publications, IMS Directory of Publications, Ayer Directory of Publications,* and *Ayer Directory of Newspapers, Magazines, and Trade Publications.*

A major source for newspapers and general and certain specialized categories of serials. Covers 39,000 U.S. and Canadian newspapers, magazines, journals from 11,000 publishers, as well as radio and television stations and cable systems; excludes newsletters and directories.

Arranged by state or province, then city, then media category, with all publications originating from a locality arranged alphabetically by title. Entries include detailed bibliographic, address, and cost/format data, plus description of type of publication (including purpose, audience, and relevant remarks) and circulation.

Separate volume of indexes by publisher, title and keywords in title and former titles, and subject. Has 17 broad subject and type categories, together with index to nearly 1,000 subject terms used within them. The major classified lists of publications include: agricultural, ethnic (black, Hispanic, Jewish, foreign-language), college, fraternal, religious, women's publications, daily periodicals, general magazines, newspapers (daily, paid community, free) , shopping guides, and trade, technical and professional publications.

Comprehensive Directories: Electronic Titles and Services

While the sources above include electronic publications, the complicated nature of these products often results in collection development librarians wanting additional information. The following tools are among the most helpful:

Fulltext Sources Online: For Periodicals, Newspapers, Newsletters, Newswires & TV/ Radio Transcripts. [1040-8258] Needham Heights, MA: BiblioData, 1989- . Semiannual.

Arranges more than 5,000 titles alphabetically. Entries include special notes, geographical orientation; name(s) of search services carrying title and the specific database, section, or file containing it; time period covered; frequency of updating; lag between online and print version; indication of full or selective coverage of the periodical if also available in print; and indications of update and archival file segments. Has subject and geographic index and listing of non-English sources. Also includes vendor listings with addresses and telephone numbers.

Gale Directory of Databases. Detroit: Gale Research, 1993- . Semi-annual print [1066-8934] and CD-ROM editions; also available on diskette/magnetic tape and online. Formed by merger of: *Computer-Readable Databases, Directory of Online Databases,* and *Directory of Portable Databases.*

Covers over 5,000 online and 4,000 portable form (CD-ROM, diskette, magnetic tape, handheld and batch access) databases from 3,400 producers, 800 online services, and nearly 1,000 vendors/distributors. Entries include name/acronym; symbol if new or significantly revised since the last edition; producer name, address, and telephone numbers; contact person or unit; coproducer and former producer; alternative and former database name, type (e.g., bibliographic, bulletin board, full-text, numeric, image, etc.); scope and coverage content; subject coverage; language; geographic coverage; year first available; time span; updating frequency; organization/vendor through which the database is available online; software and hardware requirements; alternate electronic formats; and price. Has geographic, subject, and master indexes, with the last listing all databases and related product and organization names in a single alphabetical sequence.

Directory of Electronic Journals, Newsletters, and Academic Discussion Lists. [1057-1337] Washington, D.C.: Association of Research Libraries, Office of Scientific and Academic Publishing, 1991- . Annual printed edition. Electronic update for new postings is available from NewJour listserv (to subscribe send e-mail to majordomo@ccat.sas.upenn.edu with nothing on the subject line and the simple message "subscribe newjour" or, if you want to receive a single daily message compiling all the day's notices, "subscribe newjour-digest"); archive of all postings that is updated daily and is fully searchable can be found at http://gort.ucsd.edu/newjour, which allows users to read an entry and then click and go to site described.

Covers 700 electronic journals and newsletters and 2,500 academic discussion lists (including electronic conferences, bulletin boards, and interest groups). Also includes timely essays on key issues, one of which typically is bibliographical survey.

Arranges titles into two major sections: journals/newsletters and academic discussion lists/interest groups (which are sub-divided into broad subject clusters). Journal/newsletter entries arranged alphabetically by title/name, and typically include description, ISSN, if free or the cost, when began, electronic formats, distribution method, frequency, subscription address/access method, back issue address, contact person(s), submissions address, related lists or news groups, URL, issuing agency, coverage by abstracting and indexing services, and language (if other than English). Academic discussion lists/interest groups arranged alphabetically by title and typically include description, subscription address/access method, archive address, editor(s)/moderator(s), and issuing agency. Has consolidated index of keywords/titles/institutional affiliations.

Comprehensive Library Catalogs

Catalogs of major libraries and specialized institutions with in-depth collections in specific fields have always been important sources for finding out about serials. The availability of many online catalogs (referred to as OPACs) via the Internet—together with numerous guides that allow one to locate them such as *The Internet Directory* and the Gopher Tree of Internet-Accessible Libraries [gopher://libgopher.yale.edu; ftp://ftp.utdallas.edu/pub/staff/billy/libguide]—has increased the importance of these sources and made them available to any librarian with access to appropriate computer and telecommunications equipment.

Because of the comprehensive nature of its collections and the major role it plays in providing bibliographic information on serials—including forthcoming titles—the Library of Congress's online catalog (locis.loc.gov; http://lcweb.loc.gov) is a fundamental source of information on what serials exist, despite its lack of user-friendliness. Harvard's OPAC (hollis.harvard.edu) is the largest university library collection available over the Internet. Moreover, coverage of its OPAC is growing rapidly as Harvard spends millions on a massive retrospective conversion of its bibliographic records. Harvard's OPAC also has the advantages of being easy to use and including materials on order and items received but not yet cataloged.

Melvyl (melvyl.ucop.edu) is the largest academic consortium OPAC, including not only all nine University of California campus and affiliated libraries, the California State Library, and the Center for Research Libraries but also the California Academic Libraries List of Serials. Finally, if one is willing to pay, OCLC's WorldCat (a user-friendly version of the cataloging database available via its FirstSearch system) is the most comprehensive source of information on serials to be found in library collections, although its searching options are more limited and less sophisticated than most research library OPACs.

Special

Newspapers

Editor & Publisher International Yearbook. New York: Editor and Publisher, 1921- . [0424-4923] Annual print [0424-4923] and CD-ROM editions and also available online.

    Includes statistical and directory information dealing with world journalism and is useful in collection development because of its comprehensive listing of

U.S., Canadian, and foreign newspapers. U.S. newspapers are arranged alphabetically within several major groups, daily, national, tabloid, weekly, and several special categories (black, ethnic, gay and lesbian, military, religious, and college/university) and then by state and city. Foreign press is grouped by major geographical area, then country, then city, with the individual dailies arranged alphabetically under city.

U.S. entries include title, address and telephone and fax numbers, circulation, price, advertising rates, news services subscriptions, date established, frequency, special sections and magazines included, and editorial and management personnel. Foreign entries include title, frequency, date established, circulation, and editorial and publishing personnel.

Newspapers Online: A Guide to Searching Daily Newspapers Whose Articles are Online in Full Text. [1065-8947] Needham Heights, MA: BiblioData, 1993- . Annual, with two updates during the year.

Covers 200 dailies published throughout the world (3/4 of which are in North America) that make substantially all their contents available to the public. Concentrates on general interest rather than specialized titles, although has some major business newspapers. Titles arranged alphabetically within four major geographic regions of the world. Entries contain 2-3 pages of data including publisher and address, region covered, publishing background and schedule for both print and online versions (including history/nature, newswires subscriptions carried, editions, and circulation), online and CD-ROM systems that offer fulltext versions (along with their chronological coverage and lag time), and telephone numbers for database assistance. Has index by title and alternate title and geographic locators indices. Also includes searching tips and vendor listings with addresses and telephone numbers.

Outing, Steve. "Online Newspaper Services." *Directory of Electronic Journals, Newsletters and Academic Discussion Lists*, 1995, p. 51-87. [Print version revised 4/9/1995; also electronic version at http://marketplace.com/e-papers.list.www/e-papers.home.page.html].

Arranges titles by method of access (newspaper local dial-up services/BBSs and then various services such as America Online and CompuServe). Entries include title/name/keyword, dial-up number, contact, price, when launched, number of subscribers, and description.

Newsletters

Although generally ignored as a minor class of serials, newsletters are growing in number, especially with the proliferation of electronic titles. The expanding demand for the most current information, together with the proliferation of special interest serials, will undoubtedly increase the importance of newsletters as library resources.

Newsletters in Print. Detroit: Gale, 1978-. Biennial print edition [0899-0425]; also on diskette/magnetic tape and online (which corresponds in part to the online version of *Gale Database of Publications and Broadcast Media*). Formerly: *Newsletters Directory* and *National Directory of Newsletters and Reporting Services.*

Provides information on more than 11,500 print and online subscription, membership, and free newsletters published in the United States and Canada; excludes titles of purely local interest and most house organs. Entries are arranged under seven broad categories and include title and alternate/former title(s); publisher, address, and telephone and fax numbers; editor(s); description; when began; features; illustration; editorial/advertising policies; audience; frequency; physical size and number of pages; circulation; and price. Has title/keyword, subject, and publisher indexes, plus alphabetical lists of titles that are online, free, or accept advertising.

Oxbridge Directory of Newsletters. New York: Oxbridge Communications, 1979- . Annual print edition [0163-7110] and included in the CD-ROM version of *Standard Periodical Directory*. Formerly: *Standard Directory of Newsletters.*

Is most comprehensive source for U.S. and Canadian newsletters available, containing over 20,000 titles. Titles are arranged alphabetically under 265 subject categories. Entries include title (and former title); publisher's name, address, and telephone and fax numbers; prime readership; key editorial staff; editorial description; year established; frequency; physical size and number of pages; ISSN; subscription price; circulation; and list rental and printing information. Has multi-publisher, online, title/ISSN, title change indexes plus alphabetical listing of publishers by state.

Little Magazines and Alternative Serials

These publications are quite diverse and distinct. They are also growing in number—and perhaps influence as well—as a consequence of the revolution in computers and telecommunications technology, which has made it easier to publish and distribute such materials. According to the introduction in *The World of Zines*, discussed below, these publications range from the traditional small press world of literary and poetry magazines, to periodicals espousing extreme political ideologies and causes, to the alternative and underground press publications that first came to prominence during the 1960s, to the highly idiosyncratic world of fanzines. Some of these little magazines and alternative serials are quite slick, have significant circulations, and otherwise come close to mimicking the mainstream press except for their slant; others are scrappy labors of love of a single individual and have only a handful of readers.[8]

The sources above do not cover alternative serials well, in part because librarians typically consider such publications marginal and less pertinent to their collections, especially when they express unorthodox ideas or have unusual emphases. Alternative serials are also more difficult to control bibliographically, because they are often short-lived and are not integrated into mainline publishing and database networks. A number of sources now exist that not only list alternative serials but also have annotations and indexing arrangements that make them particularly useful as selection sources:

The International Directory of Little Magazines & Small Presses. Paradise, CA: Dustbooks, 1973/74- . [0092-3974] Annual. Formerly: *Directory of Little Magazines and Small Presses.*

    Emphasizes literary publications and contains titles not found in more standard sources. Entries for serials include title; publisher's name, address, and telephone number; founding year; type of material used; additional comments by editor (including recent contributors); circulation; frequency of publication; price; back issue availability; number of pages per issue; method of production and physical characteristics; and areas of interest for review materials. Arrangement is alphabetical by name of serial or press, with a subject index by broad terms and a U.S. regional index by state.

This tool should be supplemented by more selective sources that provide additional listings and, even more importantly, annotations and other evaluative information:

APT for Libraries: Alternative Press Titles for the General Reader. [1062-0664] Gainesville, Fl.: CRISES Press, 1992- . Annual.

    Annotated selection tool that has section on periodicals, arranged alphabetically by title. Covers 70 English-language serials, emphasizing social and environmental sciences. Selection criteria include challenge to the dominant paradigm, importance for the general reader, substance, current concern and lasting value, breadth of scope, and format. Also notes if titles are included in *Alternative Press Index.*

Gunderloy, Mike, and Cari Goldberg Janice. *The World of Zines: A Guide to the Independent Magazine Revolution.* New York: Penguin Books, 1992, 101 p.

    Authored by former editors of *Factsheet Five*, this work lists hundreds of titles chosen because the editors "like them." Arranges serials by topic (including such unorthodox ones as fringe culture, hip whatnot, and spirituality). Entries include basic bibliographic information with subjective annotation and background information. Has subject/title index.

Spectrum: A Guide to the Independent Press and Informative Organizations. [0883-282X] Olathe, KS: Editorial Research Service, 1984- . Annual. Formerly: *Censored.*

    Major source covering over 1,100 alternative serials related to current affairs. Emphasizes economics, government, education, environment, foreign affairs, civil liberties, ethnic and racial issues, new and unconventional religions, cults, philosophy, and social issues. Entries arranged by subject, and each includes organization/publisher, address and phone number, serial(s) published, and a short annotation stating orientation and focus.

Periodicals with an explicitly politically-oriented focus form a large and distinct component of the world of the little magazines. Selectors whose libraries need such serials should also consult the following sources:

Guide to the American Left: Directory and Bibliography. Olathe, KS: Editorial Research Service, 1984- . 8756-0216 Annual. Formerly: *Directory of the American Left.*

Guide to the American Right: Directory and Bibliography. Olathe, KS: Editorial Research Service, 1984- . 8756-0208 Annual. Formerly: *Directory of the American Right.*

    Provide listings by title and U.S. or Canadian postal code for serials of the traditional left and right, respectively. To the side of each entry is a code indicating general category (e.g., anti-Communist, Neo-Nazi, anarchist, pro-choice, etc.), mailing address, additional or more specific orientations, and frequency. Both are followed by an annually updated bibliography.

Skidmore, Gail, and Theodore Jurgen Spahn. *From Radical Left to Extreme Right: A Bibliography of Current Periodicals of Protest, Controversy, Advocacy, or Dissent, with Dispassionate Content-Summaries to Guide Librarians and Other Educators.* 3rd ed. Metuchen, N.J.: Scarecrow, 1987.

    Contains 430 publications, almost all in English originating in the United States and Canada. Titles are grouped into generic categories such as Marxist-socialist left, radical professional, race supremacist, feminist, and gay liberation, with each section prefaced by an essay describing the field.

    Entries include title, address, frequency, price, date established, circulation, information on physical format, ISSN, and back issue/reprint/microform availability, followed by informative and non-judgmental review, often with a response from the editor of the serial. Has cessations, geographical, titles/editors/publishers, and subject indexes.

U.S. Government Serials

The federal government publishes many serials useful to libraries, especially in business, economics, politics, and technology. With the exception of librarians at regional depositories that receive every distributed title, all others must select serials appropriate to their collections. Because the standard sources cited above often do not include information on government serials, selectors must consult additional tools in order to identify all relevant titles.

Guide to U.S. Government Publications. McLean, VA: Documents Index, 1973- . [0092-3168] Annual. Formerly: *Guide to U.S. Government Serials and Periodicals.*

    Contains 35,000 entries that form an annotated guide to series and periodicals issued by the federal government. Arranged by SuDoc classification, each entry contains title, starting dates, frequency, earlier and later references, item number,

Dewey and LC classification numbers, LC catalog number, and annotations. Has agency, title, and keyword in title indexes.

Schwarzkopf, LeRoy C., comp. *Government Reference Serials*. Englewood, CO: Libraries Unlimited, 1988.
Contains titles published at least biennially, including some "non-GPO" publications. Titles arranged into broad groups, then subdivided. Each entry includes title, corporate author, series statement, frequency, SuDoc, LC and Dewey classifications, several identification numbers, publishing history background, and descriptive annotation. Has title, SuDoc, author, and subject indexes.

New Titles

Keeping abreast of new serial publications is difficult, because available sources are inadequate in at least one of the critical areas of scope, arrangement, or currency. It is particularly difficult to create a comprehensive system for the early identification of new serials comparable to that for titles already in existence. As a result, random identification by means of brochures, advertisements, publisher catalogs, notices in periodicals, user suggestions, and the comments of colleagues play an important part in the process. Nevertheless, much can be done to improve the haphazard way librarians monitor new serial publications.

Comprehensive Sources

With the demise of *New Serial Titles: Classed Subject Arrangement* (Washington, D.C.: Library of Congress, 1955-1980), librarians lost the most convenient and comprehensive print source for the identification of new titles. Unless one is the sole bibliographer for a library collecting in many subjects, it is not worth the time to go through the surviving *New Serial Titles* (Washington, D.C.: Library of Congress, 1953-). This monthly, which averaged over 1,000 serials per issue even before its expansion to include all CONSER contributions regardless of publication dates, is too massive to be an efficient identification tool. More effective and current sources do exist, however. The best print source is:

Ulrich's Update: Supplement to Ulrich's International Periodicals Directory. [1000-1074] New Providence, NJ: Bowker, 1988- . Triannual. Formerly: *Ulrich's Quarterly, Bowker Serials Bibliography Supplement*, and *The Bowker International Serials Database Update.*
Each issue contains 2,000 new and newly-added titles. Its scope, arrangement, and searching options are modeled on the main work. Is the most useful printed tool for identifying new serials because of its comprehensive coverage, currency, and arrangement of titles into broad subject categories.

The most effective electronic source for identifying new serials is:

CDMARC Serials: The CONSER Database. [1063-8784] Washington, D.C.: Library of Congress, Cataloging Distribution Service, 1992- . Quarterly CD-ROM.

>   Includes 600,000 MARC records for serials authenticated by the Library of Congress and two dozen participating major libraries, abstracting and indexing agencies, and serials vendors. Has numerous subject searching capabilities, including subject heading, LC and Dewey class number, and keyword, coupled with flexible year, language, and country delimiter options and Boolean capabilities.

Another effective means of identifying new serials is to have periodic computer searches done on the general serials databases discussed earlier. Although such a strategy probably works best for narrowly defined areas in science and technology, a carefully structured profile should identify the vast majority of new titles in almost any field. In fact, because a librarian would be concerned with only recent titles or publications added since the last search rather than all titles in the database, the searching profile can be quite broad. This approach for identifying new serials can be supplemented by searching appropriate library OPACs that allow one to segment by date.

Finally, an excellent way to keep abreast of new electronic publications is to subscribe to appropriate listservs. All collection development officers in academe should be aware of the announcement list for new and revised electronic serials offered by the Office of Scientific and Academic Publishing of the Association of Research Libraries (ARL). NewJour, discussed earlier, covers all subject areas and functions as an updating service for the Office's annual *Directory of Electronic Journals, Newsletters and Academic Discussion Lists,* which has been discussed above.

Review Sources

Reviews and notices of serials appearing in journals and newsletters provide another way to identify new titles. Inasmuch as the sources below provide more than bibliographical information about a title, they are useful in both identification and selection. On the other hand, because they list or review only a limited number of new serials, librarians must use these tools as supplemental identification sources.

The following titles are among the most useful general sources that review serials:

Choice: Current Reviews of Academic Books. Middleton, CT: Association of College and Research Libraries, 1964- . Print version [0009-4978] monthly (except bi-monthly for July-August); also available on cards, CD-ROM, and online.

>   Contains authoritative reviews of periodicals appropriate for undergraduate collections and constitutes a supplement to the fifth edition of *Classified List of*

Periodicals for the College Library (to be discussed in the section on selection). Each column reviews 4-6 titles that are usually 4-5 years old. *Library Journal.* [0363-0277] New York: Cahners, 1876- . Semi-monthly (except monthly for July and August).

Features regular column on new magazines that contains paragraph-length notices on 5-7 titles. Emphasizes general, humanities, and social sciences of interest to a public or general academic library, with an entire column occasionally devoted to periodicals in a neglected or unusual field.

Serials Review. [0098-7913] Greenwich, CT: JAI Press, 1975- . Quarterly.

Provides evaluations of all types of serials, with every issue having at least one review or bibliographic listing of serials on topics that range from gospel music periodicals to nursing research journals.

Small Magazine Review. [1068-7742] Paradise, CA: Dustbooks, 1993- . Monthly. [Published as part of *Small Press Review.*]

Contains reviews of 6-10 literary and general magazines as well as news and notes about established titles (including submission needs and upcoming issue contents), and announcements of new magazines.

Because any source has only a small minority of the reviews of periodicals, selectors need to be aware of the following guide:

Beach, Barbara, ed. *Book Review Index: Periodical Reviews, 1976-1984: A Cumulative Index to More than 15,000 Reviews of Approximately 5,300 Periodicals That Have Been Cited in 'Book Review Index'.* Detroit: Gale Research Company, 1987.

Covers "non-book publications with a continuing, specific title that are published at stated intervals, usually more often than once a year" that appeared in 530 different publications. Includes popular and specialized magazines, children's periodicals, scholarly journals, literary titles, newspapers, and some newsletters; generally excludes annuals, scholarly series, conference proceedings, reference titles, and irregular serials. Entries are arranged alphabetically by periodical reviewed, with sources of review cited below. Small "c" appearing to the left of a title indicates a children's periodical.

Retrospective Acquisitions

Unlike collection development for current or new serial titles, retrospective acquisition entails not only identifying appropriate publications but also determining what is available for purchase. Because the problems and sources of information differ substantially for each process, they will be considered separately.

What Has Been Published

Librarians have three options to determine what serial titles have existed. First, they can consult comprehensive bibliographic databases, such as OCLC and RLIN, and the print and online catalogs of individual libraries. (Because MARC rules require the notation of reprint and microform, one can easily identify these materials through a search of the library databases.)

Librarians can supplement this approach by checking library shelflists. Because of the extensiveness of its collections, the Library of Congress shelflist is the most comprehensive available.

U.S. Library of Congress. *Shelflist.* Ann Arbor, MI: University Microfilms International, 1978-1979.

>Consists of 3,306 microfiche representing nearly seven million shelflist cards and provides exhaustive coverage of serial and monographic literature for almost all fields of knowledge. Access to specific subjects is by means of the individual classification schedules or the subject-keyword volumes of the *Combined Indexes to the Library of Congress Classification Schedules.*

Librarians can supplement the Library of Congress with Harvard's older periodicals shelflist:

Harvard University Library. *Periodical Classes, Classified Listing by Call Number, Alphabetical Listing by Title.* Widener Shelflist no. 15. Cambridge, MA: Harvard University Library; dist. Cambridge, MA: Harvard University Press, 1966.

>Covers about 26,000 periodical and serial titles in 23 major subject and language classes in the humanities, sciences, and social sciences. Includes about half the serial titles in the main library at the time it was compiled and complements the Library of Congress shelflist because of the uniqueness of Harvard's collections and its different classification system. First part arranges all the serial titles by class; the second part arranges them alphabetically by title.

Second, in contrast to these empirical approaches to retrospective serials collection development based on library holdings, selectors can determine what serials have existed by consulting comprehensive lists for specific subjects. Theodore Besterman's *Periodical Publications: A Bibliography of Bibliographies* (2 v. Totowa, NJ: Rowman and Littlefield, 1971) constitutes the basic retrospective guide. It is supplemented for U.S. and Canadian titles by Gary C. Tarbert's *Periodical Directories and Bibliographies: An Annotated Guide to Approximately 350 Directories, Bibliographies and Other Sources of Information about English-Language Periodicals, from 1850 to the Present, including Newspapers, Journals, Magazines, Newsletters, Yearbook, and Other Serial Publications* (Detroit: Gale, 1987) and brought up to date by the sources found in *Guide to Reference Books* and other general bibliographical tools.

A third approach to retrospective serials collection development consists of using older editions of the tools for current serials to identify earlier titles. These lists can sometimes be of unique historical importance, as in the case of the 1947 edition of *Ulrich's*, which not only is a directory of titles being published at that time but also contains a listing of clandestine serials issued during World War II. Using these three methods collection development librarians can build a comprehensive list of nearly all serial publications in any field.

What Is Available For Purchase

Retrospective serials acquisitions can involve purchase of originals, reprints, or microforms, depending upon availability, cost, space considerations, physical characteristics, perceived user needs, and library preference.

Originals

In the area of retrospective serials acquisitions, librarians should not trust statements of availability found in the standard identification tools. Such sources tend to be incomplete or out-of-date; they are often erroneous. Librarians should contact the publisher or distributor directly in order to find out exactly what is still in print and the price.

If back issues or volumes are not available from the publisher or distributor, collection development librarians can try the Universal Serials and Book Exchange and commercial dealers who specialize in serial backruns.[9] A few of these dealers put out extensive catalogs, which have a strong bias toward major titles in medicine, science, and technology and tend to include the most heavily requested titles. Consequently, librarians should consider such catalogs mainly as indicators of stock and not hesitate to ask about the availability of other titles.

Librarians also need to be aware of Readmore's BACKSERV database (available at http://www.readmore.com). This back issues and duplicate exchange service provides comprehensive searching and ordering capabilities to a variety of listings, both commercial and non-profit. Finally, if all else fails and a librarian is determined to purchase originals, he or she can advertise. This option, however, is expensive in terms of price and staff time.

Reprints

Large-scale reprinting of serials began in the 1960s and flourished in the 1970s. At the same time basic bibliographical tools came into existence to control these materials.

Guide to Reprints: An International Bibliography of Scholarly Reprints. [0027-8667] Kent, CT: Guide to Reprints, 1967- . Annual.

Lists serials and other materials available in reprint editions from over 450 publishers worldwide. Basic arrangement is by title or author. Serial entries include title, volume numbers covered, years covered, publisher, and price for run (but not individual volumes).

Microforms

Microforms represent another major means of retrospective serials collection development. The number of titles available in microform has grown dramatically over the past decade. On the supply side, large firms such as UMI have made agreements with major serial publishers to offer their periodical backfiles in microform or, in a few cases, CD-ROM, while library preservation efforts have added great numbers of more specialized serials to the microform universe. On the demand side, librarians have increasingly turned to microforms in lieu of binding current subscriptions in order to save money and space. In response to these developments, some major serials publishers now offer special dual subscriptions in both paper and microform.

The inclusion of statements on microform availability in some of the major serials directories provides additional evidence of the continuing importance of this format. However, a librarian must still be prepared to make direct inquiries to the publisher or distributor, consult print and microfiche directories, or CD-ROM and online databases, because indications of microform availability in the general serials directories are often inaccurate. More frequently, they are incomplete.

The major sources for determining what is available in microform are:

Guide to Microforms in Print: Author -Title. [0164-0747] New Providence, NJ: Saur, 1961- . Annual.

Lists microforms available from publishers throughout the world. Arrangement is alphabetical by author or title. Serial entries include title, volumes available, dates covered, publisher, price, and microformats available. For newspapers indications of city and state (and country when non-U.S.) follow the title.

Guide to Microforms in Print: Subject. [0163-8386] New Providence, NJ: Saur, 1962/63- . Annual.

Companion work to *Guide to Microforms in Print: Author - Title* providing subject access under modified Dewey Decimal Classification, including separate groupings for major categories of serials such as non-U.S. newspapers and general periodicals. Has guide to classification, alphabetical listing of main subject categories, and index of persons as subject.

Guide to Microforms in Print: Supplement. [0164-0739] New Providence, NJ: Saur, 1979- . Annual.

> A supplement to both parts of *Guide to Microforms in Print* issued six months after they appear.

Although *Guide to Microforms in Print* is the most comprehensive source for retrospective serials acquisitions, it strongly emphasizes the products of commercial publishers. This is a significant bias, because libraries, historical societies, and other non-commercial organizations have microfilmed many titles. It also fails to list individual serials that are part of large microform collections.

Because University Microfilms International (UMI) offers so many periodicals and newspapers in microform, librarians need to supplement *Guide to Microforms in Print*, with the former's *Serials in Microform* [1069-6174] and *Newspapers in Microform* [1079-5944]. These annual compilations are free in both print and microfiche editions and provide current and detailed information on availability and price for 19,000 periodicals (including 10,000 currently published) and 7,000 newspapers. Both of these sources are now available in a combined file via the Internet from the TitleNet service (gopher.infor.com). UMI also has a toll-free number (1-800-521-0600) that librarians can call to get additional and updated information.

SELECTION

After a collection development officer has identified relevant serials, he or she makes actual selection decisions. This section discusses the value of a collection development policy, the major elements in the selection process, and the critical philosophical considerations and selection criteria influencing acquisitions. A fuller section on evaluation follows. Selection and evaluation are, of course, closely related processes, especially since the methodologies used to select a single title are also used to evaluate an entire collection. They differ in that each selection decision represents an individual evaluation, while evaluation is collective and looks at the results of many selection—and non-selection—decisions.

A collection development policy should fully incorporate serials along with other library resources. Only in this matter can librarians ensure the quality and consistent development of serials holdings that accurately reflect constituency needs and institutional acquisitions priorities.[10] As Robert Goehlert notes, "without a concrete collection development policy, one which states clearly the mission and purpose of the library, it is difficult to see how acquisitions are more than a series of unrelated decisions."[11]

Such a policy is particularly important for serials, because these materials are harder to select and demand more critically informed collection development choices than do one-time purchases such as books. Moreover, a mistake is more serious, because it comes back to haunt librarians in the form of recurrent and escalating subscription costs. As serials budgets come under greater financial pressure, the desirability of a collection development policy increases. A formal policy not only provides a guide to selection but also furnishes the basis for budget allocations and evaluation.

A deliberate and planned development of serials mandates that selection responsibility for materials in all formats supporting a particular program be vested in the same person(s) in order to ensure the most coherent collection building effort. Ideally, this selector is not only the most knowledgeable person in the library regarding resources in a specific field but also the most competent to assess local needs. He or she should also be in the best position to relate serials to other materials that the library has as well as what is available through resource-sharing arrangements and document delivery systems.

This is not to say that committees for serials selection do not have any legitimate place in the collection development process. They can be useful for soliciting suggestions and have a definite role to play in the selection of general and multi-disciplinary titles. Indeed, as Katz notes, involvement in the selection process is positive, and it is advisable for selectors to listen to constituents and colleagues.[12] Such is especially true when dealing with a clearly defined clientele, as in the case of academic and special libraries. There, in fact, user consultation should be a major factor in order to ensure that holdings consist of the most appropriate and relevant titles. However, while seeking advice, collection development officers must not abdicate ultimate selection responsibility to either users or fellow librarians.

The manner and timing of choosing new titles constitutes another important element in the selection process. Because funds are rarely sufficient to cover all requests, librarians must be content to acquire only the most valuable serials and hope that budgets will keep up with at least these subscription charges. Within this context, selectors should consider new titles as a group at specific times during the year, rather than one by one, in order to maximize the chances that a library will subscribe to only the most important serials out of a larger universe of merely desirable publications.

At the same time, librarians should anticipate constituent demand by adding important new serials as soon as they find out about them. Indeed, because the number of subscriptions a serial receives in its first two or three years often determines whether it succeeds, librarians have a special obligation to their users to subscribe to a publication that is particularly worthwhile and fills a definite need as soon as possible.[13] In addition, because print runs are not much in excess of actual subscriptions, a significant delay in a selection decision may mean that earlier issues are no longer available and librarians must secure them in the out-of-print market at a cost generally greater than the original price.[14] Although the periodicity of new serials selections depends on the individual situation, Davinson suggests that acquisition decisions be made at least quarterly in order to avoid the problems outlined above.[15]

Sample issues contribute to the high quality selection process that is at the core of effective collection development. Because possession of a sample enables librarians to make judgments about the scope, contents, format, and overall value of a serial, recent issues should be obtained before actually making subscription decisions.[16] Librarians can obtain a sample issue easily from the publisher, typically at no charge. Because even the most comprehensive library deals with only a limited number of proposed new subscriptions, a requirement that a sample be secured is not a heavy burden and may serve to discourage trivial requests.

Constituent and program needs, given the purpose of the library and the intellectual and informational requirements it is committed to meet, constitute the prime selection factor. All other criteria are of secondary concern and come into play only if this fundamental consideration is satisfied.[17] Furthermore, demonstrated demand, as evidenced by hard data, such as interlibrary loan requests, is superior to perceived needs.[18] Finally, the actual and perceived requirements of a particular library's community take clear precedence over such theoretical considerations as a title's bibliographic accessibility through indexes or its citation impact value (both of which are discussed in the section on evaluation).

Within this framework librarians have a special obligation to make sure that all legitimate needs are being met at appropriate levels—and not just those of the more visible segments of its constituency. This is particularly important in public libraries, where librarians not only have often considered serials to be relatively unimportant but also selected them on the basis of tradition as defined by the supposed interests of middle-class America, regardless of the actual user population.[19] In order to discharge this obligation adequately, collection development officers often need to solicit requests actively.

Once the prime criterion of need is met, then many of the standard selection factors such as authority, accuracy, readability, language, and subjective judgments of quality come into play. As in the case of other formats, there are review tools (discussed earlier) and selection guides (discussed later) that provide assistance in making acquisition decisions.

In the past price played a minor part in serials collection development. However, the massive inflation of the last two decades, especially for scientific, technical, and medical (STM) serials, has pushed subscription charges to such heights that above a certain threshold "the quality of the publication as well as its balance and scope, turn out to be secondary to cost—unless the journal is absolutely essential."[20] Librarians must be particularly careful with reference titles, especially the electronic serials now available, otherwise the excellent bibliographical access these tools provide will be cancelled out by the lack of funds to buy the indexed titles themselves.

Moreover, in this age of massive price increases, librarians must monitor the cost of serial commitments. On a micro-level this can be partially accomplished by a system that notifies selectors whenever a price increase exceeds a certain percentage or a specific dollar amount, so that he or she can reevaluate the subscription in light of its new cost.[21] On a macro-level, librarians interested in monitoring this situation should subscribe to the *Newsletter on Serials Pricing Issues*. (To get this electronic journal, send a message to listserv@unc.edu saying "subscribe prices" followed by your name. Back issues are available at http://sunsite.unc.edu/reference/prices/prices.html.)

There are also several essentially illegitimate considerations that may influence decisions. Selectors should never be reluctant to acquire a title just because of the presence of a great deal of advertising matter. As Katz reminds us, "American magazines are built on advertising, and those which are not, are built on high prices. Librarians can't have it both ways."[22] Except in extreme cases, considerations of physical format such as binding or ease of handling are also illegitimate grounds for rejecting an otherwise useful and needed title.[23]

Circulation, as measured by global subscription figures rather than use, also fails to qualify as a valid selection guideline.[24] Large circulations simply mean large sales and are not necessarily correlated with any pertinent selection criteria. Both the *National Enquirer* and the *Wall Street Journal*, for example, are among the serials with the largest circulation in this country; yet they differ dramatically in terms of accuracy and quality. Selectors should not refuse to subscribe to a title just because it has a small circulation, especially since a major trend in serials publishing is the targeting of titles at specific groups and special interests. In the final analysis, a library collects for particular groups of users and to support specific programs, and these needs can often be met best by a little magazine or specialized scholarly journal having only a limited circulation.

> The profession says the librarian should select material based on positive criteria. No librarian should reject for the sake of rejection. The problem comes from the librarian who sincerely believes he knows what is best for all readers. This librarian is satisfied to believe that his own attitudes are equivalent to the "proper" ones. He is likely to be the first to fight for the status quo and in good conscience deplore any magazine that threatens his sense of morality and taste. He honestly thinks, to repeat Sontag, that he knows what is best for B, and that "B isn't qualified or experienced or subtle enough," to know what is best for himself. Put another way, the avoidance of *Playboy* in many libraries is an expression of the librarian's confidence that he knows what is best for B, all six million of the Bs who read the magazine everywhere but in the library.[25]

As this passage makes clear, tradition and traditional prejudice have no place in the selection process. The widespread failure to respond to community needs, and especially the tendency to build collections of titles readers "ought" to read rather than what is wanted and needed, has been a major obstacle to the creation of effective serials holdings. While personal judgment rests at the center of collection development, selection officers must rise above personal biases and the elitist and censorious attitudes that have so strongly distorted collection building efforts in the past if they are to build responsive serials holdings.[26]

EVALUATION

The American Library Association's *Guide to the Evaluation of Library Collections* specifically warns against assuming that holdings are meeting needs and advises that "periodic evaluations should be made to determine whether the collection is meeting its objectives, how well it is serving its users, in which ways or areas it is deficient, and what remains to be done to develop the collection."[27] In addition to assessing the utility of library resources and the effectiveness of collection development programs, evaluation provides a basis for future planning and budget allocations. Collection evaluation can also serve the politically important function of demonstrating "to administrators that something is being done to change the 'bottomless pit' of library acquisitions budgets.[28] Finally, because the benefits are so great, librarians should evaluate serial holdings periodically, perhaps even every three years as Osborn recommends.[29]

Collection development librarians now have a number of techniques for analyzing holdings, and this section critically discusses the principal strategies applicable to serials.[30] The particular approach employed depends upon what information is needed, although available time and staff usually influence choices as well. However, because each method has limitations, the most informative and useful evaluations will typically combine more than one approach.[31]

Before discussing evaluation strategies, the question of quantification needs to be clarified. Although librarians traditionally have put a great deal of blind faith in numbers, especially in assuming that the larger collections are *ipso facto* the better and the ultimate aim of collection building is to amass the largest hoard of titles possible, one still finds hostility to the scientific uses of quantification embodied in the newer evaluation methods. Such opposition is often simplistically reduced to a debate over quantitative versus qualitative or objective versus subjective strategies for assessing a collection. As Mosher pointed out, these are false dichotomies that miss the point, especially since quantitative data are not necessarily superior to impressionistic information and can also be variously interpreted. He goes on to state that the real issue revolves around judgment: that is, which evaluation strategies are best in terms of gaining the desired information, and what conclusions do librarians draw from this information. Within this context, scientific methodologies provide additional and more precise information that permit the collection development officers to make better informed and less subjective decisions.[32]

List Checking

Checking holdings against standard selection guides, periodical indexes, bibliographies, and the serial holdings of other institutions is a widely used method of evaluation. If a library holds a high percentage of the listed titles, then its collections are presumably providing a good level of support to users, although it is not known what percentage translates into a good collection. Depending on the type of list employed, this evaluation strategy can also be used to determine the quality of serial holdings. List checking has the further advantage of being an easy procedure to conduct.

On the other hand, this evaluation method has been criticized on the grounds that any such compilation is highly arbitrary and fails to give the library credit for the titles it has that are "almost as good" as those on the list, the quality of the publications is not fully taken into account, the list might not be appropriate to the institution, and the compilation may be outdated. Any discussion of these criticisms must begin with the realization that significant quantitative differences exist between the universes of serial and book titles. While the quantity of books on many subjects can be large, with many new works appearing each year, the number of current serials is comparatively limited, and the titles themselves are fairly constant from year to year. As a result, the use of lists to evaluate serials holdings can avoid many of the pitfalls and limitations inherent when this method is applied to book collections.

In the first place, while lists of books can only include a tiny fraction of the total population, those for serials can reflect a proportionately larger and more representative sample, if not the entire universe of relevant titles. As a result, list-checking methodologies applied to serials tend to be less arbitrary, and failure to give a library credit for titles held but not on the list is likely to be less of a problem.

Second, the smaller and relatively stable universe of serials makes it easier to come up with an appropriate evaluation list for them, even if this entails the construction of one specifically tailored to a given library. This last course of action, which is considered to be a more effective means of evaluation than relying on standard compilations, is usually prohibitively expensive in the case of books.[33]

Third, the smaller and more stable world of serials makes it easier to control for quality than in the case of evaluation lists for books. Indeed, a selector is far more likely to be familiar with a list of serials than one of books, while the smaller universe of the former makes it possible to examine each serial personally to determine its quality and relevance.

Fourth, as Broadus points out, "The relative constancy of each periodical means that lists of recommended titles are effective for a longer period of time than are guides to the best books."[34] In fact, not only do serials evaluation lists become dated less rapidly than those for other library materials, but some, such as indexes, are by their very nature up-to-date, since serials evaluation almost invariably involves current titles.

Although list checking is a useful approach to serials evaluation, it demands a great deal of judgment and discrimination. Before beginning such a project, librarians must thoroughly evaluate the list to be used, especially for appropriateness to a given library. After finishing, the results of list checking will require additional interpretation. The titles identified as not being in a library's collection represent but a pool of potential subscriptions, all of which have to be individually judged by critical selection standards.

While the numbers of standard guides, periodical indexes, bibliographies, and library serial lists are great, several useful guides to basic serials as well as sources for identifying indexing and abstracting services now exist:

General Guides

Katz, Bill, and Linda Sternberg Katz. *Magazines for Libraries: For the General Reader and School, Junior College, College, University, and Public Libraries.* 8th ed. New Providence, NJ: Bowker, 1995.

> Is an authoritative guide covering approximately 7,000 recommended titles that "represent what the editors and consultants believe to be the best and most useful" magazines in all subject areas. Includes both general, nonspecialist titles and major English-language research journals, balancing the needs of the researcher and the layperson.
>
> Periodicals are grouped into topical categories, followed by a short introduction and listing of basic titles and abstracts and indexes, and then arranged alphabetically by title. Entries include title, ISSN, date founded, frequency, price, editor, publisher and address, information on illustrations, indexes, advertising, circulation, availability of free samples, date volume ends, if refereed, microform and reprint availability, availability online or as CD-ROM, indexing and abstracting information, number and type of book reviews in each issue, and an indication of the audience or type of library for which it is intended. Provides evaluative judgments about the value of most of the titles. Has index of titles and subject cross references in the back.

Ganly, John V., and Diane M. Sciattara. *Serials for Libraries: An Annotated Guide to Continuations, Annuals, Yearbooks, Almanacs, Transactions, Proceedings, Directories, Services.* 2nd ed. New York: Neal-Schuman, 1985.

> Is companion to *Magazines for Libraries* providing information on approximately 2,000 serials published not more than once a year, excluding periodicals, newspapers, loose-leaf services, and monographic series.

Concentrates on the more general English-language titles available in the United States, giving only limited coverage to foreign language serials and titles of interest primarily to research and special libraries.

Serials are grouped into topical categories and then arranged alphabetically by main entry. Annotations include title, former title(s), ISSN, date begun, frequency, information on bibliographies, indexes and illustrations, publisher and address, distributor (if different) and address, issue examined, price, audience level, and indexing information. Has title and subject indexes, listing of serials online, and a guide indicating the month when new editions appear in the back.

Farber, Evan Ira. *Classified List of Periodicals for the College Library.* 5th ed., rev. and enlg. Westwood, MA: Faxon, 1972.

Is high quality selection guide for the liberal arts college library covering basic periodicals needed to support the undergraduate curriculum and provide general reading as well as titles that permit faculty to keep up with their fields. Titles are grouped into subject categories. Entries include title, basic bibliographical information, subscription price, annotations on scope and contents, indexing and abstracting information, and LC catalog number. Has title index in the back. This work is supplemented by the reviews of periodicals appearing in *Choice.*

Katz, Bill, and Linda Sternberg Katz. *Magazines for Young People.* 2nd ed. New Providence, NJ: Bowker, 1991.

Formerly *Magazines for School Libraries*, this source provides information on 1,000 titles. Divided into Children's Magazines, Young Adult Magazines, and Professional Education and Library journals, with titles grouped into specific subject categories in each division. Within each section the editors list their "First Choices" in order of preference. Entries include title, date founded, frequency, price, editor, publisher and address, illustration, indexing, advertising and circulation information, whether publisher provides a free sample, if refereed, date volume ends, microform/reprint information, where indexed, inclusion of book reviews, and indications of audience (including age ranges).

Indexes

The use of indexes as guides to serials selection and as a means of evaluation has a long history and has profoundly influenced the development of collections. Librarians have traditionally considered coverage of a title by an indexing or abstracting service to be an indication not only of quality but also of potential usefulness. As a consequence, they have made indexed serials a top acquisitions priority.

The growth in the number of indexing and abstracting tools and their ever-expanding coverage, however, has seriously diminished the validity of these assumptions. The percentage of serials now indexed in one or more print or online sources has grown immensely, leaving relatively few titles bibliographically inaccessible.[35] Furthermore, this phenomenon, coupled with the encyclopedic coverage of some indexes, especially in the sciences, has long since ceased to make coverage by an indexing or abstracting service a mark of quality.[36] While indexing and abstracting tools remain useful in serials selection and evaluation, librarians should avoid exclusive reliance on them.

Serials indexing and abstracting services number in the hundreds, and the determination of which ones exist for a given subject constitutes the initial step in the employment of this evaluation methodology. While a great number of subject specific guides exist, they are selective, often concentrate on the principal English-language indexing and abstracting tools, and typically are dated. Librarians therefore should begin by consulting *Ulrich's International Periodicals Directory* and *The Serial Directory/The Index and Abstract Directory: An International Guide to Services and Serials Coverage*, which are the most complete and current general sources.

Citation Analysis

While bibliographic accessibility through indexes provides an indication of a title's potential utility, research shows that users tend to rely more on direct bibliographic citations to locate relevant serial literature.[37] In addition a relatively small portion of the serials in any given area accounts for a disproportionately large share of all citations, especially in the sciences.[38] Taking advantage of user behavior and bibliographic clustering, citation analysis measures the significance of a serial by counting the number of times it is mentioned in footnotes and bibliographies.

The major attraction of citation analysis, then, is its ability to identify current interests and the core and peripheral titles needed to support them. In addition to providing information that librarians can use to isolate the most frequently cited titles and construct core lists of serials, this method of evaluation also produces data on the temporal aspects of use that are helpful in determining retention and backfile acquisition. The general availability of citation analysis lists, especially the computer-generated commercial varieties such as the Institute for Scientific Information's annual citation impact reports, coupled with the ease of checking such lists, have made this a popular method of serials evaluation.

At the same time, some researchers have attacked the utility of general citation studies and ranked serials lists produced at other institutions on the grounds that only locally collected data are valid.[39] Citation analyses based on specific user populations avoid this objection, and the computerized databases now available make it easy to construct institutional-specific databases. Indeed, the Institute for Scientific Information now offers two such collection development services, Institutional Citation Report and Local Journal Utilization Report, whereby all the relevant citations produced through database searches are captured and can be manipulated and analyzed using off-the-shelf relational management software.

Beyond considerations of technical biases such as self-citation, co-citation, citation densities, and obsolescence rates, one must keep in mind that this evaluation strategy is most useful when dealing with research journals, where reading is generally purposive.[40] This, in turn, is linked to the fact that although citation analysis is a powerful evaluation technique, it can provide only a partial determination of needs, because users regularly use more materials than they cite.[41] In conclusion, despite the controversy over the validity and utility of this means of serials evaluation, a survey of the literature states that "it would seem fair to say that the reliability of citation analysis compares favorably with the reliability of other methods which may be used to make decisions in collection building."[42]

Circulation and Use

In his work on evaluating library services, Lancaster concludes that use represents the supreme test of the quality and utility of an institution's holdings.[43] Use is not only one of the best surrogate measurements of need, but it also constitutes the most accurate means of predicting which titles will be consulted in the future.[44] Statistics on use are particularly desirable to gather because study after study has demonstrated that a small portion of a library's titles generate the overwhelming majority of use, with twenty percent of the serials typically supplying eighty percent of the use.[45] Financial pressures generated by the serials dynamics outlined at the beginning of this chapter make it imperative that librarians measure the amount and mode of serials use. Indeed, it is hard to see how the carefully controlled and highly effective serials collections everyone claims to want can be created without adequate knowledge of what readers actually need and use.[46]

Serials use studies are an attractive evaluation method. Not only do use studies relate directly to reader needs, but the statistics themselves are generally easy to gather, widely understood, and by their very nature comparative. Flaws in research design constitute the major danger in undertaking any use study. Consequently, librarians must be careful to define exactly what is being measured and how it will be done if the statistics are to be valid.

A major criticism leveled at both use and citation studies is that they simply do not provide sufficient practical guidance. While it is important for a selector to know which titles are heavily used or cited, it would be more useful to have this information in relation to such key factors as subscription price.[47] The desirability of expanding use studies to include such data has been underlined by research demonstrating that an analysis of serials use in relation to cost produces very different results from one based solely on use.[48] Because librarians must live within definite—and often inadequate—serials budgets, such information is vital in building the most effective holdings for a limited amount of money.

Although use studies represent an important means of evaluation, they are a strictly quantitative methodology, one that does not take into account the quality or type of use. In addition, while circulation and use data are helpful in determining which subscriptions to continue or cancel, they will not provide data on how many serials libraries should acquire.[49] Finally, this evaluation strategy is, by definition, limited to titles an institution already has and, therefore, fails to provide information on serials that librarians should add.

Interlibrary Loan Analysis

Analysis of the materials requested on interlibrary loan can serve as a supplementary means of serials collection evaluation, particularly if librarians consider the results in conjunction with an overall use study. In addition to representing a simple, economical, and on-going means of serials assessment, interlibrary borrowing provides specific information on user needs not readily available elsewhere. It not only identifies titles required by users that an institution does not hold but can also indicate whole areas of the collections that do not serve users well.[50] Moreover, if librarians keep statistics on the ages of serials requested, they can use the data as a guide to backrun acquisitions.[51]

The key practical question facing a selector is how to interpret the results of an evaluation: that is, at what point do the data on interlibrary borrowing justify entering a subscription to a title. Studies consistently indicate that as a general rule it is more economical to rely on interlibrary loan if there are fewer than five requests per year for a title.[52] Conversely, excessive reliance on interlibrary loan may not only be uneconomical but can also result in violation of the fair use guidelines under the copyright law. Yet, when it comes to judging a specific serial, the cost effectiveness equation must be modified by local economic variables, actual subscription price, and any cooperative collection development or interlibrary loan arrangements.

An institution's service philosophy and level of funding also profoundly influence the interpretation of any evaluation. Users expect the funding of major research libraries, for example, to be sufficient to meet the vast majority of their potential needs, even though studies indicate that nearly three-fourths of their journals fall below the critical threshold of five uses per annum.[53] Furthermore, all collection development decisions must go beyond the simple results of serials evaluation and consider user behavior. These quantitative models all assume that serials use is purposive. While this may be true in the sciences, such an assumption is less valid in the humanities and social sciences, where the nature of research and bibliographical access tools make browsing a necessity.[54] More specifically, models of the cost effectiveness of interlibrary borrowing versus ownership do not assess user frustration and assume that all users are willing to request the material from elsewhere, even though this is often not the case. In fact, certain major populations served by academic libraries, such as users in the areas of business and undergraduates in general, show a marked reluctance to use interlibrary loan.[55]

Resources Delivery Tests

As libraries become increasingly dependent upon cooperative acquisition agreements, interlibrary loan arrangements, and fee-based document services to provide low use or highly specialized serials, resources delivery tests increase in popularity as an approach to serials evaluation, especially for time-sensitive information. This method typically involves compiling a list of relevant materials on a subject, checking to see if the library holds the titles and whether the materials are available on the shelves, and—if lacking—measuring how long it takes to get them from elsewhere. Such an evaluation strategy has the advantage of measuring not only local holdings but also remote resources and the related services needed to make them available. Although this means of evaluation is biased toward titles used in research, its chief limitation is the amount of staff time required. Moreover, the results of such a study are meaningful only when they can be compared against the performances of other libraries or units of the same library system.

Comparative Size and Expenditure Statistics

Comparisons of the number of serial titles and/or the amount of money spent on them in terms of both absolute size and rate of growth constitute another major method of evaluation.[56] While such comparative compilations with appropriate libraries provide quick, precise, and significant evaluation information if the areas of measurement are clearly defined, this strategy alone will not provide data on how well a particular institution is meeting user needs.[57]

User Opinions

Although demonstrated needs in the form of hard data such as circulation statistics and interlibrary loans are preferable, user perceptions can also constitute an effective way to evaluate serials collections. While discrete user suggestions may be valuable in the selection of individual titles, librarians must systematically survey these opinions in order to get accurate and representative assessments for purposes of evaluation.[58]

User opinion as an evaluation methodology has the advantage of representing a direct assessment of needs and being a practical option in almost all types of institutions. It can also be the most politically acceptable method in the case of academic and special libraries, particularly when librarians are forced to reduce subscriptions.[59] However, user opinions may be subjective, uninformed, and narrowly focused. In fact, surveys of faculty opinions in academic libraries are almost always inadequate, because they invariably slight interdisciplinary and general serials as well as those most heavily used by students. This strategy can also be quite expensive in terms of staff time and administrative costs, although it represents a one-time investment, whereas any cancelled titles constitute recurrent savings.[60] This method of evaluation is perhaps most useful as a first step, to be followed and augmented by other types of evaluation.[61]

Direct Examination

Direct examination of serials holdings, although quick and easily performed in any library, remains an imprecise and impressionistic method of evaluation. While a knowledgeable and alert collection development officer can learn much through direct examination, this strategy is probably best employed as a preliminary technique to help determine what other types of evaluation should be used in order to gain more accurate and detailed information.[62]

Formulas and Standards

Although generally included in discussions of evaluation, the formulas and standards now in existence are useless for assessing serials collections. In the first place, the theoretical and empirical bases used to generate their quantitative recommendations are not based on research.[63] As a consequence, even some of the most widely accepted models have not been confirmed by independent economic analyses.[64] Second, these formulas and standards generally have been concerned with book holdings and have not paid adequate attention to serials. As a result, research has shown that even such widely known models as Clapp-Jordan seriously underestimate serials needs on the order of magnitude of 100 to 400 percent.[65] Third, the dynamics of serials growth, especially as these resources become more important and consume an ever larger portion of total expenditures, make existing formulas and standards more inadequate than ever before. Fourth, there is always the danger that the minimal recommendations of these models will be considered as optimum levels, resulting in poorer holdings than before.[66]

These, then, are the major methods for evaluating serials holdings. No one approach is necessarily better than any other; rather, the most appropriate technique depends on what information is needed. Moreover, since each strategy has limitations, the most useful evaluation typically will combine more than one approach. The information gained, in turn, should influence future selection decisions. Finally, although much space has been devoted to discussions of the merits and limitations of various methodologies, librarians must not overlook the fact that from beginning to end—that is, from the choice of an approach to the interpretation of its results—informed, professional judgment rests at the core of evaluation and is the key factor in the entire collection development process.

NOTES

1.   National Enquiry into Scholarly Communication, *Scholarly Communication: The Report of the National Enquiry* (Baltimore: Johns Hopkins University Press, 1979), pp. 37 and 43-4. This shift is especially marked in the case of historians, who not only display a growing serials orientation but also "rank inadequate library journal collections among the major communication problems they face as scholars." p. 134. In fact, according to one study historians use serials almost as much as books. Margaret F. Stieg, "The Information Needs of Historians," *College & Research Libraries* 42 (1981), pp. 549-560, especially Table 3. A more recent survey found that access to journals was more important than monographs for historians engaged in research. Helen Finch, *The Research Process: The Library's Contribution in Times of Constraint*, British Library Research Paper 95 (London: British Library Research and Development Department, 1991), p. 9.

2.   Mosher, Paul H., "Collection Evaluation or Analysis: Matching Library Acquisitions to Library Needs," in *Collection Development in Libraries: A Treatise*, ed. Robert D. Stueart and George B. Miller, Jr. (Greenwich, CT: JAI Press, 1980), pt. B, p. 527.

3.   Robin Downs, "User Surveys and Development of Journal Collections," conference paper cited in Coy L. Harmon, "The Impact of Serials on Collection Development: A Report on the Conference Proceedings," *Library Acquisitions: Practice and Theory* 5 (1981), p. 95; Charles B. Osburn, *Academic Research and Library Resources: Changing Patterns in America*, New Directions in Librarianship 3 (Westport, CT: Greenwood Press, 1979), p. 129; and Gordon R. Williams, "The Function and Methods of Libraries in the Diffusion of Knowledge," *Library Quarterly* 50, no. 1 (January 1980), p. 69-70.

4.   Siegfried Feller, "Developing the Serials Collection," in *Collection Development in Libraries: A Treatise*, eds. Robert D. Stueart and George B. Miller, Jr., Foundations in Library and Information Science 10 (Greenwich, CT: JAI Press, 1980), pt. B, p. 514; William A. Katz, *Magazine Selection: How to Build a Community-Oriented Collection* (New York: Bowker, 1971), p. 48; National Enquiry, *Scholarly*, pp. 11 and 21-22; Osburn, *Academic*, pp. 126 and 149; and Herbert White, "Strategies and Alternatives in Dealing with the Serials Management Budget," conference paper cited in Harmon, "Impact," p. 97.

5.   Paul H. Mosher, "Collection Evaluation in Research Libraries: The Search for Quality, Consistency, and System in Collection Development," *Library Resources and Technical Services* 23, no. 1 (Winter 1979), p. 17.

6.   For information on the kinds of serials that lend themselves most readily to cooperative acquisition, see Patricia Buck Dominguez and Luke Swindler, "Cooperative Collection Development at the Research Triangle University Libraries: A Model for the Nation," *College & Research Libraries* 54 (1993), pp. 470-496. In terms of ownership versus access, the latest research indicates that "if a periodical is used fewer than five times per year in a given library, it is generally more cost-effective to rely on access, even if the subscription cost is modest." Eleanor A. Gossen and Suzanne Irving, "Ownership versus Access and Low-Use Periodical Titles," *Library Resources & Technical Services* 39 (1995), p. 43. These results are part of one of the most comprehensive and ambitious attempts at serials cooperation. See State University of New York University Center Libraries, "Council on Library Resources Grant: 'Policy Issues in Cooperative Collection Development and Resource Sharing': Final Report," [Albany: University Center Libraries], July 1993.

7. The classic study of how a small percentage of serials holdings account for the vast majority of use is Richard L. Trueswell, "Some Behavioral Patterns of Library Users: The 80/20 Rule," *Wilson Library Bulletin*, 43 (1969), pp. 458-61. These results have been consistently replicated in more specialized studies. See, for example, the sections on "Periodicals—Bradford Distribution, Implicit" and "Periodicals-Core" in David F. Kohl, *Acquisitions, Collection Development, and Collection Use: A Handbook for Library Management*, Handbooks for Library Management (Santa Barbara, CA: ABC-Clio Information Services, 1985), pp. 316-323.

8. For a brief, recent overview of this publishing trend, see David M. Gross "Zine but not Heard," *Time* (5 September 1994), pp. 68-69.

9. Beth Holley's *Directory of Back Issue Dealers* ([Atlanta]: North American Serials Interest Group, 1991) provides an international list of nearly 100 such vendors.

10. Strong support for formal statements can be found in American Library Association, Resources and Technical Services Division, Collection Development Committee, *Guidelines for Collection Development*, ed. David L. Perkins (Chicago: The Association, 1979), pp. 2 and 5.

11. "Journal Use per Monetary Unit: A Reanalysis of Use Data," *Library Acquisitions* 3 (1979), p. 98.

12. Katz, *Magazine*, pp. 43-44.

13. Clara D. Brown and Lynn S. Smith, *Serials: Past, Present and Future*, 2nd rev. ed. (Birmingham, AL: Ebsco Industries, 1980), p. 80; and Katz, *Magazine*, p. 31.

14. Brown and Smith, *Serials*, p. 80; Donald Davinson, *The Periodicals Collection*, rev. and enl. ed. (London: Andre Deutsch, 1978), p. 172; and Andrew D. Osborn, *Serial Publications: Their Place and Treatment in Libraries*, 3rd ed. (Chicago: American Library Association, 1980), p. 80.

15. Davinson, *Periodicals*, p. 172.

16. Robert N. Broadus, *Selecting Materials for Libraries*, 2nd ed. (New York: H. W. Wilson Company, 1981), pp. 158-159; and Osborn, *Serial*, p. 89.

17. This position has been forcefully asserted for serials by Katz in *Magazine*, pp. 43-44 and *passim*, and by Edward S. Warner and Anita L. Anker in "Faculty Perceived Needs for Serial Titles: Measurement for Purposes of Collection Development and Management," *Serials Librarian* 4 (1980), p. 295. See also John Rutledge and Luke Swindler, "The Selection Decision: Defining Criteria and Establishing Priorities," *College and Research Libraries* 48 (1987), pp. 123-131, which not only shares this view but assigns a relative value to all the decision making criteria and relates them to one another within a wholistic and prioritized schema.

18. For an extended discussion of the relationship of library collection and service configurations to demonstrated and perceived needs, see Edward S. Warner, "Constituency Needs as Determinants of Library Collection and Service Configurations," *Drexel Library Quarterly* 13, no. 3 (1977), pp. 44-51. See also Warner and Anker, "Faculty," pp. 296 and 300; and Edward S. Warner and Anita L. Anker, "Utilizing Library Constituents' Perceived Needs in Allocating Journal Costs," *Journal of the American Society for Information Science* 30 (1979), pp. 326 and 328-329. On the other hand, in another article Warner acknowledges that "data representing constituents' perceived needs, particularly if taken together with data evidencing demonstrated needs, when applied to collection development decision making begins to reveal a 'critical mass' of titles tailored to constituency needs." "The Impact of Interlibrary Access to Periodicals on Subscription Continuation/Cancellation Decision Making," *Journal of the American Society for Information Science* 32 (1981), p. 95.

19. Katz, *Magazine*, pp. 7, 13-14, 43-44, and 141. As he goes on to state, "The best of all types of magazines must be considered, not simply the best of the coffee table fare of the split-level suburban family." p. 40.

20. Bill Katz and Berry G. Richards, *Magazines for Libraries: For the General Reader and School, Junior College, College, University, Public Libraries*, 3rd. ed (New York: Bowker, 1978), p. viii. See also Katz, *Magazine*, p. 28-29.

21. Feller, "Developing," p. 520.

22. Katz, *Magazine*, p. 30.

23. Katz, *Magazine*, p. 30.

24. Katz, *Magazine*, p. 31.

25. Katz, *Magazine*, pp. 84-85.

26. See especially Katz, *Magazine*, pp. 5, 27-28, 36-37, and 39.

27. Barbara Lockett, ed., Collection Management and Development Guides no. 2 (Chicago: American Library Association, 1989), p. 1.

28. Mosher, "Collection ...Search," p. 17. See also Jane E. Fowler, "Managing Periodicals by Committee," *Journal of Academic Librarianship* 2 (1976), p. 233.

29. Osborn, *Serials*, p. 97.

30. The *Guide to the Evaluation of Library Collections* sketches the various evaluation methodologies, summarily lists the advantages and disadvantages of each strategy, and provides a basic bibliography for each methodology. This work should be supplemented by Michael R. Gabriel, *Collection Development and Collection Evaluation: A Sourcebook* (Metuchen, NJ: Scarecrow Press, 1995). Part 2 is devoted to a general essay on collection evaluation, followed by a 349-item comprehensive bibliography.

31. ALA, *Guide*, p. 2 and 15; Mosher, "Collection...Matching," p. 531; and Osburn, *Academic*, pp. 146-147.

32. Mosher, "Collection...Matching," pp. 530-531; and Mosher, "Collection...Search," p. 23. See also Warner, "Constituency," pp. 46 and 48-49.

33. Cynthia Comer, "List-Checking as a Method of Evaluating Library Collections," *Collection Building: Studies in the Development and Effective Use of Library Resources* 3, no. 3 (1981), p. 29.

34. Broadus, *Selecting*, p. 159.

35. Katz, *Magazine*, p. 28.

36. Feller, "Developing," p. 513. It is not only a question of the comprehensiveness of such major tools as *Chemical Abstracts*, whose 1995 *Source Index* claims coverage of 18,656 current serials plus another 7,486 no longer published together with 14,239 monographs containing collections of papers, but even highly specialized tools are now exhaustive, for example, *Weed Abstracts* covers nearly 1,000 titles—and even that figure excludes most annual reports and conference proceedings!

37. Robert N. Broadus, "The Applications of Citation Analysis to Library Collection Building," *Advances in Librarianship* 7 (1977), p. 307.

38. An extreme example of this clustering is provided in Martyn and Gilchrist's work on British scientific serials. They found that 95 percent of the important citations were encompassed by less than 9 percent of the periodicals, and that if a library were content to provide access to only 90 percent of the important citations, this core could be reduced by a third. Cited in Davinson, *Periodicals*, p. 42. Moreover, Eugene Garfield has estimated "that a combination of the literature of individual disciplines and specialties produces a multidisciplinary core for all science comprising no more than 1000 journals." "Citation Analysis as a Tool in Journal Evaluation," *Science* 178 (3 November 1972), p. 476.

39. See especially Maurice B. Line, "Rank Lists Based on Citations and Library Uses as Indicators of Journal Usage in Individual Libraries," *Collection Management* 2 (1978), pp. 313-314; and Maurice B. Line and Alexander Sandison, "Practical Interpretation of Citation and Library Use Studies," *College & Research Libraries* 36 (1975), pp. 393 and 396.

40. Broadus, "Applications," p. 315; Shirley A. Fitzgibbons, "Citation Analysis in the Social Sciences," in *Collection Development in Libraries: A Treatise*, eds. Robert D. Stueart and George B. Miller, Jr. (Greenwich, CT: JAI Press, 1980), pt. B, p. 321; and Garfield, "Citation," p. 476.

41. Fitzgibbons, "Citation," p. 320; Robert Goehlert, "Periodical Use in an Academic Library," *Special Libraries* 69 (1978), pp. 54-56; Paul H. Mosher, "Managing Library Collections: The Process of Review and Pruning," in *Collection Development in Libraries: A Treatise*, eds. Robert

D. Stueart and George Miller, Jr. (Greenwich, CT: JAI Press, 1980), pt. A, p. 175; and William A. Satariano, "Journal Use in Sociology: Citation Analysis Versus Readership Patterns," *Library Quarterly* 48 (1978), pp. 297-299. For a dissenting view, see Elizabeth Pan, "Journal Citation as a Predictor of Journal Usage in Libraries," *Collection Management* 2 (1978), pp. 31 and 33.

42. Broadus, "Applications," p. 322.

43. F. W. Lancaster, *The Measurement and Evaluation of Library Services* (Washington, D.C.: Information Resources Press, 1977), p. 178.

44. Robert N. Broadus, "Use Studies of Library Collections," *Library Resources and Technical Services* 24 (1980), p. 320; Mosher, "Managing," p. 174.

45. Davinson, *Periodicals*, pp. 165-166; and Lancaster, *Measurement*, p. 183.

46. The importance of this was recognized by the National Enquiry, which concluded that libraries "need to be discriminating in their subscriptions, basing decisions on studies of journal usage." *Scholarly*, p. 11

47. Line and Sandison, "Practical," pp. 394-396; Goehlert, "Journal," p. 91; and Allen Kent et al., *Use of Library Materials: The University of Pittsburgh Study* (New York: Marcel Dekker, 1979), p. 71.

48. See Goehlert, "Journal," pp. 93-95 and 97, especially Tables 2 and 4; and Kent, *Use*, pp. 116-123.

49. Goehlert, "Journal," p. 97. This is not a minor financial consideration since studies indicate that in order to accommodate each five percent increase in availability above the 80 percent satisfaction level, the total number of subscriptions must double. Davinson, *Periodicals*, p. 166.

50. Doris B. New and Retha Zane Ott, "Interlibrary Loan Analysis as a Collection Development Tool," *Library Resources and Technical Services* 18 (1974), pp. 275 and 282.

51. See, for example, Eugene E. Graziano, "Interlibrary Loan Analysis: Diagnostic for Scientific Serials Backfile Acquisitions," *Special Libraries* 53 (1962), pp. 251-257.

52. Davinson, *Periodicals*, p. 166; King Research, Inc., *The Journal in Scholarly Communication: The Roles of Authors, Publishers, Libraries, and Readers in a Vital System* (Washington, D.C.: National Science Foundation, 1979), p. 50; and New and Ott, "Interlibrary," p. 282.

53. King, *Journal*, p. 356.

54. Davinson, *Periodicals*, p. 167.

55. Davinson, *Periodicals*, pp. 166-167; and Patricia Stenstrom and Ruth B. McBride, "Serial Use by Social Science Faculty: A Survey," *College & Research Libraries* 40 (1979), p. 430.

56. Lancaster warns that both absolute size and rate of growth must be used because the latter alone can present a distorted picture. He also cites research that shows growth in absolute numbers is a more meaningful indicator of quality than percentage increase. *Measurement*, p. 168.

57. See Mosher, "Collection...Matching," p. 535.

58. Warner, "Constituency," p. 49. See especially the systematic and successful user surveys described in Fowler, "Managing," pp. 230-234, and Warner and Anker, "Faculty," pp. 295-300.

59. Warner and Anker, "Utilizing," p. 326.

60. Warner and Anker, "Faculty," p. 299.

61. See Mosher, "Collection...Matching," p. 533; and Warner and Anker, "Faculty," p. 300.

62. Mosher, "Collection ... Matching," p. 534.

63. For a good example of this, see the inside look at the evolution of standards in Diane C. Parker, "'Standards for College Libraries': Foundations," *College & Research Libraries News* 55 (1995), pp. 330-337.

64. Lancaster, *Measurement*, p. 171.

65. Lancaster, *Measurement*, p. 172.

66. See especially Lancaster's discussion of the experience of the SUNY system with such an interpretation. *Measurement*, pp. 171-173.

Chapter 6

SUBSCRIPTION AGENTS AND OTHER SERIALS SUPPLIERS

Most libraries do not purchase all serial subscriptions directly from the publisher because of the expense of processing invoices, renewals, and claim responses from multiple sources. Instead, they use intermediaries called subscription agents or standing order dealers. This chapter opens with definitions of the several types of suppliers and continues with a description of each one. It then discusses the criteria for selecting and evaluating these companies.

DEFINITIONS

One may place serial orders in a number of ways, either with the actual publisher or through an intermediary. This book defines the types of suppliers as follows:

Vendor

Vendor, meaning "seller," is a generic term for the person or company receiving the serial order from the library. Although the vendor may be the actual producer of the material, most often the word is used to describe an intermediary purchasing agent used by the library as a means of economizing through consolidating orders and payments.

Subscription Agent

Subscription agents specialize in periodical subscriptions. The library subscriber employs a subscription agent to consolidate continuing serial orders and payments and to provide other services made possible by the economies of scale.

Standing Order Dealer

The standing order dealer is to nonperiodical serials what the subscription agent is to journals. In the United States, this type of vendor is often primarily a bookseller, a specialist in monograph orders and approval plans for libraries. Most booksellers handle standing orders in a separate, less profitable department. Many of these vendors will not process subscriptions. They may stock material in a warehouse to be forwarded to the library customer, or they may order and reship it. A standing order vendor may give the library pricing concessions on serials published by large companies that allow the vendor a substantial discount. The dealer may impose a service charge on other types of standing orders, to recover costs and make the necessary profit.

European vendors are likely to handle periodicals, nonperiodical serials, and monographs equally well; however, they may have separate divisions for each.

Publisher

The publisher produces the serial. It may be large or small, from an international company to an individual working out of a home or office. In the past, most serials came from small companies or individuals; however, the trend today in scholarly serials is toward larger, well-known commercial or society publishers performing at least the production and distribution functions of serials. Most of the time they do the editorial work as well.

Distributor

Some publishers, for any of several reasons, use their own intermediary to sell their products to subscribers. Small publishers, including societies, may contract their distribution work to a larger publisher; those in one country may channel foreign orders through publishers or subscription agents in other countries; publishers of mass circulation magazines may use a fulfillment center. Use of an intervening distributor saves the publisher from investing funds in recordkeeping, currency exchange, computer equipment, personnel, customer service, and storage space.

Magazine Fulfillment Center

The magazine fulfillment center is a special type of distributor. Fulfillment centers, an American phenomenon so far, exist in areas having low labor costs and low overhead, and they invest heavily in sophisticated automated equipment. They contract with publishers of mass circulation magazines and, increasingly, with publishers of smaller circulation journals, to receive orders, payments, and renewals from subscribers and to keep circulation records and provide mailing labels for each issue. In recent years the inability of librarians (a very small percentage of all subscribers) to reach human beings at the fulfillment centers has caused serious problems. However, work done by representatives of U.S. subscription agencies has eased the problems. Each fulfillment center title now has a toll-free telephone number for efficient customer service. For a discussion of the library's relationship with the fulfillment center, see the author's 1985 article.[1]

Back Issue Dealer

Some companies specialize in serials that are not current and are difficult to locate. These booksellers probably do not accept continuing orders for current serials, only one-time orders for the older volumes. The librarian can expect to pay a premium price for material acquired through a back issue dealer, because this vendor often must go through a time consuming and expensive search to obtain the volume or volumes required. For the same reason, the library can expect to wait a long time for the fulfillment of many orders.

SERVICES OF SERIALS SUPPLIERS

Serials suppliers have different specialties and different ways of filling library orders. This section discusses in detail each type of vendor.

Subscription Agent

In the United States the library subscription agent is a specialist in filling continuing orders for periodicals. The large agents process standing orders for nonperiodical serials as well, but this is not their strength. Typically, the subscription agent receives periodical orders from many libraries, batches them and sends them to the publishers each autumn with a check covering the total cost of the subscriptions. The agent does not see the material ordered; the publisher mails it directly to the library, a process known as "drop-shipment."

When subscription agencies first automated their records and procedures during the late 1960s and early 1970s, a period of adjustment ensued for vendor, publisher, and library, while the agents debugged their computer programs. During this confusion, some libraries bypassed the agent and dealt directly with the publishers. After a few years, the automated agencies offered much more efficient order processing and detailed management reports than before they had computers. Many libraries returned to them as customers.

Until the 1960s, library subscriptions through agents were less expensive than those directly from the publisher because publishers offered substantial discounts to vendors. The subscription agent made its profit from publishers' discounts, but rising costs have eroded these profits. Today's discounts to the suppliers are not large enough to cover the agent's expenses. The publishers have lowered their discounts to decrease the rate of subscription price increases, and now librarians expect to pay a service charge to the agent. This charge represents the difference between the revenue generated by the publisher discount and that required by the agent to maintain a profitable business. The service charge appears on the library's invoice as either a percentage of the total list price of the periodicals or a charge calculated for each title. Thus, libraries pay more to use a vendor than they would ordering from a publisher directly.

There are still a few exceptions to this policy, however. School and public libraries may pay less than list price for periodicals, because the publishers of the high-volume titles they are likely to order still give the subscription agent a discount that is large enough to cover expenses and profit.

In the past, librarians were mainly concerned with the agents' performance as purchasers and invoicers, but today they have additional concerns. One of these is the need to make the best use of their serial acquisitions funds. At the same time, the number of companies available from which to choose is reduced by competition for automated services and by shrunken subscription lists resulting from libraries' cancellations. The subscription agencies that have survived provide libraries with management reports and current information about price and availability of serials; they will continue to survive only by adapting to libraries' changing needs.

The reduction in publisher discounts led American agents to expand their business by accepting standing orders for nonperiodical serials. However, they did not perform this task well. These agents handled such orders as if they were periodicals, and they did a poor job of it. Further, they imposed a service charge, where a standing order vendor might give the library a discount. Eventually most subscription agents learned to treat standing orders differently, as a bookseller would do. They continue to solicit orders for all types of serials.

Once again, foreign subscription agents, especially those in Europe, usually accommodate all types of continuing orders equally well. Their quality of service can vary from thorough and careful to totally unsatisfactory. Some of these foreign vendors are primarily bookshops and are appropriate agents only for their geographic or subject specialties. Some European agents may receive and reship all materials, even periodicals. A few will provide a consolidation service (known as "buying round" in the United Kingdom), in which the agent orders, receives, checks in, and claims (if necessary) serials for the library and ships the pieces by air freight monthly, weekly, or more often if the volume requires. There is, of course, a fee for this service.

The subscription agent engages in a high-volume, low-margin business and, quite naturally, prefers to handle periodicals that appear regularly and have liberal discounts. Problems with an agent's service are likely to come in orders for periodicals that (1) are behind in schedule, (2) are issued by single-title publishers, and (3) do not consider libraries to be their primary market. A former subscription agent comments:

> The strong side of the agency is what I used to call "the 90 percent." We have always got to realize that when an organization is geared to handle large quantities of material, there is almost necessarily less attention for (very) special things.[2]

In this era of the necessary service charge, agents compete not only on the annual cost of subscriptions, but also on the services they offer. The market for the subscription agent's services has become saturated, resulting in an expansion of services offered to the library customer. The largest agents are extensively automated and can provide almost any information or special handling the customer desires.

One of the first innovations was making the agency's database available to the library. Although the company developed the system internally for its own use, the persistent librarian could view current bibliographic and subscription data, plus payment information for one's own library. Some systems could pass on information from journal publishers regarding delivery dates and delays in publication.

The same computer was able to churn out management reports sorted in any number of ways and covering two or three years' worth of data. The agency used these reports as a selling point. Library-specific data are useful in budget projections.

Some customers had little funding for staff but were able to pay for services contracted to external agencies. This situation led to a consolidation service, including off-site check-in and processing. Having created a serials management system for this purpose, it was only natural that the agency offer to sell the system to libraries for their own use.

Subscription agencies have offered the option of early payment discounts to their customers for several years. The library pays in the spring or summer a sum roughly equivalent to the total annual amount of business with the agency. The vendor invests the money and shares the income on these funds with the library. Later, when the renewal prices are set, there is an accounting.

The newest service offered by subscription agents is journal tables of contents and the delivery of articles to either a library or an individual. For example, EBSCO has purchased a document delivery supplier, and The Faxon Company is developing its own service. Some other agencies formed partnerships with existing companies such as Uncover and the British Library Document Supply

Centre. No one has yet determined the implications of this shift from brokering subscriptions to supplying articles.

How much service an agent will provide and at what cost depends largely on how much the vendor wants the library's business. One agency may offer a great number of services at no charge but be unwilling to accommodate a special request from one single library. Another agency may charge for certain services but be quite flexible in what it will do for an individual customer, both for a fee and at no charge.

Good working relationships depend on good personal relationships. Having one person in the agent's office who is familiar with the library's account promotes a comfortable business relationship. Only one telephone call to the vendor during which no one seems to recognize the library's name, much less the account, damages both the caller's ego and the relationship with the vendor. Personal contact is the best way to ensure the communication which can promote a good working relationship. Visits to the library by interested and informed marketing (and occasionally customer service) representatives of the subscription agencies can secure and increase the amount of business a serials department does with a vendor. Marketing personnel who best understand the library's concerns are often those who have been practicing librarians.

Vendors discover the requirements of library customers and adapt their procedures and services accordingly. The competition among American vendors forces them to be creative and sensitive to the needs of their customers and potential customers. This competition has extended to foreign titles, and is forcing nondomestic vendors to offer services previously restricted to American subscription agents.

Occasionally both sales representatives and promotional literature mailed to libraries by the subscription agencies make claims about service that the company cannot fulfill. To promise a single annual invoice and a single payment for all serials is not realistic. Annual price increases are the norm and the publisher may not determine the amount of an increase until shortly before publishing the new volume. Both domestic and foreign agencies send invoices earlier than ever so they can earn interest on library money until they pay the publishers. These two trends virtually ensure that the vendor will have to send the library supplementary invoices, unless the library prepays in a lump sum and receives its renewal invoice well into the autumn or winter.

Claiming is another area in which the subscription agent cannot always fulfill its promises. The agent acts as an intermediary between the library and the publisher in claiming as in ordering. Librarians believe they pay for this service. Most library claims are handled correctly and expeditiously, but the intervention of a novice or careless account representative may slow the transmission of the claim to the publisher and sometimes garbles the message so that it becomes meaningless. Both the routine, computer-generated claim and office procedures may cause deletion or misinterpretation of crucial claiming information. However, when a library's claim is the latest of many the agency has received for a specific issue or title, the agent can respond immediately from the database without involving the publisher. The agent will already have the answer or a response from the publisher, from having processed the earlier claims. In fact, the largest agencies may already have given the claim response in their online title information files. These databases list both changes in serials (e.g., title changes, frequency changes, suspensions, mergers) and publication delays reported to them by the publisher.

The 1990s have seen heightened competition among subscription agencies. Some of them are struggling for survival. Thus, libraries have a great deal of power in negotiating with the agencies. They can decrease their service charges and increase their agency services by bargaining. Basch and McQueen have published an excellent monograph on the subject and Basch, a former subscription agent, has written articles on it.[3]

Standing Order Vendor / Bookseller

Standing order vendors, usually also booksellers (or "jobbers"), are specialists in monographic materials: firm orders for books, approval plans, and continuing orders for nonperiodical serials. Often, particularly in the United States, standing orders are not their primary interest or their most profitable service. Most of them, again in the United States, will not accept orders for journal subscriptions; some will not even consider an annual that has the word "journal" in the title. Still, within the last twenty years these companies have created separate standing order departments staffed by specialists in nonperiodical serials. These units have provided the best service available for this type of material, including approval plans for serials and blanket orders for all publications of an association or institute.

Because a large proportion of standing order serials are monographic or annual, vendors are likely to discount the list price. Publishers still give booksellers hefty discounts on these materials. However, at the same time they may charge for shipping/handling/postage which will boost the library's price nearly back to the list price. These terms are all negotiable.

Unlike most subscription agents, standing order vendors usually stock the most heavily-ordered serials and reship them to the library. For items not in stock, the vendor orders and then reships them. This procedure derives from their firm order procedures, but it is also a service to the customer. Booksellers claim that publishers make so many errors in shipment that they need to inspect the volumes before forwarding them to the library.

Publisher

Publishers of both journals and other serials will nearly always accept a continuing order directly from the library. In fact, some publishers will not work with intermediaries (e.g., the H.W. Wilson Company). Increasingly sophisticated technology makes such direct orders more attractive to the library, especially when it subscribes to many serials from one publisher.

Some publishers will still give a library the same discount they give the subscription agent or standing order vendor. At times they will offer a smaller discount. Gale Research and Reed Reference are examples of publishers offering discounts to libraries on standing orders. Springer-Verlag had such a program for journals in the 1970s; Pergamon Press recently discontinued the policy of giving a reduced rate for two-year subscriptions.

In light of the high annual price increases now common for journals, several publishers have invented creative ways to save libraries money. For example, Pergamon now credits the senior author of an article accepted for publication with 25 pounds sterling. The author can pass on the credit to a library so that the institution may pay a reduced price for a Pergamon journal. The publisher has a list of suggested third-world libraries as beneficiaries, but the author may select any library.

Gordon and Breach has two plans for reducing its journals' costs to libraries. The first is known as the "Subscriber Incentive Program," or SIP: the library may lower its price by promising not to cancel the title and by purchasing directly either from Gordon and Breach or from its designated distributor. This publisher also credits the senior author of an accepted article with $20 (15 ECU) for a library to use in subscribing to a Gordon and Breach journal.

Reed Reference Publishing introduced its "gift certificates" which anyone may purchase and give to a library for application to the invoice of any Reed Reference publication. These certificates work in a way similar to U.S. savings bonds in that one purchases them for less than the face value.

It is appropriate here to issue a warning about gimmicks. All of these programs are publisher promotions and the library should evaluate them carefully before using them. Efficient serial acquisitions relies on set procedures, and these promotions depart from the standard procedures. "Incentive plans" or gift certificates do not necessarily pay off in terms of library staff time required to handle claims, complaints, and problems with publishers' business offices. However, in the present economic climate, the number of such programs is likely to increase and the programs will probably become even more creative.

As in the Gordon and Breach situation, publishers may use distributors. Some will accept direct orders from neither a librarian nor a subscription agent. This arrangement has long been the policy in Eastern European countries, although it may be changing now. International publishers may require subscribers to order from the branch in their own country and to pay in their local currency.

Publishers vary in their retention policies for back issues and back volumes. Large international publishers have a supply of back issues and, at least in the case of Pergamon, promote their sale. Older materials may even be available at a reduced price from the publisher, because their cost has already been covered in the subscription price for the year in which they were produced; the only expenses for publishers' back files are storage, handling, and mailing. Other publishers may sell their stock to back issue dealers, often for tax purposes. Libraries must then pay a premium to acquire them.

Back Issue Dealer

The final category of serial vendor is the back issue dealer, who specializes in older serials and does not accept continuing orders for current material. Libraries may place firm orders for items listed in a dealer's printed or online catalog, or they may send lists of desiderata for the company to search in the out-of-print market and quote prices. In the latter instance, libraries can expect to pay a much higher price than they would have (or did) when the material was new. They can expect to wait a long time for fulfillment of out-of-print orders and should limit the time their order list remains valid. A six month limit is common. Requests for badly needed serials could allow a longer term.

Where institutional or state laws permit, the library may sell its unnecessary duplicates or other discarded serials to a back issues dealer for either cash or credit.

WHY USE A VENDOR?

Each librarian will decide whether to use an intermediary in the purchase of periodicals and other serials. There is not necessarily a right way for all libraries. Factors to consider include size and scope of the serials collection, existing staffing levels, and the funding available for staffing.

Economies in the Use of a Purchasing Agent

The librarian can take advantage of several economies by using a subscription agent or standing order vendor as intermediary in the purchase of serials. For example, the use of agents enables the librarian to avoid dealing with numerous publishers, perhaps in different areas of the world. Most large foreign vendors will correspond in English and invoice in the currency of choice, another distinct advantage to most American librarians. The customer receives fewer invoices and thus has fewer checks to write and to mail. The vendor should act as advocate for its library customers, using the leverage it has from the money it pays the publisher. Libraries benefit from a good vendor's services, such as automatic renewal, timely claiming reports, budget projections, and individualized invoices.

What Vendors do for Publishers

Many publishers claim that the subscription agent or bookseller is only a "factor," that is, a purchasing agent hired by the library to perform a service. On the other hand, the vendors unanimously believe that they provide essential services to publishers and earn every bit of their discounts.[4]

In fact, subscription prices of journals would increase significantly were there no intermediary. Publishers would have to expand their own circulation and distribution services to handle separate orders arriving from hundreds or thousands of libraries worldwide. They would need to invoice each subscriber individually and, as a result, would receive separate payments for each invoice. Alternatively, the publisher could contract with a fulfillment center for these services.

The subscription agency consolidates orders from its library customers and sends a check for the orders, in advance of publication. The agency guarantees payment to the publisher for its orders, and that check is drawn in whatever currency has been agreed upon.

If there were no vendors, libraries would claim missing issues and volumes directly from the publisher instead of having the agent claim on their behalf. Responding to these claims would take more staff and investment of funds for the publisher than exist now, for the agent filters library claims and sends the publisher only those that are valid (e.g., within the specified claiming time frame or the first request the agent receives for a particular piece). The vendor is also able to pass on to the library, either in writing or on its online system, distribution and delayed-shipment information that it has received from the publisher, thus heading off unnecessary claims.

Some vendors distribute promotional literature from publishers and place journal ads in their printed catalogs. They may also display sample periodical issues at their booths at library conferences.

The debate continues over whether the subscription agency provides services solely for the library customer or also for the serial publisher. In efforts to cut costs, publishers have repeatedly lowered agency discounts; some have even discontinued them. In every case, of course, the library pays more.

How the Agent Makes Money

Traditionally, subscription agencies have received a tremendous proportion of their income from publisher discounts. Even though international publishers have reduced or eliminated agency discounts, the discounts still account for a significant part of the vendor's income. Basch and McQueen document this fact:

> [T]he authors' informed estimate is that the largest agencies still derive at least half of their revenues from publisher discounts. Service charges are rapidly assuming equal importance. Miscellaneous income accounts for only a small proportion of overall revenues—probably from half of one percent to five percent of total sales.[5]

Booksellers receive deeper discounts from publishers than subscription agencies receive for serials. However, booksellers have expenses that subscription agents do not have. Standing order vendors must have one or more staffed warehouses to stock the monographs and serials that they sell. They have handling and mailing costs that subscription agencies, at least in the United States, do not have. While all vendors incur expenses in bibliographic work, booksellers handling irregular publications have perhaps the more difficult—and costly—work.

Back issue dealers have the most labor-intensive work of all, because not only must they have room to store serials, but they must very often search for a specific volume or issue for a library. The price of second-hand serials is directly related to the amount of effort that goes into procuring them.

Magazine fulfillment centers, the highly automated circulation operations hired by magazine publishers, profit from the services they provide their employers. They take advantage of economies of scale by working for many publishers, and their efficiency saves publishers money in circulation services. The fulfillment center provides specific services to publishers, including receiving subscription orders and renewals (primarily through direct mail and cards placed in magazines), processing payments and cancellations, and producing statistical reports for publishers. The publishers may contract for other services. The common end product of fulfillment centers is the mailing label that printers (located elsewhere) place on the issues when they are ready to mail.

UNDERSTANDING AND OPTIMIZING VENDOR SERVICES

From the serials manager's perspective, the issues in understanding and optimizing serials vendor relationships are cost, service, and honesty. The ideal agency-library business relationship is one of trust. When both parties understand and agree upon the issues of cost, service, and honesty, trust should be the natural outcome.

What the Librarian Contributes to and Expects from the Professional Relationship

Librarian Contribution. The librarian makes three contributions to the vendor relationship: money, information, and honesty. Revenue earned from library subscription and service charge payments contributes to the agency's profit. Both parties understand this. Marketing representatives' income is also tied to library business in their territories, so the library contributes to the representatives' earnings, as well.

Librarians are excellent resources for a vendor representative who wants to learn what is happening in the profession. And it is to the librarian's advantage to inform the vendor, because the more the agency partner knows about serials librarianship, the better the business relationship.

Honesty on the part of the librarian is essential for a productive vendor relationship. The librarian must not mislead an agent or prospective agent to gain an advantage. For example, in a request for proposal sent to competing agencies, the librarian should promise a certain level of business and follow through with the appropriate number of orders. It is equally important that the librarian not skew the truth and mislead the agent about size of account, services desired, or any facet of the relationship.

Librarian Expectation. The librarian has a right to expect the same three qualities from the vendor: a financial contribution, information, and honesty. The subscription agent assumes much of the acquisitions clerical work; this constitutes its financial contribution. In addition, a competitive service charge may be considered a financial contribution to the library.

Just as librarians inform and educate vendor representatives, so vendors can help librarians to know more about the commercial side of serial acquisitions. Visiting subscription agents put specific librarians in touch with each other when they have a mutual problem or when one librarian has resolved a problem with which the other wrestles. At the same time, librarians need to be wary of a vendor's criticisms of a competitor.

The librarian should be able to expect the agency to fulfill its promises. The sales representative should not tease the librarian with services that may not be available nor mislead him or her about the company's capabilities. The agent does not have to highlight any problems with the organization, but staff should not claim that problems do not exist if, in fact, they do.

Building and Maintaining Relationship

Education is the first step in building and maintaining a successful library/vendor relationship. Each party has a responsibility to become informed about the other. This orientation takes place during agent visits to the library and librarian visits to the vendor. The professional literature contains numerous articles about both library serial acquisitions and the workings of the subscription agency. Also, both participants attend the same national and regional conferences and can strengthen working relationships there.

A trusting agent/librarian relationship, like a good friendship or marriage, does not just happen. Both parties must work on it. Again, honesty is the key. A librarian should be worthy of trust; follow through on promises and keep confidences.

The serials manager must be realistic. The vendor is in a very competitive business, and he generates as much revenue from the publisher as from the library. Thus, the agency must satisfy both the librarian and the publisher. The librarian's job is to ask questions and to verify information.

Contracts, Agreements, Requests for Proposals

In today's economic climate librarians are being held accountable for their materials funds to a far greater degree than ever before. Acquisitions librarians must make business decisions instead of letting personalities and perquisites sway their choices. Many serials librarians have been guilty, as has the author, of saying, "Service is more important than cost." This adage no longer remains true.

Just as the librarian must be honest with the vendor, so must the agent be honest with the librarian. That is, honesty requires no misleading requests for proposal submitted by the library and no obsolete prices from the vendor. It does not mean that the agent should not make itself look as good as possible or that the librarian should not make the account as attractive as possible. It means that both should represent the truth about themselves.

To make certain that agreed-upon terms and concessions are understood and adhered to, they should be detailed in writing and signed by both parties. There may be a formal contract, examined and approved by institutional attorneys, or there may be a letter spelling out the details. A vendor's response to a request for proposal is not sufficient; it should be followed by a formal written agreement.

Ethics

The topic of ethics in the librarian/vendor relationship has been much discussed in recent years. Here again, honesty on the part of both parties is crucial. This means no pricing games from the vendor; no accepting agency concessions and taking business elsewhere for the library.

Librarians often discuss the ethical issue of meals and parties paid for by the subscription agent. The vendors' efforts to survive in a low-margin business and a saturated or shrinking market have reduced the number of these events in the last few years. Some libraries allow no vendor-paid meals; others accept them from current vendors but not prospective ones. In the author's view, these meals (and to a lesser degree, parties) are usually opportunities to talk business and meet other librarians with similar interests and concerns.

A comparable situation is the invitation to a librarian to visit the present or prospective vendor's headquarters, meet customer service personnel, and see how the company works. The author has visited several vendors, domestic and foreign, at their expense and at her library's or her own expense. It is her opinion that such visits are valuable in establishing a relationship with the subscription agency and its personnel. On occasion other librarians may be visiting at the same time, enhancing the opportunity to learn. In the author's view there is no reason to decline an agent's or a prospective agent's invitation to visit the headquarters at his expense for the purpose of mutual edification.

In conclusion, both parties need to know their reason for doing business: mutual financial advantage. They should be open about the services they need and services they offer. Each should learn about the other through personal conversations, visits, journal articles, and conference presentations. They should state their agreements in writing, either as a formal contract or in a letter. Knowledge, awareness, and honesty will lead to trust between the vendor and the librarian.

PRINCIPLES FOR VENDOR SELECTION

Every serial acquisitions unit should have a written vendor selection policy. It should devise its own, not simply adopt another library's policy, for there is no single correct way to select a serials vendor.

One Vendor, Many Vendors, or No Vendor?

One should not necessarily place all library orders through a subscription agent or standing order dealer. The library may more easily acquire some titles from a magazine fulfillment center by ordering directly. This is particularly true for multiple copies, because of the very strict rules concerning length of subscriber address for these periodicals. Small circulation titles such as literary magazines may be published by a single person who has never heard of a subscription agent and will not know what to do with an agent's order. Certain commercial publishers do not work with vendors and accept orders only from the subscriber. The librarian must exclude these types of orders, then, from the "list" of those placed with vendors.

Just as vendors differ in the services they offer, so libraries differ in their vendor needs. The decision of whether to use a subscription agent or standing order vendor as an intermediary or to deal directly with the publisher is one each library must make based on its own needs and priorities. The decision may govern all serial orders, or it may govern specific types of orders or individual orders. Some of the variables to consider in selecting a vendor are size of the library's continuing serial financial obligation, distribution of titles by country of origin, geographical location of the library, and services required of the vendor. When a decision has been made to place all or part of the library's serial orders with an agent or with several agents, the librarian has several choices to make. Written policy statements should formalize this process. The library policy needs to be continually evaluated as computer technology and library budgets change and as vendors and their promised services change. Some libraries may best use a single vendor; others will need to work with several.

All Orders with Single Vendor

For many libraries the ideal situation is to place all serial orders with one vendor, particularly if the titles are relatively standard and predominantly domestic. The only orders not placed with the agent would be those for which the publisher will not accept orders from agents, such as the H.W. Wilson Company titles. This consolidation permits the library to process the fewest number of invoices and to deal with only one agency.

The library subscribing primarily to domestic publications will probably be able to use a subscription agent in its own country for all serial titles, including the relatively few foreign ones. Many vendors claim to be able to deliver foreign titles, but they often fail to do so. Libraries having no satisfactory domestic vendor may perhaps place all their orders with one of the truly international agents. These companies are large and established, and they offer a full range of services to the library, often including a consolidation and reshipping program. If a library requiring an international vendor has funding for a consolidation program, this may be the ideal means of acquiring serials.

Particular advantages of using a single vendor may tip the scales in favor of this policy. Unless the library has its own automated serials management system, the vendor-produced management reports will be more useful than if the orders are divided among several sources, since the reports will include nearly all of a library's current serials orders. Claims could, with few exceptions, be sent to one source.

Especially for a large account, the vendor may make concessions or offer inducements to the library to acquire the business. When a library consolidates its subscriptions and standing orders with a single, domestic vendor, it may pay a lower service charge than when the agency handles only its periodicals, because publishers still typically give agents a discount for nonperiodical serials. Even so, there may be disadvantages to the use of one vendor. Periodicals and nonperiodical serials are different types of publications with differences in pattern of appearance, and in billing and fulfillment procedure. An automated American subscription agent sometimes may attempt to apply routines which are successful for periodicals to other serials, and they do not work. Irregular publications usually are not paid annually in advance, but are invoiced upon publication to the agent and, in turn, by the agent to the library. Libraries combining subscriptions and standing orders with one vendor should demand a separate account for each type of order. Experience and careful attention can minimize the foul-ups, but vendors have personnel turnover just as library serials departments do, and the risk of unfilled orders is a consideration when standing orders are placed through a periodicals subscription agency. Unless a library has very few or very straightforward nonperiodical serial orders, it is better to have a separate source for each type of order and to place standing orders through a vendor specializing in that form of serial.

Further examples of vendor enducements are database access at no charge, and customized management reports. The degree to which the vendor will go with concessions depends on how attractive the account is, that is, how much revenue the orders will bring to the agency.

In spite of all these benefits there are those who say a library should not restrict itself to a single agent. That company, they believe, will come to take the library customer for granted and will cease to compete for the library's business; performance will drop and service charges will increase, because it would be an impossible task for the library to move its orders to another vendor or to place them directly. An article by Doris New indicates that such a change may not be as difficult for the library to effect as agents insist.[6] New's article was written before most serial acquisitions units were automated; the task is much easier today than in the 1970s. There is evidence that when a library serials department monitors the performance of its vendors and gives new business to the ones which rate highest, the agencies involved respond with improved service. Such a change, however, is not without problems. This chapter has a later section entitled "Vendor Change," that discusses ways to minimize disruption.

Use a Variety of Vendors

There are fewer subscription agents in the United States to choose from than there were just a few years ago. Some of the first vendors to disappear were those that could not afford to automate. Larger American agencies purchased smaller ones, and foreign vendors bought still other agencies.

Libraries having large and/or specialized serials collections may be successful using both subscription agents and standing order dealers. Librarians may divide titles by type of serial, subject matter, and/or geographic location of publisher. Some vendors restrict themselves to, for example, standing orders, a single language, or medical serials—whatever they do best. Many others will accept an order for any title and do their best to supply it. This attitude is commendable, but a library with a strong collection of German or African serials should have a vendor in the country of origin, or at least one specializing in that region. In general, domestic vendors will produce results inferior to those from an appropriate specialized or foreign vendor.

American subscription agents often use a foreign vendor themselves for certain difficult material, adding another step between library and publisher. The loss in completeness of management data with the use of more than one vendor may not be a problem, as librarians have continued to develop their computer skills and to take advantage of sophisticated automated management systems.

The librarian may not be willing to risk placing all orders with a single vendor, especially if the account would be in the range of a million dollars or more. In this case, the orders can be distributed according to whatever criteria the library cares to use.

Ordering Directly from the Publisher

The librarian should examine a decision not to use a subscription agent as carefully as the decision to use one or more agencies. One uses an intermediary in the purchase of serials when to do so offers a financial advantage. The vendor takes over clerical tasks, and the library should receive either a price break on its titles or service worth the price paid. Unlike subscription agencies, publishers do not yet invoice on tape, disc, or the Internet. The librarian must balance issues of convenience and cost. The vendor can save the library time and money in claiming, receiving issues, accounting, and postage. However, the library must pay the service charge. With inflation making all cost figures invalid before they appear in print, calculating invoice expenses is difficult; but certainly the cost is significant. And there is no difference between the local payment procedure for a ten thousand dollar chemistry journal and that for a $7.00 newsletter.

One must consider whether saving a vendor's service charge by ordering directly is not negated by the required clerical work. A library can use direct orders selectively. On occasion a publisher gives a significant discount to the library. Some publications cost more when purchased from a vendor. The agents try to convince societies to offer member prices on vendor orders, but they are not always successful. Some societies will give the member discount if the agency gives the library's membership number, a more workable situation for the library.

Now that the Decision is Made

In summary, each serials librarian needs to decide what is best for the library—one agent, several agents, or no agent. There is justification for each choice, because every library is a unique institution with individual requirements. Each librarian must set priorities and decide what is best for the library. Once the decision is made, the next step is to select the best vendor or vendors for the library's situation.

VENDOR SELECTION CRITERIA

This section covers the qualities the librarian should look for in a vendor. In some instances the list will be brief and uncomplicated, but for a research library, the requirements are likely to be extensive and demanding. New's article cited in the previous section and one by Harry Kuntz[7] have checklists containing questions a serials librarian should ask of prospective subscription agents. The author's own checklists for vendor selection are given in Appendix 6-A and 6-B.

Cost of a subscription agent's service includes not only service charge, but also possible fees for such exceptions as cancellations and rush orders. Service details include the time required to process orders and claims, agency-supplied claim forms, flexible invoicing, and various reports. In addition to investigating cost and service, Kuntz questions the management, fiscal condition, and facilities of the company. Serials librarians are glad to talk about their own experience with particular agencies, and such discussion represents a legitimate aspect of vendor selection and evaluation. A marketing representative presents his or her agency in the best light. A telephone call or letter to serial acquisitions librarians working with a collection of comparable size and scope to one's own will either support or refute the company's statements about itself.

For serial acquisitions personnel without direct experience with a variety of vendors, and for those considering changing or adding agents, two books provide guidance. A 1975 book by Bill Katz and Peter Gellatly, *Guide to Magazine and Serial Agents*,[8] reports the results of a survey of vendor policies of 850 libraries of various size and type. While this work is more than twenty years old and should have been revised long ago, its principles remain valid. *International Subscription Agents*[9] is revised every few years. Recent editions have expanded the definition of "international" to include many American vendors who accept orders for serials published in foreign countries, even though the bulk of their business is with American publishers. One should not use those agents for complicated foreign serial orders, because they probably do not have procedures for this type of order, and the library takes an unnecessary risk of not receiving the material. The scope of *International Subscription Agents* now includes back issue dealers. The information comes from recent vendor questionnaires, and the book contains a geographical index. On the whole, the directory is quite useful.

Questions for Subscription Agents

The library selecting a vendor should ask specific questions in a number of categories, many of them concerning speed and cost. The topics below match those in the checklist in Appendix 6-A but cover only selected questions on that list.

Order Placement. One should know how long it takes the agent to place orders with the publisher after it has received them from the library. While subscriptions placed for next year's journals may go to the agent several months in advance of the first issue, a vendor's delay in contacting the publisher presents an opportunity for loss of the library order. Many agents send an acknowledgement of new orders.

Does the vendor send a check with the orders and renewals, or is there some other arrangement? In this low-margin business, agents may place the order in good time but pay later or accompany the order with a postdated check. Separating the order from the payment could mean that the publisher will never reconnect them and the library will not receive its material. Some publishers will not accept orders without payment and will not accept a postdated check.

Are there restrictions on the type of materials a library can order through this vendor? Some subscription agents do not want to accept library orders for material that is difficult to acquire or orders with publishers considered difficult to work with. United States government publications fall into both of these groups. Other agents may accept such orders but charge an extra fee for handling them. The librarian should be aware of such policies.

One should also ask whether the vendor informs the library when there is a delay in processing the order. That is, what kind of reporting system does the agency have if it cannot, for example, identify the publisher on the library order?

Claiming. Again, the librarian needs to ask how quickly the vendor forwards library claims to the publisher? And what type of verifying does its staff do before sending the claim? How does the agent notify the library of claim responses? When does the agency cease to process a repeated claim routinely? Does the vendor have any stock of back issues from which to fill library claims without contacting the publisher? What information does the agent include on a claim? Will they send a sample of their claim form?

Service Charge. The service charge is presently the most negotiable item in the vendor/library agreement. Competition has decreased the rate within the past several years, as has vendors' increased reliance on the use of customers' prepayment of renewal funds. The librarian should determine how this charge is calculated and for what term it is guaranteed. It is also important to investigate hidden fees for certain types of serials and the possibility of paying no service charge either for high-priced scientific journals or for the library's complete list of serials.

There has been talk of "unbundling" vendor services. Unbundling is basing the service charge on the actual services (e.g., claiming, management reports, access to database) that the agency provides. Joe Barker has written about this policy, based on conversations with vendors and librarians. He says:

> I discovered that serious dangers may lurk around the unbundling of service charges— threatening libraries and vendors alike. I discovered too some alluring possibilities. But, for the latter to materialize without being outnumbered by the former, serials managers clearly need to develop a "cold-cash" understanding of the whole topic of packaging vendor services, and become more wary and willing to dicker than what I heard....[10]

Invoicing. Nearly all large subscription agencies can supply invoices in electronic formats such as tape or computer disc. It is now possible for the library to receive invoicing information over the Internet. If the library is capable of receiving and processing electronic invoices, the librarian should investigate this possibility, including any increase or decrease in the service charge. Other variables the librarian should investigate are rates of interest or credit for prepayments and late payment charges.

When a library uses many funds for serials, it must know how flexible the company is in its invoicing. The library may need several levels of subtotals for accounting purposes. Some libraries wish to renew only when they know the firm price of a journal, and they need to know how the agent handles this stipulation.

In-House Service. One customer service representative should work with the library's account, a single, accessible person with whom acquisitions staff can establish a good working relationship. This person also needs a back-up representative or team. The librarian may question the qualifications and authority of the representative. By the same token, at times the agency may ask the library staff members to adapt their own procedures, to improve in-house service of the account.

Management Reports. Depending on the sophistication of the library's automated system, management reports from the vendor may or may not be valuable. One should ask about the agency's fee structure, frequency, and data included on the reports. The agent should be willing to send the library sample reports for examination and discussion. If the library does not need the reports, it may negotiate a reduction in the service charge.

Database. Subscription agencies' databases have become an essential source of current information about serials. The librarian should ask the agent about various means of accessing the database, service and communication charges for access, information available on the database, and its currency. Any fee for database access can be a negotiating point for the library.

Transfer of Orders. When the library selects a new vendor, existing orders are likely to be transferred to the vendor, from publishers or other vendors. Even with automation, such a transfer is time-consuming (i.e., expensive). It is reasonable to expect the agent to assist in these transfers. This help may include preparing transfer orders at the library and sending letters to the publishers informing them of the transfer.

Cancellations. In today's economic climate, nearly every library is forced to cancel subscriptions. The librarian should know the prospective vendor's policy on cancellations. Does the agency actually notify the publisher of cancellations, or does it simply not renew? How does it confirm cancellations to the library? What about refunds if the library must cancel during the term of a subscription? Is there a penalty for late cancellations?

Questions for Librarians about Agencies

Appendix 6-B is a list of questions for the librarian to ask other librarians who already are customers of an agency. The librarian can compare or contrast the answers with the vendor's own response to the library's questions. Subscription agents may offer a list of customers who are willing to speak with the librarian. However, take note that the vendor will suggest only those persons they know are satisfied with their services. If the librarian is able to identify other librarians using the vendor, the responses might be different and revealing.

The libraries chosen for this purpose should be comparable in size, complexity, and vendor selection policy to one's own library. It is particularly crucial either to select libraries with a similar size and type account or to remember the differences in vendor policy for different sized accounts when evaluating the answers to the questions.

VENDOR EVALUATION CRITERIA

In evaluating one's own current vendors, the librarian can usually respond to the questions without consulting either the vendor or other librarian customers. The same questions used to select a subscription agent are valid for evaluation, although the librarian might want to compile another set for this purpose. Key questions target services and service charges.

Service

One wants to determine whether the agent receives and renews the library's orders in a timely manner. Is renewal done correctly? Several years ago the author's library had a vendor who renewed several titles for the *preceding* year instead of the following year. The customer service representative could not understand why the library objected to paying for the incorrect year when the publishers would not refund the agency's money. Needless to say, that experience contributed to the decision to change agents.

Do library staff members have a good relationship with agency representatives? Do these persons visit the library? Do they make an appointment to visit? Are both marketing and customer service representatives knowledgeable about their company's services? Can the agency deliver what its representatives promise? Does the library work with a single in-house person, and is this person easy to reach by telephone, fax, or electronic mail? Is he or she responsive to the library's requests and needs? Are the library's claims effective? Are claim reports timely?

Is the vendor's database up to date with bibliographic changes? Having a current subscription price is particularly crucial. Librarians have mounted a campaign to receive publishers' renewal prices in time to evaluate the journals for renewal or cancellation. Most librarians learn these prices from the vendor database, and the agent has a responsibility to enter the new prices quickly. When a vendor delays entering new prices the librarian may suspect that the vendor is playing games. Recently one major US subscription agency issued its printed catalog for one year, but the catalog contained the previous year's prices. The agency gave an embarrassed explanation, but the suspicion remained.

Service Charge

In calculating the service charge, compare it to both the agent's quote and other comparable agents' charges to the library. Has the vendor raised the service charge without consulting the library? Talk to other librarians to determine whether their charge is similar. Finally, does the library actually receive the services it pays for?

VENDOR CHANGE

There may come a time when the librarian feels it necessary to transfer serial orders from one vendor to another. Or, the librarian may have no choice. A subscription agent may go out of business, and either cancel or unilaterally transfer the orders to another agency. On occasion, a vendor may cancel or transfer the library's orders even though it is not going out of business. It may decide that the library's account is too small to be worthwhile. Alternatively, the scope of the vendor's business may change. A bookseller, for example, may decide that it will no longer handle standing orders.

The librarian who decides to change vendors should have a valid reason for doing so and should be able to document that reason. Usually this will be poor service, excessive cost, or a change in the library's vendor selection policy. A valid reason to transfer orders from one vendor to another is to consolidate the library's business with fewer agencies. If an agency is not automated, its service problems and costs will probably exceed those of a larger, more modern company. In order for a library to gain maximum benefit from its own automation, its agent must also be automated.

It is usually unwise for the librarian to make the change abruptly; it is much better to work with the vendor to try to resolve the problem. If this action does not improve the situation, the librarian might express dissatisfaction by placing new orders with another vendor. If neither of these efforts is successful, the librarian should still not be in a hurry to make the change. One year is not too long to be certain that the transfer is necessary and will be smooth. There are, of course, exceptions to this rule, such as a severe deterioration in service. However, librarians must remember to base their decisions on fact, not on rumors. One should make the choice of a new vendor as carefully as the initial selection.

No matter how carefully the librarian conducts the transfer, problems will occur. Some orders will be lost, others will be duplicated. Invoices will arrive from several sources. Care in selecting the new vendor and close communication with this supplier should minimize trouble. It is essential that the new agency know that the orders are transfers from another vendor, so it can pass that information on to the publisher.

The new agent should be willing to assist in the transfer of orders, to avoid problems both for itself and for the library. The account may be large enough that a staff member from the agency will come to the library to help create order records, or at least communicate with the publishers on behalf of the library.

CONCLUSION

A good relationship with one's subscription agents and other suppliers is essential for a successful serial acquisitions program. It is a business relationship that should be entered into only after careful assessment of the library's needs and the vendors' services.

APPENDIX 6-A

Questions for Subscription Agents

Objective: To get the best service for this library at lowest cost.

Scope: U.S. and Canadian periodical subscriptions.

Essential services: timely order placement and payment; timely and efficient claiming; competitive service charge; accurate electronic invoicing; specific, experienced in-house person to handle account; updating information for titles placed with agency; access to database of bibliographic and subscription information about serials published worldwide.

1. Order Placement
   1.1. How soon after receipt at your agency are new subscriptions placed with the publisher?
   1.2. Do you acknowledge orders? All? Some? Only exceptions?
   1.3. Can you hold orders and release them later to meet delayed start date requests (e.g., order received in July for January start)? Is this your current practice?
   1.4. Does payment accompany the order for new subscriptions? NOTE: Postdated check is not considered payment.
   1.5. Does payment (not postdated check) accompany renewal orders? Exceptions?
   1.6. Do you accept orders for single issues? Back runs? Samples?
   1.7. Do you place any restrictions on the type of materials ordered (e.g., memberships, GPO, order directs, continuations, etc.)?
   1.8. When and how is the library notified if the publisher does not accept an order or the publisher cannot be identified?
2. Claiming
   2.1. How long after receipt of a claim is it dispatched to the publisher?
   2.2. What does your claim processing involve? Confirmation of library order? Check cashed by publisher? Review of publisher reports? Etc.? (i.e., do you review, or just forward?)
   2.3. What is your schedule of dispatch of claims to publishers? Daily? Weekly? Less frequently?
   2.4. How and how often are claim responses communicated to the library?
   2.5. At what point does a repeated library claim generate other than the routine passing of information to the publisher? What options are available to the in-house service staff?
   2.6. How can you supply missing issues not available through claiming?
   2.7. Please send a sample of a completed claim form for a publisher.

3. Service Charge
    3.1. How is the service charge calculated? Does the same charge apply to all invoices?
    3.2. Please comment on the stability or guarantee of quoted service charge, listing factors which influence charge. Under what circumstances will the quoted service charge change?
    3.3. Will you guarantee your service charge for more than one year? For how many years?
    3.4. What does the service charge cover?
    3.5. What services cost extra?
    3.6. Is there a dollar cap on the service charge for an individual title? How much?
    3.7. How do you handle the so-called "zero percent service charge" titles from STM publishers? Is there a service charge assessed on these titles?

4. Invoicing
    4.1. Are you able to supply electronic invoices for automated systems? What electronic methods are available: tape? disc? ftp? other? How does the service charge differ from that for paper invoices?
    4.2. What are your current rates for early payment discount? How have these changed over the past five years?
    4.3. Please explain late payment terms.
    4.4. How often are supplementary invoices sent?
    4.5. Are you able to identify and distinguish title-by-title on an invoice or renewal list: current year prices, last year's prices, next year's prices, estimated prices, "firm prices" (i.e., prices established for next year by the publisher)?
    4.6. Can you separate firm prices from estimates and bill them separately? Do you charge extra or increase service charge for this practice?
    4.7. What mechanism do you have for billing firm prices only?
    4.8. Describe the number of levels of subtotals, totals, and invoice presentation format available from library-supplied codes.
    4.9. Under what circumstances will the invoiced price exceed the publisher's price that appears in the publication?

5. In-House Service
    5.1. Is there a specific person in-house to handle the library's account?
    5.2. How many accounts does this person handle?
    5.3. Explain the responsibilities and authority of the assigned person (e.g., issue credits, call publishers, call back to libraries, staffing levels, issue checks to publisher).
    5.4. To whom does the assigned person report?

5.5. What backup to this person is provided?

5.6. What hours is this person available?

5.7. How long has this person been with your company?

5.8. How are rush/priority requests/situations handled?

5.9. Are there preferred practices that the library can follow to improve in-house servicing of a library's account (e.g., call at specific time each day, use agent's title numbers, use electronic mail, batch claims)?

6. Management Reports

6.1. What is your policy and fee structure for standard and customized management reports?

6.2. Are management reports self-explanatory, or must they be explained to the library personnel? How do you familiarize library staff with your standard reports, formats, etc.?

6.3. How frequently and in what format do you communicate to the library updating information for titles handled for that library?

6.4. What data can you supply to a library on disc for library usage?

7. Database

7.1. What access do you provide to your bibliographic and subscription database? What is the charge for this access?

7.2. What information is available through this database? Can it be downloaded to library systems?

7.3. How often is the database updated with bibliographic and subscription information?

7.4. What is the source of the bibliographic data? MARC (LC)?

7.5. Are tables of contents available through your database? Copies of articles?

8. Transfer of Orders

8.1. What assistance do you offer for transfer of subscriptions?

8.2. What are your recommended procedures to identify current expiration dates and to notify publishers of the transfers?

9. Cancellations

9.1. What is your policy for informing publishers of cancellations; do you simply not renew, or do you notify the publisher of cancellations?

9.2. What are your procedures for cancelling a subscription either at expiration or immediately? Is there follow up? How do the procedures differ when a publisher has been paid or not yet paid?

9.3. What are your refund practices?

9.4. What is the last date that cancellations are generally accepted? What exceptions can be accommodated?

APPENDIX 6-B

Questions to Ask about Vendor over the Telephone

Objective: To learn what experience libraries comparable to ours are having with the vendor as a supplier of US and Canadian periodicals.

1. Order Placement
   - Accurate and timely order placement and payment?
   - Accurate and timely renewal and payment?

2. Claiming
   - Claims processed quickly internally and to publisher?
   - How are claim responses communicated to library?
   - Take initiative in resolving repeated claims?
   - Reports accurate, complete, easy to understand?

3. Service Charge
   - Competitive?
   - Guarantee for multi-year period?
   - Notify before changing?
   - What is covered?
   - What costs extra?
   - Dollar cap on service charge for single title?
   - What about service charge for STM publications?

4. Invoicing
   - Use electronic invoices? Successful?
   - Different service charge, or same as paper?
   - Use early payment, no bill-back options? Successful?
   - Late payment terms?
   - Supplementary invoice volume and frequency?
   - Invoice formatted as library wishes?
   - Firm prices noted?

5. In-House Service
   - Specific person handling account?
   - How many other accounts for this person?
   - Satisfactory service from in-house person?

6. Management Reports
   - Easy to interpret?
   - Fee for any reports?

- How is updating information communicated to library?
- Get data or reports on tape? Useful for your own reports?

7. Database
   - Access? How? Charge?
   - Accurate? Current?

8. Other
   - Vendor strong points?
   - Vendor weak points?
   - Same strengths/weaknesses as several years ago, or change?
   - Use other agents for same type of material?
   - What percentage domestic subscriptions with this vendor?
   - Overall, how does this vendor compare?
   - Specific ways better?
   - Specific ways worse?
   - Size of account?
   - Length of time doing business with this vendor?
   - Place new orders with this vendor?
   - Plan to do more/less/same business with this vendor in future?
   - Anything else I should ask?

Thank You!

NOTES

1. Marcia Tuttle, "Magazine Fulfillment Centers: What They Are, How They Operate, and What We Can Do about Them." *Library Acquisitions: Practice and Theory* 9 (1985): 41-49.
2. Jos van Ginnekin, Personal communication.
3. N. Bernard Basch and Judy McQueen, *Buying Serials* (New York: Neal-Schuman Publishers, 1990); N. Bernard Basch, "The Business of Subscription Agencies: A Look at Maximizing Profitability," *Library Acquisitions: Practice & Theory* 13 (1989): 129-131.
4. Mary Devlin and Ronald Akie, "Publisher/Vendor Relations," *Advances in Serials Management* 5 (1995): 113-123.
5. Basch and McQueen, *Buying Serials*, 64.
6. Doris E. New, "Serials Agency Conversion in an Academic Library," *Serials Librarian* 2 (1978): 277-285.
7. Harry Kuntz, "Serial Agents: Selection and Evaluation," *Serials Librarian* 2 (1977): 139-150.
8. Bill Katz and Peter Gellatly, *Guide to Magazine and Serial Agents* (New York: R.R. Bowker Company, 1975).
9. Lenore Rae Wilkas, *International Subscription Agents*, 6th ed. (Chicago: American Library Association, 1994).
10. Joseph W. Barker, "Unbundling Serials Vendors' Service Charges," *Serials Review* 16, no. 2 (1990): 34.

Chapter 7

SERIALS PRICING

Serials pricing is currently the most crucial issue in serials management and perhaps in all of scholarly communication. Journal prices are too high, and they keep rising. Annual, double-digit inflation is the rule for subscription prices, with twenty to thirty percent increases for scientific journals not uncommon. At the same time, there has been an explosion in the number of science journals available. Scientific disciplines subdivide into new fields and require new journals. As an area of research grows more specific, the market for its journals also shrinks, forcing the cost of production to be spread among fewer subscribers. Science articles include plates, graphs, and formulae, all of which increase the cost of producing the journal. This chapter concentrates on scientific journals and their impact on serials pricing.

High prices have generally not affected humanities journals; those periodicals are not nearly as attractive to commercial publishers as science journals. Other entities, including associations, university presses, and individuals continue to publish humanities journals. These journals do not contribute to the pricing problem, but often they are its victims, as librarians cancel them in across-the-board reductions.

Social science journals, formerly carrying the qualities of humanities periodicals, are becoming akin to scientific journals in composition and in price. They are growing in size and in number, and they have become the target of takeover by commercial publishers. The increase in quantitative research is a factor in this evolution. Here, as in the hard sciences, the use of computers in research has increased the number of articles to be published.

On the whole, however, the scientific journals are the problem. Ann Okerson gives several reasons:

1. Science journals are generally more voluminous per title than those of other disciplines.

2. The science professions (also law) offer more jobs at higher salaries than the social sciences and humanities. They are associated with greater prosperity.
3. There are more emerging and advancing research areas in the sciences; many of these have commercial and industrial (profitable) applications.
4. Higher grants are awarded for scientific research.
5. Higher costs (such as refereeing, composition) are frequently associated with science publications.
6. Scientists are more number-conscious; the emphasis on citations has accelerated pressure for publication.[1]

As a result, libraries cannot provide the same coverage of the literature that they did in the past. The pricing crisis, however, is not limited to libraries; it has implications for publishers and subscription agents as well. The journal pricing situation requires that librarians and journal publishers meet and learn about each others' professional constraints. At the same time, the escalation of the crisis has disrupted this communication. "Why are Elsevier's profits so high?" wonders the librarian. Pricing issues affect the stability of the subscription agent, who is caught between the publisher and the librarian. In a sense the pricing issue hurts vendors as much as librarians. Although higher journal prices bring them additional revenue, agents receive nothing for subscriptions that librarians cancel. "Why can't the librarians get more money?" asks the publisher. Arlene Sievers explains that "the topic of serial prices...is one where perspective matters greatly," because the major players "approach the subject in very different ways."[2]

This chapter briefly covers the history of the serials pricing crisis and analyzes the situation today. It details how librarians, publishers, and subscription agents fight the high prices, and it speculates on what will happen to serials pricing in the future.

HISTORY OF SERIALS PRICING

Two essays cover the history of serials (i.e., journals) pricing through the mid-1980s very well. Deana Astle and Charles Hamaker investigated discriminatory pricing by German publishers between the two world wars,[3] and Ann Okerson analyzed serials pricing from 1970 until the mid-1980s.[4] Both articles show that the issue of high journal prices is not new. Instead, it has been causing controversy intermittently throughout the twentieth century. Today the issue involves many of the same aspects as it did historically.

In the years before World War II most periodicals were published by associations, institutions, and individuals. With the exception of a few commercial publishers, mostly in Europe, societies published the scholarly journals. During the war years national governments sponsored scientific research for military purposes and published the results.

The current serials pricing crisis actually began at the end of the Second World War. Sievers describes what happened:

> The growth of, and support for, scientific research in university campuses was driven by the increased resources directed towards these programmes. This new funding emphasis arose to some degree in response to the US commitment to technological and military superiority after World War II. The Sputnik era of the late 1950s, during which US education was found wanting, and American students were found to lag behind the Soviets in the study of mathematics and science, marked the beginning of a period of unrestricted funding for education in these areas, as well as for research in technology.[5]

At that time, the means of disseminating the results of scientific research changed dramatically. Scholarly scientific activity required a new outlet, although some governments, especially the United States, continued to fund research. Society journals, the traditional pre-war outlet for research, could no longer accommodate all the articles worthy of publication, but the societies were reluctant to risk publishing more journals. A few societies did expand their list of journals. The American Chemical Society and the Royal Society of Chemistry are examples. But smaller societies did not take this risk. This situation opened the door for the new commercial publishers, nearly all of which were located outside the United States.

The established scientific publishers (e.g., Springer-Verlag of Germany and Blackwell's of the United Kingdom) found themselves in competition with new entrepreneurs, some of them persons displaced by the war, who formed competing science publishing houses. Both established and new publishers realized that their primary market lay not in Europe, but in the United States, and they worked to develop that market for both subscriptions and authors. By successfully tapping the American market, they became truly international publishers.

These international publishers then were at hand to provide new serials. They launched journals rejected by the scientific societies, and they found editors for other new journals. By the 1960s, with U.S. government support for education at its highest level ever, these publishers were experiencing exponential growth and profits. Gordon Graham, formerly chairman of Butterworth's, has detailed the growth of the European scientific publishers in his article "Reflections on the Origins of European Journals."[6] It expands upon this section.

In August 1970, President Nixon fueled the fire by suspending convertibility of the U.S. dollar. This action led to wide fluctuations in exchange rates and in libraries' cost for journals priced in foreign currencies. At the same time, the post-war baby boomers grew up, completed their formal education, and began to research and write articles. Many more scholars, especially scientists, needed a publisher. To respond to this need, commercial publishers continued to enlarge existing journals and launch additional ones.

ANALYSIS OF THE SITUATION TODAY

Today, in the mid-1990s, the greatest number of scholarly, scientific journals is in the hands of large commercial publishers, most of whom are located in Europe. Prices for these journals are usually established in the domestic currency of the publisher, although there is a trend toward setting a U.S. dollar price for the large North American market. The international publishers concentrate on scientific titles, because that is where the money is. The sciences are growing, "twigging" (dividing into ever smaller branches), and growing again. Scientists are increasing in number. Scientific researchers have grant money to support their activities. Science journals are the cause of the pricing problem; it is only there that relief can come. Concentrating on cancelling science journals would be fair to humanists and social scientists, but would it be fair to the scientists? They say not.

This section explores eleven factors contributing to the growth in the number of scientific periodicals and to their escalating prices.

Falling Circulation

Declining circulation of scholarly journals has been a concern for many years. Since World War II, subscriber characteristics have changed. Researchers who have become active since the war no longer build their own libraries, but instead use journals in research libraries or departmental offices. Personal subscriptions to society journals began to drop in the late 1940s and continued to decline as older scientists retired from their positions. Edwin Shelock documents this startling "change in social habits and outlook"[7] within the Royal Society of Chemistry.

It is likely that the decline of personal subscriptions led to the practice of having two subscription prices, one for individuals and the other for libraries. "Why," the publishers asked, "should the copy of the journal that many readers use not cost more than the copy used by one?" They also realized that libraries were better able to pay higher prices than individuals. Publishers began to claim that the institutional cost reflected the true cost of the journal; the individual price was just to attract a few more subscribers. Librarians finally let this issue die, and the dual pricing continues. Today a different reason exists for falling journal circulation, the financial inability of libraries to continue to subscribe to all the journals they formerly received.

Stagnant Library Budgets

Since the halcyon time of ample government funding in the 1960s, libraries have never had adequate materials funding, and their serials collections have suffered. Journal prices increased faster than monograph prices and faster than the Consumer Price Index, a fact demonstrated by Michael Kronenfeld and James Thompson in 1981.[8] Various price indexes show that the trend continues. In response, librarians first cancelled duplicate subscriptions, then unique titles that were marginal to their collections. Still, the percentage of the materials budget spent for serials climbed in many cases to well over 75 percent. Robbing the monograph collection to support serials generated a cry of protest that continues today. Libraries at public institutions such as state universities depend on tax revenue for their allocations; private institutions rely on endowments and the stock market. Both types of institutions have undergone fiscal crises in recent years, and libraries have lacked adequate funding not only for materials but also for staff and facilities. With particularly high inflation for journal subscriptions, the same amount of money buys less each year, a situation which contributes heavily to falling circulation.

Librarians must consider escalating journal prices in light of the whole budget. Reduced funding for monographs has probably led publishers to issue fewer of them. Monographs may be published in series more frequently now, making them appear to be serials. Sometimes the library may transfer funds from other budget lines for journal purchases, reducing the money for postage, supplies, and salaries. Librarians cannot do this indefinitely.

More Researchers

The "baby-boomers," born just after the Second World War, graduated from college in the late sixties. Many of them went to graduate school and entered teaching and other research professions in the early- to mid-1970s, just when government support for libraries declined. The sciences were especially attractive to the new scholars. Young scientists, as well as their older colleagues, published journal articles in order to earn tenure. The increase in articles repeated what had happened at the end of the war and again led to new journals and more competition for the library dollar.

Tenure Process

A further factor contributing to the serials pricing crisis is the tenure process. Competition for a tenured position—security from dismissal without cause—brought about frantic writing and publication by younger scholars. There is at least a perception that promotion and tenure committees regard quantity of published articles and monographs more highly than their quality.

Some institutions have begun to limit the number of publications considered in promotion and tenure decisions. This trend may reduce the amount of "salami publishing:" dividing research results into as many articles as possible to accumulate the highest number of publications. As long as the quantity of published articles and books is highly valued, scholarly journals will continue to multiply, grow in size, and increase in price.

Specialization

With all of the factors fueling the explosion in scientific publishing, together with the tendency or the necessity to specialize, it was inevitable that both scientific disciplines and their journals would break into smaller, more manageable pieces. Some commercial and society journals have divided into lettered sections; others have spawned "daughter" journals (sometimes a mandatory purchase with the "parent") or have simply transformed one title into two or more very specific titles reflecting subdisciplines. Some publications have just gotten fatter and fatter.

When questioned, publishers claim that their increase has been only "x" percent (3, or 4, or 5; something low)—except for the increase in size. They mean that the price per page or per issue remains nearly the same, but that they have added more pages and/or issues. Again, even though the library is getting more, it is paying more. Librarians try to explain that there is a limit to what they can afford, and publishers keep expanding, pushing them past that limit.

Electronic Technology

The technological advances of the last decade have undoubtedly contributed heavily to the explosion in scientific publication. Computers are faster and less expensive. With the large capacity of today's minicomputers and supercomputers, researchers can do quickly what used to take them months, freeing them for more research and more writing.

Free-Floating U.S. Dollar

After President Nixon suspended convertibility of the U.S. dollar in 1970, librarians could no longer predict subscription prices. The performance of the dollar added uncertainties to Americans for European serials and to Europeans for American serials. Journals have on occasion increased in price twenty to thirty percent one year and decreased slightly the next. Such irregularity can lure librarians, in the year of a price decrease, to add more journals to their collection, only to face another year in which the dollar reverses its direction.

Publishers raise journal prices for many reasons, but it is not fair to blame foreign publishers for increases resulting from the poor performance of the U.S. dollar. An unfavorable exchange rate hurts the library just as much as any other price increase, but the publisher is not the cause. In fact, many publishers try to minimize increases in journal size when it appears that the dollar will be weak.

Increased Publishing Expenses

Publishers complain to librarians about the increased cost of publishing. The culprits have shifted recently from paper, printing, and postage costs to editors, computers, and telephone charges. Services that formerly were underwritten by editors' institutions are now charged to the publisher. Further, publishers relate stories of the demands made by editors for higher-quality paper, color plates, and the like. They must meet these demands to retain a good editor. Naturally, this effort increases the subscription price of the journal.

It is not just commercial journals that have escalating expenses; society journals have rapidly increasing prices for the same reasons. In addition, some societies are eliminating or reducing "page charges," that is, the amount a society assesses an author per page for publication of the article. (Ironically, because of a policy change at grant-awarding bodies, commercial publishers may now impose page charges.) Societies claim that their prices are so much lower than commercial journals that the percentage rise hardly matters. But no matter what the price, an increase means librarians must find more dollars or pounds to acquire that title.

Ownership of Publishing Houses

In days gone by publishers were "book people," scholars whose interest was communicating information, as much as making a profit. In the last two decades some publishing houses were bought by other publishers, some disappeared, and others became part of huge, international conglomerates. An example of such a corporation today is Reed-Elsevier, which owns not only Reed Publishing and Elsevier Science, but Butterworth, Bowker, Pergamon, and other publishers. These companies represent only the publishing arm of the organization; it owns much more. The overriding motive of the conglomerate is to make money for its shareholders. This motive is worlds away from that of the scholar who published journals in former times. Today the marketplace puts publishing houses under great pressure to increase their profits.

Photocopying

Since the advent of the coin photocopier, publishers have claimed that librarian and library patron copying cost them subscription revenue. However, much of the copying in libraries replaces taking notes; it is easier to photocopy the article than to summarize it. Few of these persons would have purchased a journal instead of taking notes!

Interlibrary loan is another sensitive point with publishers. Copies of articles do travel from one library to another, but the 1976 U.S. Copyright Act permits this copying. As a rule, librarians are very careful to keep the required records and to forward to the Copyright Clearance Center any payment due the publisher. Their recordkeeping can attest to that.

Professors may cause greater concern by copying multiple sets of documents for course packs (collections of required readings in lieu of a textbook) and for reserve. Commercial copy services such as Kinko's have been lax in their attention to royalties, but recent lawsuits by publishers have caused them to tighten their procedures. It is the author's opinion that few, if any, librarians violate the fair use provisions of the law.

Research Grants

At least in the United States, scientific, particularly medical, research is funded liberally by government grants and support from other foundations. As important as this funding is, it probably leads to more research and to more articles being published than if there were fewer grants.

WHAT LIBRARIANS ARE DOING

Librarians do a number of things to combat escalating serial prices. They increase communication with all parties concerned with the crisis. Publishers are pleased to hear that librarians are finding more money for books and journals. Serials specialists take better care of materials money and are beginning to use document delivery to ease the damage caused by cancellations. Finally, librarians evaluate their collections; they conduct use studies to determine what is essential.

Communication

Increased communication is a positive response to the pricing crisis. Librarians explain their situation and their actions to publishers and vendors, and in return they learn about the constraints under which the commercial sector operates. Opposing parties are beginning to understand each other. Librarian/publisher/vendor interaction occurs at meetings; at NASIG, ALA, and SSP conferences; and at publisher or vendor librarian advisory groups and visits to libraries.

Librarians talk more among themselves now, sharing experiences and horror stories. Budget difficulties serve as a catalyst to promote communication among librarians, institutional faculty, and administration. All can work together to determine which cancellations will damage library collections least. Library newsletters inform the university community of actions and problems. As much as they may want to aid the library with its journal problems, administrators also work under constraints. At one university, for example, the chief academic officer, pressured by faculty members to give more financial help to the library, responded: "I will be happy to do so; where can I cut your budget to get the money?"

When faculty members learn about the library's need to cancel serials, they may offer the library gift subscriptions. Many librarians resist such gifts because of the problems that can occur: the professor leaves or decides to keep one or more issues, the copy stops coming and no one notifies the library. But when needed titles are being cancelled, it may be best not to turn down these offers, especially if the journals are used by the donors' classes. They may not understand why the library does not leap at the chance to have these free periodicals. The author's library resolved the problem by creating a faculty gifts policy, where the donor gives the library complete volumes of journals. Library holdings records do not reflect a continuing order, and there are no check-in records.

Creative Funding

The author once attended a seminar sponsored by the Society for Scholarly Publishing. In a small group discussion, one publisher asked somewhat angrily why librarians don't find creative ways to get more journals funding. Librarians *are* being creative, and those at the table convinced that publisher. Here are some examples.

Along with all other state agencies and university departments, librarians at the University of North Carolina at Chapel Hill continue to plead for more funding. But their success comes from more creative fundraising. After extensive lobbying by library staff members and the university development office, several senior classes made their class gift to the library endowment. The goals, each of which was larger than the previous one, were in the $350,000 range.

The university has a very active and successful group of athletic boosters. It has been persuaded to give funds to the library, as has the Athletic Department when the Tar Heels go to bowl games or the NCAA Basketball Tournament. The Panhellenic Council of a few years ago gave the library enough money to restore the hour between 11:00 p.m. and midnight, which had been cut because of a reduction in student wages.

Senior library staff members and development officers travel across the state to explain to alumni and friends about the plight of the library. For the recent Bicentennial Campaign, the library's goal was ten million dollars. The alumni were responsive; their pledges and those of library staff members and other friends met the goal. For the last two years the library has been fortunate enough to receive gifts in the half-million dollar range from a special donor. Not all of this money can be used for journals, of course. One-time funding cannot be used for subscriptions. But it does ease the pressure on all other lines of the budget and makes the library less dependent on uncertain state funding.

When the library is not forced to cancel serials in an emergency situation, it offers an enticement to academic departments to cancel journals that are not as valuable to them as those they want to acquire. When a department initiates cancellation of a title, it receives back for new journals eighty percent of the price paid for the cancelled title in the previous fiscal year.

In another effort to combat escalating journal prices, a binding supervisor came to the author with a year's worth of an 8-page monthly newsletter. "This costs $297.00!" she said. I asked her to show it to the social sciences bibliographer, which she did. He cancelled the newsletter. The staff member realized that this $297.00 newsletter cost us $40.00 an issue, or $5.00 a page. Incidentally, the first volume about fifteen years earlier had cost $18.00. The serials department is the place where any staff member can put the price and the material together, notice excessive charges, and call them to the attention of a selector.

Taking Better Care of Money

Librarians are spending materials money more carefully now. More than ever parent institutions are holding librarians accountable for these funds. Automation helps librarians by permitting them to monitor expenditures and recognize where the money goes. Librarians are aware now of the prices and pricing history of journals. They know which publishers have high prices and large annual increases, and they make these facts known to their constituents in the context of review and selection.

More and more often librarians are refusing to pay renewal invoices unless they contain updated prices. The Association of Research Libraries Working Group on Firm Prices asked science publishers to set their prices early.

Demand Early Pricing

In 1992 a cry arose for journal publishers to set their prices for the following year in the summer and to release these prices to subscription agents by August 1. Librarians want to know what a journal costs before they pay for it, and they can get this information from the subscription agents' databases. The August 1 date allows the agents time to get the prices into their databases and therefore available to their customers before order renewal. Some libraries determined that they would pay only "firm price" invoices, while others just wanted to know which prices were for the term being invoiced and which were not. The August 1 date gives librarians enough time to review price increases and make any cancellations they feel are necessary before paying the renewal invoice.

Under the leadership of Donald Koepp, Librarian at Princeton University, the Association of Research Libraries campaigned with certain international science publishers and large subscription agencies to meet the late summer price deadlines for 1994 renewal prices. In most cases they succeeded.

Some librarians, the author included, do not believe this process will ease the pricing situation, partly because the publishers involved do not delay setting their prices. The international science publishers set their prices (except for some society publications that must be approved by a board of directors) in the late spring, and they release the prices in plenty of time for librarians to evaluate the increases. Not only do these companies distribute the prices to subscription agents, they also publicize them in other ways, such as letters and price lists sent to their library subscribers.

In fact, for many years some subscription agents have pressured these same publishers to set their prices earlier and earlier, so that the agents could invoice librarians midyear with the updated price. As stated earlier, the library gets back a small percentage of its deposit for the next year's renewals, but the agent has the use of the library's money for several months before the publishers must be paid. This situation promotes higher prices because the publishers must predict not only their costs for six to eighteen months ahead, but also the size of the journals and the performance of the dollar. The earlier one makes these predictions, the more protection must be built in and the higher the price. This position, one must admit, is not widely held among librarians, publishers, or subscription agents.

Document Delivery

Libraries forced to cancel journals that their patrons need are turning to document delivery, either commercial, interlibrary loan, or through special arrangement with a nearby library. Chapter 14 discusses document delivery in detail. Librarians are aware that massive widespread cancellations will jeopardize this avenue, because someone must own the journal for others to be able to purchase article copies. The catch phrase has changed from "access or ownership" to "access *and* ownership."

Use Studies

Finally, librarians are conducting use studies of their serials collections. One can no longer buy for possible use; collection management must be based on actual use. Because most academic libraries do not circulate journals, any use study is labor intensive. Various methodologies exist, from a simple "green dot" reshelving count to barcoding volumes to the very detailed cost-effectiveness procedure used by Dorothy Milne and Bill Tiffany at Memorial University of Newfoundland.[9] In the latter study, cost per use is compared to the cost of document delivery, in their case, interlibrary loan.

WHAT PUBLISHERS ARE DOING

Because scholarly publishers depend on library subscriptions, they make serious efforts to retain library business. These publishers have not always acknowledged that the library is their market, claiming instead that it was the scientist or other researcher—the end user—who made the decision to purchase journals. In most cases today librarians determine which serials to acquire, and the publishers know this.

Cutting Production Costs

While editorial costs may be rising as a result of academic and research institutions cutting their own expenses, publishers are trying to reduce their production costs by negotiating for the best rates for paper and printing, distribution, and communication. At the same time, suppliers of paper and ink, for example, are finding ways to increase the quality of their products and decrease the costs. Publishers work with subscription agents to use electronic data interchange (EDI) for transmission of subscription and fulfillment data. Like libraries, publishing houses use "outsourcing," the contracting out of some processes (such as circulation), to reduce costs.

Cutting Agent Discounts

Over the years liberal publisher discounts to subscription agents (as much as twenty percent) have diminished to single-digit concessions or have disappeared entirely. Most large commercial scientific publishers recognize the services subscription agents provide and have reduced the subscription amount they charge the agent. Because scholarly societies and small publishers refuse to allow an agency discount, the international publishers felt that their discounts subsidized the smaller publishers' prices. They therefore insisted that the agents assess their customers no service charge at all on their own journals.

Publishers had agreed to the large discounts when journal prices were much lower. However, the cost of journals has risen much faster than the cost of the subscription agency's expenses, and by the late 1980s the publishers felt that it was fair to reduce the discounts.

Setting U.S. Dollar Prices

Formerly, publishers outside the United States had accepted payment in either the currency of the country of origin or the currency of the subscriber. However, the added uncertainty of exchange rate fluctuations jeopardized some of their American orders. In addition, vendors in the country of origin often had special arrangements with the publishers that gave them a pricing advantage. American subscription agents felt that this was an unfair practice and insisted upon having the same terms. This situation caused the publisher to set a U.S. dollar price and to require American subscribers to pay it. Springer-Verlag is an example. The decision also meant that American vendors would order from publishers' branches in the United States instead of the home office in Europe and would pay in American dollars instead of being able to choose their currency.

Communicating with Librarians and Agents

Recognizing that the librarian is the one who selects journals to be purchased and that librarians work through subscription agents, large publishers have established professional relationships with these vendors. Increasingly, they attend and participate in SSP, NASIG, UKSG, and ALA. They realize, as do librarians, that opportunities for informal communication are among the greatest benefits of conferences and workshops.

Some publishers have formed library advisory groups that meet annually, either at a national library meeting or at the publisher's office. Here they are able to solicit librarians' advice about how to produce and market their serials. When both librarians and subscription agents participate, the interaction is especially valuable.

One result of communication with librarians was the use of alkaline instead of acid paper for periodicals. When publishers realized that librarians looked for alkaline paper as a criterion for selection, they made the switch. At almost the same time, the higher price of alkaline paper fell to about the same as acid paper, something that must have resulted from testing and experimentation on the part of paper-makers.

Experimenting with Electronic Technology

As electronic publication becomes more common and as the so-called Information Superhighway looms closer, commercial and society publishers have invested financially in experimental projects designed to determine how they will make the transition from paper to online publication. They have also employed electronic technology in their editing and peer review processes by using first floppy discs and then the Internet for exchange of manuscripts. Although the interval depends on the attention reviewers give to their assessment of articles, electronic transmission has shortened the lag time between submission of an article and its publication. Publishers are taking steps, sometimes working with librarians, to reduce costs through technology.

Partnerships with Librarians and Agents

Some of the electronic test projects involve partnerships of publishers and librarians; others involve publishers and subscription agents. Elsevier's TULIP (The University LIcensing Program) was an example of such a partnership. The publisher delivered articles on materials science to a selected group of universities. The universities, in turn, designed the means to make the data accessible to their communities. Springer-Verlag worked with Bell Laboratories' Right Pages software and the University of California at San Francisco (also John Wiley and Company) to make certain Springer and Wiley biomedical journals available electronically in page-format. This project featured a "page turning" effect in the system.

Publishers and subscription agents work together in SISAC (Serials Industry Systems Advisory Committee) and ICEDIS (International Committee for EDI for Serials) to develop standards for the transfer of information about pricing, subscriptions, claiming, dispatch, and other details, all of which can reduce costs. Librarians will soon be able to take advantage of EDI through their automated management systems.

Subscriber Incentives

Some publishers, trying to retain subscriptions and increase profit, have offered librarians (and authors) incentives to continue to renew their journals and to order additional titles. Haworth Press, for example, offers a 5 percent discount and free claim fulfillment to libraries accepting their offer to subscribe direct with the publisher. Gordon and Breach and Pergamon offer incentives to libraries through authors of articles in their journals. Both give the author a credit which a library may use to reduce the subscription price of one of the publisher's journals. Reed Reference offers price breaks by means of certificates (e.g., for $100) that a patron may purchase for less than the face value and give to a library. The librarian must decide whether these offers are gimmicks that cost more in hassle than they save or are real cost savers.

WHAT SUBSCRIPTION AGENTS ARE DOING

The subscription agent is involved in a very competitive, low-margin business. The agent is in the middle between the journal publisher and the subscribing library. The crisis of serials pricing has definite revenue implications for the agent. These often take the form of reduced discounts from publishers and cancellation of library orders.

Cutting Costs

In order to survive, subscription agents have had to cut costs for several years. Some have needed to reduce their work force, both internal and external, and they have attempted to do this with minimal deterioration in service to their customers. Electronic technology enables the vendors to streamline their work and reduce their costs. An example is the electronic transfer of funds between the agency and the publisher.

Subscription agents used to have lavish parties for their customers at library meetings, but cost-cutting has ended this practice. These large gatherings are no great loss, in the author's opinion, because they were usually overcrowded and were not conducive to productive discussion.

Reducing Service Charge

In a furious battle to retain existing customers and attract new ones, the major American subscription agencies have waged a service charge war, each attempting to undercut the others. Libraries benefitted from this competition, so long as they did not suffer a loss of service. As a result, service charges have dropped significantly in the last few years. However, reduced agency discounts from publishers combined with massive library cancellations, makes one wonder if some vendors are not buying business or taking a loss on some accounts. They might do this to increase future business and perhaps for the publicity from winning a desirable library's account.

Broadening Services

In the face of a stagnant market, subscription agencies have chosen to diversify the range of services they offer and to increase their revenue by charging separately for these services. Customer use of the vendor database was the first expansion of services. Some agencies permit use of their computerized files at no charge, and this is always a point of negotiation with vendors who do charge. Despite the fact that most of these files were compiled for internal use, they are exceedingly valuable for the customer because of their up-to-date information about pricing and fulfillment data. Having customers able to determine such details for themselves reduces the workload on in-house staff members and thus reduces expenses of the agency.

The serials vendors were among the first companies contracted as outsourcers by librarians when, during the 1970s many agencies offered check-in, claiming, and reshipment services. From this consolidation program it was only natural for the agent to adapt its internal check-in and management system for sale to libraries.

Most recently, some vendors have developed journal contents and/or document delivery services as a further source of revenue. Some have become intermediaries for other such services. These efforts appear to be investment in the agency's future, as the library and academic world turn to the purchase of individual articles as their own economy measure.

Increasing Income

From its location between the library and the publisher, the subscription agent has made extensive use of another means of increasing income, but one that is less beneficial today than in times of higher interest rates. The vendor has had some success in convincing librarians that it is to their advantage to prepay (as early as March!) for their next year's subscriptions in return for a share of the interest generated by the library's payment. The vendors also pressured journal publishers to set their prices very early, ideally in the spring, both so that librarians would receive fewer added charges (an expense to both agent and librarian) and so that their prepayments would be larger. In the late 1980s the agents began to extend the period during which they controlled the money by delaying payment to publishers beyond the customary late October or early November. Unfortunately for libraries, the publishers' loss of the renewal payments could only serve to increase subscription prices.

Partnerships

Subscription agents work in partnership with both publishers and librarians in efforts to combat high serial prices. The vendor may provide a channel for publisher advertising and may serve as a distributor for journals originating in a foreign country. As noted above, they work with publishers to develop standards that can enhance their services to libraries and publishers and also reduce expenses for all parties. Examples of agency partnerships with libraries include using customers' libraries as test sites for new products. Far more common are partnerships with individual librarians in workshops and articles. Serials vendors, as well as journal publishers, have increased their efforts to communicate with librarians, to learn about their needs and constraints and to explain their own.

NEWSLETTER ON SERIALS PRICING ISSUES

This chapter has explained measures librarians, publishers, and subscription agents have taken to combat the runaway subscription prices for, especially, scientific journals. Although it began as a library publication sponsored by ALA, the electronic *Newsletter on Serials Pricing Issues* evolved into a forum for all parties, as well as authors and other scholars.[10] Its 2,100 subscribers come from 30 countries. Since February 1989 this online serial has been a forum for information about price increases, strategies to combat these prices, publishers' defense of their prices, and general news that affects serial prices. Gradually the scope of the newsletter broadened to include electronic publication.

The *Newsletter on Serials Pricing Issues* received the following charge: to gather and disseminate statistics and other data on the rising costs of journals to libraries; reduce duplication of effort among persons and institutions studying the impact on their collections of unprecedented serials price increases; identify trends in serials pricing; and determine what additional data need to be gathered. It was to serve as a clearinghouse for information about serials pricing: news, studies, questions, and other concerns.[11] These objectives still guide the editorial board.

From its beginning the newsletter has been a success, because of its responsive readers. The bulk of the Newsletter's content is brief notices: questions, complaints, solutions. Most of the submissions come by electronic mail. The editor (who is the author of this book) tries to stay away from publisher and vendor bashing, although she prints letters and reports concerning excessive rates and practices that appear to raise journal prices needlessly. Although the December 3, 1991 newsletter was not the first electronic publication to print what has come to be known as the "Princeton Letter" protesting Pergamon Press journal prices, it is probably the only one to follow up with comment from librarians, vendors, and publishers. Such discussion is a favorite of the readers.

WHAT WILL HAPPEN IN THE FUTURE?

What are the implications of escalating journal prices? In the short term, present trends are likely to remain. The volume of scholarly research will continue to increase and library budgets will not catch up. Paper journal circulation will continue to decrease and prices will continue to rise. But, will loss of circulation perhaps not end the twigging of journals? Perhaps print journals will begin to merge instead of split. Paper journals might become more general, leaving the esoteric subdisciplines to online-only publication.

Electronic Publishing

Both commercial and society publishers will continue their experimentation with various forms of electronic, online publishing, often in partnership with libraries and perhaps with subscription agents also. We do not all drive the same kind of car, and we may not all choose to receive information in the same format. On the other hand, it is possible that one means of distributing scholarly information will prove to be preferred by publisher, librarian, and reader. There is no doubt that, having taken the plunge into electronic dissemination of information, publishers are committed. The question remains, will electronic publishing relieve the serials pricing crisis?

Copyright

Copyright will remain a controversial issue. Many publishers either assume libraries and individuals abuse fair use or they refuse to recognize fair use. Every so often another publisher attempts to require that subscribers agree to pay a stated amount for a specific number of photocopies—any copies made by anyone. Such provisions cannot ever be enforced. Copyright or royalty fees set by publishers, although no substitute for the traditional advance renewal subscriptions, must increase and become a significant source of publisher revenue as subscription levels decline. Royalty payments may be the resolution to the copyright issue.

Presently, the United States Government is preparing to face the copyright issue as it relates to electronic copies. The administration has produced a report on this topic that would amend the 1976 Copyright Act to include electronic copying in its provisions. However, the report does not address the problem of enforcement.

Document Delivery and On-Demand Publishing

In the author's opinion, document delivery and on-demand publishing (see Chapter 14) can only increase. Widespread reports of many thousands of dollars saved by individual libraries underscore the success of this means of acquiring information. Comparatively few suppliers exist now: UnCover, BLDSC, OCLC, ISI, EBSCO, and UMI appear to be the largest. New players will likely appear on the scene, and all the suppliers will compete based on cost and service. The variable costs involved can only be the amounts charged by the delivery company for access, the per-article charge, and any delivery charge; publishers will continue to set royalty fees and the charges will continue to rise. It seems safe to speculate that the percentage rise in royalties will outstrip the rate of increase of subscription prices. Users will judge service not only by speed, but also by the quality of image, ease of access and ordering, and scope of journals covered.

In five or ten years librarians may deal with document suppliers as they deal now with subscription suppliers: most articles will come through an intermediary, but some will be ordered directly from the publisher. On the other hand, it may be that the librarian is not often involved in this process; individual users order and pay for the articles they need now, and this trend could grow. In the latter case, ease of ordering assumes critical significance.

Decline in Paper Subscriptions

If the above discussion about document delivery is accurate, and if library budgets remain relatively static, the decline in paper subscriptions will plummet to the point where journal publishers can no longer afford to issue some titles in that format. Or, stated another way, libraries can no longer afford to purchase the paper journal. Improving electronic technology, especially speed and computer capacity, will make online receipt of scientific articles as satisfactory as paper—perhaps more so.

The trend will also affect popular magazines. Consider that *Time* is available through America Online and readers can access much of the *Chronicle of Higher Education* through gophers at universities across the world. The *NASIG Newsletter* is available to members through the NASIG gopher, and the author, for one, has cancelled her paper subscription to it.

Increased Activism

As librarians increasingly must account for the expenditure of materials funds, as publishers see their traditional revenue sources diminish, and as subscription agents face the prospect of being squeezed out of the information process, all must expand their activism. Ideally, this energy would develop some communication system that would satisfy all parties, as well as the researcher. Such a system, however, seems a long way in the future.

NOTES

1. Ann Okerson, "Periodical Prices: A History and Discussion," *Advances in Serials Management* 1 (1986), p. 121.

2. Arlene Moore Sievers, "Serials Prices and Scholarly Publishing," in *The International Serials Industry*, ed. Hazel Woodward and Stella Pilling. (Aldershot, England: Gower Publishing, 1993), p. 187.

3. Deana Astle and Charles Hamaker, "Journal Publishing: Pricing and Structural Issues in the 1930s and the 1980s," *Advances in Serials Management* 2 (1988): 1-36.

4. Okerson, "Periodical Prices," pp. 101-134.

5. Sievers, "Serial Prices," p. 191.

6. Gordon Graham, "Reflections on the Origins of European Journals," *Advances in Serials Management* 4 (1992): 1-14.

7.   Edwin Shelock, "Learned Society Publishing in the United Kingdom," *Advances in Serials Management* 2 (1988): 173-183.

8.   Michael R. Kronenfeld and James A. Thompson, "The Impact of Inflation on Journal Costs," *Library Journal* 106 (1981): 714-717.

9.   Dorothy Milne and Bill Tiffany, "A Survey of the Cost-Effectiveness of Serials: A Cost-Per-Use Method and Its Results," *Serials Librarian* 19, nos. 3/4 (1991): 137-149; Dorothy Milne and Bill Tiffany, "A Cost-Per-Use Method for Evaluating the Cost-Effectiveness of Serials: A Detailed Discussion of Methodology," *Serials Review* 17: 2 (1991): 7-19.

10.   Full reports of the newsletter's origin and early history may be found in three articles: Marcia Tuttle, "The *Newsletter on Serials Pricing Issues*: Teetering on the Cutting Edge," *Advances in Serials Management* 4 (1992): 37-63; Marcia Tuttle, "The *Newsletter on Serials Pricing Issues*," *Public Access Computer Systems Review* 2:1 (1991): 111-127; and Marcia Tuttle, "The *Newsletter on Serials Pricing Issues*: An Electronic Publication," *Serials* 3 (November 1992): 25-32.

11.   Letter to the author from Caroline Early, June 29, 1988.

Chapter 8

ACQUIRING SERIALS

Serial acquisitions is a complex and challenging responsibility. The work increases and never appears to diminish; patrons abandon the library seasonally, budgets are cut, staff members resign, but still the serials come into the department for processing. There is a notable difference between serial acquisitions and monograph acquisitions. A monograph order produces one easily defined piece or predetermined group of material that is requested, received, paid for, and sent to be cataloged. On the other hand, the serials standing order or subscription is intended to continue until someone at the library acts to stop it. The usual monograph· order is a self-contained transaction that is complete when the monograph arrives and is paid; a serial order carelessly handled can cause repercussions for years.

The position of serial acquisitions librarian provides a continuous learning experience because of the changing nature and variety of both serials themselves and the ways to handle serials. Work which on the surface seems to be routine, somehow is not. Serials themselves change, and collection policies also change, financial situations change, vendors change, means of keeping records change. There is not enough time to monitor these changes and their documentation in the literature or to evaluate thoroughly one's own procedures and policies. The definitions in Chapter 1 introduce the scope of serials types. This chapter and the next illustrate the variety of ways to process serials. Serials change and variety result in an unlimited number of challenges and opportunities for growth as a librarian in serial acquisitions. Those who feel that the preceding thought is overly positive and who don't enjoy a challenge should, perhaps, avoid serial acquisitions.

This chapter does not emphasize "correct" procedures but centers on the factors a serial acquisitions librarian considers in determining local procedures and on the decisions each librarian makes to ensure effective processing. Specifically, the chapter covers receiving, checking in, and authorizing payment for serials. Chapter 9 treats other acquisition functions. The first edition of this book emphasized manual procedures. Now, however, most libraries have or plan to have automated serials management systems, so automated procedures receive more attention here.

SERIAL RECORD

Some libraries still have manual serial systems, by choice, for financial reasons, or because they have not discovered a system that suits their needs. Because most librarians have converted their serial acquisitions functions to an online system, this discussion of the manual record illustrates "the way it was."

What It Was

For most libraries the serial record was for years a visible, manual file of cards commonly known as the Kardex. "Kardex," though, is not a generic term, but the copyrighted name given by one manufacturer to its visible files. The tall metal cabinets often intruded as a physical barrier within the serials department.

The manual check-in record contained enough information about the standing order or subscription to identify the order. The amount of information varied with the size and complexity of the library and of the check-in card. Small academic and public libraries managed with fewer details than research and special libraries. The serial's cataloged main entry—title or corporate body—determined where a record filed in an alphabetical check-in system. That single access point showed on the visible record. In libraries that did not catalog serials, the publisher's name and address on the check-in card distinguished between identical titles. The International Standard Serial Number (ISSN) later identified one title among the universe of serial literature. At times, notes on the card facilitated identification of the material: "pink cover," "be sure volume says 2nd edition," for example.

For ease of communication with patrons and other library staff members the manual serial record needed the same form of entry as the card catalog or COM (Computer Output Microform) serials catalog. Consistency could be the rule if order preparation included verification of entry in a database such as OCLC or in a Library of Congress publication. This effort ensured that the entry under which a serial was ordered would be, in most instances, the entry under which it was later cataloged. Differences between the two records could be reconciled quickly if there was a procedure for communication— perhaps a special form or a copy of the catalog record—between serials cataloging and serial acquisitions, whether they were in the same department or not. In a manual check-in record the liberal use of cross references served somewhat the same purpose as multiple access points in an automated database. Cross references enlarged a serial record, but they saved time and money.

In a successful manual file, each card showed details about the serial title and the specific library order. At the same time, most serials units needed to maintain other files, for example, a numerical file of orders, and a source file arranged by vendor. Some libraries, however, attempted to make the serial record a comprehensive file showing all information about all titles in the collection. They made the manual acquisition file into a multi-use record. Library staff members found this policy frustrating because of congestion, both of data on cards and of people trying to use the file. Eventually they resolved this problem by creating serials order and receipt records in the developing automated systems.

Early Automation of Serial Acquisitions

When librarians began to consider using computer technology, serial acquisitions seemed to be a natural area to convert from manual to automated operations: periodicals are published regularly, they are numbered consecutively, and their processing requires much routine and clerical labor. All of this is true; but any person who works with serials will characterize their processing not as routine, but as "fraught with irregularities!" or some equally emphatic and emotional phrase. Indeed, it is the problems and the unexpected happenings that make serials work fascinating. These same things make the intelligence and flexibility of human beings necessary to successful serials processing. None of the early automated check-in or serials management systems swept the library world. However, some of the early integrated systems, most notably those of Northwestern University Library (NOTIS)[1] and the Biomedical Library at the University of California at Los Angeles,[2] had successful local online check-in. A few networks, such as PHILSOM and OCLC, developed somewhat satisfactory cooperative systems, which were used by a limited number of libraries.

Many libraries had automated ordering and most included searching some database as part of preorder processing. COM catalogs of serial holdings were in vogue several years ago but now have given way to online catalogs. Some local databases included more than location and holdings—for instance, accounting information—and could, therefore, be considered automated serials management systems. The check-in aspect of acquisitions was the least successful early computer application to serials work. In the 1980s technology was not responsible for the slow development of automated check-in systems; instead, the culprits were the funding required and the low priority library administrators gave this aspect of computerized library operations.

What It Is Now

When library automation specialists finally learned to manage serials processes, acquisitions personnel's work changed for the better. In the manual environment, the check-in card duplicated much information found on other records, as well as showing order and payment data. Today's check-in record can be limited to details concerning receipt. An integrated library system links check-in records to order records and the bibliographic records available to all library users through the public catalog.

TYPES OF ORDERS

Subscriptions and Standing Orders

Not all serials are alike, and not all serial orders should be treated identically by the librarian. As noted in Chapter 1, serials divide into "periodicals" and "nonperiodical serials." These two categories are often defined differently by librarians and vendors, with the librarian using frequency as a criterion and the vendor using type of payment. In other words, librarians are likely to consider any serial published more often than once a year a "periodical." Subscription agents may define "periodical" as any serial that is paid once a year. Both definitions include journals, newspapers, and magazines; however, the vendor's definition includes annuals.

There are a variety of ways to obtain a desired serial. Periodicals—journals and newspapers—are paid in advance once a year, or every two, three, or five years if the publisher and local accounting system permit. Periodicals are usually mailed directly from the publisher to the library. This book designates continuing orders for periodicals as *subscriptions*. Nonperiodical serials, on the other hand, are paid upon receipt, whether they appear regularly or irregularly. Monographic series are nonperiodical serials, as are the annual "advances" and "progress" survey publications. This book designates continuing nonperiodical serial orders as *standing orders*. The vendor often receives standing order materials and reships them to the library, sometimes in large batches. Continuations or sets—works published over a period of years, but having a planned conclusion—are not true serials; they are most easily and economically acquired as serials, however, through a standing order. In fact, for some German sets the vendor must place a standing order with the publisher to receive any volumes.

Subscriptions and standing orders account for the majority of a library's serial orders, but sometimes there is need for special arrangements. Besides the basic paid subscriptions and standing orders, there are other ways to acquire serials. These orders are often the responsibility of serial acquisitions for ease in processing; the library makes a commitment to accept certain material until the agreement is formally ended.

Serials Services

Serials services, frequently updated publications where currency of information is essential, are another periodical-like type of publication and are particularly valuable in business administration, law, and other social sciences. Payment is annual or every two years, in advance, usually sent directly to the publisher. The material arrives weekly or daily, perhaps in looseleaf format. Standard directories and price lists do not usually include these services. However, most of the large publishers of serials services, such as Commerce Clearing House, Standard and Poor's, and Prentice-Hall, have regional representatives who visit both the library and interested faculty members to solicit renewals and promote new services. The representatives receive a commission on their orders and prefer that the library deal directly with them instead of with the home office or through a subscription agent. This arrangement can work well for the library, because there is an interested local person with whom to communicate if service is interrupted or duplicated. However, if that person is not interested, works for several companies, or changes jobs, the system may break down.

Membership

A *membership* in a society can be the most efficient, and sometimes the only, way to obtain serials published by an organization. Memberships are paid annually, in advance, as are subscriptions. This payment may produce not only the journal the library needs, but also newsletters, directories of members, pamphlets, ballots for choosing officers, and registration forms for the annual convention. More significantly, the membership may confer the privilege of purchasing the organization's monographs at reduced prices or of receiving them at no charge. The serial acquisitions librarian should make an effort to determine the scope of a membership to ensure that marginal items are identified and procedures set up for their disposal. It is also necessary to ensure that other benefits such as members' prices are used. Some organizations, realizing that libraries neither need nor want every mailing that goes to individual members, have devised the "library membership" which brings only the substantial publications. Such organizations are to be commended for their sensitivity to library procedures. If the library membership were promoted in the appropriate literature and by subscription agents, perhaps more organizations would adopt it.

A pseudo-membership type of order is akin to the book or compact disc club: the library must return a notice each time it does *not* wish to receive a publication, or it must select from a group of titles and notify the publisher. This procedure has no place in a serial acquisitions unit because of the risk of a staff member's neglecting to return the announcement on time. Serials work is full of exceptions to the routine. The "book club" type of standing order is an exception which one should avoid.

Blanket Orders and Approval Plans

Many libraries have blanket orders or approval plans with publishers, organizations, or vendors so they will receive automatically such classes of material as university press publications, Western European language works in particular subjects, or titles to support a special program. Under the terms of a *blanket order* the library accepts, with few returns, all works issued by the publisher or organization and included in the agreement. In an *approval plan*, the library receives material which the vendor selects under an agreed-upon profile with an understood right to return the portion that it does not require. These arrangements can easily exclude periodicals; however, annuals, sets, and numbered monographic series are likely to come on these orders.

There is more than one way for a library to process blanket order and approval plan receipts, and the one chosen may or may not involve serial acquisitions records and staff. When blanket order serials are identified elsewhere in the library and routed to the serials department, staff can easily check them in and process them in the same manner as regular orders. If the program works smoothly, there should be minimal claiming. Only the payment may be different because it probably is handled outside the serials department. On the other hand, serials received through an approval plan are likely to cause confusion when processed through serial acquisitions. The approval plan, with its right of return, is not consistent with standing order procedures, and it is appropriately managed elsewhere in the library.

Other types of blanket orders are predominantly serial in nature (very similar to memberships) and can be managed entirely by serial acquisitions. Examples include publications of international agencies, such as the Food and Agriculture Organization and the Organization of American States; those of research organizations, such as the Rand Corporation and the Brookings Institution; and depository arrangements with the Government Printing Office, or a state government. The agreement may be all-encompassing, or either the library or the supplier may tailor it to conform to certain characteristics of the library, such as the scope of its collection or the internal division of responsibility.

Before this type of order begins—before it is placed, in fact—those library units involved must determine the appropriate means of processing the material. If it is to be held together as a special collection, such as in a documents unit, perhaps that section should receive and record the shipments directly.

Serials would handle only the payment. Or, if one prefers to use a single shipping and invoicing address, publications received in serials can be routed to the other section for recording of receipt on the serial record or on its own check-in system. It is crucial to plan in advance and in writing before a single piece arrives how the library will process the order; otherwise that first piece is likely to be passed around until it disappears. Before long the department will be floundering in the bulk of "insignificant" publications for which frustrated patrons express their need elsewhere in the library. A depository library or one that collects heavily in government documents may be better off to do all processing and service in a central documents department or section, although this is open to question.[3]

Exchanges

A library can often increase its serials holdings at reasonable cost by establishing an intelligently administered *exchange program*. Exchanges may be managed entirely within the serials department, by a separate department, or by a section of another department; or responsibility may be dispersed among acquisitions and collection development personnel. Whatever the administrative organization of exchanges, periodicals and other serials coming on exchange are appropriately received by serials either through the mail or indirectly through an exchange program staff member in another library unit.

There are two common categories of exchange programs. The first is a simple exchange of available publications between two libraries, with no payment of any kind required of either partner. Except for the absence of payment, these incoming materials are processed as regular serial orders, so long as the library upholds its exchange obligation by sending the partner what it promised. Communication is essential in an exchange agreement and involves the receiving and the sending personnel in each library. One detail of this communication is the return of small cards often enclosed in material from foreign libraries. The card is an acknowledgement of receipt and its return is both a courtesy and an assurance that the next issue will arrive. Disregarding this task may quite justly lead to the inadvertent end of the exchange agreement.

The second type of exchange occurs when one library subscribes to serials that are mailed to the partner library, usually a foreign library with no funds to acquire American serials. That library in turn either subscribes to equivalent serials published in its country and has them mailed to the American library or, more commonly, sends titles to which it has free or low-cost access. This type of exchange involves payment, but the payment goes to a source other than the one from which the library receives compensatory material. A check-in record serves to record serials received on this kind of exchange, but a payment record must document payments for publications mailed to the foreign library. The outgoing material is most easily handled, from the library's perspective, if the publisher mails it to the exchange partner. When serials are shipped directly to a foreign library, the local library cannot confuse the exchange serial with its own copy.

The purchase of a domestic title for shipment to a foreign library is a fertile area for problems, so a direct order with the publisher may be preferable to an order with the library's subscription agent. Often, though, the domestic vendor is willing to open separate accounts for each foreign address, having serials shipped to the foreign partner and billing the donor library. Sometimes, however carefully the librarian acts, there are problems of nonreceipt, and the only solution is for the local library to collect issues and volumes and reship them to the exchange partner.

In this second type of exchange program good communication is even more necessary than in the regular type. Exchange records need to show complete terms of the exchange, full addresses, and notes citing related serials. This is the place to go overboard with detail in records, rather than to risk losing essential data. All specifics need not be on the receipt record, so long as there are current full records easily accessible to serial acquisitions personnel. If these records are outside the serials department and are not adequately detailed or maintained, the check-in and payment records in serials need more facts. This is not a luxury!

For the past several years many libraries having exchange programs have reduced or eliminated them. Usually this is because they no longer have free or reduced-cost access to their institutions' publications and do not feel that it is the best use of materials funds to pay for them. This trend is among American libraries only and not those from Europe or developing countries.

Gifts

Enhancing the library serials collection through *gifts* is similar to the exchange programs, but simpler. Gifts come either unsolicited or as a result of a request from the library to be placed on the mailing list for a publication. Gift subscriptions and standing orders are checked into the serial record in the same manner as paid orders, except that there is no need for a payment record. Unfortunately, because of economic conditions, many publishers who had gift lists are cutting them back or eliminating gifts entirely. Sometimes they inform the library, sometimes they do not. In either case, when a staff member realizes that a gift title is now available only on subscription, that person needs to notify selectors, so they can decide whether to subscribe or place a standing order, or to stop receiving the title.

One-Time Orders

All types of transactions discussed until now are continuing orders: the title should arrive until someone acts to stop it. Three kinds of serial orders are not continuing, but are one-time orders for specific items; they are similar enough to monograph orders that some libraries place them through the monograph acquisitions department.

Back File. The first of these types is for a serial *back file*, perhaps in connection with a new order; for example, volumes 1-3, when the subscription begins with volume 4. Some dealers specialize in serial back files and may not handle continuing orders at all. Often the publisher can supply older material, especially if that publisher is small and issues only one or two journals. Large, international publishers may also retain back volumes of their titles. Back files tend to be less expensive directly from the publisher than from a back issues specialist, perhaps because material available from the publisher is not considered as rare as that from the dealer. Nor does the publisher need to search beyond its warehouse for the volumes. Certainly one reason for higher prices through back file suppliers is the imposition of an intermediary in the transaction.

The librarian may have the option of alternative formats for the back file. Publishers sometimes reprint large-circulation serials when the original supply is exhausted. Much of the body of serial literature is available in microform; microfilm has been the popular choice, but microfiche has gained respect among librarians and library users. The compact disc back file may become popular, but this format does not lend itself to small runs or individual volumes.

Inevitably librarians will have to order some issues or volumes of serials that should have arrived but did not. When claiming is not successful, these serials are ordered in the same manner as a back file.

Replacement. Orders for serial *replacement volumes* or issues are similar to orders for back files: one time orders for specific material. The difference is that the library has already received these serials and they were lost or damaged. The sources for replacement orders are the same as for back files, but some second hand dealers will not break up volumes. Missing only one or a few issues, the library may have to accept and pay for a complete volume. If the replacement is required a short time after the original copy is received, an order to the publisher may be successful in obtaining just the pieces needed. As with back file orders, the librarian may have a choice of formats for the replacement. If the order is for one or two paper issues, the original format, even a photocopy, is definitely preferable to microform. If the order is for complete volumes, film or fiche can be acceptable, despite the fact that it must be cataloged as a separate title.

Thus, *replacement orders* are for specific issues, volumes, or pages that were received but were lost or damaged. *Serial backfile orders* are for issues or volumes that the library has never owned. Both types of orders may be (1) for recently published material that is easily obtainable from the publisher or a back issues dealer, (2) available only in a reprint edition or in microform, or (3) out of print, unavailable in reprint, and difficult to acquire. Work with these orders requires a different knowledge of the publishing trade than that for continuing orders; there is an entire network of publishers and vendors for these types of orders, and unique procedures exist for determining the best source. NASIG has published the *Directory of Back Issue Dealers*[4] as an aid to this type of order. Further, the Duplicates Exchange Union, sponsored by the American Library Association, circulates lists of available material and supplies back issues and volumes to its member libraries. The Universal Serials and Book Exchange (USBE) is often a fruitful source for these items as well.

Two American subscription agencies have online files of serials wanted and available. The Faxon Company supports Faxon Quest, a two-part service that includes an online database of "wants" and "trades," and a comprehensive back volume fulfillment service. For more information, contact an agency representative. Readmore, Inc. offers BACKSERV, an unmoderated electronic list that acts as a forum for listing available and desired materials, both serials and monographs. For further information consult the Readmore World Wide Web site at http://www.readmore.com.

Samples. Sample *issues* of journals are the best means of evaluating a title for possible purchase. Often one orders these single issues directly from the publisher, because they are likely to be free of charge. Some subscription agents have a stock of sample issues to distribute upon request, or they may be able to acquire them on behalf of the library. Many vendors provide the sample issue at no charge, while others impose a fee. Requesting a sample issue is appropriate only for periodicals, that is, serials published in separate numbered issues making up a volume. The librarian who wants to examine a title published in complete volumes or as a series of monographs should either place a purchase order for one volume and expect to pay the normal price for it or attempt to borrow it through interlibrary loan.

As is characteristic of serial publications, there are exceptions to all the routine acquisition procedures. Some publishers will not sell through serials vendors, nor will they accept a direct continuing order. The library may not need serials such as almanacs and statistical yearbooks every year or it may find them too expensive to purchase annually. In both instances it may be possible to have the online serials system alert personnel when it is time to order one of these titles. If the system does not have this capability and if the vendor will not do it, the librarian may create a separate file as a reminder to order these titles. A card file in a box will do, although a small database is also appropriate. For the manual file, one card is filed under the month the title is to be ordered and gives specific instructions. An index card showing only title and month of purchase is filed alphabetically. For efficiency, this responsibility belongs to one person.

PREPARING AN ORDER

When a library places new subscriptions and standing orders, it is most efficient to determine certain facts about the serial before sending the order. This care ensures that (1) the library does not already receive the requested title, (2) the title ordered is actually being published, and (3) what is requested will be received. A further reason to know exactly what one is ordering is to record facts about the serial that will be useful to the cataloger. *Searching* and *verifying* are the two procedures used to determine this preorder information and record it. Each order needs a separate request form or order card with adequate space for symbols and notes.

Searching Procedures

When an order request arrives in serials it needs first to be *searched*; that is, the title asked for needs to be checked against library records to see if the serial is already on order or if the library has any portion of it. There are two reasons for searching. Primarily, one wants to ascertain that there will be no inadvertent duplicate orders. If, however, someone requests a second or third copy intentionally, the information on the new order should duplicate that already in the serial record and public catalog. If a new order is to duplicate an existing subscription or standing order, we want to know it, because this linking makes processing and cataloging more efficient. Orders for multiple copies of serials should go to the same vendor to avoid confusion at the time of invoicing and receipt. A second reason for preorder searching is its function as precataloging searching. Data that can be passed on to serials catalogers about the new title's relationship to library holdings save time and effort.

For the library with an integrated system, one search determines whether the serial is being or has ever been received. For other libraries, the logical starting point for a preorder search is the serial receipt record. If the title appears there, the searcher verifies or adds publisher, price, and source, and the searching procedure may be complete. If one-time orders for specific issues or volumes are placed by monograph acquisitions personnel, then the searcher checks any separate order file for duplication and for the purpose of communication. The only remaining task for additional copies is to determine from the requestor whether a duplicate is intended.

In most cases the title being searched does not appear as an active order. The next step for librarians without integrated systems is to check the COM catalog, serials catalog, public catalog, or database—whatever record is the official union catalog of systemwide serial holdings. The library may previously have had an order for the title or may have received some volumes as a gift. Part of a series may be cataloged as a monograph and not be in serial records; it can be identified from a series access point in the public catalog. If earlier volumes are already in the library, an indication of the call number and holdings speeds processing when the new order begins to arrive, because the title has already been cataloged. Finally, the searcher determines whether any part of the serial is currently on order but not yet received. If the serial record or public catalog serves as an order file for every kind of serial order, then this final step has already been taken. When one-time serial orders are not recorded in the public catalog, one may need to search a separate monograph order file. Recording pertinent information ensures that the two orders are brought together for processing when they arrive; otherwise, the title may be cataloged twice, or part of the holdings may be cataloged while the rest collect dust in the backlog.

Sometimes serials arrive at the library without having been searched, for example, gifts from patrons and material which comes as part of a membership or blanket order. These titles are searched quite easily before cataloging, using the same procedure as for preorder searching. The advantage here is that the searcher has in hand a volume or an issue of the serial.

Verifying Procedures

After determining that an order request is not a duplicate in the library system and that no part of the title is in the library or on order, the searcher needs to *verify* the serial. Check the title and publication information against an authority—at best, Library of Congress cataloging in the OCLC, RLIN, or other database—to ensure that it is consistent with what is accepted as a standard. An order needs to show not only the title, but also the place of publication and the publisher, the beginning subscription volume and date, the ISSN, and (for encumbering funds by accounting) the approximate price. If the order duplicates a title already in the library, no further verification is necessary.

Much of the verification procedure for serial orders takes place today at the computer terminal, ideally through a database containing the CONSER file. Records that have been authenticated by the National Serials Data Program (NSDP) at the Library of Congress (for United States publications), the National Library of Canada, or another approved cataloging center, have listed in the record a key title—a title unique to that serial—and the ISSN. In most cases, these data are enough to identify the specific title one is about to order. Such a record also supplies the beginning date, as well as other information necessary for cataloging, for example, subject headings and linking notes. Some very complete records even give publisher's address and price. However, publisher and price data should be confirmed elsewhere; only a price entered very recently is valid. The database record identification number documents the verification of the publication information and later leads the cataloger to the bibliographic record for the new title.

Today it is not necessary to go to OCLC, RLIN, or WLN for CONSER records. Both Faxon and EBSCO make them available in their online systems, and the Library of Congress publishes a quarterly compact disc version of the CONSER database. *CONSER on CD*[5] is searchable by sixteen data elements, far easier than using any other means of accessing these records. It has, however, some problems. Title search appears to be most successful.

Should the title requested not be in any database, or should the details not be sufficient for verification, one can go to standard printed sources such as *Ulrich's International Periodicals Directory* (or *Ulrich's Plus* on compact disc), national or subject lists of serials, or publishers' catalogs. Serials that have begun publication very recently will not have had time to appear in printed sources, so the procedure for verifying new titles may be abbreviated.

At times during the verification process, the searcher finds information that changes the name under which the serial will be ordered. Whenever this happens, it is necessary to re-search the title under the new entry.

Final Preparation of Order

The final order, as sent to the vendor, should identify clearly what title the library wishes to receive, the vendor's title number if available, the volume and date when the order is to begin, the shipping and invoicing address(es), the library's order number, and the library's account number with the vendor. Essential internal data, such as fund, routing, and searching history, are recorded for future use. This internal information can confuse the vendor, so if it must be visible on the final order, separate it as clearly as possible from the bibliographic data and instructions to the agent or publisher. The best location for local use data is on the back of an order form or on a copy of the order that remains in the library.

If the library's serial orders are not computer-produced, there is nearly always a need to retype the order before sending it to the vendor. The searching and verifying procedures produce corrections and additions, and a newly searched order is generally cluttered and confusing to everyone except the searcher. A library places comparatively few serial orders each year, so there should be time for this effort to reduce the possibility of misinterpretation.

RENEWALS

This section covers the continuation of serial orders after initial placement. The easiest type of ongoing order, or list of orders, is known as "automatic renewal" or "until forbid." Under this direction the subscription agent continues to invoice the serials as long as the librarian does not ask to cancel the order. To facilitate such an agreement, the vendor may send the library a list containing all the titles due to be renewed. The librarian then reviews the list, adds and subtracts titles, and returns it to the vendor.

Renewal lists usually do not have prices, because the vendors send the lists before publishers set the next year's prices. Careful review of the renewal list can eliminate problems later. Among the errors one may find are listings for titles cancelled previously, transposed or otherwise incorrect order numbers, and an incorrect number of copies ordered. Subscription agents do not necessarily use the library form of entry for standing orders, and in these cases, it is useful to insert an alternate title into the bibliographic record.

If automatic renewal of subscriptions is not acceptable to the librarian or the parent institution, it may be possible to place orders for multiyear subscriptions, where a title is renewed and paid for two, three, or five years in advance. Usually, this practice ensures that the library will not have to pay price increases that occur during the time covered by the advance payment. It may also be possible for the library to place standing orders for a specific multiyear term, say for five years. This practice, although not as satisfactory as automatic renewal, is far superior to an annual bid requirement.

Some librarians cannot place true continuing orders, because they must always accept the lowest price offered. In this instance one prepares a list of the serials (either journals alone or all serials) and submits the list to more than one subscription agent. Each vendor submits a "bid," the lowest price he can charge for this list of serials, and a list of services (claiming, access to database, etc.) covered by the service fee. The annual bid list is not a satisfactory procedure for subscription renewals because of the possibility of having to change subscription agents frequently. Changing one's source of supply always creates some problems in lapsed and duplicate subscriptions, in claims going to the incorrect vendor, and in general confusion on the part of librarian, agent, and publisher. The more scholarly the library's list of serials is, the more problems are likely in a bid situation. If possible, the contract should be for a term of several years.

RECEIVING SERIALS

After library serials are ordered, they must be paid for and, when they begin to arrive, they need to be checked in. In manual systems, clerks wrote details of both functions on the card. Automated systems may have separate, expandable records for order/payment and receipt, both of which may be attached to the same bibliographic record. Payment is covered in the next section.

The serial record, manual or automated, must show certain bibliographic details, so that one can verify receipt of a specific item. Foremost among these data is numbering; the record must be flexible enough to provide for whatever numbering system the publisher chooses to use. The most common methods of numbering serials are volume, volume and issue, sequential number, or date. All of these appear in various ways and in many languages. They can be made more comprehensible to a check-in assistant who lacks extensive language skills if there is at hand a multi-language or polyglot dictionary of terms used in the description of serials and in the book trade.[6] When entering a monographic series in the serial record, it is most useful to have space for author and title of each monograph as well as for the series number, if there is one. Then, when a patron who knows a volume only by series title and number fails to locate it in the public catalog, the check-in record links serial title to the title of the individual volume.

Other details about the serial and the library's order prove useful if they can be listed on the check-in record. Most systems automatically enter date of receipt for all serials. Some libraries datestamp journal issues instead, which means that one must examine the piece to know when it arrived. Each practice and every variation of it has advantages and disadvantages, so a serial acquisitions librarian must decide what to sacrifice and what is needed at hand. Internal routing of serials needs to be on the record for composition of routing slips and for aid in retrieval when a piece has strayed along its route. Of increasing importance is the access number to the local bibliographic record in the database, if this file differs from the acquisition system. Check-in assistants may prepare some serials, such as softbound annuals for binding; if this is the case, binding specifications need to be available on the record. It is useful to note the intended frequency of the serial. This may be done through words or codes, or through the predictive format of the check-in system. Often a note on the record calling attention to some peculiarity of the serial, such as "two years late," or "return card acknowledging receipt," prevents unnecessary claiming or other problems. Notes, such as "Issue no. inside back cover," aid in recording receipt.

All of the above data are not required in every library or for every title. However, they can and should be recorded if needed for accurate, speedy processing of serials and invoices. Local use of the serial record determines what items can be omitted. For instance, if the serial record is a public service as well as a check-in resource, such data as call number, monograph title, and publisher's full address have greater significance than if it is not.

A notation of claims placed and responses from publishers is not only useful for follow-up purposes and for answering questions from patrons and other library departments, but it is required for an automated claiming system to function. In subsequent claims or claim letters, specific information lends weight to the complaint. Chapter 9 discusses claiming in detail.

PAYMENT AND PAYMENT AUTHORIZATION

It is essential that the serial record show payments, as well as receipts. If these two acquisition functions are not held together, two records should be, but probably are not, consulted before sending claims and paying invoices. Having the two together reduces the likelihood of a title's being paid year after year, but never being received. It also alerts the claimer to request an invoice as well as current issues when a lapsed title has not been paid. A library that uses a single vendor for all, or nearly all, its orders may try using the annual invoice or a vendor-generated printout of payment records as the official verification of payment, instead of entering the data on each record. If this shortcut is to be successful, staff members must examine the annual invoice very carefully, to make certain that it includes all charges and that all are valid. When a library does not enter the prices of serials on a payment record, price increase trends are not so easily apparent.

Much information on the serial record relates to payment. At a minimum, this includes the source of the order (to ensure that payment is made to the proper vendor), the amount charged, the period or volumes covered by the payment, and the date on which payment was processed. It is useful to include the invoice number on the serial record, so it can be cited as documentation of payment. Use of the vendor's own identification number for the title facilitates communication in correspondence concerning payment or nonreceipt. Finally, if the library's budget for serials is divided by subject, this funding information is useful on the payment record for management reports and so the vendor can include it on the invoice, to let accounting know which fund is to be charged.

Payment of serials invoices requires consideration of three rules: pay promptly, check carefully, and follow accounting principles.

Pay Promptly

Serial acquisitions personnel usually do not actually "pay" invoices; instead, they authorize them for payment by accounting department staff members. This process needs a high priority. Checking in received materials and processing invoices are one-two in priority. Payment for serials the library has ordered is the most serious part of the business relationship with suppliers and may be compared to an individual's paying his or her own bills. Institutions have more involved procedures, more red tape, than a person, but the repercussions of failure to pay are the same.

Nonpayment, or delayed payment, of charges incurred damages the reputation of the institution and, if lasting an extended time, interferes with its ability to do business with its suppliers. While large companies may be able to accept slow payment of their invoices, smaller ones may not have resources that enable them to carry the library's debts for any length of time. For this reason, when serial acquisitions assistants must prioritize invoice payment, they often process those from smaller suppliers first.

Most libraries have occasional periods when they cannot pay invoices immediately. Perhaps the funds are not yet allocated from the state or city; perhaps the books are closed for the fiscal year. When the delay will be several weeks, suppliers appreciate a memo explaining the situation.

Check Carefully

Paying the wrong invoice or paying an incorrect amount is expensive to both the library and the supplier. Careful processing of invoices reduces errors significantly.

First, be sure the source of the invoice, the company sending the bill, is the source from which the library ordered the serial. Occasionally, material ordered through a vendor will produce not only that company's invoice, but also an invoice from the publisher. Or, the charge from the publisher may not be a true invoice; it may be something designed to look like an invoice, perhaps a pro-forma invoice for a future volume, and its purpose may be to persuade the library to change the order from a vendor to the publisher. On occasion a publisher will inadvertently send an invoice to the library instead of to the vendor. In any case, a staff member's recognition of erroneous invoices before payment, saves time and expense for both the library and the publisher. One may forward these invoices to the vendor for resolution, or a supervisor may communicate directly with the publisher about the matter.

At times a second invoice comes from the vendor. It may be the result of an error on the part of the vendor, or it may be a second notice if the vendor has not received payment of the first invoice. The payment record indicates a previous payment. If there has not been sufficient time for the check to reach the vendor, the second notice may be ignored, otherwise, someone needs to investigate and determine what happened to the first invoice. Was it lost or was it paid? If a check has been drawn, was it cashed? Erroneous duplicate invoices (where the check has been cashed) may be returned to the vendor with check number and date that it cleared. One of the greatest benefits of library and institutional automation is the ease with which persons may now determine payment details. Ten years ago this would not have been possible in most libraries.

The best time to compare current price with previous price is when one processes the invoice. The library should have a policy regarding subscription price increases to alert the staff member to one that is excessive. The rule may be twenty percent or fifty percent; it may be $50.00 or $100.00. Review these guidelines occasionally, because as prices rise, $50.00 may not be considered a very large increase. At the same time, one should use common sense in determining excessive increases; a fifty percent jump in a $25.00 journal is not necessarily unreasonable today.

Finally, one must recognize statements of the library account and separate them from invoices. Not all statements are labelled as such, but in most cases they list outstanding invoices by number, not by title. Sometimes companies send statements automatically every month and, for most libraries, unpaid invoices appear. The statement may also give the dates of the invoices and perhaps list the number of days they are overdue. Items for payment that have not had time to reach the publisher may be ignored, but those that are, for example, more than 90 days late should be investigated. The statement can indicate problems before they become expensive problems.

Follow Accounting Principles

In most libraries, financial records are subject to auditing by a representative of the university, state, or other parent body. Thus, the audit trail must exist clearly. The auditor is liable to select a group of invoices and expect to be shown the order, the payment record, and the material received.

To protect against the possibility of fraud, the person who orders serials or any other library material does not authorize payment. Serial acquisitions librarians must be sure to separate these two functions.

In an automated management system, do not delete records showing payments unless they are archived. Institutional policy may vary as to retention of financial records, so archiving must be planned in accordance with that policy.

Library accounting follows the fiscal year of the institution, and the rhythm of that year determines actions of serials personnel. For example, there may be a period of a month or more when they cannot make payments. At other times accountants may want invoices processed even more speedily than usual, because of their need to expend funds that may otherwise revert to the parent body. An understanding of this rhythm is necessary for smooth payment of invoices. Open communication between the accounting and the serial acquisitions units is essential.

WHAT TO DO WITH THE MAIL

Every day the mail comes. It comes whether anyone is around to open and distribute it. It comes on weekends and legal holidays and during school vacations. Staff must process the mail accurately and promptly before it becomes an overwhelming burden. Serial acquisitions receives two types of mail: (1) individual issues and packages of books and journals, most of which were ordered and can be checked in; and (2) "letter mail," a euphemism which includes not only letters, but invoices, claim responses, ads, requests for funds, publishers' catalogs, questionnaires, contest entry blanks, and, often, communications addressed to some other part of the library, someone in another library, or someone totally unrelated to any library—especially at Christmastime. Some person must look at every piece of this mail and make a decision as to its disposal. In their book *Serials: Past, Present and Future*, Clara Brown and Lynn S. Smith have a lively chapter entitled "Mail Information," which discusses all the things that can happen to mail before it gets to the library.[7] This section concerns what happens to the mail after it has survived the hazards Brown and Smith detail.

There are decided advantages to having all mail—letters and packages—delivered to the check-in area unopened. Addresses on wrappers aid in resolving problems of duplicates or titles for which there are apparently no check-in records. Acquisitions assistants can examine the address on both copies of a duplicate and on all problem material. Sometimes it seems that the local post office workers see a magazine and throw it in the library pile. It is not unheard of for serial acquisitions to receive properly addressed journals destined for a library across the country. Nearly every staff member has his or her version of the "University of California, Cambridge MA" garbled address! This only compounds the chance that the serial will be delivered to the wrong library. Even when both copies of a duplicate issue are addressed and delivered to the department, the addresses are frequently different and the mailing labels probably have different numbers at the top. These labels can be the key to a publisher's or fulfillment center's correction of the problem and should be retained when there is trouble. In both a large check-in area where the serial record is divided among several persons and a small one where a single staff member processes all incoming serials, the person who records receipt of a title learns quickly to recognize it and to make certain that it goes to the correct destination. Longstanding problem titles, those which have taken much searching time in the past, are easily recognized when check-in assistants open the package mail.

Likewise, a seasoned staff member needs to review the letter mail. Experience teaches this person to distinguish between invoices and statements, ads and renewal notices, publishers' catalogs and newsletters, and it teaches him or her to realize when something is not quite right and to question and investigate. One develops a sense of what to throw away and what to keep, what goes to collection development and what goes to monograph acquisitions. Opening the mail does not sound like a very responsible task, but accurate sorting and evaluating of the mail requires experience and care. Curiosity is a valuable quality in any staff member, but it is especially beneficial in the one who processes letter mail.

Each serials department can reduce letter mail problems by establishing written procedures based upon local library organization and stated division of responsibility. Much of the bulk of this mail is ads—ads for journals, series, monographs, audiovisuals, conventions, automobile seat covers, and worse.

What can be thrown away at once? And where is the rest routed? If there are duplicate ads, is one discarded or is it sent to a different person than the first copy? The same staff member who evaluates the ads can decide what to do with sample copies of serials which arrive unsolicited. Is the subject matter of the piece within the scope of the library's collection? If so, which librarian or faculty member should see it?

There is often a fine line between an ad and a renewal notice. Some of both are complicated by special subscription offers, which are nearly always for arbitrary time periods, such as forty-one weeks or seventeen months. Accepting these offers probably costs the library more in confusion than is saved in price, because library records are geared to regular, annual cycles, not artificial terms. If a communication from a publisher says, in effect: "Your subscription is about to expire," it probably is a renewal notice. If the library has no orders direct with the publisher, one can discard the notice after determining that the expiration date on the mailing label corresponds to library records. But if there are direct orders, it is safer to examine the notice more carefully for possible payment. If any notice arrives well after the renewal date, one should investigate fully to see if the order has stopped.

Invoices and statements, likewise, can be practically indistinguishable. An invoice is to be paid; a statement is a record of what has been invoiced and should already have been processed for payment. But some publishers do not recognize these definitions and reverse the terms. Publishers may print "INVOICE—DO NOT PAY!" or another contradictory message on the form that contains a figure to be paid. Whatever the communication is called, do not ignore it. Statements that list outstanding invoices identify unpaid charges. Partially approved invoices can get buried in a mail basket, lost at the photocopying center, or misplaced outside the serials department before the check is sent. It is unlikely that all such mishaps can be avoided, but care in evaluating and processing the mail can reduce missed payments and, thus, the patron and staff frustration that occur when serials do not arrive because the invoice was not paid.

In summary, it pays to be overcautious when checking the mail. Extraneous communications can be discarded at whatever point this is verified. There will be invoices or other notices discarded in error. Every serial acquisitions unit will plead guilty to the emotional charges made by faculty members or other patrons unjustly deprived of research material or of the latest issue of *Playboy* or *Road and Track*. The likelihood of such a situation, even though it is an excellent learning experience, is minimized by having written procedures designed to promote careful evaluation of the mail.

MANAGEMENT RECORDS

The collection development librarian wants to know the subject breakdown of the current serials budget. The botany librarian needs to know the total amount spent annually during the past five years for botany periodicals. The reference librarian asks for a list of all German language periodicals. The library director must tell the university president the percentage of increase in foreign serial prices since last year. The serials librarian believes it would be more efficient to consolidate foreign orders with one vendor and needs to know what foreign serials the library receives and what the source is for each order. If the library has a functioning automated serials management system one may comply easily with these requests. The amount of time and the degree of effort required to produce the pertinent information manually depends upon the type of management records the serials department has, as well as the size of the serial record. The control of management data is the greatest advantage of an online serials system.

A record of serials received is a management record when it contains data beyond entries for issues and volumes received. Examples of these data are (1) payment information, including invoice number or date, period or volumes covered by the payment, amount, and date paid; (2) publisher's name and address, source of order; (3) fund and classification number and routing instructions. With these kinds of facts at hand it is possible to describe the active serials collection according to subject, country of origin, source, cost, location, or any combination of the above, and to document pricing trends by using payment data over two or more years. In a large collection, an automated system makes such analysis feasible. For example, the time required to identify from a manual serial record of 20,000 entries, Swiss titles placed with non-Swiss vendors is likely to cost more than the value of the data or savings resulting from a projected consolidation of orders.

An alternate manual approach to management records is to have multiple files, each with a specific kind of information—source file, shelf list, holdings list, fund lists, and so on. Each of these files describes the collection from one aspect and can be examined with less human effort than the complete manual serial record. However, the group of single purpose files not only occupies space, but also requires a significant amount of maintenance.

Computerization is essential for efficient management records. Fortunately, this does not always require the library to invest in a crash program of entering its serial records into a new database. Libraries that have placed all their orders with one of the large subscription agents can benefit from its management system. Vendors worldwide can now provide management data. Many such services are supplied upon request at no extra charge to the library; some are available only at additional cost. For libraries using more than one vendor, partial information is useful, but it may be possible to have a single agent provide data for a library's total list, even for titles placed direct or through another agent. Some vendors can provide total serials processing as well as management records, for instance, Faxon's MICROLINX.

THE FUTURE

Serial acquisitions is in transition, which is not unusual for this area of librarianship. Much is possible through automation, even with the irregularity of serial publication and receipt. Automation does not necessarily mean staff reductions; it usually enables more to be done using existing staffing. The progress made through automation is having as dramatic an effect on serials operations as it did on other library operations. But on the other hand, there is the problem of money: inflation raising the cost of everything from salaries to scotch tape; instability of the dollar creating even faster increases in the cost of foreign titles than of domestic serials; competition within the library and the parent organization for priority in funding for materials, staff, and automation. These are situations serials personnel have faced before and they have adapted. This need to adapt and explore is one more reason why serial acquisitions will always be a challenge to serials librarians and support staff.

Having to make serials available in new, electronic formats adds a different aspect to the serials manager's role. Librarians no longer just purchase information; now they also provide access to information by leasing it and paying for electronic access. The need to examine, approve, and sign leasing contracts developed with the first CD-ROM resources. Serial acquisitions librarians now consider these contracts a fact of their professional life.

As commercial document delivery, discussed in Chapter 14, becomes a significant factor in expending materials funds, serial acquisitions personnel often order, receive, and pay for copies of journal articles. These transactions have some similarity to firm, or one-time, orders, but frequently staff members pass the copies on to individual patrons; the articles do not become library property, even temporarily.

The current period of experimentation with electronic publishing forces serial acquisitions personnel to determine the future role of the serials specialist in providing access to journals in electronic format. These publications may reside in the library on a local area network, or they may be housed remotely. Publishers may send issues to the subscribing library or they may only send a notice, perhaps a table of contents, that another issue or article is available for retrieval. Serial acquisitions staff members are already having to adapt to a variety of delivery methods, a trend that will continue.

Librarians and publishers are predicting that, ultimately, scholarly information will not be published in serials or in paper format at all, but will be available electronically only as articles upon request. When and if this happens, serial acquisitions personnel will adapt to drastically changed conditions. Until that time, however, the need for accurate, written manual or computer acquisitions records retains its importance. Flexibility and curiosity, as well as accuracy, are the personal qualities that enable staff members to meet the challenge of serial acquisitions.

NOTES

1. William J. Willmering, "On-Line Centralized Serials Control," *Serials Librarian* 1 (1977): 243-249.

2. James Fayollat, "On-Line Serials Control System in a Large Biomedical Library." *Journal of the American Society of Information Science* 23 (1972): 318-322, 353-358, and 24 (1973): 80-86.

3. Karen D. Darling, "Integrating Depository Documents Serials into Regular Serials Receiving and Cataloging Routines at the University of Oregon Library." *Advances in Serials Management* 5 (1995): 91-112.

4. *Directory of Back Issue Dealers.* Compiled by Beth Holley. (New York: North American Serials Interest Group, 1991).

5. *CONSER on CD.* quarterly. Washington, D.C.: Library of Congress, 1993- .

6. For example, Jerrold Orne, *The Language of the Foreign Book Trade*, 3rd ed. (Chicago: American Library Association, 1976).

7. Clara D. Brown and Lynn S. Smith, *Serials: Past, Present and Future*, enl. (rev.) ed. (Birmingham AL: EBSCO Industries, Inc., 1980), pp. 253-264.

Chapter 9

SPECIAL SITUATIONS IN SERIAL ACQUISITIONS

Would that serial acquisitions were only ordering and receiving! But that would be so dull. All acquisitions units experience "special situations," some of them routinely (e.g., claiming) and others in problem times (e.g., cancelling).

CLAIMING

A library claims, or asks for, a serial that was ordered and should already have arrived, but has not. Serials departments place continuing orders—subscriptions and standing orders—so they can receive each part of the serial automatically upon publication. When the material does not reach the library, someone must ask that it be sent. Claiming missing issues and volumes is one of the most time-consuming and neglected aspects of serial acquisitions. Few libraries are able to give enough attention to claiming, even though automation has made the process easier by identifying potential claims. This section treats both automated and manual claiming, with emphasis on automated procedures.

There are today several excellent automated serials control systems, and most of them feature automatic claiming. The best of these offer claim alerts and permit library staff members to review each potential claim before actually printing it or sending it electronically to the vendor.

Types of Claims

There are six categories of claims, each requiring its own investigation within the library and its own procedure for communication with the agent or publisher.

1. *Skipped Issue.* The most obvious claim and that most easily apparent is the skipped issue or volume: number nine is being checked in, but number eight has not arrived. Several years ago Frank Clasquin stated that claims for "single missing issues" accounted for 74 percent of all Faxon claims.[1] This type of claim can be processed routinely, often electronically.

2. *Lapsed Subscription.* Sometimes a periodical stops coming, either at renewal time or during the course of a volume. One recognizes this type of claim either through systematic automated or manual review of the serial record or at a patron's or staff member's request, because there is no reason to examine this check-in record when processing the daily mail. The first action to take when one becomes aware of a lapsed subscription is to look at the title's payment record to make sure that it was renewed. When the serial record lists payments, consultation becomes automatic and details of the payment can be transferred to the actual claim message, if appropriate.

3. *Dormant Standing Order.* This type of claim is similar to the lapsed subscription, but it is not as obvious, since many standing orders are irregular publications. In systematic review, one questions a standing order in which significantly more time has elapsed since the arrival of the most recent volume than between the next-to-last and last volumes. Monographs in series and annuals often appear in publishers' catalogs, vendors' databases, national bibliographies, bibliographic utilities, and catalogs of in-print books, so a staff member can sometimes confirm the necessity for a standing order claim by verifying that the missing volume already exists.

4. *Inactive New Order.* There is necessarily a delay of several weeks to several months in receiving the first piece of a new serial order, but sometimes titles are not received a year or more after placing the order, even if the library has paid. In manual systems, a file of order copies, arranged by date, facilitates monitoring of new orders. When the first piece arrives, the order copy can be discarded. In an automated system new order claims may need different procedures than continuing orders, but the system should identify those needing to be claimed. For example, one can create a check-in record at the time of ordering so a claim alert is generated after a specified number of days. If necessary, new continuing orders may be coded so they are easy to extract from the database and process for claiming.

5. *Replacement.* A different category of claim is a request for replacement of a serial that is imperfect or that was damaged in transit. Sometimes this condition is apparent to the check-in assistant, but occasionally the defect is not noticed for several years. As a rule, the quicker the claim, the more willing and able the publisher is to supply a replacement.

6. *Invoice.* The previous types of claims have been for library materials; this claim is needed when the library should have paid for a subscription but has not received an invoice. In almost all cases the lack of an invoice means

that the material has not arrived either. In fact, it is usually the missing serial that reveals the missing invoice, and both can be claimed together.

Factors to Consider Before Claiming

Claims originate in several ways: in the process of recording receipt; as the result of a request by a patron, a serials department staff member, or a departmental library staff member; in bindery preparation; and during a systematic review of the serial record. Systematic claiming is an examination of serial orders, entry by entry or section by section, to discover claims needed. When most serials departments had manual records, an increasing number of orders and additional duties were assigned acquisitions personnel. This situation caused many libraries to reduce or eliminate systematic review and to rely on other library units to inform them of needed claims. Libraries with automated check-in systems do not have this problem, for either the computer program can produce a list of potential claims (and this is the case with a good system), or there is no efficient way to review the orders.

The check-in assistant or other staff member who processes claims may prepare the actual claim message. Consistent with the low priority often given to claiming, librarians who assign this responsibility to one person usually classify the position at a lower grade than that of check-in assistant positions. To be sure, many claims, particularly those for skipped issues, are routine. However, much claiming requires a decision about whether a claim is needed, the use of bibliographic resources, and the occasional resolution of long and complicated misunderstandings. This kind of claiming is at least as difficult as serials check-in and authorizing of invoices. Because claiming demands knowledge of the title's publication pattern, and because claims can easily develop into full-scale acquisition problems, the job is done better by the check-in assistant. A clerk or student assistant can prepare routine claim messages once the check-in assistant has determined that the claim is a straightforward one.

Some libraries have centralized ordering of serials but decentralized receipt, where branch libraries receive and check in their own serials. In such a situation a decision must be made as to which unit dispatches claim messages, the receiving location or the ordering one. Although some libraries have the receiving location send claims and have no problem, it would seem that the ordering and paying site is preferable because this unit is responsible for invoice processing and payment. On the other hand, the claimed material should come to the shipping address. The library needs to document whatever decision it makes.

Serial acquisitions is governed by the uncertainties of serial publication, and the library policy for timing of claims can be only a set of guidelines based on experience. The best online systems allow for automatic generation of claiming alerts when a specified number of days has passed without the expected issue's being checked in. While it is usually possible to change this number of days, the default set by the system's designer is a good figure based on librarians' experience and may be accepted with confidence for all except unusual cases.

Publishing delays are not unusual; many times there is no explanation or warning from the publisher. The length of time publishers or their distributors retain back issues varies. One must also take into account political disturbances, mail and transport strikes, the weather, and even the reading preferences of institutional or library mail room personnel. Whatever guidelines a serial acquisitions unit employs to determine timing of claims, it seems certain that some inquiries will be too early, risking publishers' anger or causing them to ignore the claim, and some will be too late, requiring expensive replacement orders. Some claims, both because of chance and because of care and common sense, will be timed correctly and will produce the missing serial at no extra cost. Developing and following guidelines with respect to the timing of claims will increase the library's rate of successful claims.

Serial acquisitions personnel can follow certain principles to improve claiming success. Above all, the claimer should use common sense in following the rules for timing of enquiries. One does not claim the 1995 *Proceedings* if earlier volumes correspond to even-numbered years. If the 1996 *Annual Report* arrived in June 1997, then February 1998 is too early to claim the 1997 edition. An awareness of the date of receipt of the latest piece of the serial and of the past pattern of publication can nearly eliminate inappropriate claims. If there are published citations to the serial in question or if a publisher's catalog lists a volume, then certainly a claim is in order, whatever the previous schedule of publication. Occasionally, serials that fall behind pick up the pace again, but one cannot assume this will happen.

A selector may submit a Cataloging in Publication (CIP) proof slip as evidence that a monographic series volume is published. Do not consider this as firm evidence unless it is supported by another listing, because much can happen to a serial volume between the time the CIP cataloging is done from page proofs and the piece is published. For example, if the title changes before actual publication, the library may already have received the volume being requested.

Occasionally a publisher actually distributes issue number five before issue number four and may send a message stating this fact. Unfortunately, the publisher sometimes undoes this good work by inserting the notice inside the serial, where the check-in assistant may not find it. Even when there is a separate announcement about out-of-sequence issues or a delay, the piece of paper may be inadvertently discarded, so the claimer does not know that the problem has been explained. However, if the agent has already received the same message or a claim response from the publisher, this information has been entered in the vendor's database and subsequently reported to the library in an electronic or a computer-produced printed updating list. In this way the agent replies to librarians' claims, often before they are aware of the problem.

All this information is of no use to the claimer unless he or she uses it. The investment of time required to consult the vendor's updating list brings a reduction in both total number of claims and number of inappropriate claims sent. When there is adequate time for claiming activities, the best use of the list is to enter relevant data in a note on the check-in record. This task may be done by a check-in assistant, a clerk, or a student. Perhaps it is more practical to check all potential claims against the vendor's database before preparing the claim form. When one finds an explanation, the information should be transferred to the check-in record to prevent premature initiation of later claims and to provide an answer to patron enquiries.

Every library has an occasional clash between the serial claiming guidelines and the needs of public service staff members. One of the benefits of an integrated serials department in which staff members do both public service and technical processing is the understanding of the other person's position. Those who produce accurate and informative check-in records use these records to respond to patrons' questions. Persons whose primary job is assistance to patrons experience the difficulty of creating and maintaining good serials check-in records. A pre-crisis program of staff development should minimize resentment of special requests and help limit them to urgently needed serials. It is especially in the claiming situation that a reasonable sense of humor can ease tension.

The claimer can increase the rate of success by reading the library's communication from the publisher's or agent's perspective. Can the recipient tell what is requested? Vagueness and misspelled words are not conducive to positive responses, nor are clutter, several remotely related questions in the same letter, or bad grammar in a foreign language. The ability to see claims from the recipient's point of view improves the success of acquiring missing serials.

The entire claiming system depends upon the library's knowing the approximate date of arrival for each serial. Arrival date equalizes differences between foreign and domestic serials, between air mail and surface mail, and between on-schedule and behind-schedule titles. Timing of claims depends on the interval between issues, not the date on the cover. Table 9.1 gives guidelines for the timing of claim requests for periodicals. It is more appropriately used by the staff of departmental libraries and binding preparation units than by claimers, because there are more factors to consider in sending a claim than merely a delay in receipt. A notice that a serial is late, according to these guidelines, can alert the claimer to investigate further to determine whether a claim is appropriate. The staff member responsible for placing claims needs to have an awareness of world events, such as strikes and revolutions, that

Table 9.1. Number of Days to Wait for
First Claim After Expected Arrival Date

Frequency	Domestic	Foreign
Daily	30	75
Weekly	45	105
Monthly	90	150
Bimonthly	120	180
Quarterly	150	210
Semiannual	240	300

Note: For second claims allow six weeks to two months
after the first claim for domestic titles and three
months for foreign titles.

delay mail delivery, and the realization that there is no agreement among vendors or among librarians as to timing of claims.[2]

These guidelines can be ignored for rush claims. However, the claimer or a supervisor should evaluate immediately each request for an exception to claiming policy and determine both that special action is required to obtain the serial and that this action has a good chance of being successful. When a rush claim is appropriate, the telephone, electronic mail, or telefacsimile are far better means of communication than the mail. American representatives of European subscription agencies can relay a rush claim overseas as effectively as the local claimer, although fax communication has become relatively inexpensive, even to overseas suppliers. Today most foreign vendors respond to claims, however sent, via fax.

Information on Claim

The variety of claim forms used by library serials departments has been nearly as large as the number of libraries multiplied by the number of types of serial orders, times the number of agents. All of them state that the library has not received a specific serial and ask that it be sent. Some of them are letters or preprinted forms that can be used for purposes besides claiming. Libraries that have automated ordering can also have computer-produced claims. This variety of forms could have been reduced, for in 1983 NISO Z39 approved a standard claim form to be either purchased or made the standard format for a locally produced manual or automated claim. However, the standard did not catch on and has disappeared from NISO's catalog of publications. General use of such a claiming device would have gone far toward facilitating communication between serials staff and their suppliers. For the present, a new serial claim form or revision of an obsolete one needs several types of information.

Each automated serials management system has its own way of producing claims and its own format. Some allow more alterations by the librarian than others, and some permit—or require—more notes to be added by the acquisitions staff member. For all claim forms, however, certain data need to be printed.

1. *Title of Serial.* A claim must state what serial the library is requesting. In the past librarians and nonlibrarians have often used different forms of entry; publishers and agents are not concerned with consistency of library records. It is easier for the claimer to use the library form of entry from the check-in record than to change it. Use of the official entry means that the claim response can be assigned quickly to the correct record. Addition of the ISSN and/or the vendor's title number will clear up any inconsistency in title.

2. *Library Order Number.* The use of the library's order number benefits both the library and the vendor. It enables each party to identify the title and copy, if relevant, being claimed. Order number is also a sure way to connect the claim response to the correct online check-in record.

3. *What is Missing.* State the specific issue(s) or volume(s) and date(s) the library is claiming. If the request is for a lapsed subscription or new order that has not begun, explain this situation concisely, including the relevant volume and date.

4. *Payment Details.* Evidence supporting the payment for claimed material is appropriate for standing orders and inactive subscriptions, but it is not needed for skipped issue claims. Specific facts a library can report are date and amount paid, period covered by payment, and invoice number and date. When payment details are recorded on the serial record, they can be transferred easily to the claim form. When a claim is for a serial that has not been paid, the absence of payment is as significant as is proof of payment; it signals the claimer to ask for an invoice.

5. *Date of Claim.* The date a library sends a claim can tell the vendor or publisher whether the claim was made too early. Date is particularly important for claims to foreign vendors, who must take into account the delay caused by serials dispatched by sea mail.

6. *Library Address.* Each claim should contain the receiving unit's complete address. Do not hide this address or put it in very small print, but make it obvious to the person who responds to the claim. The library's fax number is helpful, as well.

7. *Supporting Documentation.* Any evidence the library has that documents publication of the claimed material will aid the vendor in resolving the claim. Evidence may be a notice from the publisher, an ad from a journal, proof (copy of a check-in record) that another library has the piece, or a photocopy of the actual volume or issue title or contents page.

Some libraries claim through their agents, using either the agent's form or their own, and some send all claims directly to the publisher. Claiming is covered in the vendor service charge, and the agency can send a copy of its cancelled check as proof of payment when necessary. Some subscription agents supply claim reports on which the librarian can request further action, and some provide paper notices of changes that they have learned about from publishers and customers. Still, the claim does not reach the publisher quite as quickly as when it is sent direct from the library. One librarian tested his suspicion that claiming through the agency was not as efficient as claiming with the publisher and found that there was an identical success rate in his study.[3] If a local experiment gives this result, the library should take advantage of the agent's claim service, but if direct claims are significantly more productive, then the library should claim from the publisher, negotiate a reduced service charge, or consider changing agents. Claims for foreign titles will almost certainly go to the agent, since the freedom from language problems is one of the strongest reasons for using an intermediary.

Not all vendors must send all claims to the publisher. Several subscription agents, among them EBSCO, Swets, and Harrassowitz, have supplies of back issues that they have acquired for one reason or another, and they are sometimes able to fill a library's claim from this stock. These agents are also happy to receive a library's duplicate issues to supplement their existing back issues supply.

What Not to Claim

It is as important to know what not to claim as to know what to claim. Serials that were not ordered should not be claimed. This seems obvious, but many times the acquisitions unit receives a request to claim a volume that appeared before the library's order began, and the claimer will not notice that it preceded the order. Care in processing the request would have shown the discrepancy. However, in defense of claimers, there are times when the library has changed vendors during the course of an order and the exact point of the change is missing or unclear on the check-in or order record, so the claimer can be blamed only for not questioning.

Libraries do not need complete files of all serials. Titles whose latest edition updates the earlier one, such as *World Almanac* and *Encyclopedia of Associations*, are examples. Likewise, serials which are not retained by the library, such as some newsletters and newspapers, need not be claimed unless the order has lapsed. Titles which are held for only a year or two do not need to be complete.

Recording Claims and Claim Responses

The library needs to keep a record of claims so as not to duplicate the work. The record should show date of first claim and issue(s) or volume(s) claimed;

agent's or publisher's response, unless the transaction was completed by receipt of the claimed material; follow-up claims and dates; and notice of composed letter sent and location of letter copy. Retain this record as long as the claim is active, but discard it when all requested material is received or declared unavailable from the publisher. Note "out-of-print" claim responses in the serial record along with a decision about an out-of-print order.

Libraries differ in their preference for location of the claim record, and each system has advantages and disadvantages.

1. *On the Check-In Record.* This method is preferable for automated serials systems. Keeping claim information on the check-in record makes it accessible immediately to any person who looks at the record. One does not have to go to another file to verify that a serial has been claimed. However, in a manual system, unless this method is supplemented by a chronological file, follow-up claiming cannot be handled systematically.

2. *Local Claiming Database.* Libraries without a satisfactory method of tracking claims on its automated system, or those with a manual acquisitions system, may create a claiming database on a personal computer that will alert the librarian when an order should be reclaimed.

3. *File of Duplicate Claim Copies.* This file can be arranged by main entry, which facilitates verification of a claim, or it can be arranged by date, which provides a simple way to monitor unresolved claims. Its disadvantage is that no record of the claim appears on the check-in record.

4. *Claim Diary.* A list of claims sent, with dates and issues, may be a practical record for a small library to keep, but it is a time-consuming procedure and is not efficient for a library having a large number of active serials. The diary also has the disadvantage of being separated from the check-in record. One librarian suggests that keeping a claim diary temporarily to monitor vendor performance is a worthy project and that the information revealed justifies its expense.[4]

The library need not restrict its record of claims to any one of the above methods; it can use two, three, or all four of them, or it can keep two or more copies of claims filed in different arrangements. Whatever works for the library is the best claim record.

When Claiming Does Not Work

Several of the problems associated with serials claiming have been discussed earlier: the difficulty of timing the request, the need for particular alertness in evaluating potential claims, the time and care required to keep informative records of claims sent, and the frustration of having the claimer's careful work ignored by an agent's customer service representative. In addition, a claim can cause a library to receive duplicate serials. A second copy of a $2.50 newsmagazine is no real problem, but when the duplicate is a $275.00 yearbook, the check-in assistant needs to act. The obvious course is a letter or telephone call to the agent or publisher acknowledging the duplicate and asking permission to return it. If there is an invoice with the volume, there should be arrangement for its cancellation. Sometimes there is no response to the letter, and the serial may stay around for years, unless another letter states that unless direction is received by a certain date, the library will dispose of the duplicate. The presence of an invoice with a duplicate volume ensures that the vendor will not ignore the situation, so long as the library does not pay. Duplicates that the publisher does not want returned may be added to the collection as second copies, sent to USBE, put on the library's duplicates list, or sold or traded to a back issues dealer.

The claiming aspect of serial acquisitions links library, agent, and publisher in a common effort to resolve a problem. Several works explore this three-way relationship, and a section of Chapter 6 discussed library/agent relations. But what is the publisher's reaction to library claims? In the first place, supplying missing issues to libraries is not the publisher's main purpose. It is expensive to respond to claims, just as it is expensive for the library to initiate claims. Customer service personnel receive inappropriate claims which careless library staff members and agency clerks send, just as library claimers receive thoughtless answers from publishing companies. In other words, we are all human and make mistakes and get angry. Large publishers often seem less than human, because of our difficulty working with their highly computerized operations. In fact, many large publishers have transferred the distribution of their periodicals to fulfillment centers, which are located at some distance from the editorial offices and which depend so heavily on automation that it seems nearly impossible to break into their routine. However, through NASIG and UKSG programming librarians have an opportunity to meet serial publishers and discuss claiming and other matters to their mutual benefit.

According to Frank Clasquin, publishers estimate that 50 percent of library claims are premature.[5] He does not explain whether "premature" means before actual publication or before expected publication based on past performance. Clasquin states that a publisher's attention to library claims is in proportion to the amount of library business it has.[6] He cites examples of publishers to whom library subscriptions are significant who fill without question single issue claims. Investigation into the problem is reserved for lapsed subscriptions, because of expense.

In a study of the reasons for library claims, European publishers listed poor postal service, postal and transport strikes, and misdirection of mail within a large company or university, all beyond the control of the publishers. Only one reason suggested that the publisher might be to blame: poor wrapping.[7] There was no recognition of garbled mailing labels, unannounced title changes, publication delays, or any of the other publisher practices that prevent the serial from reaching the library and being recognized. There is a need, perhaps within

NASIG, for a forum for open discussion of the claiming problems of libraries, subscription agents/standing order vendors, and serial publishers.

It is not easy to determine an acceptable percentage of titles requiring claims, because library collections differ as to type of serial received. Katz and Gellatly suggest 5 to 8 percent per year of the number of periodicals as a reasonable rate[8] and cite three studies to support their statement. What does a serials librarian do if claims exceed an acceptable percentage? The first step to take, before blaming outside factors, is to look at the department's procedures, records, and staff performance. In addition, agents and publishers should know the exact address to which serials are to be mailed, and it should be given them in a format that will fit computerized label requirements. Although there is at this time no standard computer label, it is better for the librarian to abbreviate a long address than to leave the decision to the vendor. Receipt of a correct mailing address does not guarantee that the publisher will use it, though, and sometimes repeated requests for correction have no effect.

At times the difficulty is not with the check-in record but with the check-in assistant. Careless recording of serials and failure to investigate every possible entry for an apparently unordered piece cause both inaccurate records and claims for serials the library has actually received. The latter problem is alleviated if the supervisor or senior acquisitions assistant reviews incoming serials for which no check-in record can be located. Carelessness in claiming, including inaccurate or insufficient information on the request, also results in more claims than necessary, since each request must be sent again when the wrong material arrives.

Library mail often comes through the Postal Service, the institutional mail system, and the library mail room. At any of these points a serial may be misrouted or held out of the mail until it can be read, then returned to the process. The author's library changed from having mail room personnel pick up library mail at the post office to using the university's "new, efficient" mail system. With this change, acquisitions assistants noticed that popular magazines began to arrive several days or weeks later than formerly, if they arrived at all. This occurrence, along with other deterioration in service, caused the library to remove itself from the campus mail system and return to picking up its own mail. Despite that experience, the most likely place for intentional delay of journals to occur is within the library, because the volume of mail is smallest there. However, mail room personnel are held responsible for serials reaching the acquisitions area and are valuable allies; most of them have no interest in delaying the mail. Also, inadvertent misrouting is corrected more quickly after, rather than before, mail reaches the library.

United States mail service appears to be slowing and a noticeable amount is misrouted, but reports indicate that mail service in many other countries is far worse.[9] Rough handling of packages and single periodical issues can cause them to be separated from their address labels and sometimes to arrive in the library damaged. Unless mail is wrapped and labelled securely, it may not reach its destination and have to be claimed. Currently United States Postal Service employees are making a sincere effort to determine the destination of damaged mail, and publishers are paying more attention to wrapping, as anyone having to open shrinkwrapped journals can verify.

Occasionally, lapsed subscriptions and standing orders result from poor service by the agency. It is the subscription agent's responsibility to enter the library's order with the publisher and to pay the publisher promptly. The agent's instructions should reflect the library's requested starting volume and date and correct address. Anything less than this is poor service and causes excessive claiming time and expense for the library and the agency.

One possible reason for excessive unsuccessful library claims is the use of inappropriate check-in records. Each one should indicate what is expected (frequency) and what is received. If a journal changes from a monthly to a bimonthly, or vice versa, note this fact and adapt the record to show the new frequency. Another cause of unsuccessful claims is staff members giving too little time to claiming. Delayed claims may reach the publisher too late for the missing piece to be available. The ninety- (or fewer) day limit some publishers impose is not an arbitrary one; it is often the length of time they keep back files before shipping them elsewhere for sale.

Everyone wishes library serials would come as they should and there would be no need for claiming. Unfortunately, this will never happen. At the same time, there is much that library staff members can do to ensure that their claiming is effective.

CANCELLING SERIALS

Today's economic climate, specifically the extremely high rate of subscription price increase for journals, has forced serials cancellations for nearly all libraries. Even in times of adequate funding libraries cancelled serial orders; now such action is almost routine. Each library must establish policies and procedures for cancelling serials. This section does not cover the criteria for selecting serials to cancel; that is discussed in Chapter 5. Instead, it covers the reasons why the library cancels serials, when to cancel, and how to cancel.

Why Cancel Serials?

Unacceptably high pricing is the predominant reason for cancelling library serials today; see Chapter 7 for full discussion of this issue. Suffice it to say that serials, particularly commercial journals, have increased in price to a point where most libraries cannot continue to pay for all their subscriptions. However, there are other longstanding reasons that libraries cancel serials.

Many libraries are running out of space for their collections. Very few new library buildings are being constructed at this time, and, short of transferring materials to an off-site storage facility, cancellation of journals may be the only relief. Runs of journals are often the reason libraries are short of space, because the serials increase in size either by adding pages or by dividing into sections or separate journals covering more specific and esoteric topics than the parent title.

A library, probably because of either pricing concerns or bulk of its serials, may devise a policy of offering access to some journals instead of trying to have on site every title its patrons need. Commercially supplied copies of articles are available with a very short turnaround time, and some librarians feel that they can reduce serials expenditures by paying for individual articles instead of continuing to subscribe to high-cost, low-use journals. See Chapter 14 for a full discussion.

Other reasons for cancelling serials are not new. A curriculum change may eliminate the need for journals on some topics. The single user of a narrowly-focused journal may retire or leave the institution. Sometimes the journal itself changes scope or slant and is no longer relevant to the mission of the library. Often in this time of static or diminishing materials budgets new journals are needed more than some of those currently received.

Finally, when a library decides to change subscription agents, it is best to cancel the existing order (i.e., not to renew at expiration) and place a separate order with the new vendor. A clean break with the old order leaves a clear trail in the event of future problems.

When to Cancel Serials

The appropriate time to end a continuing order for a periodical is at the conclusion of the term already paid. Minimizing library requests for refunds prevents strained relations with vendors and publishers. Some journals may be difficult to cancel neatly, because the library pays for a block of volumes that may not correspond to a calendar year. In this case, the periodical may continue to arrive for many months before all that the library has paid for arrives. For nonperiodical serials, one sets an arbitrary end to the order and notifies the vendor.

Many subscription agents send either automatically or upon request a list of all periodical orders held, for the library's approval of renewal. Usually the renewal list arrives a few months before payment date and new orders are placed by the vendor. This was in years past an excellent time for a review of the collection, or that part of it covered by the vendor's list. It was even better if cancellation decisions had already been made from the previous year's renewal list, so the new list could be returned immediately with instructions about which titles were renewed and which cancelled. When journal prices did not increase with double-digit inflation nearly every year, the renewal list was an efficient tool to use in the cancellation process. Now, however, without the new journal prices, such a list is much less valuable, unless decisions have already been made on the basis of prices paid for the current year.

The recent "firm prices initiative," begun in 1993 by the members of the Association of Research Libraries, urged journal publishers to inform subscription agents of their new prices by August 1 at the latest. Most of the commercial publishers of scientific journals (the type of serial that increases in price fastest) conformed to ARL's request. The librarians' objective in this effort was to provide time for review of new prices and for evaluation leading to possible cancellation of the journals that had increased in price.

If the library asks for its renewal invoice after the next year's prices have been set, there is rarely time between receipt of the invoice and the vendor's ordering period to compare prices (i.e., to calculate increases) and then evaluate journals that have increased excessively in price. An invoice earlier than about mid-September will have very few of the following year's prices. Subscription agents place renewal orders in November and December, and need to process any cancellations before that time. Many agents request notice of cancellation by the beginning of September. Cancellation instructions to the supplier after the renewal process has begun are likely to be ineffective and can endanger a business relationship. The management reporting function of automated systems can speed the time for calculating price increases, but if faculty members, for example, are to be consulted before any cancellations, six weeks is not a long time. Some publishers inform agents of their prices in July. This policy helps librarians recognize journals that should be evaluated, but at the same time it tends to increase prices. See Chapter 7 for discussion of this issue.

Cancelling standing orders smoothly can be either easier or more difficult than cancelling subscriptions. Since standing orders are paid upon receipt, one can set an arbitrary future termination of the commitment (such as at the end of a calendar year or after a specific volume). Flexibility and the willingness to accept an occasional extra volume eliminate the expense of correspondence, returns, and refunds. On the other hand, if the vendor confirms cancellation of the library's order and continues to send and invoice succeeding volumes, the library should insist upon returning the serials and receiving credit. Usually such vendor actions are inadvertent, but occasionally they are deliberate and continue as long as the library tolerates them.

How to Cancel Serials

As noted above, when cancelling journals, one should select carefully the time of notification to the vendor. It takes little effort to consider the effect of the cancellation on the agent or the publisher and to make it as easy as possible. The worst time to send cancellations to the vendor is while renewals are being processed. It is best if journal cancellations are done before the first of September. Some libraries prefer to send cancellation notices to their vendors throughout the year, as decisions are made; others want to use the renewal list.

The cancellation request should give title, order number, ISSN, and any other data that would be useful to the vendor, and it should state clearly the point at which the order is to be discontinued. The notice should ask for the vendor's confirmation of the cancellation. Retain or record the confirmation for documentation in the event that the serial continues to arrive.

Consider stating the reason for cancellation on the notice sent to the subscription agent or publisher. If an extreme price increase caused the action, both the vendor and the publisher should know that the library's staff and patrons consider it unacceptable and have acted. The survival of both businesses depends on libraries continuing to subscribe to journals. The librarian might explain to the vendor that a subscription is cancelled to use the funds for new titles. This message tells the vendor that the cancellation does not necessarily mean a loss of revenue from that order. If the library cancels a serial placed direct with the publisher in order to place the order with a bookseller, let the publisher know that the library will continue to purchase the title.

Communications to serials vendors regarding cancellation of orders has usually been done by letter or other paper message sent through the postal service. Increasingly, cancellation is being done electronically through the Internet.

It is essential that the acquisitions assistant retain a copy of the cancellation request, be it a photocopy of a letter or a printout of an electronic mail message, until it is obvious that the vendor has taken the requested action. If there is no confirmation from the vendor within a reasonable time (a month or two), the assistant can follow up one or more times. Sometimes the vendor will never respond, but the serial stops coming, and one can assume that the order has been cancelled as asked. If there are separate order and check-in records for the cancelled serial, both should be annotated in whatever way is appropriate to show the end of the order.

For the cancellation procedure to be effective, good communication is essential with the accounting unit of the library. Acquisitions personnel must know how to annotate records so the accounting staff member can close the order; they must know what data to send to accounting for this purpose; and they must understand the cycle of the library's fiscal year to ensure timely communication and reconciliation of financial records.

The crucial thing to remember about cancelling serials is that for everyone's protection—serial acquisitions, library accounting, departmental library, vendor, and publisher—the request needs to be recorded and retained, whether it is electronic or in writing, and the vendor should confirm the cancellation electronically or in print. In this way all parties can refer to a copy of the transaction if questions or misunderstandings arise.

Transferring Orders

The transfer of orders from one agent to another or from the publisher to an agent or vice versa are best treated as cancellations followed by new orders, to ensure that staff members can determine where one order ends and the other begins. Effective claiming depends on such detail. The library can retain both a confirmation of cancellation from the first source and a copy of the new order with its own order number. Having these records at hand simplifies resolving the problems of duplicate receipts. Transfer demands that serial acquisitions carefully mark its internal records concerning the change, so that there are no loose ends. When two agents are involved, the old and the new, accurate recordkeeping is even more necessary than when one order is or has been direct. Serial acquisitions records involving cancellations and transfers are the place to go overboard on detailed recordkeeping.

DUPLICATE SERIALS

In serial acquisitions work duplicate copies or duplicate subscriptions are enough of a problem that they merit a separate section here. Serial acquisitions personnel must remember that duplicates that will (or might) be returned to the publisher or vendor should not be marked with a library stamp, a location code, or in any other way. The reason the vendor wants the material back is to resell it, and marking the serial prevents reselling.

This discussion covers occasional duplicates (one or a very few extra copies of either a periodical or a nonperiodical serial) and continuing duplicates (multiple pieces of orders that arrive repeatedly). One treats occasional duplicates and continuing duplicates with different policies and procedures.

Occasional Duplicates

Occasional duplicates may be either excessive copies of periodicals or extra volumes of a serial on standing order. The first case usually does not require detailed treatment, but the second case must be taken more seriously. Because they are treated differently in libraries, this section treats periodical duplicates and other serial duplicates differently. Some time may elapse before it becomes apparent that the duplicates are "occasional" duplicates, and for this reason none should be discarded without permission unless it is certain that the unneeded copies will stop coming shortly.

Overlapping Subscription Periods. Receipt of one or a few duplicate issues of a periodical usually occurs around the time one order ends and the next begins, that is for most libraries at the end or the beginning of the calendar year. There are several reasons for these duplicates. Usually the publisher sends a "grace" issue or issues anticipating a late renewal. Among the reasons for this disruption of the order are changing subscription agent or going from an order with the publisher to one with an agent, delayed renewal by the agent or the library, or sometimes a change of publisher. A further reason for overlapping subscription periods is fulfillment center procedures, which extend the library's subscription in lieu of supplying a missing issue or fulfilling the obligation to the Audit Bureau of Circulations to supply a certain level of subscriptions.

In all cases, but especially with fulfillment center titles, one should examine mailing labels to determine the expiration date of the orders and to compare these dates with the dates library records show as the end of the term paid. Where there is a difference in the two dates because the renewal has begun early, one can be sure that a gap in the subscription will occur at the end of the term if no action is taken. In the case of differing expiration dates, the acquisitions assistant should notify the subscription agent, who is responsible for ensuring that the library does not miss any issues.

Other Occasional Duplicates. Occasionally a mailing label prints twice, generating two copies of a serial. In this instance the mailing labels are exact duplicates. With periodicals this is no problem, but other serials may be expensive and should be returned. The staff member processing the duplicate should refrain from marking the volume, or the publisher or vendor may not accept its return.

Sometimes the library receives a serial addressed to another library, to an individual elsewhere in the institution, or to a person or library in another city or state. Once recognized, these duplicates should go back in the mail to be forwarded to the correct address.

Because most standing orders are paid at the time of arrival, when a duplicate volume comes, one should expect and look for a duplicate invoice for that volume. Standing order invoices may be mailed separately from the volume, so the staff member recording payment needs to watch carefully and avoid duplicate payments. Sometimes the first request for payment comes from the wrong source, for example, from the publisher instead of the vendor. For this reason, one should compare the source of the order with the source of the invoice.

The acquisitions assistant should write, fax, or telephone the publisher or other source of the expensive duplicate serial to determine whether to return the volume. This is the publisher's (or other source's) decision; some want the material returned, and others do not want the volume back. Those who ask for return often specify address and means of transporting the volume. They may give the librarian a Federal Express or UPS account number and absorb the postage.

The library must enquire about the return of any duplicate material that has a duplicate invoice, especially a numbered invoice. If the problem is not resolved at once, the publisher or vendor will send reminders about the unpaid invoice, and it will appear on statements and have to be cleared up at a later date. It is simplest and most efficient to settle the account at the time the problem is recognized.

Duplicate Subscriptions or Standing Orders

When duplicate issues or volumes continue to come, the problem is more serious than with occasional duplicates, and it must be investigated thoroughly. Again, the sooner one resolves the problem, the better for all parties concerned. The three primary types of these duplicates—paid order vs. apparent gift or exchange, publisher-entered error, and vendor-entered error—are treated separately.

Paid vs. Apparent Gift or Exchange Subscription. At times the library may begin receiving duplicates of a periodical to which it has subscribed for years. The vendor has not invoiced a second copy of the magazine, and the mailing label offers no useful information. Very likely the duplicate copy is an unsolicited gift or a new exchange subscription. In the former instance, an explanatory letter may have come in the letter mail and be in a pending basket. Unsolicited gifts are likely to be magazines having a specific political, religious, or ethnic position. When exchange agreements are managed in a separate library unit, someone may have forgotten to notify serials of the new subscription. It should not be difficult to check with exchange personnel to determine whether they initiated the duplicate. When exchange is not the answer, a letter or call to the publisher can confirm the gift and the supervisor can consider cancelling the paid subscription. When it is not possible to confirm that the duplicate subscription is a gift, one must decide whether to continue both subscriptions or to cancel the paid order and take a chance that the gift will continue.

Publisher Entered in Error. Sometimes a serial publisher inadvertently enters a duplicate subscription or standing order for the library. Procedures for resolving this error vary according to whether the library paid for one or two copies. When the vendor's invoice verifies that only one copy was paid, a staff member can either notify the vendor of the problem or do nothing and continue to receive duplicates. The first procedure is recommended. All duplicates need to be held unmarked for possible return.

If, on the other hand, the library has actually paid for an unintended duplicate order, the acquisitions staff member should, as soon as the problem is confirmed, communicate with the publisher. In the case of a duplicate standing order, one requests cancellation and a possible refund of the payment. For a duplicate subscription, the correct procedure is a cancellation and either a refund or an extension of the library's correct subscription. A duplicate invoice that the library has paid, even if the error is the publisher's, must be resolved before it becomes a long-term problem.

Vendor Entered in Error. When the vendor enters an inadvertent duplicate subscription or standing order, the library has paid for either the correct number of orders or the correct number plus one. When only the accurate number of orders is paid, the library may ask the vendor to correct the error or not, depending upon the value of the serial. For a hefty scientific journal or for a standing order, the vendor will want to correct the situation. But for a popular magazine or low-priced journal, it may be better to let the extra subscription run its course, so long as the vendor gives assurance that the error will not be repeated for the next year. Follow the vendor's advice regarding the duplicates, but be sure not to mark them in any way.

Procedure for Disposing of Duplicates

Whatever causes duplicate serials to arrive in the library, they must be evaluated and disposed of either within the library system or outside it. Not all libraries have the full range of options available to them; for example, state or other public libraries may not be able to sell publicly-funded materials. In any case, the procedure for disposing of duplicate serials begins with evaluation.

Evaluation of Material. In any but the smallest libraries, serial acquisitions personnel do not select and evaluate library materials. Thus, one should consult the appropriate selector concerning the disposition of the piece. This person may be a bibliographer, a reference librarian, or another staff member with expertise in the serials's subject. Instead of, or in addition to, the library selector, one may wish to consult a faculty member or other library user who recommended purchase of the original continuing order. It is likely that in the case of periodical duplicates of one year or less, the selector will recommend that the library not retain the material. For a substantial volume of a nonperiodical serial, the decision may be either for or against retention.

When the selector has determined that the library should have the extra copy of the serial, that volume is processed according to the procedures for any added copies. Serials that are not retained may be disposed of in one of the following ways.

Return to Sender. If serial acquisitions personnel have not already contacted the source of an expensive duplicate serial regarding return instructions, they should do so at this time. Never send back duplicate serials without the vendor's permission, unless the library and the vendor have agreed to a blanket policy about returns. Write first and ask for instructions. This writing-to-return procedure applies to serial volumes, not to periodical issues.

Exchange. If the library has an exchange program with foreign libraries, particularly if some of the exchange partners are from Third World countries, the duplicate serials may be appropriate to send in return for material for one's own collection. Members of the American Library Association's Duplicates Exchange Union or another cooperative program may circulate lists among themselves or on the Internet (e.g., Readmore's BackServ) listing serials available for exchange or for the cost of transportation. A third possibility is to send the volume or volumes to a cooperative facility such as the Universal Serials and Book Exchange (USBE), where it is available for purchase at a very low price by another member.

Sell to Back Issues Dealer. Some libraries may legally sell unneeded materials to second-hand and back-issue dealers; some may not sell for cash but may exchange monographs and serials for credit toward future library purchases. There may be libraries that prefer to receive credit instead of cash, if the cash would not come to the library but go to the institutional or state general fund.

Not all library duplicates are attractive to these dealers; they accept only what they think they can sell. The most efficient procedure for working with back issue dealers for these serials is to wait until the library has a good number of duplicates and create a list of titles and volumes. Send the list to one or several dealers to see which they are willing to buy or accept for future credit. After working with a few lists, it is not difficult to recognize the type of material dealers will purchase.

Discard. Although discarding duplicate serials comes last as a means of disposal, it is not necessarily the least preferable. When "discard" means "throw away," then it is the last resort. However, there are creative ways to discard serials. Libraries that cannot sell duplicate materials may be able to give them to another library. There may be a preferential list of libraries to be consulted. For example, in a state university system, other libraries in the system may have first chance to claim unwanted materials.

Other productive ways to discard serials are to give them to the library book sale or to library patrons or staff. Someone may very well want what the library does not need. After all, duplicates are extra copies of serials that the library already subscribes to and probably pays for. They are not junk!

SUMMARY

To recap, one uses different disposal procedures for periodicals and for nonperiodical serials, with the latter generally requiring more attention. Do not waste time on occasional inexpensive duplicates. Be sure to check invoices for duplicate payments, either both charges from the vendor of record or one from the vendor and one from either the publisher or a former vendor. Duplicate periodicals require that one examine the mailing label for an altered expiration date caused by either extension of the subscription to compensate for missed issues or a second subscription having been entered instead of a renewal. Consult the appropriate selector for retention decisions on expensive duplicates. Finally, dispose of unwanted serials by the most productive method, using discard as the last resort.

NOTES

1. Frank F. Clasquin, "The Claim Enigma for Serials and Journals," in *Management Problems in Serials Work*, edited by Peter Spyers-Duran and Daniel Gore (Westport CT: Greenwood Press, 1974), p. 76.

2. Katz and Gellatly's *Guide to Magazine and Serial Agents* has a helpful discussion of the differences which appeared in agencies' responses to their questionnaire. See pp. 137-138 and 171-173.

3. Calvin D. Evans, "An Experiment in Periodicals Claiming," *Stechert-Hafner Book News* 25 (1970): 26-27. However, vendor claiming procedures have become much faster than they were in 1970.

4. Katherine R. Smith, "Serials Agents/Serials Librarians," *Library Resources and Technical Services* 14 (1970): 11.

5. Clasquin, "Claim Enigma," p. 75.

6. Clasquin, "Claim Enigma," p. 70.

7. Paul Nijhoff Asser, "Some Trends in Journal Subscriptions," *Scholarly Publishing* 10 (1979): 285.

8. Katz and Gellatly, *Guide to Magazine and Serial Agents*, p. 134.

9. Asser, "Some Trends," p. 286.

Chapter 10

CATALOGING SERIALS

Frieda B. Rosenberg

SOME INTRODUCTORY THOUGHTS[1]

Surveying serials cataloging in the mid-1990s is something like surveying a sandbar: the shape changes as it is measured, and the surveyor had better not stand in one place too long. The job is, in fact, parallel to that of trying to describe serials.

Catalogers puzzle a lot (that's why they like cataloging), and serials catalogers are no exception. Many catalogers in the field are not sure what the future will require of them. As they struggle to keep up to date with their traditional tasks, they take note of continuously rising expectations for the comprehensiveness of the catalog they are building. Users expect to find there records for articles in periodicals as well as for the full-text files of electronic journals in Lexis and the Internet—and, wherever possible, an easy bridge to that full text. And as the catalog begins to provide part of that—as it has—expectations will only rise again!

Libraries today are accessing and transmitting today's proliferating new forms of communication. Amorphous sources of information containing serials or parts of serials have arrived, some of them replacing the library's time-honored serial subscriptions. New kinds of serials are pushing the envelope of serial bibliographic control. They change titles, publisher and content even more rapidly than traditional serials did. They lack traditional bibliographic information as well as traditional places such information is found. They come out in multiple simultaneous versions. Their stay in the library may not be permanent, and some of them may not really be there physically at all! It has been a struggle, and sometimes a feat, to find the ways to accommodate many of these new types of serials into our traditional catalog.

Serials catalogers can point to several important achievements in the last decade:

First, on the local level and on the national and international level, we see online serial cataloging records accompanied by holdings. The presence of these holdings (whether serials are in a general catalog or a separate database) has meant that everyone, from the reference desk staff to the dial-in user, has simultaneous access to both cataloging records and holdings. Such access benefits libraries large and small. Especially in research libraries, catalogs accessible through the Internet convey information about holdings of serials all over the globe. In a few of these files, data about the disposition and availability of particular volumes or issues is visible. In some libraries and networks that have mounted separate databases with article citations, vendors or programmers have provided links (called "hooks to holdings") to the local or network-wide holdings file, so that catalog holdings serve the users of both the catalog record and the citation.

Another bright spot is the quality of the national serials database: the records for cataloged serials which libraries share, and build cooperatively, through their memberships in online networks such as OCLC. Once ridden with unidentifiable, incomplete and inaccurate records, it has been transformed through the vigilance of the cooperating libraries and the groundbreaking work of CONSER into an extensive and reliable tool for the management of a broad serial collection. CONSER, composed of a selected group of research libraries, federal and institutional, working with the national libraries and OCLC, has the privilege (and responsibility) of modifying existing cataloging records put into the database by other libraries, and conferring on them its "authenticating" seal of approval. It is also shaping the way serials are cataloged with its companion publications, the *CONSER Editing Guide* (*CEG*)[2] and the *CONSER Cataloging Manual* (*CCM*)[3]. The CONSER database is now accessible over OCLC as well as via tape, CD-ROM, or in printed form in *New Serial Titles*.

A third positive development for serials catalogers is the availability of advice and information, not only from national libraries and official policy-setting bodies, but from the wider world of their colleagues everywhere. BITNET and the Internet offer their users the electronic discussion groups Autocat,[4] a cataloging forum, and Serialst,[5] a forum on serials management with a strong component of serials cataloging. Digest subscriptions are available for those who wish to read selectively. Any subscriber can, by following a few rules, pose questions and offer help with the questions others pose. Anyone, subscriber or not, can search the archives with subject keywords. Beyond these lists, many serialists will benefit from exploring the Library of Congress's gopher site, MARVEL, with its archives of serials and cataloging documents to read onscreen, download to disk, or mail to their own accounts. Newest and fastest-growing are the resources of the World Wide Web, where searchers can find technical services policies and procedures along with serials- and cataloging-related information.[6]

In a few academic libraries so far (Carnegie-Mellon University and the College of Charleston, to name two), plans are underway for the routine cataloging of articles within journals.[7,8] Another few support a Web-browser interface to the catalog which accesses the full text of electronic documents and electronic serials by means of embedded hypertext links.[9] These and other advances will continue to occur. They have come in time to meet the upsurge in importance of periodical literature in modern life, in research, and in instruction in our schools and colleges. For all these reasons, the use of serials (and serials cataloging records) in such libraries has climbed sharply.

Before proceeding, the reader should realize that the approach of this chapter is quite different from the textbook or "rulebook" approach. It avoids instructing readers (who may or may not be catalogers) to "use this field in this way" or "describe this example in thus-and-such a manner." There is a guide which does just that, the *CONSER Cataloging Manual*, which will enrich any cataloger's life with pages and pages of lucid instructions and illustrated examples. Trying to emulate it in a restricted space would be ludicrous. Literal descriptions of processes belong elsewhere, too, since the variances among libraries are too wide. The goal is instead to open a window onto serials cataloging concepts, including contemporary practices, broader reference points, issues, and challenges, and a little history to underpin it all.

WHY CATALOG SERIALS?

Not that long ago, serials cataloging was viewed with some skepticism among library professionals. In library schools through the years, some smart cataloging teachers have challenged the need to "catalog" serials in the traditional sense. Many libraries, especially smaller ones, did not catalog serials at all; they maintained a list of serials with library holdings in printed or card form; serials service at the Kardex, too, was once a norm.

Some experts on serials management were enigmatic at best in defense of cataloging. Osborn's list of "basic reasons" for cataloging serials, found in the revised third edition of his *Serial Publications* (1980), granted the need for cataloging "to permit all units in a library to concentrate on normal functions without let or hindrance caused by unrecorded serials."[10] To the question whether a reader, or anyone, really needs most of that cataloging information, the answer was firmly negative. "If they [the reasons for cataloging] are weighted heavily on the administrative side, that is because service to readers depends to a high degree on the catalog record. Insofar as any of them do not apply in particular circumstances...the cataloging can be simplified or even dispensed with."[11] Indeed, for current titles, information on the check-in records, such as frequency, should not be "duplicated" on catalog cards at all.[12]

Osborn conceded a further advantage: cataloging "facilitates cooperative undertakings such as *New Serial Titles* and the *Union List of Serials.*" That list of cooperative undertakings, like the roles of the cataloging record within the library, would be today not so much expanded as exploded. A focus on sorting and housekeeping of individual files is giving way to the concept of one integrated file. A datum that comes into the library, for example, as an order request is gradually expanded as the role of the material which it describes for the collection is determined. Different versions of the record are available for different purposes: order, check-in, circulation, binding, holdings. Even union lists are often built on a base of full bibliographic records. Cataloging information is added with a view to its ultimate utility in all the arenas where it is used. With new channels of transmission, some of these have impact far beyond the library walls. To achieve its true potential, cataloging information must be enhanced with information that promotes the use of the material, whether this be local holdings notes or enhanced levels of cataloging.

Before assuming that the serial cataloging record has regained a permanent place in the information chain, we might take into account some contemporary counterparts to Osborn's negative view. In one scenario, "the catalog will disappear as a separate entity. Instead, ...catalog data would be part of a much broader set of data elements, and the catalog function would be one feature in a suite of related functions in online library use."[13] A clientele (seemingly composed of autonomous, technologically skilled researchers) would query external bibliographies, enhanced with local holdings, to access a range of possibilities including physical volumes, machine-readable full text, and the ability to request copies online. Catalogs and catalogers would disappear with "the local bibliographic superstructure,"[14] and libraries would presumably need only control numbers and copy-specific local information in order to process acquisitions and circulation transactions. (Human beings seem optional.)

But, viewing likewise the future research environment, others see endless possibilities for catalogers. It was only a little over ten years ago that the link between the catalog and the scholar's workstation heralded a new level of library service to research, and only a little over five years ago that OCLC and various libraries committed themselves to enhancing cataloging records with "deeper" indexing and analysis of content to reveal collections beyond their surface levels. Today, some who explore "virtual libraries" foretell a need for tasks akin to cataloging to provide authority structure and user assistance in navigating a hugely expanded universe of information.[15] Walt Crawford and Michael Gorman have, of course, sounded the call to librarians to remember their "proud record" of "making sense of massive quantities of disparate information," which the authors laud in their book *Future Libraries.*[16] They also provide a reminder to us all that there are many kinds of libraries with many different needs and tasks, some of which will be carried on for the foreseeable future in the traditional print environment. We may be in danger of being paralyzed by our many options. It is up to us, working with our library leaders, to chart our future direction.

So, then, how fares our sandbar; that is, what does the future hold? Libraries are still buying serials, and both they and their records see heavy use. Catalogs are being broadened in scope. Users of catalogs say they will be even better off when catalogs contain still more serials information, including records for serials not owned but accessible. Now that we share records with other libraries, networks, utilities, union lists, and the world at large, we have many people beyond our walls who get serials information from us. All the traditional goals are still there: the bibliographic identification and description of serials; their control in files; service to readers. We talk positively about our standards: in the process of communication, standards guarantee that others are able to find and interpret our messages, which in this case are bibliographic records. Only if libraries mean the same thing by the same punctuation, or numeric coding, or text, can sharing of this kind of information succeed on a global scale.

None of this should lull us into inaction. No responsible serials staff today can be laggards in the proactive study of the approach people make to information. Serials catalogers, in particular, must not hang back to let someone else do the thinking and planning. They should be at the forefront of efforts to incorporate previously uncataloged collections, and link the catalog with such new resources as remote databases and electronic journals. Finding new ways to facilitate and ensure efficient access to the information that appears in serials in any format, using any possible approach, is part of the cataloger's job, even though nothing is said about that in the *Anglo-American Cataloguing Rules*. This means that we must regularly examine our practices for usefulness, whether they are prescribed by standards or not, and develop in ourselves the will to lead constructive change. With all that at stake, why should our serial records not have a future?

THE BACKGROUND

Serials In (and Out of) the Catalog

Libraries have spent many years with different forms of the catalog, those in the form of written or printed books as well as those composed of cards or microfiches. The card catalog, in particular, was widely welcomed as an infinitely interfilable, browsable (but not portable!) index. Many are still in existence, though few are still receiving new cards. At their zenith, card catalogs were filed with sets made from "unit cards," carrying full bibliographic information for an item. The original unit card was used for the main entry; it was reproduced as many times as was necessary to put one card in each place in the catalog where it was needed. To mark additional cards in the set for filing, subject and added entries were typed above the bibliographic information. At first, there was some attempt to update cataloging information as changes took place, especially on the main entry; in the end, even that effort was abandoned as impractical.

Some card catalogs included serials; others did not. At libraries where the list with holdings served as the sole access to serials, only the holdings, the changes in title of the serials, or the names of the bodies that issued them, needed maintenance. Of course added access points were absent or severely limited. Even some libraries that cataloged serials segregated the cataloging records into a separate card file, in some so that holdings could also be located and maintained there. Even the Library of Congress, with its hundreds of thousands of serials, once followed this practice.[17] As libraries grew, however, library-wide serial title and holdings maintenance in printouts and card files became less and less feasible. Particularly in large libraries, it became common practice to locate the bibliographic information in one place (the general catalog) and the holdings in another place (typically, a printout or a set of microfiches, sometimes with additional user access to the check-in records). Osborn welcomed this solution.[18] Carefully crafted cataloging records were more or less orphans in the general catalog, since the microfiche or printout (often maintained by non-cataloging staff) was the only place to find the all-important holdings.

The Online Catalog

From the seventies to the early nineties, however, a slow but steady migration to online catalogs has taken place. Unlike the card catalog, online catalogs can be available any time of day, wherever a phone line can reach and the receiving and viewing equipment exists. Vendors market a variety of integrated or modular systems. Libraries buy carefully but are limited by their budgets. Some libraries have migrated two or three times as their past system vendor left the business or the files outgrew the capacity of the old system. The market has presented ever more powerful systems at a more affordable price. Few libraries have been able to start from Day One with an integrated system, wherein the OPAC, acquisitions/serials, cataloging, and circulation subsystems are all present and able to update one another; but interfaces between modular programs from different systems are also possible. Though almost all library staff members (or library users!) could name some things they wish their system did, there have been considerable strides in integration, standardization, and customization of library systems.

The MARC Format and its Adoption by Libraries.   The name "MARC" derives from MAchine Readable Cataloging, and the format was invented by the Library of Congress in the late sixties as a protocol by which to communicate its bibliographic records internally among operations.[19] The development of MARC provided the impetus for the major online library networks or "bibliographic utilities" to form, to contract with the Library of Congress, and begin to build multilibrary databases, sharing not only Library of Congress cataloging but their members' cataloging in the MARC (in this country eventually called USMARC) format. Especially in the United States, OCLC (Online Computer Library Center), RLIN (Research Libraries Information Network), WLN (Western Library Network), and Utlas (a Canadian utility, which evolved into ISM CATss) adopted and extended LC's seven MARC bibliographic formats and used them to market automated shared cataloging to libraries here and abroad. Other bibliographic utilities have developed in other regions of the world. Local online catalogs, home-grown or provided by a commercial vendor, have also implemented some or all of the MARC formats (become "MARC-compatible") so that they can accept MARC records and both read and write them "without loss of content, content designation, or structure."[20] Some have adopted the related authority and holdings formats. MARC for serials was released with its second edition (1974) and implemented on OCLC in late 1977. Recently achieved as this is written is the merging of the seven bibliographic formats and the validation of all field content designation for all types of materials. These developments, called "format integration," will be discussed below in a special section, and in relation to special types of serials.

THE SERIALS CATALOGING PROCESS

Tools Serials Catalogers Need

In order to adapt and edit existing cataloging (copy or adaptive cataloging) or create cataloging for a serial for which no existing record is found (original cataloging), British and American catalogers, and some others, use as the basis for all current cataloging the *Anglo-American Cataloguing Rules*, second edition, revised (1988), called *AACR2* or *AACR2r*. Along with this book, the American cataloger needs the Library of Congress Rule Interpretations, available in the quarterly *Cataloging Service Bulletin*[21] and also in a cumulated, helpfully indexed looseleaf edition, updated semiannually.[22] The Rule Interpretations, called "LCRI's," elaborate upon the succinct Rules and Options of AACR2, and in general express Library of Congress decisions about what they mean and policy on how (and in some cases whether) the Library will implement them. Almost all American libraries have adhered to "Library of Congress practice" in implementing the latest cataloging rules.

Most guides described here are continuously revised and thus published in a looseleaf format; AACR2 itself offers a looseleaf option. *The CONSER*

Cataloging Manual develops information from the rules and interpretations into a comprehensive, profusely illustrated guide to all the decisions that must be made in order to catalog a serial or edit existing cataloging. Each set of decisions about particular aspects of a serial or about particular types of serials is explained in a *CCM* "module," which can be consulted on a reference basis or studied as part of a training program.

Concurrently, most catalogers today will be dealing with MARC content designation: deciding how to "tag" the various pieces of cataloging information in order to make them machine-readable, or evaluate the existing tagging of MARC serial cataloging records. The standards for MARC content are found in the *USMARC Format for Bibliographic Data*,[23] and those are adapted for use by the major utilities in their own manuals, for example, *OCLC's Bibliographic Formats and Standards*.[24]

The definitive tagging guide specifically for serials catalogers is the *CONSER Editing Guide* (*CEG*). It has been a traditional inconvenience to go from the Rules to the Formats and back again to answer cataloging and tagging questions.[25] This situation may be remedied, for libraries that can afford it, in the evolving *Cataloger's Desktop* from the Library of Congress, a networkable workstation product on CD-ROM which already contains the LCRI's, the USMARC Concise Format, and several other tools, fully text-searchable and with hypertext links between the documents at appropriate points.

There are several different ways catalogers may be integrating new cataloging records into the catalog. The four utilities named earlier can be directed by commands to deliver cards for card catalogs, magnetic tape to be loaded later into a local system, or an electronic version of the record to be transferred in real time or in batch into the system. Other catalogers may be working on one of the other bibliographic utilities, in vendor-provided cataloging databases, or with CD-ROM databases, and may work with them in several different modes: downloading records and editing locally, searching records and editing remotely, and other variations. Information about these possibilities is available from utility headquarters and from regional networks. And small libraries still order sets of cards from vendors or type them manually, using printed sources of cataloging such as the *National Union Catalog* (NUC) in book or microfiche format.

The Workload

One might assume that because many serials enter the library regularly and steadily, the workflow of a serials cataloger has a regular and steady quality. A new cataloger may be surprised (and disappointed?) to learn that his or her chief role (unless the cataloger performs other tasks too!) will be to step in at the beginning of the library's relationship with the serial, and thereafter intervene only when change occurs or problems arise. Traditionally, what the serials cataloger tries to do is to regularize the information about a serial by means of a complete catalog record with enough bibliographic and technical information so that future issues of that serial will be handled with ease, regularly and steadily, by whoever is assigned the task of adding them.

Material in print format on subscription or standing order is the most predictable. If an integrated serials control system is in place, serials acquisitions staff generally key in an interim record on first receipt so that issue and volume control can be maintained. The record may display in the online catalog ("online public access catalog," or "OPAC"), if the system supports it. In some libraries, staff download a record from a bibliographic utility, which reduces the cataloger's task. When final cataloging is done, some management or relinking of these interim files is often necessary.

If such a system is not in place or if it is not interfaced, cataloging staff ordinarily add the first record to the OPAC. If the library desires timely representation of the serial in the OPAC, cataloging will be done from the first issue; this is probably the usual procedure today. If adequate data for the unbound issues already displays in the OPAC, some libraries might choose to defer final cataloging until a bindable unit is compiled in order to make binding, holdings, and cataloging decisions at one time and on the basis of firmer data. The latter method, however, usually involves retrieval of the issues from wherever they are shelved (which may be a branch library).

Furthermore, in some libraries, part of the cataloger's work comes from outside the check-in system, and is therefore unpredictable. There is a gray area between serials and monographs into which many types of materials fall, and it often takes a while to decide how that material should be handled. Any serial, but especially the non-periodical serial, annual, or reference work with an ISBN, is likely to enter the library as a one-time order. (Even when standing orders are available, not all libraries can afford to establish standing orders for each such work.) The new acquisition may be routed first through the monographic cataloging workflow. In libraries where there are teams handling both workflows at once, this may not be a problem. In routing a new acquisition, special training may be needed to recognize that a work with an ISBN and a monographic record on the utility could be treated as a serial. In some cases, a previous issue or edition of the same work may already be in the library, cataloged under a serial or monographic record. Each library must judge for itself what expenditure of staff time it is willing to invest in careful searching of library files (optimally, pre- and post-order) to minimize duplicate orders and assure consistent cataloging. For those new "gray area" publications, the guidelines catalogers use in deciding whether to catalog as monograph or serial (Library of Congress Rule Interpretation 12.0A) can be adapted for use by receiving staff; but is often simply difficult to gauge the publisher's intentions from a single issue in hand.

These ambiguities raise a philosophical question as well as a practical one. Monographic and serial records coexist for the same items in databases. It is not yet possible to hold and link in an understandable way both types of records. Though it is possible (under format integration) to store ISBNs on serial records, even that would not help many searchers for the monograph to find the material cataloged as a serial. In choosing one option, we must to some extent impede access from another direction. This is a problem most acute for interlibrary borrowing and lending, and for those libraries that have monographs and serials in separate databases, but own many materials that could be logically searched in either one.

Because AACR2 prescribes that when the title or main entry changes, issues after that change must be cataloged as a separate serial—this cataloging method is called *successive entry* cataloging—serials catalogers see the title again at least whenever those changes occur. Receiving staff must spot the situation and route the material, photocopies, or whatever notice is decided upon, to the cataloging workflow. The procedure involves at least two serial records, more than two in the case of mergers or splits: one or more old ones to close out, and one or more new ones to create. Title changes occurring in the middle of a volume have implications for binding, above all if volume holdings are (or will someday be) used on the records involved. And naturally, works acquired as one-time orders on monographic funds may *also* turn out to be volumes of a serial whose predecessor is in the library, cataloged under an earlier title. Successive entry will be discussed in some detail at various points in the chapter (including the next section), and also illustrated later on by an example.

Searching for Copy

Cataloging, whether all-paper, "paperless," or the usual combination of paper and screen, begins with searching for a cataloging record, or "copy." A medium-sized general library using OCLC or most other utilities should find fairly good copy for a very large percentage of serials searched. Very specialized libraries may find a much smaller percentage. Unlike printed sources of copy such as the *National Union Catalog*, OCLC may hold unintended duplicate records for the same title. Choosing a record according to specific criteria, preferring CONSER authentication and a higher number of holding libraries, will facilitate the interlibrary loan subsystem. In OCLC, certain types of duplicates are found and merged by CONSER libraries. RLIN users, on the other hand, have as many records available as libraries who have cataloged the item. Information from any record in the "record cluster" may be used by another library in "deriving" its own record; the resulting record remains separate in the database.[26]

One category of serial record present in the database, and of course, in the printed *NUCs,* should not be used for current cataloging according to AACR2 and CONSER guidelines. This is the "latest entry" record used under ALA cataloging rules. Under the latest entry cataloging method, recataloging was done whenever the title or main entry of a serial changed. Instead of making a separate record, the existing record was altered to file under the new title or main entry, with information about former titles relegated to a note (the famous "Title varies:"), and an added entry (USMARC 247) was given for each title. This type of record now is permitted only under very restricted circumstances where old manual cataloging already exists and is being "retrospectively converted" for an online catalog. The question of latest entry and other alternatives to successive entry is discussed further on in this chapter.

Apart from new and unusual formats, proportionately less cataloging copy is available for reprints, microformats, and other reproductions, partially because many libraries append their holdings in those versions to their print holdings without making the separate record that AACR2 prescribes. This whole question is part of the ongoing Multiple Versions debate, which is discussed in the section on microform serials.

Any serial for which no copy is found needs original cataloging. Original cataloging may be a large proportion of the work in specialized libraries. Most libraries are careful about accuracy of data and choice and form of access points when contributing original cataloging; but far-ranging research into details of publishing history is rarely cost-effective. Nonetheless, good original cataloging does involve some time and care. It is recompensed by the knowledge of how important the work is to the building of the shared cataloging database; availability of a record—especially a clear and informative record—helps all libraries.

BUILDING THE RECORD

Bibliographic Description Under AACR2

Description of serials under AACR2 is based on ISBD(S), International Standard Bibliographic Description—Serials. This is another product of the 1970s, compiled under the authority of the International Federation of Library Associations (IFLA), which has now added "and Institutions" at the end of its name. The standard has been expanded from its first version to include elements used by ISBD(M), the standard for monographs; ISDS, the International Serials Data System; and the MARC formats in use by national libraries. The complex punctuation used in AACR2 serial records, for example, Title : other title information/statement of responsibility, is part of ISBD(S) in its final form. This punctuation distinguishes different types of information in such a way that records can be interpreted and transcribed internationally.

HF5801
.A21   Adweek (National marketing edition).   <ACCESS POINT>
    Adweek. -- National marketing ed. -- Vol. 1, no. 1 (July 1, 1985-
    ---1--   ---------2-----------   ------------3--------------
    v. 27 (Sept. 1, 1986). -- [New York, N.Y.: A.S.M. Communications,
    ----------3----------------   --------------------4-----------------
    Inc.], 1985-1986.
    --------4----------
        2 v. : ill. ; 28 cm.   (Advertising series [fictional])
        -------5------------   ----------6-----------------
    --- Continues: Ad forum.
    Continued by: Adweek's marketing week.
    Title from cover.
    Indexed in its entirety by: Business periodicals index, 1985-1986.
    Indexed selectively by: ABI/INFORM, 1985-1986.
    Issues for <July 22, 1985>-Sept. 1, 1986 called: <Vol. 26, no. 26>-v.
    27, no. 41 in continuation of the numbering for the Eastern ed.
    Some nos. issued jointly with: Adweek (Eastern edition).
        --------------------7--------------------------------
    ISSN 0888-3718 = Adweek (National marketing ed.)
        --------------------8------------------------
    1. Advertising--United States--Periodicals.   2.   Commercial products--
    United States--Marketing--Periodicals.   I. Series.   <ACCESS POINTS>

Note: The series in Area 6 is fictional and added to illustrate the series area. The added access points
    above Area 1 and below Area 8 are not part of the description.

Figure 10.1.   Eight Areas of Description

The "rulebook," AACR2, may look unusual at first. The missing chapters
14-19 are reserved for new formats, but the introduction is silent on the subject.
AACR2 is thus a "work in progress." Amendments are regularly proposed by
standards committees, approved, compiled and eventually disseminated. In
general organization, AACR2 has two parts, the first devoted to description,
the second to the selection of access points. The book covers the description
of most serials in either Chapter 1, the general chapter, or Chapter 12, the serials
chapter. Other chapters in Part I may also be used if the serial being cataloged
is also one of the types of materials treated. The procedure recommended by
AACR2 (Introduction to Part II, Rule 20.1) is to establish the description first,
and then add "headings and/or uniform titles" to that description, based on
guidelines from Part II (Chapters 21-26). The *CONSER Cataloging Manual*,
however, puts determination of main entry first, because on that decision
depends the decision whether to make a new record (Module 4, p. 8).

The first eight rules in each chapter in Part I of AACR2 cover the eight "areas" of the cataloging record prescribed by ISBD(S). Serial records use all of the areas, which are: 1. Title and Statement of Responsibility; 2. Edition; 3. Material (or Type of Publication) Specific Details; 4. Publication, Distribution, etc.; 5. Physical Description; 6. Series; 7. Notes; 8. Standard Number and Terms of Availability. By contrast, monographic records, for example, do not ordinarily use Area 3. That is where serial catalogers put the numbering and dates of the serial. These areas are illustrated in the catalog record shown in Figure 10.1.

In several major ways, AACR2 for serials departed from its predecessors:

(a) Serials should be described on the basis of the first available issue; information taken from later issues should be given in notes. If the issue cataloged from is not the first, the record should state which issue was used.

(b) Description and access points are based as closely as possible on the wording as it appears within the works cataloged, with the minimum of changes necessary to identify the works clearly and facilitate their collocation and retrieval.

(c) Since each form of material should be cataloged by the same rules as every other form, there should be no "special rule for serials" determining what the main entry of a serial should be. (In the real world, a few distinctions, such as the discouragement of entry under personal author, re-entered through rule interpretations by the Library of Congress.)

(d) In accordance with paragraph c, the concept of corporate authorship, which had been used extensively for some kinds of serials in the past, was entirely removed, replaced by the new concept of "emanation," explained as *issuance from* or *origination with*. The content of the publication, rather than either the type of serial or the nature of the title wording, determined whether it should be entered under the heading for the body issuing it or under its title. Many more serials than in the past, by this rule, ended up under title entry, since they could go under body only if they both emanated from the body and dealt with the body's administration, resources, collective thought, or other specific content.

AACR2 was written, also, with some areas only vaguely sketched that had been explicit in earlier codes. That slack was taken up by the Rule Interpretations ("LCRI's"). AACR2 presents four levels of detail in cataloging; the Library of Congress prescribes an "augmented level 1" of cataloging for serials, which means that in terms of descriptive detail, a serial record falls between lowest and second lowest complexity. (Serial catalogers will be stunned when they hear that.) What is really meant by that assignment of level is that because of the potentially enormous amount of information there is to communicate about one serial, some of the details that might be given on a monographic record: subtitles, the presence of indexes or bibliographies in individual volumes, the specific types of illustration in the work, are not ordinarily given for serials. Some of these restrictions, which were quite inflexible in the early to middle 1980s, have been eased considerably by means of rule interpretations so that catalogers can use their judgment to a greater extent about communicating pertinent information. For example, the latest LCRI to Rule 12.1E1 allows the cataloger to include information from the title that is not included in the title proper as "other title information" as long as it would be useful and add to the understanding of the title.

Some early bibliographies described serials issue by issue; how, after all, does one describe something that changes? It should be noted that some theorists are still trying to devise ways to return to that practice.[27] In our catalogs, however, we describe at the "title" level; that is, while the title remains the same, we consider there to be one recognizable, describable published entity. Our cataloging rules "freeze a moment" in this serial, called the "first available issue," and describe that. If there happen to be later issues of the serial with changed information, that information almost always should be placed in the "note area," area 7. If later issues are not on hand at the time of cataloging, time goes by, and an out-of-date bibliographic record can mislead the seeker of information in literally dozens of ways. Because changes in bibliographic information not affecting the main entry are usually not brought to the cataloger's attention, once the cataloging has been done, until the serial title is being laid to rest, any element of the bibliographic description can be out of date without the fact coming to anyone's attention. Records completed in the past may simply not contain vital information such as the names of new corporate bodies associated with the serial, a newly assigned ISSN, or a recently acquired parallel title, any one of which could be the object of a catalog search.

Getting hold of new information to enhance bibliographic records already in the catalog is not always easy. Issues being checked in are often not scrutinized for changes in the name of the issuing body, series, or subtitle unless the changes affect filing or ordering. Further, in many libraries the only reward for noticing and reporting this sort of change is a good conscience and a lot more work to do! Sometimes the cataloger has not set up a good communication system for changes noted by other staff or by users. Proactive serials catalogers can encourage communication from acquisitions, reference, and other staff, explain its importance, and suggest a means such as e-mail. Some state-of-the art catalogs have built-in user e-mail message systems so that users can report errors and difficulties they encounter; other libraries must make do with strategically placed "suggestion boxes."

And as though that were not enough, the *presence* of a note or an access point could possibly mislead as well. "Ownership" of a serial can mean ownership of one volume out of, say, a hundred. For example, the user viewing the record for a recently entered subscription may very well see in the details about the history of the publication in the 1920s an affirmation that the library owns issues from that era. In his book *Serial Reference*, Joseph Puccio says: "The most prevalent mistake made is the assumption that if a serial title is listed in a library's catalog, then the library has a complete set of the publication. This is a problem especially in serials catalogs where the holdings are not shown."[28] While the bibliographic utilities and the comprehensive research library will keep as definitive a bibliographic record as possible in the database, it is not considered a violation of standards to shorten a bibliographic record, to eliminate access points that index redundantly, or keep only those notes found necessary by the staff and the users. Deleting should not be done short-sightedly; after all, we will soon be living in an era when the materials in the world's libraries can be brought to hand, perhaps almost instantly. But each library, in the end, should be the judge of whether a note, added title, or corporate body entry should be retained in its local record. In any case, regular communication with colleagues and users should enhance the usefulness—and cost-effectiveness—of cataloging records.

Making it MARC

A MARC record is composed of two types of data: fixed, or fixed length, fields, which are the system-specific translation of fixed-length numeric codes, and variable, free-text fields. Most of the editable codes are one to three characters in length. They compress a lot of information into a little space, some of which goes to codify information expressed as text in the record. Variable fields contain primarily textual information used to record the description given for the serial and the access points assigned to it in the catalog, so that it may be searched. On an individual utility, added non-MARC fields may allow entry of local notes and other information, and the full-MARC coding appears to the user in an easy-to-read formatted display. It may, for example, look like Figure 10.2.

Both fixed and variable fields are designated or defined by tags or field markers. Indicators control the way the computer acts upon the tagged fields, regulating such matters as what to display or print, and which characters will be filed upon. Subfields set off by delimiters further subdivide and specify content within the field.

Establishing the Title

Of all the problems that arise when cataloging serials, problems concerning the title are thorniest. The task of choosing the source of the title (called the

---

▶ OCLC: 11824189   Rec stat: c
Entered: 19850310 Replaced: 19950219 Used: 19950823
Type: a Bib lvl: s Source: d Lang: eng
Repr: Enc lvl: I Govt pub: Ctry: ii
Phys med: Mod rec: Conf pub: 0 Cont: ^^^^
S/L ent: 0 Ser tp: Frequn: a Alphabt: a   ← 1
Desc: a   Regulr: r ISDS:
             Pub st: d   Dates: 1935-1950
▶ 1 040   NDD ≠ c NDD ¶
▶ 2 092   954 ≠ b A832a ¶
▶ 3 090   ≠ b
▶ 4 049   NOCC ¶
▶ 5 245 00 Journal and proceedings of the Royal Asiatic Society of Bengal. ¶   ← 2
▶ 6 246 13 Jounral of the Royal Asiatic Society of Bengal, ≠ f 1935-194 ¶
▶ 7 260   Calcutta: ≠ b Royal Asiatic Society of Bengal, ≠ c 1936-1950.¶
▶ 8 300   16 v. : ≠ b ill. ; ≠ c 25 cm.
▶ 9 362 0 3rd ser., v. 1 (1935)-v. 16 (1950). ¶
▶ 10 515   Each vol. issued in three parts (with separate t.p. and paging): pt. 1, Letters; pt.
2, Science; pt. 3, Yearbook, called also Year-book of the Royal Asiatic Society of Bengal. ¶
▶ 11 651 0 India ≠ x Periodicals. ¶
▶ 12 710 9 Royal Asiatic Society of Bengal. ¶
▶ 13 710 22 Royal Asiatic Society of Bengal. ≠ t Year-book of the Royal Asiatic Society of
Bengal. ¶
▶ 14 730 02 Year-book of the Royal Asiatic Society of Bengal. ¶
▶ 15 780 00 ≠ t Journal & proceedings of the Asiatic Society of Bengal ≠ w
(OCoLC)11824035 ¶
▶ 16 785 00 ≠ t Journal of the Asiatic Society ≠ w (OCoLC)7102772 ¶
        ↑ ↑ ↑
        785 00 ≠ t

Notes: 1. Fixed Field. 2. Variable fields. 3. Tags (field markers). 4. Indicators. 5. Subfield
delimiters.

Figure 10.2. OCLC Record

chief source of information) comes first; second comes selecting the title itself.
The first problem is the lack of a title page on most periodicals, so that the
title proper (USMARC 245) ordinarily must be taken from the cover, where
the art director has often given his imagination free play. There are the
publishers who put their last names or their firm's initials at the beginning of
the title for one issue, and remove them with the next issue in an attack of
modesty. There are the variations in title between the cover, the masthead,
and the editorial page; which should be chosen and what should be done with

the others? There is the name of the organization right before the word "BULLETIN," but in a different typeface. Is it part of the title or not? There is the title itself, dwarfed by its initials, which take up half the cover. There is the multilingual symposium which shifts languages from year to year. Some of the conundrums are cataloger-made, too. If there is a title page with contents or editorial information, it may be not a title page at all, but a contents page or editorial page and therefore defer to the cover as a chief source for title (*CCM*, Module 3, p. 10-11). If a volume title page appears when issues are completed, presenting a different title, that title could appear only in a note/ added entry under AACR2, because such a page does not present the title of an issue, but of the volume as a whole (LCRI 12.0B1).

These problems in themselves are not insoluble. In fact, when it is difficult to make a determination, the instruction to consider the formal presentations of the title apart from the chief source is certainly the one most likely to lead to a resolution. The titles in other places may be used as additional access points (variant titles, appearing in USMARC 246 fields). The real difficulty arises when the chosen title, a few issues down the road, disappears and is replaced by one of the titles not chosen. LCRI 12.0B1 allows the cataloger with more than one issue in hand to choose a title from a less preferred source if it is known to be the stable title, as long as there is no true title page. When the change occurs after the title is cataloged, however, following that instruction would mean reevaluating and undoing the previous cataloging. This option probably seems less attractive than declaring a title change and making a successive entry. This is an example of a common decision catalogers confront in a shared cataloging environment: between conforming to existing practice (which may be outdated or unsuitable for local conditions), or else ignoring that practice (while perhaps increasing labor and impeding resource sharing).

Successive Entry and Its Alternatives

For years serials catalogers—and others in the library field—have bemoaned title changes, as the literature on serials testifies.[29] The argument on the cataloger's side, however, would be more compelling were it provable that (a) we had not exacerbated the problem by the way we handled the changes, (b) that we were more concerned about irreparable bibliographic confusion in our catalogs than we were about extra work for catalogers (catalogers *like* puzzles, remember?) Figure 10.3 shows some deliberately simplified (and invented) cataloging records of each of the three types.

As the first AACR had, but the three previous ALA codes had not, AACR2 required that when a serial title or author changed, the record for the old title must be closed off and a new record made, beginning with the first issue of the new title. Notes beginning Continues: and Continued by: (or other appropriate wording) linked the *successive* titles, and the resulting records were

Successful library catalogs. v. 1- 1956- Boston,
Library Press.
    v. ill. 27 cm.
  Title varies: 1968- Vision of online catalogs.
  Imprint varies: 1968 Santa Monica, Calif., Automated
Library Press.
    1. Catalogs, Card--Periodicals 2. Catalogs,
Online--Periodicals. I. Title: Vision of online catalogs.
      (Earliest entry record)

Vision of online catalogs. v. 1- 1956- Santa Monica,
Calif. [etc.] Automated Library Press [etc.]
    v. ill. 27 cm.
  Title varies: 1956-1967, Successful library catalogs.
  Imprint varies: 1956-1967, Boston, Library Press.
    1. Catalogs, Online--Periodicals. 2. Catalogs, Card--
Periodicals. I. Title: Successful library catalogs.
      (Latest entry record)

Successful library catalogs.--Vol. 1	Vision of online catalogs.--Vol.
(1956)-v. 11 (1967). -- Boston :	12 (1968)- . Santa Monica, Calif. :
Library Press, 1956-1967.	Automated Library Press, 1968-
11 v. : ill. ; 27 cm.	v. : ill. ; 27 cm.
Continued by: Vision of online	Continues: Successful library
catalogs.	catalogs.
1. Catalogs, Card--Periodicals.	1. Catalogs, Online--Periodicals.

    (Successive entry records for first and second titles)

Figure 10.3. Latest, Earliest, and Successive Entry Records
for a Two-Title Sequence

called *successive entries.* All the ALA codes had required that, as long as the
numbering remained continuous, the serial be described in one record based
on the latest title, with the former titles listed in notes and either traced (given
added entries in the catalog) or referred from.

In adopting successive entry, the AACRs were following international
standards. Successive entry had been endorsed in the Statement of Principles
of the International Conference of Cataloging Principles in Paris, 1961.[30] Of
course, these Paris Principles were stated in the era of manual catalogs, which
were time-consuming and difficult to update. In card catalogs, for example,
the pulling, erasing, retyping and refiling of entire card sets to accommodate
changed titles was a monumental task. To catalogers, the successive method

seemed cleaner, neater, and more succinct; information for each title could be sought under its own entry; no title not owned needed to be described at all.

The cataloger wanting to decide which title changes were major enough to warrant making a new record would have found little guidance in AACR2. A flood of new serial records triggered by inconsequential title changes ensued; many are still in the CONSER database. At the same time, LC took note that the International Serials Data System (ISDS) *Manual* of 1983 exempted certain sorts of changes from being considered title changes, including minor punctuation, spacing, spelling and other changes. Eventually LC issued rule interpretations extending these same provisions to AACR2 records. The new restrictions helped stem the flow, and they were incorporated into chapter 21 of AACR2 revised (Rule 21.2).

For the automated library, the picture has changed. From the technical point of view, updating a latest entry record could be as easy as changing old title field markers (tags), making sure the description, such as place and publisher, still matched the item, and adding a new entry at the top of the record. Making an *earliest* entry record would be even easier. This last method was described by Charles Cutter[31] and used in American catalogs before 1908; it was also prescribed by the British edition of the 1908 code. Though seemingly not used at present, it has supporters.[32, 33] The cataloger records the earliest title in the title area, the description of the first issue in the description area, and all later bibliographic information in notes, with tracings for later titles. (Earliest entry cataloging requires staff training to deal with the differences between entry in the catalog file and in the order file.) For either earliest or latest entry cataloging, the presupposition is that unless the publisher does something really drastic, like starting a new Volume 1, we have only one serial. The best argument for both methods is *not* cataloger convenience, but elimination of irrational fragmentation; consolidation of bibliographic, management, and holdings information in one record.

In the United States, there has been one striking experiment (in terms of staff and user acceptance) at Northwestern University, using the latest entry method as one means of handling serial title changes. The staff there has published their rules for making the decision and for describing publications using this method.[34, 35] One of the important provisions is that latest entry is used only for straightforward title changes: not for a merger, split, or break in numbering, for example. As of 1992, the staff reported having over 800 latest entry records in the online catalog, and after a survey which asked patrons to answer specific questions from both kinds of records, found that latest entry records seemed easier to interpret.[36]

Defenders of successive entry warn that abandoning it implies abandoning national and international standards, including ISSN; jeopardizing consistency in union lists; distorting series added entries; confusing users who approach the catalog with an article citation; diverging, in general, from the way the bulk of libraries catalog titles. It also may mean using shared records in non-standard ways or doing double entry, so it's not a choice without cost and administrative implications. In addition, some simply find successive entry clearer;[37] and collectively, successive records do usually offer more bibliographic information about the serial as a whole.

To the question of which kind of cataloging is "best" for access in a *local* catalog, the only answer is a mixed answer. If in a serial where title changes have occurred, a library holds, for example, only the later volumes because those are in scope for the collection; or, say, only a volume from the middle of the run, a successive entry record would be clearer; a long serial history would probably fulfill only a rare and esoteric need and at worst might be misleading. If an entire run is held, or particularly if a long incomplete run is held, either an earliest or a latest entry record would provide the advantage of giving a full picture of the serial and its holdings. Incomplete runs are a problem because missing titles will break the chain of "Continues" notes and/ or control numbers in successive entry records, and the trail vanishes; in unclassified collections, there may be no thread to follow by which to pick it up again. And in classified collections, call number searching—which would pick up a common element—is still very seldom used.

Some hope for making successive entry work better in the future lies in the capability of the computer. North American librarians might well envy the ease with which the German International Serials Data System Centre (ZDB) accesses linked titles, as described by Günter Franzmeier in a 1987 article: "In our system, by simply asterisking...[the earlier or later title] in the notes, before the first title word, and depressing the SEND key, the program switches the user to the respective record."[38] To enable the user to know beforehand whether a linked title is held, utilities and system vendors could add an "ownership" subfield (a place to give either a local control number or zeros to indicate that a linked title is not owned by the library), as proposed by Melissa M. Bernhardt [Beck] in 1988.[39] If such a subfield were available, a program could be written for today's catalogs to examine all serial records for linked titles, follow the links in both directions (by means of the national control numbers in the fields), and set the ownership or non-ownership subfield in each linking field. Subsequently other programs could be written to generate notes and instructions for retrieving linked titles. For example, the holdings screen of today's serial record could alert users to the presence or absence in the library of earlier or later titles, give the titles themselves, and direct their retrieval by the easiest method, and all without using the computer resources of a new database search until the user specifically invoked it.

Better still than traversing one record at a time through the linked titles would be viewing a coordinated display of all linked serial information like the one Beck suggested in her article. A system could provide this display by repeating the search of control numbers (either national or local) in each direction until the chain ends, and making resultant groupings of titles. To aid future systems in using numbers and enable guidance to users, it is important to supply them in the linking fields of all records wherever available, as Robert Alan urged in a follow-up to Beck's article.[40]

This long and necessarily sketchy account of the title change and earliest/ latest/successive entry question has been given in order to invite every serialist and serials cataloger not only to take a critical look at the local catalog, but to join the debate and work with others to improve access in all catalogs. The question of using one of the alternative methods is very likely to come up in libraries with many long runs of serials, especially when recataloging or converting to machine-readable form. CONSER permits the use of existing latest entry records, if no successive records exist. CONSER may even input such latest entry records (*CONSER Editing Guide*, C10).

If we are to use multiple records for a serial run, as standards now direct, we must be concerned that this technique may contribute to some search failures. The bottom line is that to most users it is not obvious, when they accidentally retrieve a wrong title because of an unrecognized title change, how to get to the correct record or even that there is a correct record. Solutions such as indexing the 780 and 785 fields on each record or including them on a "related works" screen accessible with a special command fall short to varying degrees. Ease in retrieving linked titles is one of the things this chapter suggests that the serials manager scrutinize when judging OPACs, as will be re-emphasized at the end of the chapter.

Linking technology in catalogs has made another step forward in the recent past. "Web" interfaces applied to catalogs offer the possibility of hypertext links embedding searches for related data within the data in bibliographic records. In these techniques, perhaps, lies another potential for aiding our search for related serial titles.

The Uniform Title Problem

Another matter left out of AACR2 was the question of a unique identifier for serial titles. The lack of unique identifiers is important, because many serial titles are identical. The potential confusion caused by this fact can be imagined in considering that many serial titles are used as series added entries on records for both serials and monographs. Without something to distinguish them, identical titles would all interfile.

International standards bodies (ISO, the International Standards Organization; IFLA, the International Federation of Library Associations and Institutions) focused intensively on this question in the 1970s, as AACR2 was being compiled. The reconciliation of the several standards did not take place, however, until after the publication of AACR2. At this point the international standard and the standard propounded by the Library of Congress and CONSER parted company.

The Library of Congress's solution was the uniform title, which is assigned by the cataloger to serve as the entry for the serial in files and when referred to in other records. The MARC tag is 130 (or, more rarely, 240, used with corporate or conference main entry). The particular use for serials is nowhere described in AACR2's original chapter on uniform titles (Chapter 25), but was formulated in the rule interpretations to Rule 25.5B, Conflict resolution, in time to be used under AACR2. Over the years the interpretation has been altered and refined. The latest AACR2 Amendments (1993) contain provisions for serial uniform titles. The provisions call for a qualifier in parentheses to any title being cataloged which conflicts with another already in the file. The preferred qualifier is place of publication:

Geological bulletin (Tokyo, Japan)

unless (a) the title consists solely of a word or phrase indicating type of serial and/or "periodicity":

Quarterly bulletin (Missouri Historical Society)

or (b) qualifying by place alone still leaves a conflict. In both of the latter situations, a and b, the heading for the issuing body, if present, becomes the qualifier of choice.

Place of publication was picked as the first-choice qualifier, not immediately upon adoption of AACR2, but two years later, because its use had a corollary: if the place of publication changed, it was not necessary to make a new record, as it had been when the first choice was a more "meaningful" qualifier, the issuing body. The perception that qualifying by place adds no helpful information has nagged at both theorists and practitioners;[41] but few wanted helpful uniform titles at the price of more successive entries. In the last reissue of this Rule Interpretation 25.5B, the prescriptive wording was removed, and the cataloger is given more latitude to make a choice of qualifier.

If the preferred qualifiers cannot be used in a uniform title, any information which can distinguish the serials may be used as the qualifier. Date (or place : date) and edition (geographic, subject, or language) are common qualifiers. Qualifiers may be combined, but only certain types—one cannot combine place and name of an issuing body in a qualifier.

Reduplication of nearly identical title fields in serial records also causes redundant retrievals in searching online catalogs. The international identifier called the *key title* is assigned to all serials submitted to national ISSN Centers. This title may or may not be identical to the uniform title and/or title proper, but appears with them on most full-level authenticated records in the national database (USMARC field 222, which, under ISBD-S, appears with the ISSN in Area 8 of the catalog record). Corporate qualifiers in key titles are taken from the form of name on the publication, while those in uniform titles use the "authoritative" cataloging form of name, which may be quite different from the way it appears on the serial. A uniform title entry is often puzzling, even to library staff. It has struck some theorists here and abroad[42, 43] as unnecessary in that this title is often similar to, but inferior to, the key title as a search argument. Incidentally, records following LC practice may not contain a qualifier in a variant-title field (USMARC 246, a further title entry for the same publication, supplied as necessary by the cataloger).[44] Unfortunately, this prohibition excludes one procedure that could resolve some of the problems, because the variant title is one place to supply the user with a title search otherwise lacking in the record.

The *CONSER Cataloging Manual* explains the basis for the uniform title but does not specifically compare it with the key title concept. It states that the uniform title "assist[s] online searching by making search displays more intelligible" (Module 5, p. 5-6). In local catalogs, to reduce retrieval overload, some systems drop the key title from the title index—in which case a tradeoff must be reckoned with in the loss of access to some title information.

Even when a library accepts whatever choice of entry appears on cataloging copy, there will still be work to do to make files, links, and entries consistent throughout the catalog.

Numbering

Possessing numbering and/or dates of issue is one of the important criteria distinguishing a serial from other types of publication. Beginning and ending numbering and dates of the entire serial—not just of the portion held by the library—are recorded in Area 3 of the bibliographic record. The numbering and/or date, as a unit, is called a "designation:"

Vol. 1, no. 1 (Jan. 1972)-v. 10, no. 12 (Dec. 1981).

To be recorded in this way, the designation must be "identifying;" that is, it must identify the issue on which it appeared. Since the identifying designation often carries a different date from the date of publication, catalogers often use such terms as "issue date," or "coverage date" to distinguish it. The designation is recorded in the USMARC 362 field, while the date of publication, usually found in conjunction with the publisher name or copyright statement, is recorded in Area 4 (USMARC 260, subfield c). The holdings are often on a completely separate screen; because of the potential confusion between numbering and holdings, holdings placement is another evaluation criterion for OPACs.

The example shows a formal transcription of a beginning and ending designation; that is, the parts surrounding the hyphen are each complete issue designations. Only complete issue designations are recorded formally.

Information which locates the serial in time is very useful, so if it can not be recorded formally, it should be given in notes even if these notes must be incomplete or speculative (followed by a question mark). Notes also carry information about "peculiarities" or irregularities in numbering that are found in many serials.

Access Points

Titles. Much has been said in the sections above about titles. They are extremely important access points for serials. Additional title searches need to be provided in many records because of the presence of various titles on parts of the serial, in issues of the serial, or in citations to the serial in other works. The USMARC 246 field does double duty as description and access, in that it can generate either a note or an entry, or both. It has indicators to provide specific wording for several common kinds of notes describing the source of variant titles, for example, Cover title: ...; Spine title: ...; and a subfield i (new with format integration) to contain explanatory wording composed by the cataloger. On the other hand, many titles found on copy will be redundant access points in the local catalog, because either the software or local indexing decisions may differentiate their retrieval in a specific catalog. Managers would do well to be aware of how title headings file in the local catalog and set policies and procedures that suit those conditions, always recording their decisions to aid in future migrations.

Other title access points enable access to the serial from searches for related works. A 730 field is used for any separately cataloged work to which the serial is related, but is particularly used to name such separately cataloged works as supplements, "companion publications," and differently titled editions. In these cases, the 730 field may duplicate linking title fields (numbered 770, 772, 775, 776 or 787) for these closely related publications.

Linking title fields, like 246 fields, may generate notes based on indicator values within the fields, describing the relationship of the linked titles. These fields are not designed to be access points, though some online systems index some or all of them. Their purpose is to provide a "machine link" to the control number possessed by that related title in the database.

A less common kind of title access point for serials is a series title. When some or all issues of a serial come out within another publication series, catalogers record an access point for the more comprehensive title. In a few series there is a complicated relationship to the serial, involving dual numbering systems, which requires much labor to chart and then represent clearly on both bibliographic and holdings records.

Subjects. Just as the description omits details that would be given for a monograph, subject headings assigned to serials have traditionally been broad and general. Both beginning catalogers and theorists (e.g., Osborn)[45] find fault with the lack of specific subject headings in serial records. Osborn recognized that the remedy was not "better" subject cataloging but indexing, that is, article-level access; even he did not foresee that within a few years of his writing, the catalog itself would begin to provide that access.

The subject subdivision "Periodicals" is assigned even to annual reports and similar works, to set off serials as a group within the subject structure. Only monographic series, very irregular serials, pseudoserials, and types of serials with their own subdivision, such as congresses, directories and catalogs, do not use this subdivision.[46]

Names. Always less common on serial than on monographic records, personal name access points are now rarer than ever. Only when an individual's responsibility for a serial is equivalent to authorship, rather than mere editorship, would main entry under personal name be considered. The best guideline for making personal name added entries is their usefulness in retrieving either the serial record or the record of the author's activity.

Corporate body names are closely associated with many serials, and some of them involve considerable work to establish and apply. Establishing a name involves determining a valid form to serve as an access point for bibliographic records, and making sure that any different forms of the name that might be the object of a search are covered by cross references. AACR2, chapter 24 gives rules for the formation of corporate name headings.

Just as titles do, corporate names change over time. If the name is not used as the main entry, the procedure is simple. Name changes over the course of one serial are described in a note and traced with a separate added entry for each change of name:

Issued by: Body A, 1900-1924; by Body B, 1925- (Note, USMARC 550)
I. Body A. II. Body B. **(Entries, 710 or 711)**

When the corporate body name is either the main entry or the qualifier of the uniform title, however, a change in the name calls under present rules for making a successive entry for issues appearing after the change. The method of linking these entries is thus the same as that for changes in titles: the linking entry field. Obviously, since not the name itself, but the title is linked:

Review (Body A).—Vol. 1-v. 25.—Continued by: Review (Body B)

the relationship of the name is not stated directly, but would have to be inferred through a complicated thought process. Such links are usually reinforced through parallel links in the authority structure between forms of name. A catalog that contains name authority records can display cross references with special wording to signal the relationship between Bodies A and B:

Body A.
For titles published by this body under its later name, see Body B.

Classification. Not always thought of as an access point, a call number places material on the same or related subjects near each other. Except in special libraries, larger North American collections of serials tend to be classed by one of the two major classification systems (Dewey Decimal System and Library of Congress Classification). Many online catalogs allow the call number to be searched, so it becomes an alternate form of subject access. Call number searching can aid in retrieval of linked titles. Smaller libraries and special libraries, however, may often choose to shelve their main serial collections in alphabetical order by title.

SPECIAL TYPES OF SERIALS

Microform Serials

The reign of AACR2 faced one rebellion: U.S. research libraries disagreed almost unanimously with the new cataloging policy toward reproductions of already existing works. The new rules (see especially *AACR2*, Chapter 11, Microforms) asked libraries not only to catalog reproductions as separate bibliographic items instead of appending them ("dashing them on") to records for the original; they were also to emphasize the information (publication, physical description) about the reproduction by giving it in the body of the record, while relegating information about the original to a note. The libraries' protest was that cataloging should emphasize intellectual content over physical form; and users seek the bibliographically familiar original rather than the unfamiliar reproduction. The national libraries decided to go back for the time being to the AACR1 rule, emphasizing information from the original, with information about the reproduction in a note (USMARC 533). Both serial and monographic reproductions in the United States are cataloged according to this policy (LCRI 11.0A), which is not followed, for instance, by the National Library of Canada.[47] Hard copy reprints, on the other hand, are cataloged in a hybrid, compromise fashion, taking their title and numbering from the original serial reproduced, but their publication data and physical description from that of the reprinted item.

There were two more levels to the microform problem in serials cataloging: Since OCLC and RLIN required that new cataloging conform to AACR2, and AACR2 required that serials be described from the first issue rather than the latest, a record for the original could not simply be "cloned" to serve as the record for the microform. That burden was seen as a discouragement and extra expense in preservation microfilming. Though this problem was solved by the acceptance of records for these materials cataloged using the standards by which the original had been cataloged, that left the ultimate problem to be solved: what would we do about the proliferation of records for essentially the same item in our catalogs?

On the local level, almost all libraries give some information about reproductions on the record for the original, especially when the reproduction merely fills in a brief gap in a run. In addition, there is the precedent of the U.S. Newspaper Program (see the next section on newspapers). A Multiple Versions Forum, convened under Library of Congress and Council for Library Resources sponsorship, debated the question and ultimately decided that a master record approach should be adopted for true reproductions. Individual versions would be adequately described by the use of the *USMARC Format for Holdings Data*, extended and restructured to contain more descriptive fields for each separate reproduction. This possibility would require that system vendors and bibliographic utilities adopt the format widely, which is far from occurring as yet. A subsequent Multiple Versions Task Force sponsored by ALA's Committee on Cataloging: Description and Access has decided to apply the technique to any reproduction where it is possible to determine that the content is equivalent.[48] Instructions for this practice may be found in the committee's recommended *Guidelines for Bibliographic Description of Reproductions*.[49]

Microform and other reproductions are covered in Part III of the *CONSER Cataloging Manual* (Module 32), published in 1994. This module does not yet endorse the multiple versions technique, citing the lag in technology. How this question will be worked out in the future is as yet unknown.

For certain complete sets of historically significant periodicals in microform, it should be mentioned that OCLC provides bibliographic records on tape to be bulk loaded into online catalogs (the Major Microforms Project). During loading, local designations and call numbers may be added.[50]

Newspapers

Newspapers are purchased on the street corner as sources of up-to-the-minute information, to be scanned and then discarded. If collected and preserved in library collections, they become sources of unique historical information unlikely to have been recorded anywhere else. In many libraries, both uses of newspapers exist together. Because the bulk and poor paper quality of newspapers preclude their being archived, as in the past, in their original form, most newspapers that are retained are purchased in microform, often in addition to a printed version that is retained for a limited time.

Since libraries acquire so many newspapers in two formats, and AACR2 mandated that separate records be provided for each physical manifestation, the "multiple versions" question was brought into high relief with the question of cataloging newspapers. *The Newspaper Cataloging and Union Listing Manual*[51], issued by the Library of Congress for participants in the United States Newspaper Program and others who wish to follow their guidelines, departs from AACR2 and general library practice in its response to this question. It has adopted a "master record convention" whereby all forms of reproduction, along with locations and holdings of individual libraries, are given in local data records—a feature of OCLC's Union List Subsystem—attached to the bibliographic record for the original.

Aside from the multiple versions question, newspaper cataloging has some interesting and distinctive aspects, most of which are not brought out in the standard works on cataloging. What is a newspaper, by the way? As the *CONSER Cataloging Manual* quotes the ISO definition (Module 2, p. 10), only "general news" publications appearing at least weekly meet the definition, not, for example, *Women's Wear Daily*. Usually a "masthead, nameplate or flag"[52] (equivalent to a caption in other types of serials) is the source of title; there is no title page or cover. Not only frequent title changes but multiple editions, supplements and other cataloging problems are characteristic of newspaper collections.

Because title changes loom so large, the USNP extends the new Rule 21.2 restricting criteria for title changes, to exempt also changes in title lasting less than one year. Titles of lesser duration are given in notes and traced. Defining the serial and its editions should be done carefully. Terms for frequency, geography, and language given in the title or edition statement are regarded. Chronological terms such as "Late City" or "Sunday" are not regarded, and title statements or edition statements with these terms are never an indication for separate cataloging. Changes in edition statements (as with regular serials) do not ordinarily call for successive entry.

Direct Access Computer File Serials

"Computer file" is the present AACR2-assigned term for the format previously denoted "machine-readable data file" (MRDF). The file itself as an item to be cataloged is as often a collection of files as one file; it may be programs, or data, or both; data may be numeric, textual, or other, such as sound or graphic; and the file may be carried on magnetic tape, diskettes, computer optical discs (CD-ROMs), or other. (A peculiarity of official computer orthography honored by catalogers: diskettes are disks, CD-ROMs are discs.) Serial computer files have most of the standard characteristics of serials; they are intended to be continued indefinitely, they bear numbering or dates. Direct access serial computer files have physical carriers which are present in the library (even though they may be housed permanently on a LAN and be accessed through a menu, just like their remote access counterparts). These definitions, and guidance for catalogers, are included in Module 30 of the *CCM*. As this is written, the guide prescribes the use of the USMARC serials bibliographic format until the second phase of format integration in late 1995, when CONSER will switch. The delay is due to the CONSER distribution program, which can presently transmit only serial records. Non-CONSER libraries may use records in either format, since both record types can contain any necessary fields.

The mutability of these media that troubled catalogers so much in the planning stages is now looking minor in comparison to the mutability of remote databases and the Internet! At the same time, it highlights the limitations of a concept like first-issue cataloging for new formats. Since a large proportion of these serials, particularly on disk, will be either discarded or returned to the publisher as an updated issue is received, accounting for the disk as it was first issued by that publisher—the version number or hardware requirements of the program or amount of data in the files—is of less concern than facilitating access to and efficient use of the data as it will be found now. The latest issue of most disks/discs will be the latest version of a program or the largest cumulation of data. The version number and system requirements should be updated as information changes; numbered releases are not cataloged separately. If the newest issue of a 5 1/4 in. diskette serial is on a 3 1/2 in. diskette, the change would not warrant a new record; the size range is merely recorded in the physical description area.

The protean nature of computer file serials, like that of newspapers, is further demonstrated in their editions, which might be defined as simultaneous manifestations differing in various ways. Differences based on carrier (diskette/ CD-ROM), hardware platform (IBM/Macintosh/etc.) and/or operating system (MS-DOS/Unix/OS2/etc.) are possible; so are all the textual variations of a print serial (geographic/audience/etc.). Rules for distinguishing between these are being hammered out. Because of frequent differences such as the addition of a search engine, a record for a computer file version of a print serial will not be appended to the record for the printed form. On the other hand, some types of direct access computer files for varying platforms may be adaptable to description on a single record, provided their data can be used with either platform (CCM, Module 30, p. 17).

Other problems often mentioned include the lack of reading equipment at the cataloger's worksite. Since the chief source of information is the title screen, if available, it may be desirable for the cataloger to go where there is equipment to view the files. Alternately, the electronic reference center or owning location can mount the files (perhaps while permanently installing them), print out the title screen, "readme" files, and any other material agreed upon, photocopy appropriate pages of any documentation, label the sheets as to the source of each, and send this material to the catalogers. This method has some advantages: it does not remove the serial itself from use, it enables the owning location to get a look at it first, and it organizes important information for the cataloger (an inducement to get on with the cataloging, and a welcome beginning to consultation about the best ways to provide access to the material). CD-ROMs can be photocopied, as well, so that the disc label may be used as a source of information. The static electricity in photocopiers is unofficially reported to affect data on diskettes, however.

According to *AACR2*, Chapter 9, the record should always name the chief source of information, even if it is the title screen. Title screens of some new products don't stand still. Perhaps it is just a bit amusing to meditate on the perversity of basing the description on something that is scrolling by too fast for one to get a look at it in one go (*CCM*, Module 30, p. 11). Non-commercial disks or tapes, especially those with numeric data, are quite likely to have no title screens at all, so the description for those is more often based on external sources: disc label, tape cartridge or box, user's guide, accompanying codebook. Variant titles are common on external sources for any computer file serial, and are given in USMARC 246 fields with subfield i's specifying source.

Relationships with other serials or other versions of the same title—printed, remote access, and so forth—can be encoded with USMARC linking fields 772, 775, 776, 780/785, 787, as appropriate. The *CCM* enjoins common sense in linking, since links can be numerous and complex.

Electronic Journals and Remote-Access Computer File Serials

The library is poised amid an ocean of information, where metaphors like surfing and navigating are commonly used by enthusiasts who venture out on it. We are only in the dawn of this era, where providing the remote serial is often on no one's agenda until suddenly it is on everyone's. Better to get the feet wet early in learning about what is already accessed in the library and what would be accessible, if someone were actively making it available.

Two pioneers in provision of access to electronic journals, and reporting about it to the library community, were Virginia Polytechnic Institute and State University (VPI)[53] and the Massachusetts Institute of Technology (MIT).[54] Their plans were drawn up in concerted effort by interdepartmental task forces who brought various kinds of expertise to the project. Both chose to assemble and locally mount a collection of electronic texts chosen specifically for their suitability for accession by various electronic transaction modes, and for storage and display by available means. Decisions about the texts had to be made from the ground up: how to mount and maintain them; who would process them and update the processing information as new issues arrived; and whether and how to make a permanent local archive of the backruns. MIT, in addition, analyzed various client/server modes of patron access (Gopher, WAIS, etc.), eventually achieving a combination which would allow users to choose through a menu either to search files interactively or browse them in the usual way. Though MIT reported it would provide catalog records only for locally mounted e-journals, its second report argues the economic benefits of relying on remote information on networked servers, and evokes the vision of a long-term solution in a "seamless interface" between the catalog, local electronic files, and access to material at other locations.

The cataloging record for a remote access computer file will lack physical descriptors. There will be a common core of bibliographic information, and a large component of access information. Classification is an option both VPI and MIT found useful for measurement of collection strengths, call number browsing by users, and links between earlier and later titles; it is also recommended by the recently released *CCM* Module 31. National-level records and local records must contain up-to-date information and instructions about accessing the files, but the function of this information at the two levels may be quite different. The master (national) record, which is increasingly used as a guide by departments wishing to order the titles, should give subscription information in detail. The MIT report urges that the record list the precise commands used to subscribe, as well as the address of the host server.[56] Depending upon the access that the local library intends to provide, however, these instructions, if they appear at all, may have to be identified as personal subscription information for those with accounts only, and accompanied with a note reminding the user to check elsewhere for instructions on library access. The latter instruction was at first assumed to be destined for the holdings screen, where precise commands needed to access current files and any archived backfiles could be given in natural language. With the advent of Web-browsable catalogs that turn fields into "hot buttons," attention has shifted to the 856 field, which is actually defined for both the bibliographic and the holdings formats. This field contains encoded information about the location and access of the online resource. The *CCM* instructs that it should contain information "sufficient to connect to a service, transfer files electronically, or subscribe to an electronic journal or newsletter" (Module 31, p. 25.) However, the coded, subfielded nature of this field lends itself poorly to clear guidance for users. Documentation for the 856 field is available from the Library of Congress gopher, MARVEL.[57] It uses indicators to distinguish between the different access methods, such as Gopher, ftp, e-mail; it uses subfields for information about the technical aspects of the files (compression, text formatting) as well as location information. The field may contain a subfield u for the Universal Resource Locator (URL), which is used in a few catalogs already to make a direct connection to an electronic file. There is still another place in the record where access information belongs (the Mode of Access note, USMARC 538); *CCM* examples vary in their explicitness from a complex guided search to a simple "Electronic file transfer ftp via the Internet." In the opinion of this writer, detailed, user-oriented repetition of instructions on the holdings screen would be much better than the message "No holdings" that one sometimes finds now.

While the library community may bear the primary responsibility for keeping the master record up to date, the responsibility for maintaining the local record rests with the local library, and it can be a toilsome one. Particularly if the electronic file is *not* maintained by the library, new identifying and tracking mechanisms are needed for monitoring the file location, content, and possible changes in access methods as well. The difficulties and possibilities for solution have been sketched in the online *Public Access Computer Systems Review* in a column by Priscilla Caplan, who also addresses the important question of how widely in the Intersurf the cataloging net should be cast.[58] Her columns are well worth searching out in the online archives of the *Review*. In addition to the *Review*, the would-be expert should probably consider two other resources: the online forums Intercat,[59] on cataloging the Internet, and VPIEJ-L,[60] on managing electronic journals.

Format Integration and Serials Cataloging

The need to allow information from any of the MARC formats to be used while cataloging any item was recognized early; but the idea crystallized around the problems of seriality. In the A/V and sound recording formats, serials catalogers could not use accustomed fields for frequency and numbering of the serial, or for defining and controlling relationship information between one serial and another; on the other hand, some of the definition fields A/V catalogers were accustomed to using were missing when they used the serials format to catalog. For systems, the multiple defining of fields and maintenance of tables in separate formats was costly; with new types of library materials appearing, there was the specter of still more formats ahead. In the early eighties, MARBI, a joint committee of librarians and information scientists, redefined the formats as a single format in which any definition should be valid across the board. Over the next few years, besides publishing the united formats (called *USMARC Format for Bibliographic Data*[61], in preparation for this merger they reassessed all the coding, and deleted fields and subfields that were undefined, unused, or unnecessary for manipulation, indexing or other structuring of the record.

At the center of the new concept was the rethinking of the record "leader," containing identification of record and material type, which determines some of the fixed field content. For items sharing aspects of more than one format, a supplementary field, called 006, has been defined so that it can be coded for multimedia items, or items that share serial or archival aspects with some other aspect. The 006, whose display is not set, is scheduled for late 1995 as the last element of the changeover to be implemented.

Field integration is already complete, though serials catalogers have had fewer adjustments to make than their monographic colleagues. Bibliographic utilities have removed obsolete fields from validation tables and recoded the data, though local systems still carry many of the old codes. Changing fields, remapping content, and validating new fields mark the first phase.

Format integration will not necessarily bring about a merged workform or record on the screen of the online network. The overwhelming majority of serials are still in the text medium. When cataloging one medium, catalogers still want the convenience of having frequently used fields displayed and default codes filled in. Serials catalogers, however, will have to learn to think in terms of primary and secondary characteristics when they catalog non-print serials. All non-textual formats: A/V, sound recordings, and computer files, for example, will have as their primary aspect their non-textuality. Seriality is in that case a secondary aspect. Those values of seriality that are coded in such cases will be coded in the 006 field, while the coding for the visual material aspect, for example, will belong in the primary fixed field (USMARC 008). Serial catalogers will no longer automatically catalog on the serials format; CONSER guidelines mandating the serials format will be changed so that one of the non-textual formats will be used instead.

OTHER RESPONSIBILITIES

Serials catalogers have many responsibilities closely related to cataloging. They also have primary responsibility for several activities related to serials that do not involve cataloging per se. In smaller libraries, they may work with all aspects of serials, or even work with serials themselves only part time. But in general, here are some of the activities very closely related to serials cataloging and commonly part of serials catalogers' routine or left to their care.

Serials Retrospective Conversion

If a library wishes to have its former manual cataloging records display in an online catalog, they must be retrospectively converted. Retrospective conversion ordinarily does not involve pulling volumes from the shelf (though it may, with problem material); and it ordinarily does not involve making new cards (because at that point it becomes recataloging). Quite often conversion of the serials collection is considered separately from the monographic because of the special complexities involved in serials. The conversion itself can be done in house, by regular staff as time permits or by specially hired staff; or it can be done by a bibliographic utility or commercial service, for a fee. In either case, the serials cataloging unit will have to set goals and timetables, choose a method, and plan how to accomplish the task. Much guidance is available in converting a collection of records of any size in the literature on serials. Procedures will depend on what method is chosen and what records or combinations of records exist to work from; shelflists, kardex records, separate serial catalogs with holdings.

Active subscriptions are prime targets for retrospective conversion, and are likely to have first priority. If they are being converted to an integrated system, a coordinated conversion project involving bibliographic records, holdings, item, order, and check-in records may be realistic; but it will take much planning and communication between all the library units involved. In conversion of current cataloging—or for that matter of older records—it is not unusual to find out that title changes have occurred since the last cataloging of the serial. In that case, those records may need special attention so that new cataloging can be provided and the holdings reconciled.

Retrospective conversion of dead serials inhouse will need decisions made. What standards will be used, and how much checking will be done? How will the right copy be chosen? Will staff use successive entry cataloging exclusively? If so, what files will need to be updated for the broken-out titles? How will any necessary original cataloging be handled? Will full authority work be done? If the LC authority file indicates a change of entry for a monographic series, who is responsible for changing series entries on the monographic analytical records? Module 22 in Part II of the *CCM* deals with the accommodation of pre-AACR2 records into AACR2 catalogs.

Once the conversion is accomplished, serials cataloging staff will probably have at least some job security as toilers in database cleanup; expertise in the special problems of serials is helpful in this task. In spite of the best planning...no conversion is perfect.

Series Decisions

Even though the majority of series are encountered on monographic titles, the series themselves are serials or serial-like. Some of them are not serials but sets: multipart monographs.

Unless a library has decided upon some blanket treatment (such as allowing whatever series form is on the record to stand, or, contrariwise, tagging all series not to be traced), the determination of shelving, access and form of entry for series will be a rather complex procedure. Serials catalogers are ordinarily required to make treatment decisions for some or all of the series that surface in the course of monographic cataloging, as well as those that pop up as supplements or other oddities in the check-in routine.

A series may be anything from a vague aggregation of items put together for marketing convenience, to a painstakingly planned gathering of works expounding on a chosen subject or entire field, to the sequentially published reports or papers of a research body. Like a serial, it may run to hundreds of numbers or end after the first volume is published. It is distinguished from a serial in that its component parts have distinctive titles. Most are monographic, hence the term, "monographic series." They can be serials, however. There are new hybrids, too: several publishers have found they can sell collections of articles twice by publishing them as journal issues and then again (supposedly to non-subscribers) as "journal monographs."

Control over series may range from nonexistent to draconian. In one beautifully organized manual operation recorded in 1985, policy required that *every* item entering the library that looked like a serial itself, that had a series on the item, series on the cataloging copy, or even an added entry for a serial on the copy, had to tour through the Serials Department for the typing of detailed authority instructions.[62] In many libraries, there is no documentation of series except the instruction to "follow LC practice," which works when LC has established a practice, when it is correctly interpreted, and when it fits the needs of the local library. In other libraries, all series are documented, but the documentation is done by serials catalogers only when LC practice is not found or not clear, or when there is no established LC practice and a bibliographic search of the database using the series as a search argument turns up inconsistent practice.

What this "practice" consists of is three decisions: (a) analyzing, whether to provide a record for each item within a series; (b) shelving, whether to class the series together in one call number or separately in the call numbers appropriate to each piece; (c) series access, whether to give a series added entry on the record for each item. A fourth decision not included in "practice" is (d) form, what the cataloging entry for the series should be. Decisions can be recorded in any of several files, including a series authority file, a name authority file, a separate series catalog, an online catalog, or a serials control system.

Most libraries make some kind of overall policy about the handling of monographic series, and use it as a guideline to decide treatment as new series appear. In the Library of Congress today, if a decision is made to provide full analysis (creation of separate records for each volume in the series), the series is almost always classed separately (according to the subject of each volume). Many libraries adhering to Library of Congress practice follow this practice as well. In other libraries, at least when there is no national decision, catalogers will decide to hold some monographic series together, but still provide access to individual volumes. In my library, a series received on standing order, whose volumes are closely related in subject matter, in a discipline such as history or literature where series have greater traditional importance, is more likely than most to be shelved together. Full analysis is usually given if the monographs are substantial, particularly if indexing in standard reference sources is inadequate; if some volumes are of minor importance, or lack distinctive titles, the series will probably be analyzed "selectively" or "monographic numbers only." For all other series, the preference is separate shelving and classification—though recent proposals by the Library of Congress to save classification time by keeping more series together may reverse that trend once more. (This rough model is intended to elucidate the nature of series decisions rather than to provide a guideline for any contemporary library.)

Factors governing whether to provide series access are related to those that govern shelving and analyzing, but criteria are broader. Under Library of Congress policies, all analyzed series are traced since August 31, 1981, though tracing decisions have not been changed for series established before that date (LCRI 21.30L). Encountering a new wording that looks like a series, the only questions catalogers ask are, "Is this wording a series?" and "Is this one series or more than one?" The criteria for determining that are in LCRI 1.6. Presumably, CONSER members, or other libraries contributing series authorities to LC, and institutions supplying original cataloging online, should routinely provide a series access point for each series in records for the national database. For local catalogs, however, practices probably vary more widely on the treatment of series than on any other section of the cataloging rulebook.

The Local System Purchase

When it is time to buy an OPAC (Online Public Access Catalog) from a library system vendor, there will be a formal process in which all catalogers and serials managers should take a lively interest. The online catalog can help users find serials information if it is well designed and provided with instructional aids, preferably onscreen. Most library software should be MARC-based, and should provide MARC format storage in addition to input and output. Most systems can append limiters to author, title and subject searches (or combinations of them) so that only serials will be retrieved. If keyword searching is available, the program can relate multiple criteria with "operators" such as "and," "or," and "not," to achieve optimum balance between recall and precision. It cannot be stressed enough, however, that serial records are complex and easily daunting to the searcher. If the display is flawed, or the indexing of too many or too few titles (since serial records tend to have many titles) leads to confusion, patrons will be easily frustrated in serials searching, and it will become the cataloger's job to compensate for the defects of the system, which is always a poor idea. The requirements of the system almost inevitably influence the quality of the cataloging. Serials catalogers must be ready to present their proposals for indexing and display when a new online system is considered. Each library may have its own desiderata, but some of the concerns might be:

Since searchers must often track holdings from title to title, how easy is it to access the former and later titles from a record?

Are the elements of the catalog record displayed correctly? In particular, are linking relationships displayed in full from the linking fields? Is all note information displayed or displayable at the library's option? Are display constants displayed from indicator values in variant and linking title fields?

Can the user determine easily whether there are further screens of information not yet seen?

What adjustments will be made for format integration in searching with a limitation by format? for display of bibliographic information?

Can holdings information be made available for display at an early point?

Would the vendor consider ("have implemented" is too much to hope) using the control numbers in linking fields in the future as a mechanism to aid in retrieval of related serial titles?

Of course, a well-designed technical editing program, linked to an advanced serials control system, linked to an OPAC and to all other modules of an integrated library system for real-time mutual updating and accessibility of information, would be very desirable, too.

Finally, since a library may wish to migrate to another system as the technology advances further, it would be foolish to choose a vendor who does not provide a way to do this without rekeying data.

SOME FINAL THOUGHTS

What is the next frontier? Linking and transparency. Technological advances have raised expectations, and libraries will have to live up to them. The finding of a citation will be expected to lead with the least possible delay to accessing the resource. The user will need more tools to judge the availability of the resource or document and its relevance to the inquiry. The delay before acquisition of the information itself will have to diminish and in some cases disappear. The library may have to be a very active participant in this process. It may create or extend links between resources, initiate document delivery services, and design current awareness programs.

Whither serials cataloging? It will diversify as the material which it records diversifies. Our careful construct of cataloging rules and interpretations will be useful to record information at the broadest level about serials that appear in traditional form—and, as always, for the serials that already exist. Newer forms of description and access will be needed, to locate and track new forms of information that possess common recurring elements, but our older ways will have to be completely rethought in order to cope with items that possess seriality or are related to serials but are not serials as we have known them.

What is the biggest challenge? Publications which, in an online environment, can be customized and altered in content without acknowledgment: a problem that we have experienced before, but now magnified. Fortunately, we will have help from specialists in other areas in making the necessary decisions about preserving and providing access to this material.

Will cataloging disappear? Only if we fail to learn and to adapt. Our discipline seeks to order information for use, and it need not stop with the tools it has today. If we keep our goal firmly in mind as we continue to build the database and import, refine, and invent new tools to exploit it, we have a basis for growth, not defeat.

NOTES

1. My first introductory thought is that I owe a great deal to Crystal Graham, who did a very thorough critical reading of the manuscript about a year after I completed it, inspiring me to add many things, clarify others, and delete some things (probably less than she wished). She corrected errors in definitions. She reminded me to consider the reader first; for instance, by explaining my terminology at all points. I hereby acknowledge all her help and nonetheless retain ownership of my own faults.

2. *CONSER Editing Guide* (Washington, D.C.: Library of Congress, Cataloging Distribution Service, 1986-)

3. *CONSER Cataloging Manual.* Ed. Jean Hirons. (Washington, D.C.: Library of Congress, Cataloging Distribution Service, 1993-).

4. To subscribe to Autocat, send an e-mail message to listserv@ubvm.cc.buffalo.edu. Send as sole text (with no subject line or signature): subscribe autocat Firstname Lastname.

5. To subscribe to Serial(i)st, send an e-mail message to listserv@uvmvm.uvm.edu. Send as sole text: subscribe serialst Firstname Lastname.

6. Only a sampling can be given here. Try out Ann Ercelawn's *Tools for Serials Catalogers* at http://www.library.vanderbilt.edu/serials.html; and George Janczyn's *Technical Processing Online Tools* at http://tpot.ucsd.edu. These will provide links to many other interesting sites as well.

7. Wilma Reid Cipolla, "Users of the Brave New Catalog: Electronic Access to Periodical Articles," in *Advances in Serials Management,* vol. 4 (1993), p. 128.

8. David Cohen, "A National Networked Solution to Improving Access to Journal Articles," *Journal of Academic Librarianship* 15, no. 2 (May 1989): 79-82; "Scholarly Communication and the Role of Libraries: Problems and Possibilities for Accessing Journal Articles," *Serials Librarian* 17, no. 3/4 (1990): 43-48.

9. The serials pioneer: North Carolina State University's Mr. Serials system, created by Eric Morgan. Its highlight for catalogers is the hypertext link embedded in the catalog record leading directly to the issue archive. With a Web browser, access http://www.lib.ncsu.edu/mrserials.html, search t=alawon or t=pacs review.

10. Andrew Osborn, *Serial Publications,* 3rd ed., rev. (Chicago: American Library Association, 1980), pp. 217-218.

11. Osborn, *Serial Publications,* p. 218.

12. Osborn, *Serial Publications,* p. 213.

13. Michael Buckland, "Bibliography, Library Records, and the Redefinition of the Library Catalog," *Library Resources and Technical Services* 32, no. 4 (Oct. 1988): 306.

14. Buckland, "Bibliography, Library Records," 308.

15. Jennifer Younger, "Virtual Support: Evolving Technical Services," in *The Virtual Library* (Westport, CT: Meckler, 1993), pp. 81-82.

16. Walt Crawford and Michael Gorman, *Future Libraries: Dreams, Madness, and Reality* (Chicago: American Library Association), 1995, p. 7.

17. Osborn, *Serial Publications,* p. 71.

18. Osborn, *Serial Publications,* p. 216.

19. Walt Crawford, *MARC for Library Use* (Boston: G.K. Hall, 1989), p. 3.

20. Crawford, *MARC,* p. 263.

21. *Cataloging Service Bulletin* (Washington, D.C.: Library of Congress Cataloging Distribution Service).

22. *Library of Congress Rule Interpretations,* 2nd ed. (Washington, D.C. : Library of Congress, Cataloging Distribution Service, 1989-).

23. *USMARC Format for Bibliographic Data, Including Guidelines for Content Designation* (Washington, D.C.: Library of Congress, Cataloging Distribution Servoce, 1994).

24. *Bibliographic Formats and Standards* (Dublin, OH: OCLC, 1994).

25. Crystal Graham, "What's Wrong with AACR2" (draft), forthcoming in the 1995 *Proceedings* of the American Library Association Annual Conference.

26. Mary Monson, "The Use of RLIN in Serials Cataloging," *Serials Librarian* 12, no. 1/2 (1987): 163-165.

27. Sheila Intner, *Interfaces: Relationships Between Library Technical and Public Services* (Englewood, CO: Libraries Unlimited, 1993), pp. 77-87.

28. Joseph Puccio, *Serials Reference* (Englewood, CO: Libraries Unlimited, 1989), p. 186.

29. See, for example, *Title Varies* 1, no. 1 (Dec. 1, 1973)-6, no. 3/5 (Dec. 1980). For a (belated) rebuttal, see Carol Monroe Foggin, "Title Changes, Another View," *Serials Librarian* 23, no. 1/2 (1992): 71-83.

30. International Conference on Cataloguing Principles, Paris, 1961, *Report* (London: Organizing Committee of the ICCP, National Central Library, 1963).

31. Charles A. Cutter, *Rules for a Dictionary Catalog,* 4th ed., rewritten (Washington, D.C., Government Printing Office, 1904), p. 59.

32. Marjorie Flaspeter and Linda Lomker, "Earliest Online...," *Serials Review* 11, no. 2 (Summer 1985): 63-70.

33. Jim Cole, "The First Shall Be Last: Earliest Entry Cataloging," *Serials Librarian* 11, no. 1 (Sept. 1986): 5-14.

34. Priscilla Andre, et. al., "Serials Control in an Online Integrated System: Can Latest Entry Cataloging Help?" *Cataloging and Classification Quarterly* 7, no. 2 (Winter 1986): 39-53.

35. Mary M. Case, et. al., "Rules for Latest entry Cataloging: Northwestern University Library Supplement to AACR2," *Cataloging and Classification Quarterly* 9, no. 2 (Winter 1988): 41-49.

36. Mary M. Case and Kevin M. Randall, "Latest Entry Cataloging Locally and Nationwide: Some Observations," *Serials Librarian* 22, no. 1/2 (1992): 336-338.

37. Beth Reuland, "Successive Entry: Another Look," *Serials Review* 9 (Fall 1983): 92-99.

38. Günter Franzmeier, "Multiplication of Serial Titles Forever?" *Serials Librarian* 12, no. 1/2 (1987): 72, Endnote 3.

39. Melissa M. Bernhardt [Beck], "Dealing with Serial Title Changes: Some Theoretical and Practical Considerations," *Cataloging and Classification Quarterly* 9, no. 2 (1988): 25-39.

40. Robert Alan, "Linking Successive Entries Based Upon the OCLC Number, ISSN, or LCCN," *Library Resources and Technical Services* 37, no. 4 (Oct. 1993): 403-413.

41. Mitch L. Turitz, "Uniform Titles for Serials: The Controversy Continues," *Serials Review* 16, no. 1 (Spring 1990): 85-89.

42. Günter Franzmeier, "Multiplication," 63-72.

43. Jim Cole, "Key Title and the Entry of Serials," *Cataloging and Classification Quarterly* 10, no. 3 (1990): 45-47.

44. Jim Cole, "ISDS: The Unfinished Revolution," in *Advances in Serials Management*, vol. 4, p. 85.

45. Osborn, *Serial Publications,* p. 454.

46. A broader use of this subdivision in order to set off all types of serials is under discussion by CONSER, according to Crystal Graham, who kindly forwarded information to the author.

47. Crystal Graham, electronic mail message to the author, 5/16/95, quoting Ralph Manning at the Library of Congress.

48.   Almost all information in this section was found in Crystal Graham, "Microform Reproductions and Multiple Versions:" U.S. Cataloging Policy and Proposed Changes," *Serials Librarian* 22, no. 1/2 (1992): 213-234.

49.   *Guidelines for Bibliographic Description of Reproductions* (Chicago: American Library Association, 1995).

50.   Kathy Carter, et. al., "Bulk Loading of Records for Microform Sets Into the Online Catalog," *Cataloging and Classification Quarterly* 13, no. 3/4 (1991): 201-209.

51.   Todd Butler, *The Newspaper Cataloging and Union Listing Manual* (Washington, D.C.: Cataloging Distribution Service, Library of Congress, 1990).

52.   Butler, *Manual*, p. 58.

53.   Gail McMillan, "Embracing the Electronic Journal: One Library's Plan," *Serials Librarian* 21, no. 2/3 (1991): 97-108.

54.   Marlene Manoff, et al., "Report of the Electronic Journals Task Force, MIT Libraries," *Serials Review* 18, no. 1/2 (1992): 113-127.

55.   Marlene Manoff, et al., "The MIT Libraries Electronic Journals Project: Reports on Patron Access and Technical Processing," *Serials Review* 19, no. 3 (1993): 23-24.

56.   Manoff, "Report of the Electronic Journals Task Force," p. 118.

57.   An electronic copy of *Guidelines for the 856 Field* may be obtained by sending an electronic mail message to listserv@loc.gov with the sole text GET 856 GUIDELINES. Alternately, gopher to Marvel (marvel@loc.gov) and follow path: Libraries and Publishers—Technical Services/ Cataloging at the Library of Congress—Programs and Services/Library of Congress Cataloging Policy and Practice.

58.   Priscilla Caplan, "Cataloging Internet Resources," *Public Access Computer Systems Review* 4, no. 2 (1993): 61-66.

59.   To subscribe (Intercat): send an e-mail message to listserv@oclc.org. Send as sole text: subscribe intercat Firstname Lastname.

60.   To subscribe (VPIEJ-L): send to listserv@vtvm1.vt.edu the sole message: subscribe vpiej-l Firstname Lastname.

61.   *USMARC Format for Bibliographic Data Including Guidelines for Content Designation* (Washington, D.C.: Library of Congress, Cataloging Distribution Service, 1988) now revised and reissued (1994).

62.   Susan Matson, "Series Authority Control," in *Projects and Procedures for Serials Administration* (New York: Pierian Press, 1985), pp. 125-179.

Chapter 11

MANAGING SERIAL HOLDINGS

Frieda B. Rosenberg

USES OF SERIAL HOLDINGS[1]

Few libraries with serial collections can get along without some record of their holdings. This record has many potential uses. It shows the public what parts of each title are available in the library, how to find them, sometimes even how to use them. It can form the basis of a report which, combined with reports on the same serial from other libraries and mounted on a union list, can be consulted by users in an entire region or even beyond. In addition, like the bibliographic record, it is needed in many functions of serials management.

In previous chapters of this book, the reader may have noted the resources and planning needed for selecting, acquiring, and cataloging serials, and for automating these operations. Libraries can benefit from the years of intensive focus and analysis that have been devoted to these tasks, and take advantage of the many forms of guidance available. By contrast, there is much less documentation, uniformity in practice, or understanding of concepts on the part of most library administrators, to assist the planner of the provision, maintenance and sharing of serial holdings.

Belatedly, in the last fifteen years, there have been two successively developed, modestly sized standards in the United States for the display of serial holdings: the ANSI (American National Standards Institute) standard Z39.42 (1980), for holdings at the summary level;[2] and its replacement, Z39.44 (1986), for holdings statements including both the summary and detailed levels.[3] These were followed by ANSI/NISO Z39.57 (1989), for non-serial holdings statements.[4] The forthcoming ANSI Z39.71 (if approved) will combine the serial and non-serial display standards.

In addition, there has been for ten years a MARC format, now called *MARC Format for Holdings Data*[5] a communication standard which covers serials and other formats. It provides for local, regional or national-level automated transmission of holdings information. (Like the bibliographic standard, it is, where implemented, widely used also as a format for storage of data within systems.) This standard is, like other MARC documentation, published in looseleaf with occasional updates. It is often called "MFHD" or simply MFH. MFH has been implemented on relatively few systems, however, and even fewer of those implementations are at all complete, as attested by a non-show of hands at the American Library Association Convention in June 1995.[6]

The holdings display and communication standards bear roughly the same relation to each other as the Anglo-American cataloging rules and the MARC bibliographic format. Unlike those bibliographic standards, holdings standards were designed with serials foremost in mind. Still, there is a great deal of uncertainty about what adopting holdings standards would mean to individual libraries where they are not fully followed, not fully available, or not available at all. Libraries are concerned about costs, system functionality, obligations of individual libraries in recording data, training, integration of older data, user satisfaction, and the effects of standards on all the tasks which depend on holdings maintenance.

Most libraries agree that in an automated system, automating the serial holdings makes sense. Manual maintenance of holdings is time-consuming, and, especially as serials collections grow, hard to keep up to date. Online bibliographic serial records will get little use if the user has to go somewhere else for the holdings. If the former are going to be in the catalog, the latter should be too. Inclusion of holdings fulfills the expectations of users that they will find essential access information in one place.

But further steps, such as giving holdings in full detail and in full accordance with standards, or sharing them with other institutions, may not be so readily perceived as beneficial. Evidence is hard to gather where neither the data nor the means to transmit the data may yet be at hand, and cooperative efforts among all sectors are lagging. It may be harder to make the case to library administrators, and (in a vicious circle) it will be harder to persuade vendors to design the programs that will make full compliance possible. For most libraries, the following proposition still needs to be demonstrated: In moving toward fully integrated systems, the inclusion of standard coded serial holdings in the system (preferably cooperatively developed, like bibliographic records) will eventually have a beneficial impact on serial and monographic acquisitions, circulation, inventory, preservation, ILL, resource sharing, remote searching, and the addition of article databases to the OPAC.

If early forecasts still hold, that prospect of system integration, cooperative database building and remote communication makes holdings not only worthy of more attention than they are getting now from researchers, system designers, utilities and national bodies, but actually full of exciting new possibilities. These are visible even as we struggle with inflexible, non-standard holdings modules, obscure documentation, non-integrated functions all in need of holdings, and our own incomplete retrospective data.

DIFFERENT FILES FOR DIFFERENT USES

Levels of Detail

As serials on active subscription or standing order come into the library, most may be received and recorded in a central file; others—documents, newsletters, gifts—may come directly from a publisher or other contact to a specific area of the library without passing through the central control. Most of those may then be forwarded there; some may not be. Recording, traditionally done on cards, is increasingly being done in an automated serial control system or integrated system. The result of this recording is an issue-by-issue holdings record—a *detailed holdings record*. The record of receipt in manual files can be held indefinitely if there is space for it. On an automated system, the time limits may be different. The issue receipts may be merged, for example, when the binding or cataloging function is run, and the entire record of receipt may either be consolidated or moved off the system altogether for reasons of disk space or cost of record storage.

The binding process generates another record. In many libraries, there is a central serials binding unit. In a manual system, a record is kept on specialized binding cards, on a shelflist, or in a public serials catalog or other file. In some automated systems, binding information updates and consolidates the check-in record. In libraries with decentralized binding operations at each holding location, there may be a file at each holding location and no centralized file at all. There are thus many different circumstances. The end result of most of them—either in addition to the issue-level records or as a replacement for them—is volume-by-volume holdings records—*holdings records at the physical piece level.*

It may surprise some serialists today to know that the part of the serial catalog card now used for a record of what was published, that is, the numbering and dates of the serial, was in the early days assigned to "Local holdings." This area on catalog cards had blank spaces where library holdings could be pencilled in. Since there was not much space in that area, this kind of notation was summarized, often ending with a hyphen in the case of serials on subscription or standing order. This was a form of *holdings records at the summary level.*

For reasons of staff time, space and complexity, summary holdings disappeared from public catalog cards long before public card catalogs themselves began to vanish. Card notations were succeeded by typed lists, and those made way in the 1970s for computer-output paper printouts and microfiche. In these lists, as on cards, space considerations and difficulty of updating limited the amount of detail that could be given. A typical holdings printout might give the following information:

JOURNAL OF SOAPBOX ORATORY
MAIN LIB 1 1963 (2) 1964 3- 1965-

This information can be translated as follows: Main Library has the first volume, an incomplete second volume, and the third and all following volumes of the *Journal of Soapbox Oratory*. Notice the absence of captions (no equivalent for "vol." or "v."). Placement of numeration vs. dates could vary. Some libraries opted for putting all numeration first, followed by all dates.

Some libraries did not even note an incomplete volume 2, but simply stated the holdings for the public as 1- 1963-. Other libraries could give more information, such as 1 1963 2 NO 4-6 1964 3- 1965-. It all depended; it was left up to the library.

More importantly, however, different files of holdings were accumulating: on the check-in record, on the binding record, and in many libraries, on the back of the shelflist to be consistent with the way monographic holdings were recorded. If a library were also reporting to a union list, and perhaps beginning to input a computerized record for a printout or COM file, there was considerable duplication and reduplication of effort going on.

Of course, there were different emphases in the different files. The type of holdings most common for public display was the summary, in terms of unbroken ranges interspersed with gaps (notation of incomplete volumes, as stated, being optional). Summary holdings were used in local lists and union lists. They could be extremely rough to fairly detailed. Usually, even at their most detailed, they did not show checked-in issues or physical volumes. Thus the automation of serial holdings began with a dilemma: wouldn't ALL these holdings forms, all necessary for different functions, have to be automated? And if so, would they require separate processes to input? Was there any way to coordinate them so that one holdings file could serve all purposes?

Public Use of Holdings

In the past, users approached holdings from the record or listing of the serial title; nowadays they may be taking a direct route from an article citation. This vantage point can alter dramatically the expectations of the public for holdings information. In a printed periodical index, a user locates specific references or browses by subject. Issue and page citations to serial publications have to be jotted down, then matched against a list or catalog of titles with library holdings in another manual or automated file, where a shelf location must also be sought. The relevant issues are then retrieved at their physical location, and read, or copied for later reading. As millions of students can testify, these laborious tasks are time-honored exemplars of library use. Online and CD-ROM indexes have brought remarkable new dimensions to index searching in the form of sophisticated term matching, browsing by keystrokes, instantaneous downloading and printing. But even today, in many libraries, the ease vanishes on leaving the CD-ROM or electronic search workstation. To escape the extra step of looking up the serial title in the catalog, many users take their chances at the shelves. But libraries have never had the luxury of assuring their users that the entire run of any, much less of each and every serial publication in the catalog will be immediately and uniformly available. Not only are there gaps in runs in even the best-funded library, but there are a number of things libraries do with issues that may delay their getting to the shelf or remove them from it for a substantial time: shelving in a current-issues area; sending to a bindery; sending to be repaired; loaning to another library branch; loaning to a patron; sending to be microfilmed for preservation purposes.

Therefore even annotating a periodical index with a pencilled check mark or call number for those titles the library owns (a job often done by reference staff) was no guarantee that any particular issue in an index citation will be owned, or if owned, found on the shelf. Similarly, it is possible to annotate the source journal list on many article databases with local holdings so that these will show up whenever an owned title appears during an article search. Usually, though, there is space for only a few characters or digits—not enough to give full details on a run with many gaps. No more attractive is the prospect of keying the same information into each vendor's program—and then watching out for changes in the information, which then must be entered, as well, into each database. Not surprisingly, some services give libraries the option of stating only, "Library may have this article. Consult [source of holdings] for details."

A small but increasing number of online systems use the interconnective power of the computer to produce a direct and transparent link between an external article database and the holdings screen of the serial record, as does NOTIS's MDAS (Multiple Database Access) system.[7] This link operates through the International Standard Serial Number (ISSN) of the serial. There are also add-on data management programs which libraries have used to enable different databases to "hook to" the serial holdings: an example is Stanford's SPIRES.[8] For any "hook" to work, of course, the database must be mounted alongside the OPAC or on a computer server which has direct communication with the OPAC server.

Thus, in library networks, the OPAC and all of its attached systems are gradually becoming, as they once were, places to look for articles as well as for serial titles. And this is good news—if after finding a citation, it is possible to tell in short order that the article is available. Users who go from a citation to holdings want the display and status of the particular issue they were seeking. What is usually displayed to them is the entire holdings for the serial, with or without data on the availability of particular volumes.

While the serial bibliographic record is at least based on a "national" level record, implying that the bibliographic data will be the same in every place the serial is held, serial holdings have always been considered "local," implying that they could vary from place to place. We have already seen some variations. In a sense, variation is only a matter of perspective; if holdings are viewed in the sense of of world holdings—which equal the universe of what has been published under that serial title—the variation disappears. This perception of holdings as local information may have delayed the attempt to standardize the display.

STANDARDS

The ANSI Holdings Standards for Content and Display

Z39.42. The first U.S. standards did not attempt to provide for all uses of serial holdings. Many of our earliest online holdings systems, as well as some of our paper and microform products, were built on the basis of the standards defined in Z39.42 (1980), for serial summary holdings, begun in 1975 by Subcommittee 40 of Committee Z39—the library and information standards committee—of the American National Standards Institute. The standards claim to "define the data elements to be included by libraries, information centers, and other institutions when they record and report serial holdings statements to union lists at the local, statewide, regional, or national level" (Foreword, p. 3.).

The Subcommittee defined three levels for reporting data. At any level, the holdings display must be linked to a serial identifier, which may be, for example, an ISSN, a CODEN, or a bibliographic description. At Level 1, only the institution or collection code was mandatory; Level 2 added a date of report and codes to show roughly how complete the holdings were and whether the title was currently received and retained. Actual *enumeration* and *chronology* (the serial's numbering and dates) were included only at the highest level (Level 3). This was the first standard to enjoin "positive reporting only," that is, only statements of what was held, not what was missing.

Enumeration and chronology as set by Z39.42 recalled the "rough" holdings style of the manual era. Enumeration data had no *captions* (such as v., t., or no.). Only the highest level of data was included in either enumeration or chronology (exception was made only for cases of ambiguity). That is, for a publication consisting of volumes with numbers within the volumes, the report would not include information below the volume level. Gaps were reported, at the volume level only, when 50 percent or more of the bibliographic units in a volume were missing. For example, if one or two issues were missing from a volume whose issues were published quarterly, the volume was reported as though it were complete; if three were missing, it was reported as not held. No provision was made for recording of supplements and indexes. This standard also set the meaning of certain punctuation, most of which would be carried over to later standards: hyphens, slashes, colons, semicolons, and question marks all had specific meaning. Here is an example of enumeration and chronology at the summary level, Level 3 (the highest level):

Copy 3 1,3-8,12/13;15- 1950,1952-1957,1961;1963-

In this statement, all the enumeration is grouped, followed by all the dates. Vols. 2 and 9 are reported lacking (though conceivably less than half of each may be owned), but 14 was never published; more than half (at least) of each of the other volumes is held; Vols. 12 and 13 were published as one volume; the title is still being received.

The standard allowed copy-specific information at the local level to be reported with all copy information combined at the institutional level—to a union list, for example. This kind of reporting was called "composite" holdings (combining all copies) (Section 5.3 and Table 3).

An important generator of many union listing products in various on- and off-line formats, OCLC's Union Listing Subsystem, adopted Z39.42 conventions for its Local Data Records. These were and are used widely for resource sharing and interlibrary loan. OCLC did not adopt the standard which supplanted this one, Z39.44 (1986), until 1994, and continues to host the older Z39.42 data.

Z39.44. While the first Subcommittee was still working, a second Subcommittee (Subcommittee E) started working on a standard for detailed serial holdings. As it became evident that the detailed standard would conflict with the summary one, the Subcommittee was asked to establish a standard that combined all levels of reporting. This is often called the NISO holdings standard, since the ANSI Z39 committee that drew up both standards became NISO (the National Information Standards Organization) in 1983.[9] NISO SC E was asked to define data suitable for check-in systems as well as for reporting to union lists, and to allow for the derivation of summary holdings statements from the detailed level. In this work the Subcommittee had to coordinate its decisions with other bodies, including SC 40 (author of Z39.42), and the unrelated group working simultaneously on the MARC format for holdings.

The NISO standard, Z39.44, redefined the lower three levels of reporting with additional data elements, and added a fourth level, that of detailed reporting at the issue level. The "status data" was now called "general holdings data," and contained codes for holdings type, acquisition status, retention policy, completeness. At Level 3, the lowest level which contained specific enumeration data, captions were now required where such captions appeared on the publication (Section 4.6.1.3.). Gaps were defined differently, too; in a summary statement, a holding was to be recorded if any part of a volume was held (Section 7.2.4.). Data in a summary statement was to be recorded using one of two options: each numeric element followed by its corresponding chronological element in parentheses (Option A), or all numeration followed by all chronology (Option B). (Section 4.6.) Composite holdings statements at Level 3 could now include a combination of print and microform holdings.

In 1994, OCLC adopted Z39.44 at Level 3 as its union listing standard, using Option B. The display at this level is close to the previous, Z39.42 display, with the addition of captions. A greater difference between this data and the former data is that a volume is now reported if any of the volume is held, instead of only when 50 percent or more is held.

In the standard itself, the greatest change was that at the new fourth level, holdings now could be recorded as they would be checked in in a serials control system. The Foreword to the standard (p. 3) states the intent to provide for this new use. Level Four required each volume number, and so forth to be followed immediately by its chronological designation (year, etc.—there were no options as at Level 3); it also forbade open-ended holdings like those permitted in Level 3 (Section 8.3.4.) Supplements and indexes constituting separate volumes were now provided for, at least within the detailed fourth level of recording. A statement of numeration and chronology for basic units from the last page of examples in the Standard's Appendix A (Ex. A11) is presented here at Levels 3 (both options) and 4:

Level 3, Option A: no.4(1954)-no.9(1957)
Level 3, Option B: no.4-no.9 1954-1957
Level 4: no.4(1954:May)-no.9(1957:Mar.)

The derivation of "detailed summary" statements, that is, summary statements at Level 4, from detailed data—for example, check-in data—is done by compressing data. Compression may be performed only as long as no gap exists at any level. Compressed holdings are statements that have intermediate levels and/or ranges omitted. A compressed statement (say, of a monthly publication) could look exactly like a Level 3, Option A statement:

Uncompressed: v.1:no.1(1991:Jan.)-v.1:no.12(1991:Dec.)
  Compressed: v.1(1991)

but unlike the latter, a compressed Level 4 statement certifies that holdings are complete within the range specified.[10] In order to avoid ambiguities concerning which level is being reported, sometimes one must invent the means. One union list with massive amounts of retrospective data that could not be filled out in detail distinguished the latter by the use of Level 3, Option B, ending up with a mixed format in the database, but a clear key to the meaning of the data.[11]

Libraries examining the standard may find some parts of it questionable, particularly for local purposes. The NISO statement is at its best when holdings can be expressed in compressed form. When many gaps, particularly gaps within volumes, require each volume to be given in several statements full of repetition and punctuation marks, we reach that nadir where both the information provider and the information seeker have extra labor. It is especially difficult when local requirements demand that the holdings be given in terms of physical volumes, because the long string simply does not look like a volume:

Z39.44, Level 4: v.1:no.1(1991:Jan.)-v.1:no.3(1991:Mar.),v.1:no.6
    (1991:Jun.)-v.1:no.8(1991:Aug.),v.1:no.10(1991:Oct)-v.1,no.12(1991:Dec.),

could be expressed more simply and legibly as: v.1, no.1-3,6-8,10-12(1991:Jan.-Mar., Jun.-Aug.,Oct.-Dec.) (or just 1991). It is possible to encode fully, but choose a modified display, as will be explained below.

The USMARC Format for Holdings Data

The development of a MARC format for holdings began with a group of eight research libraries[12] within the Association of Southeastern Research Libraries (ASERL). They desired to improve the communication of serial holdings information for purposes of collection development, resource sharing, and interlibrary loan. In October 1981, the group obtained a Title II-C grant to develop a machine-readable database to show regional strengths and gaps in current serial holdings.[13] At an early point, the group envisioned a standard in the form of a machine-readable (MARC) format. Several years of work involved common input into a regional holdings database (LAMBDA) designed by contract with SOLINET (the regional OCLC network), and increasing cooperation with the ANSI Z39.44 committee, with the Library of Congress, and with ALA's MARBI committee. In the end, though the shared database did not continue, the group produced a communications vehicle and standard for machine-readable representation of the data in holdings statements which was implemented, with variations, in their separate databases. A first edition of the documentation was produced in 1984. The revised and expanded edition in use today is called the *USMARC Format for Holdings Data, Including Guidelines for Content Designation (1989)*.

The format covers both serial and non-serial bibliographic items (*Introduction*, p. v.) After specifically relating the content designation to the serial and non-serial display standards, the introduction states: "Other *USMARC Holdings* content designators allow the potential of using the format to interface with such automated control systems as union catalog, serials check-in, and interlibrary loan systems." With the second update (July 1994), the *Format* also maintains a data structure for the management and communication of data about physical items (e.g., volumes) separate from the data structure for display.

It is one of the purposes of this chapter to give an overview of serials- related functions of this format, and highlight enough features to give serialists a good basis to evaluate whether a given implementation is likely to provide the necessary benefits.[14]

Structure. The holdings format echoes previous formats in its basic structure: leader, directory, control and data fields. An array of *tags* (field identifiers), *indicators* (limiting definitions and signalling potential ways to manipulate data) and *subfield codes* (subdividing fields into pieces of significant information) organize the data for formatting in local or union list systems. This structure, however, is distinctive in the great complexity and interdependency of the information it tries to convey by means of these codes, which leave a great deal of work to individual implementations. It presents an economy of means, with some new features such as *paired fields* containing constant data and variable data that must be presented together. The format is very tightly constructed, so that a non-working feature or piece of missing data can have real impact. For example, the importance of indicators for manipulating and changing the display of the data (e.g., suppressing some fields in favor of others) may represent a special challenge for system designers.

The format can be used at four levels which coordinate with the NISO standards, giving an increasingly specific report of holdings. One code identifies the encoding level. Others provide the "general holdings" data of the NISO standards, and a few more define the holdings statement and policies particularly applicable to union listing or to interlibrary loan.

The format is designed to be either separate or embedded in the bibliographic record. The latter is not possible for serials with multiple locations or call numbers if location-specific piece holdings fields—or any similar data—are present. Location and shelf number are reported in an 852 field, which can also contain general notes for either staff or public.

For actual enumeration and chronology, two structures exist. The most specific consists of the "paired fields," 853/863, 854/864, and 855/865. The first of each pair encodes captions along with other details. The second encodes actual enumeration and chronology data and may carry piece-specific notes. The three sets of pairs are used for "basic bibliographic units" (e.g., volumes), supplements, and indexes. These fields are subfielded to define each part of the holding, and are linked to each other by a special subfield, $8, which contains a link number. Each line of holdings data repeats the link number and adds to it a sequence number. Changes in the caption definition or

Current review.

852   ELXI ≠b 1111 ≠h AP2 ≠i .C9

853 00 ≠8 3 ≠a v. ≠b no. ≠i (year) ≠j (month)

853 00 ≠8 4 ≠a n.s., v. ≠b no. ≠i (year) ≠j (month)

854 00 ≠8 4 ≠a v. ≠i (year)

863 40 ≠8 3.1 ≠a 1-10 ≠i 1974-1983

863 40 ≠8 3.2 ≠a 2 ≠b 1 ≠i 1984 ≠j Mar.

863 40 ≠8 4.1 ≠a 1-4 ≠i 1985-1988

864 40 ≠8 4.2 ≠a 1 ≠i 1987

Current review.

Exum Library—Main Stacks Call no.: AP2.C9

Holdings:

    v. 1 (1974)-10 (1983)

    v. 2: no. 1 (1984: Mar.)

    n.s., v. 1 (1985)-4 (1988)

    Suppl. v. 1 (1987)

Figure 11.1. USMARC Holdings Record (Location/Enumeration Portions) and Hypothetical Local Display Derived from It

publication pattern require a change in the link number, which is then repeated in the next holdings sequence. Figure 11.1 shows a sample (simplified) USMARC format holdings record (the location and enumeration portions) and resulting hypothetical, modified NISO Z39.44 local display. Details will vary depending on the local system.

A second option is to use *free-text holdings* fields 866/87/88. Here captions and enumeration/chronology are both present in each field. Free-text fields are often used for retrospective holdings, especially when complete information is lacking. Such holdings might be encoded at Level 3. Paired fields encoded at Level 4 can be used in the same record for current receipts. For serials no longer received, free-text holdings are often used by themselves, and are very typically used when converting holdings data into the MARC format from a non-MARC display. A third way of using free-text holdings is more complex: when paired fields do not provide an optimal display, they can be set by means of indicators to be suppressed, and the free-text fields can be used to give the same data in a form more appropriate for display.

It should be kept in mind that free-text fields are, as Priscilla Caplan put it, "basically inert, and can only be reformatted with extensive technical analysis."[15] However, if the local system (such as NOTIS at this writing) does not yet create a display from paired fields, they are untestable. When results are undisplayable and untestable, there is no immediate benefit and some long-term risk in the intensive labor required in double input. Free-text fields used alone are then a reasonable alternative.

Functions

1. Order and Check-in—Detailed Holdings. In order to serve the acquisition function, the serials control and order system must have direct access to the MFH data. If the implementation supports it, *publication pattern data* embedded in the 853 field of the MFH record can be accessed to predict the next issue and update the summary generated as the issue is received. Publication pattern is the term specified, but never verbally defined, in MFH to cover the concepts of frequency, intervals of expected issue, numbering scheme, and so forth, that enable a library to set up a predictive check-in record and identify each arriving issue. The pattern includes codes which, at each level, define the number of issues required to make up the next higher level, plus a code to define whether the numbering restarts or is continuous, and the calendar points when publication (or nonpublication) is to be expected. Not only prediction of receipt is dependent on pattern information: automatic compression of holdings statements also depends on pattern values. There is a wide range of variations among systems which have implemented the Format. In fully integrated systems, check-in data automatically updates the total holdings file. Some systems operate without any link at all between these files. Receipt of an issue may in other systems trigger a display in a "latest issues received" area rather than in the specific holdings area, thus providing a distinction between unbound and bound holdings. Staff compress the issue data to the volume level (or higher) and transfer it from the check-in to the holdings screen at point of binding. Systems which cannot even display the full range of data to staff using either the check-in or the holdings module are bound to impede efficient workflow.

Developments long envisioned should enhance check-in functions. One is already being used on some publications: the SISAC (Serials Industry Systems Advisory Committee) barcode. The barcode, which appears on each issue, consists of the ISSN combined with specific issue numeration and date. Unfortunately for those pioneering publishers that have included SISAC barcodes on their publications, few systems yet can take advantage of them. It will be up to each system designer to incorporate a way to translate SISAC barcode information in terms of the MARC format.

The second is the ever-elusive vision of a national (or international) publication pattern database. This database of publication patterns needs a host, source of data, standards, and economic rationale. The vision is this: The pattern for each serial being received is transferred to each subscribing library's serials control system, where it predicts the next issue. Without such a database, each library must separately input pattern information. In combination with the SISAC barcode, check-in is possible by "waving a wand." The trouble with publication patterns is that they are always changing, and, since the publication pattern is the same for all libraries, the inevitable conclusion is that changes should be monitored and new patterns disseminated from one place, or at least in one action.

The third component is less often discussed: an accompanying database of actual enumeration and chronology (also unchanging data in relation to what was published or to world holdings, as has been pointed out previously).[16] Such a database would facilitate orders and make accurate holdings possible even in retrospective projects. The three together (whatever the coverage) would represent a step toward control of past and future publication data.

In libraries today, customers of certain vendors (such as Dynix) can share or even sell/purchase the publication patterns of other customers, but benefits are limited to the contracting libraries.[17] CONSER, unfortunately, specifically excludes holdings from its purview,[18] so we must create leadership in the enterprise of finding a broader approach to control.

2. Public Display of Holdings—Local or Union (Summary Holdings). As we have seen, until the 1980s approximations of holdings were the rule rather than the exception. The union list was the prime impetus to summary holdings development. The *Union List of Serials* and its successor *New Serial Titles* put their official stamp on the brief summarized notation. The need to give a broad overview of many serial collections limited the detail that could be given for any one, and the card, microfiche, and primitive online catalog had little space or sophistication for details.

In the 1990s, those who work with serials perceive a need for "full disclosure" of actual holdings. Both staff and users expect more guidance and more precision than in the past, and do not understand why the detail given for serials should not be comparable to that given for monographs. The essential tool to perform this task is the MARC holdings format with its ample space, specificity, and automatic holdings compression and expansion. The "early adopter" pioneer libraries have now been able for a decade to rely on their systems to give varying amounts of detail according to purpose, and have the means to extract their information for communication to union lists.

The effort in maintaining holdings at Level 4 is considerable and can be even more considerable if the technology does not give some assistance. Some libraries where none of this is automatic have nonetheless decided to give fully detailed, Level 4 holdings, and to work around the limitations of the system they may be using by inputting more than once at different levels of detail. And there are many more who compromise, giving Level 4 data for newer volumes, Level 3 for older holdings, or who follow Level 4 except for leaving a hyphen to indicate unbroken current receipts. There are special areas in the

MFH fixed field which permit the display of a note to inform users about special retention periods for some serials that are not permanently retained.

To be able to compress and expand, the system needs to be able to work with the pattern data to manipulate the holdings data. Automatic updating of holdings from check-in data is highly desirable; but since direct input will also be necessary, the library must evaluate the ease of entering data, the means of reviewing the coding, and the testability of the functions. A fully developed system with active paired fields and publication pattern is the only kind that is fully testable. Other desiderata for a MARC holdings implementation are:

1. ability to receive input and extract data for output in MARC format;
2. a choice of display capabilities, including but not limited to NISO;
3. ability to keep track of and move together, if necessary, the different links and sequences throughout the record for legible display of data with minimal recoding but without loss of accuracy.
4. ample space for notes and the means to enter commonly used ones by codes or shorthand;
5. a way to work with the numeric equivalents of months (1-12) and seasons (21-24) in conjunction with the language code, necessary for proper operation of the 853 (pattern portion);
6. a way to derive a correctly sequenced ordinal number display (such as 1st ed.) from field content consisting of a cardinal number (not part of MARC format);
7. ability to display free-text fields as sole holdings, in combination with fully coded holdings, or as a substitute display for fully coded holdings;
8. clear, easy-to-interpret interface to aid coders, with all relevant information from other parts of the online system readily available;
9. correct linkage with acquisition and item information;
10. GOOD DOCUMENTATION is a must!

Some systems (VTLS, in particular) are especially commendable for making a coded MFH display available to other libraries viewing their records; this will help increase understanding of the format.

3. Physical Piece Management—Volume-Level Holdings.   Often, at the time the physical volume is bound (if received unbound) and sent to permanent shelving, the library barcodes it. Since annual and non-periodical serials are often received publisher-bound or sent immediately to be bound, at least part of the collection can be barcoded almost immediately. Other formats such as microformats and electronic formats can also be barcoded on receipt, if the library barcodes such materials. Some libraries do barcode their unbound issues (and delete superfluous barcodes when they are bound), and others maintain a special array of reusable barcodes to control issues in a temporary location.

The first thing to say about barcodes is that "they're not just for circulation anymore." They can also be used to identify a piece for other purposes such as preservation or inventory. They serve as well as a copy number to distinguish copies of the same piece, so the latter maintenance-intensive piece of data is often expendable—if the system allows. Management and use of the physical piece can be monitored, and the data stored in a part of the record called the *item record*, a record for a physical as distinguished from a bibliographic item. Item records in use in many systems can store dates (of acquisition, loan, etc.), temporary locations or statuses, statistics, or other data of local importance.

The new MARC fields for item information are 876, 877, and 878.[19] As local processing data, item information was at first excluded from both editions of the holdings format (though barcodes could always be recorded in piece holding fields). Only with Update 2 (July 1994) did the new fields enter the format.

In the item fields, subfields are defined for date, source, and cost of acquisition, temporary location, item status (coded only for permanent, not temporary, changes in status), use restrictions, and various control numbers. This list contains the item information most important for resource sharing; but certainly not the complete range of information that a library might consider important for management. The purpose of the new item fields is expressly "communication of holdings information rather than local concerns" and emphasis is "on only including the information of permanent value and that is not too transaction oriented."[20] Increasingly, however, libraries are finding it necessary to coordinate circulation and other transaction data, and the statistics that result from it, with holdings. Keeping track of all this data is a challenge that library systems must to be ready to meet.

If research on holdings is hard to come by, research on item information is nearly nonexistent in the literature on serials. There is a great deal of variance in how this information is handled in online catalogs and in existing MARC holdings installations: separate and unlinked, or tied to and dependent on the individual lines of holdings. Most existing MFH implementations do not have 876-878 fields, and some system vendors will find it difficult to make any change in their present ways of handling items. It remains to be seen whether the item fields will provide a sufficiently flexible scheme. In the end, it is up to our standards committees and our libraries to explain in clear language how an implementation of the USMARC format is supposed to work, and to improve any parts of the standard that our community finds unsatisfactory. After that it is up to system designers to make the format work in all the functions—local and beyond—that it is designed to fulfill. It is a task well worth the effort: libraries will support and implement the format if they know that it will work in their individual circumstances. The system that provides an efficient means to control the various levels of holdings and to provide the needed display options will be seen as an invaluable tool for managing the collection.

ISSUES IN HOLDINGS MANAGEMENT

Multiple Formats in the Holdings Record

Earlier in this book, in the chapter on cataloging, the question of "multiple versions" was addressed. One library may hold several versions of a single serial. The holdings in each format may be complementary, or duplicative. It is crucial to collocate the holdings statements of each version lest the user go away empty-handed, unaware that the library holds the needed piece. Union lists, also, sometimes prefer the information on one title to be presented in one composite, institution-level statement rather than several statements.

In a limited way, the USMARC holdings format lends itself to a combined statement, in that several holdings records can be linked to one bibliographic record. Furthermore, the format includes two fields specifically for descriptive information about reproductions: the 007 (also defined for the bibliographic record) and the 843, which contains the same information as the 533 in the MARC bibliographic record. It is therefore possible for libraries to include under one bibliographic record the holdings for all their different versions, as sanctioned in the *Guidelines for Bibliographic Description of Reproductions,*[21] as long as the descriptive data needed for the reproduction is brief and the system can handle any necessary links between the holdings records and other modules with which they need to interact.

Virtual Holdings

Should there be holdings statements for serials which are only accessed, not owned, by the library? Most libraries have reported only on making records for those electronic serials which they have mounted or made accessible. Even check-in records have been established for such journals, and as issues are mounted, they can be added to the holdings screen.

When a library substitutes remote access for a printed resource it has cancelled, however, the problem becomes more acute. There could be at least three choices: to place a note on the holdings record for the printed form explaining the situation; to set up a separate holdings record for the electronic resource linked to the bibliographic record for the printed form, with an 856 (Electronic Location and Access) field to point to the resource (perhaps reinforced by a more user-oriented note in natural language on the holdings record); or to catalog the electronic resource, again using an 856 field in either the bibliographic or holdings record. The second option, using a multiple versions technique, has advantages in theory because it both collocates the different versions and enables some detail about the remote resource; but the answer for each library will partially depend on how the remote file will be accessed: in fact, these days, there may be several methods of accessing a single electronic file, and more than one electronic file with the same content available.

Hooks to Holdings

Citation databases mounted alongside the public catalog often lead to electronic versions of resources. When they do not, they can still point users toward available resources if they feature the ability to display local holdings on command. The "hook" in the ISSN forms a bridge to the display of location, call number, order information, and holdings. With NOTIS MDAS and a printer, a user can print a formatted citation along with holdings information from the OPAC.[22]

Even more powerful for this purpose would be the SICI (Serial Item and Contribution Identifier), which starts with the ISSN, adds issue and date information as in a SISAC barcode, and finally adds information from the article level (article title identifier). SICI data in the permanent record could be accessed to select the very line of holdings needed for display in a citation search. And perhaps we need to ask ourselves whether we could provide for specifically targeted holdings information and document retrieval by making a place for the permanent storage of that data within MARC holdings data.[23]

VIEWING THE FUTURE OF HOLDINGS

Don't give up! We are going to continue to need holdings data, and we will need it in our online systems. We sometimes avoid automation out of uncertainty, waiting "until we get a new online system," "until we get a serials check-in system," "until the holdings are cleaned up," "until we decide what kind of holdings we want." (For there are choices!) If there are available means, and especially if some kind of machine conversion is possible, it makes sense to make holdings machine-readable, even if the display must initially be a non-standard display of some kind. Careful planning helps to minimize mishaps, and sometimes it is possible to clean up during the process (if it isn't, cleanup is usually easier once the holdings are automated.) To make later migration easier, all information should be categorized, and the categories distinguished by coding, especially the actual holdings themselves.

When we then implement holdings standards, we must educate ourselves to use them correctly. In doing so, we should push for clarification, unambiguous interpretation of the standards, and the widest possible distribution of expertise. Only after this is done can we demand from everyone equal attention to that given our bibliographic standards.

Holdings are multipurpose data. The goal of the holdings manager and serials staff should be to minimize variance from the original intent, minimize the need to duplicate data in different places, and maximize the data's usefulness and intelligibility. As professionals, we must work with other librarians, our bibliographic utilities, our local system vendors, our contacts in the publishing industry, and our library organizations to promote the use of standards and to test them reciprocally to make sure they continue to work. And since our changing environment is the context against which they must work, the testing never really ends.

NOTES

1. The author is grateful to Linda Visk of Emory University for her kindness and her time in aiding research about the early stages of serials holdings standards development, especially the MARC Format project in which she was involved.

2. *American National Standard for Serial Holdings at the Summary Level* (New York: American National Standards Institute, 1980).

3. *American National Standard for Information Sciences. Serial Holdings Statements* (New York: American National Standards Institute, 1986).

4. *American National Standard for Holdings Statements for Non-Serial Items (ANSI/NISO Z39.57-1989)* (New York: Transaction Publishers, 1989).

5. *USMARC Format for Holdings Data, Including Guidelines for Content Designation* (Washington, DC: Library of Congress, Cataloging Distribution Service, 1989-).

6. *MARC Format for Holdings Data: An Implementation Status Report by Local System Vendors & Utilities,* joint LITA/ALCTS/MARBI meeting at ALA Annual Conference (tape transcription), June 30, 1995.

7. Mary H. Monson, "The NOTIS Opac and Serials: The University of Iowa Experience," *Serials Librarian* 22, no. 1/2 (1992): 163.

8. S. Manojlovich, "Mounting Commercial Databases Using the SPIRES DBMS," *Public-Access Computer Systems Review* 1, no. 3 (1990): 51-57.

9. Mary Ellen Clapper, "Standards for Serials," *Serials Review* 12, no. 2/3 (summer/fall 1986): 122.

10. Marjorie E. Bloss, "The New! The Improved! Standard for Serial Holdings Statements," *Library Resources and Technical Services* 31, no. 1 (Jan. 1987): 30.

11. Judith M. Brugger, "How the NISO Holdings Standard Works: The Findings of an Investigation at CUNY, 1989," *Serials Librarian* 20, no. 2/3 (1991): 20-22.

12. Emory University, University of Florida, Florida State University, University of Georgia, University of Kentucky, University of Miami, University of Tennessee, Virginia Polytechnic & State University.

13. Nolan F. Pope, "Developing a Format for Holdings and Location Data," *USMARC Format for Holdings and Locations: Development, Implementation, and Use* (New York: Haworth,, 1988), pp. 3-6.

14. The author acknowledges great indebtedness to Gail McMillan's *Coded Holdings Manual: Applications of the USMARC Format for Holdings at University Libraries, Virginia Polytechnic Institute and State University,* 3rd ed., 1993. though it is based on VTLS's implementation of USMARC holdings, which is itself based on the first edition of the standard, since altered, the *Manual* goes a great part of the way to provide an unambiguous interpretation of many of the codes.

15. Priscilla Caplan, "Implementation of USMARC Format for Holdings and Locations at the Harvard University Library," *The USMARC Format for Holdings and Locations: Development, Implementation, and Use,* ed. Barry B. Baker (New York: Haworth, 1988), p. 63.

16. Mary Ann Van Cura, "A Step Beyond Shared Patterns: A Shared Holdings Record Database," *Serials Review* 17, no. 3 (fall 1991): 72-73.

17. Ed Riding, speaking for Ameritech in *MARC Format for Holdings Data: An Implementation Status Report by Local System Vendors & Utilities,* LITA / ALCTS / MARBI joint meeting at ALA Annual Convention, June 30, 1995 (tape transcription).

18. Bill Anderson, "History of the CONSER Project," *Serials Review* 21, no. 2 (summer 1995): 3.

19. *MARBI Proposal 92-21: Addition of Fields 876-878 (Item Information) to the USMARC Holdings Format.* Available in the Library of Congress MARVEL archive (gopher:// marvel@loc.gov); also available by sending an e-mail message to listserv@maine.maine.edu, with message GET 92-21 DOC as sole text. Previous proposals centered around a separate format are recorded in *Discussion Paper No. 48: Considerations for an Item Level Record Format* in the same archive.

20. Ibid., sec. 1, Introduction.

21. *Guidelines for Bibliographic Description of Reproductions* (Chicago: American Library Association, 1995).

22. "NOTIS Links Library Holdings with Locally-Mounted Database Records," *Public-Access Computer Systems News* 1, no. 9 (Sept. 6, 1990).

23. "Serials Industry Systems Advisory Committee," [fact sheet]; available on Faxon web server; access http://www.faxon.com and link to section: Library and Publishing Standards.

Chapter 12

PRESERVING LIBRARY SERIALS

Preserving library serials is not the same as preserving books. Most serials are not rare, they are not encased in fine bindings, and they are not published in editions. Preserving library serials is nearly always a matter of finding a correct balance between accessibility and security, so that library patrons may locate the information they are seeking.

Preparing for use and housing are pre-preservation steps. Librarians differ in the ways they prepare materials for patron use. In some libraries, unbound journal issues are ready with only an ownership stamp; in others, new issues show classification number on a label or replace older issues inside tough plastic covers. Good preservation practice is doing as little as possible in the way of marking and labelling unbound journals. Some libraries house unbound, single-piece volumes in the book stacks alongside bound materials; others would not consider such treatment. Whatever the policy, shelve volumes upright and support them with a bookend. Shelve unbound issues flat or upright and supported.

Preserving library serials consists of three aspects—binding, retaining in another format, and security—and it encompasses the various functions of serials management. Preservation is, first, a collection development responsibility; it also depends on network relationships and cooperative agreements; it influences the selection of options in acquiring and cataloging; and finally, it determines the means of access for serials.

Before the 1960s most librarians practiced one type of serials preservation: binding. They combined loose journal issues in a buckram, cloth, or cardboard volume and protected single-piece paperbound volumes with more substantial covers. Then, with growing space and money problems came the popularity of microforms and later compact discs. Later some librarians became more concerned with binding and some with microform or electronic format. The emphasis depends upon the local policy for retention of serial backfiles. During the 1970s librarians recognized a number of new ways to preserve their collections; these included selecting the appropriate type of microform, studying the acidity of paper, using electronic security systems, and developing disaster-response plans and preservation standards. Disaster response plans are beyond the scope of this chapter; suffice it to say that serials are as susceptible to bugs and mildew, fire and water as other library materials.

A library should coordinate its policy concerning preservation of resources with other aspects of collection development so that the written statement reflects the purpose of the library. For example, a branch of a public library system may restrict its funds to current serials, because the main library can supply older volumes when they are needed. A research library needs both current and retrospective serials in the fields in which its patrons are working, so a portion of its materials and equipment budget must be dedicated to preservation, including preparation, storage, and security.

A selector should evaluate each subscription and standing order in terms of the collection development policy to determine what is retained and in what format. When the selector decides as part of the ordering process, no titles are retained or discarded without evaluation. The decision can also be made or reviewed as part of precataloging procedures. The advantage to the latter practice is that the selector has recent issues in hand. Factors to consider in the retention decision are, in part, those used for initial purchase, discussed in Chapter 5.

Few libraries can finance the optimum degree of preservation and must reach a balance between acquiring and preserving. Not all preservation costs can be isolated in budgeting. The decision to purchase an item in alkaline paper or on silver halide microfilm instead of vesicular may add hidden costs to the subscription. Preservation is expensive, and a commitment to it requires financial support. For this reason librarians must frequently compromise and sacrifice optimum preservation in order to acquire or access a greater number of resources.

At the same time, one must realize that not every serial needs to be preserved. Duplicate copies within a library system or consortium, complete files of annuals on topics peripheral to the curriculum or areas of interest, and daily newspapers acquired only for current events are examples of categories to consider for discard or weeding.

The preservation of library materials is a lively topic within the profession. It fits well with energy conservation and ecology, matters of concern to librarians and nonlibrarians alike. For many years the former Resources and Technical Services Division of ALA had a Preservation of Library Materials Committee. In 1980 this committee advanced to sectional status and formed its own committees and discussion groups. Fifteen hundred RTSD members joined the new section in its first year. In an era of concern for the continued existence of material things, preservation of serials is a legitimate interest, although the concern may be primarily with preservation of information, not necessarily of fine bindings and first editions.

BINDING

Commercial binding is still the most widely used method of preserving serials. An understanding of the librarian's options and the binder's procedures should be included in on-the-job training of serials librarians. Binding has traditionally been a labor intensive industry, but now many processes are computerized, and others are performed by sophisticated machinery. Not all commercial binders are willing to accept the expenses of automation and mechanization at the same rate, so there are differences in the way they process serials.

Not all libraries bind serials. Some libraries, usually small ones, elect to retain periodical issues unbound (perhaps for a stated number of years) either loose, tied and stored, or boxed. Others prefer to convert some or all of their periodicals to microform. Still other libraries purchase prebound complete volumes for retention and dispose of worn individual issues. Every library must consider and resolve binding questions: Shall we, or shall we not bind serials? How can we best serve our patrons? What are the costs of each alternative?

Most research libraries bind or otherwise routinely draw together in volumes every periodical title that they retain. If a serial is worth keeping, it deserves better treatment than leaving issues loose. Unbound nonperiodical serials, which usually appear in single pieces appropriate for binding separately, are exempt from the problem of loose issues, but the library needs a policy regarding their preservation treatment.

The cost of binding rises along with the cost of obtaining materials, and the library administration must recognize the binding budget as an increasing, continuing commitment just as the serial allocation is. Not only is the price of a bound volume rising, but increasing costs of paper and postage have forced publishers to cut expenses wherever they can. They have narrowed margins and may use a poorer quality of paper, changes that mean the library can bind fewer issues in the customary way. The library may have bound a typical weekly newsmagazine, for instance, in one or two physical volumes a year initially; later it required quarterly volumes. Now one must bind the title bimonthly or monthly if all the text is to be readable and copyable. In this case, binding costs have at least tripled, without considering increases in cost per volume. Library binders are working on these matters, but at binding time, the librarian must evaluate each problem title and decide on binding, retention in microform, or discard.

Although other libraries' binding manuals may be available for use, no library should accept without question any other institution's practices. Binding policy depends upon the function of the library. Does it collect current serials and dispose of older volumes? Does it support the parent institution's curriculum and, perhaps, limited graduate study? Or is it a research library which collects exhaustively within an explicit profile? Is the library a regional or national resource with a heavy interlibrary loan and photocopying program?

The function of the library determines the degree of permanence necessary for its serials collection and the subject emphases that guide binding policy.

If a serial is of recognized value to the library collection, there is a limited number of binding alternatives from which to choose. It can be bound by a commercial binder, according to Library Binding Institute (LBI, discussed later in this chapter) standards and become a permanent part of the library's holdings. Options for a serial of questionable retrospective value include a semi-permanent commercial binding, placing in cardboard covers or otherwise drawing it together in the library, or retaining it unbound until it falls to pieces or is lost. Even for a library that has elected to preserve serials in their original format, there are times when microform is appropriate, such as for titles produced in newsprint. Finally, the serial may be discarded at a specified time, perhaps after one year or two years.

Types of Binding

When a library selects a member of the Library Binding Institute as its primary binder, it has a right to expect certain standards of quality, as specified by LBI, and to have a variety of choices. LBI publishes the *Library Binding Institute Standard for Library Binding*,[1] with the latest edition issued in 1986.

Before the mid-1980s, the most commonly used means of binding was *oversewing*, which is defined in the LBI Standard as "a method of sewing thin sections (i.e., piles) of leaves, one to another in succession, to create a semi-flexible text block."[2] Oversewing is no longer the binding of choice because it diminishes access to the volume's contents and promotes damage to the text. In the oversewing process, the thread travels diagonally through the back of each section of the book, taking up at least one-quarter inch of the inner margin; this loss is in addition to what was ground or cut away to separate the book into single leaves. Oversewing prevents the volume from lying flat when opened. If a serial volume with inner margins of less than five-eighths of an inch is oversewn, any use, but especially photocopying, is likely to lead to broken stitches or torn pages as the reader attempts to see words close to the inner margins. Thick volumes require much wider inner margins than thin volumes if they are to be readable after they are oversewn. As journal margins became narrower, oversewing became less satisfactory as a means of binding issues and signatures together. The amount of space required by oversewing makes rebinding virtually impossible.

An alternative to oversewing is *sewing through the fold* by hand or by machine, if the text to be bound is composed of one or more separate signatures. Single-signature serial issues are good candidates for this type of binding. Thickness of signatures and nature of paper may determine whether the binder uses hand or machine sewing. In this procedure the binder uses a saw to cut notches in the spine edge of folded signatures or issues and sews the text to cords or tapes placed in the notches. The notch enables the bound volume to be opened flat, so that even the innermost words are visible. The hand binder uses a good quality linen thread to stitch the leaves and issues together and to the supporting cord. The binder uses thread for machine sewing through the fold that is specified by the manufacturer of the machine, and it may be cotton, nylon, or polyester.

During the past ten to fifteen years, so much improvement has occurred in the quality of glues used in library binding that sewing is no longer a prerequisite for a strong volume. Most libraries bind their serials today by the *double fan adhesive* method. On a machine, inner edges of a volume are slightly spread and passed across glued rollers on first one side and then the other. Gluing can now make as strong or stronger a binding as stitching, and it does not require more than a one-sixteenth inch margin. The process covers only 1/64" of the binding margin. For successful double fan adhesive binding every leaf of the text must be separate from the next so that each one receives the glue coating. The volume should be no more than two inches thick.

A commercial binder should be able to offer each of the above methods of preserving a serial volume, as deemed appropriate by the library, based on the volume's thickness, width of inner margins, and projected use. It is the binding librarian's responsibility to select the best method. The two editors of the LBI standard, Jan Merrill-Oldham (a librarian) and Paul Parisi (a binder) published a very useful aid to librarians responsible for binding, *Guide to the Library Binding Institute Standard for Library Binding*.[3] The guide uses numbering parallel to that of the standard. It interprets the standard for librarians and gives much more detail than is possible in this chapter. Both the Guide and the Standard itself are well illustrated.

For low use titles, an economy cloth cover may suffice instead of the standard buckram; the volume within this case may be either sewn or glued. For annuals or thin serials, the binder may be able to provide a mylar covering, but one should use this binding carefully, because it will not adhere to serials with slick covers. Single issues of serials and thin single-piece volumes which will be used lightly are often stapled or glued between cardboard covers. This "pamphlet" binding is frequently done within the library, and it can be considered either permanent or temporary. Some libraries have a policy of gluing the serial's cover to the outside of the front cardboard; many attach a typed label. Other kinds of binding that can be done within the library include *spiral binding*, in which pages are held together by a plastic or metal ring backing; *post binding*, where metal or plastic fixtures are inserted through holes in the material; and *portfolios*, folders that hold together loose issues or pages.

Among original-format alternatives to commercial or in-house permanent binding of serials are boxing, which at its best includes the purchase of acid-free boxes and at its worst, Princeton files or cartons from the grocery store; bundling, trussing with cotton string or cotton tape; and placing loose issues between cut-to-size cardboard and tying them securely. The above are methods of retaining serials; by no means can they be called preservation!

Every library has some material that will be used for so brief a time or so seldom that it does not warrant the expense of permanent binding; guidelines will be determined by the individual library. Most libraries provide for on-site repair and temporary binding, involving cardboard covers, tape, and staples. There will be local processing of materials that do not need commercial binding because of low projected use or low cost. The type and amount of binding (sometimes combined with repair) done within any library can vary from simply stapling between cardboard covers to the use of devices which punch and sew, available from library suppliers, or even the use of some types of specialized binding machinery. So long as the in-house treatment does not require the purchase of expensive equipment justified only by heavier use than the library makes, this is probably an economical means of preserving some materials. Serials that do not have to leave the library to be bound are more quickly available for use, and the procedures employed within the library are completed faster, provided there is not a large backlog. It is important to remember that any local binding that is considered to be temporary must not preclude permanent binding in the future. Temporary binding must not alter the piece to the extent that it cannot be bound commercially if the need arises.

When to Bind

The appropriate time to bind serials varies according to both library priorities and subject of the material. For example, a library with low patron use for a specific period during the year, for example, a library at a high school where there are no summer classes, may hold all unbound issues and volumes until that low use time to ensure that serials are always available to patrons. A library having more consistent, year-round use may bind whenever the volume is complete, sacrificing patrons' immediate access for the relative security of hard covers. Some librarians make a special effort to have certain subject categories of journals available at a particular time; for example, university library education journals may be kept on the shelf unbound during summer school when public school teachers are enrolled and then sent to be bound. One librarian sends a volume to the bindery as soon as the last issue arrives, while another feels it is important to wait until the first piece of the next volume appears, so the most recent issue will always be available to patrons. Certain titles that are published in bindable units, such as annuals, may upon request be held for review by a faculty member, or they may be shipped immediately to the commercial bindery.

A further consideration in timing of sending large numbers of serials to the bindery is the work flow at the binder. Binding of public school textbooks must be done during the summer months, and if one's binder holds the state contract for textbook rebinding, the library should plan to send large batches of materials at other times of the year. If serials must go to such a binder during the summer, expect delays in the return of shipments and possible lowering of quality because of a heavy workload.

Every library system should be able to work out a procedure whereby multiple copies of a serial go to the bindery in succession, not all at the same time. One library is designated the first to send a volume of a multi-copy subscription. The other holding locations agree to wait until notified that the first copy is back from the bindery before they send their copies. Or, one library can wait to bind until at least one other copy has returned from the bindery. This policy ensures that a patron will always have access within the system to a title that is used heavily enough to justify more than one subscription.

When should one rebind a serial? As soon as possible after someone realizes that it needs rebinding. The longer the wait to rebind a deteriorating volume, the greater the risk of loss and permanent damage to the pages. Rebinding may, however, be scheduled to fit the cycle of library use in the same way as the initial binding was. In-house repair of a volume may provide a temporary resolution of the problem, but the work must be done carefully for materials that will go later to the commercial bindery. Tape, holes, trimming, and staples cause problems for the binder both by mutilating the piece so badly that it cannot be rebound and by damaging binding machinery. A library may want to consider limiting the availability of a deteriorating volume through closed shelving instead of risking more damage by "repairing" it carelessly.

When a thick serial volume goes for rebinding, the librarian may want to consider splitting the piece into two physical volumes. Heavy use, particularly copy machine use, of a volume more than about two inches thick, even with three-quarter inch or larger inside margins, causes damage quickly. It is more economical to rebind in two volumes that will survive heavy use than it is to rebind in a single volume that will neither last nor take rebinding again.

Binding policies and their details are unlimited, and each library will determine the optimum time to send journals to the bindery by considering such variables as public service, security, cycle of use, budget, and binder's schedule. Whatever the specifications of the written policy, it proves beneficial to retain enough flexibility to account for unexpected situations—a change in the school calendar, an international institute meeting on campus, patrons' publishing deadlines, and equipment breakdowns at the bindery.

Bindery Preparation

Many of the routine operations used a generation ago to prepare serials for binding are no longer considered practical by some librarians. Such tasks as removing advertising, collating every unit to check for missing pages, and deciding for each title whether to retain or discard covers are often dropped in the interests of economy and efficiency through standardization. Even the choice of color and lettering may be made once, for all a library's serials, instead of for each title.

What remains essential is collecting pieces of a serial that comprise a bindable unit, not necessarily corresponding to a bibliographic volume; arranging them in numerical order, top to bottom; securing them temporarily with cotton string or cotton tape; marking the bundle so the binder can identify the title; and recording that the volume is being bound. These things are done according to guidelines which support the library's public service and collection development objectives; thus, the guidelines vary from library to library.

The first step in preparing a serial for binding is to get it to the staff member responsible for the succeeding steps of this operation. A one-piece volume may be routed from serial acquisitions to the correct person, or the check-in assistant may do the preparation. The latter practice may gain a few days' time, but it probably sacrifices the care given by one whose chief responsibility is binding preparation, as well as delays claiming or some other primary responsibility of the check-in assistant.

Periodicals that have accumulated in a current issues reading room and are ready to be bound can be gathered by a clerk or student assistant working from either binding records of these titles or notices sent by check-in assistants reporting that a volume is ready to bind. Many online serials systems have binding modules that can produce a pull-slip. The clerk who gathers the issues can easily place them in chronological and numerical order and check to see that all pieces are present. When there is a missing issue or the subscription appears to have lapsed, the clerk can notify the supervisor in writing so a search can be made and a claim or replacement order placed if needed.

It is at this point that a trained binding preparation assistant should take over the procedure and examine each volume according to the library's guidelines. If pages are missing, photocopies are ordered and inserted when they arrive. Replacement pages usually are in front-and-back photocopy on archival quality paper with binding margins. There are problems with this method of replacing pages even before binding, for sometimes the operator copies the pages carelessly, and they are out of register. For work done within the library, recopying is done quickly. If the pages came from another library, one must decide whether to delay binding until an acceptable copy can be obtained, to go ahead and use what is at hand even though the copy extends beyond the page edge or into the inner margin, or to bear the expense and time required to have the pages carefully recopied within the library. Missing pages contain articles that people use, and the replacement pages will be read and photocopied and, perhaps, cut out and stolen again. It might be practical to keep a master file of replacement pages for particularly high-risk articles.

In any libraries where advertising pages and covers are still removed before binding, this is the time for that operation. In-house removal is less expensive than leaving this task for the binder. Also, the library staff member may take more care than the bindery employee. This policy saves money if the binding budget is tight, for the cost of removing covers and ads comes from the library's personnel budget. If, however, the personnel budget is tighter than the binding budget, the library may prefer to have ads and covers removed at the commercial bindery. In fact, most libraries have abandoned entirely the removal of covers and advertising, for economic reasons.

Sometimes a volume cannot be completed, at least not in paper format. When an issue is not available from the publisher or a second-hand dealer and when a photocopy is too expensive, the librarian may decide to bind the volume in its incomplete state. Sometimes there is a request for the binder to "stub" the volume (leaving room within the casing by filling in the space with narrow pages, similar to checkbook stubs), so the missing issue, if it is ever located, can be bound in. However, often there is so little chance of acquiring the missing issue that stubbing is not feasible. For essential missing issues not available in the original format, it may be preferable to purchase a microform copy, annotate the incomplete volume, and forget about obtaining a paper issue. Binders sometimes use top stubbing for very short serials, to give the piece enough height not to be lost on the shelf. Another use of stubbing is to fill in gaps at the top of a volume having issues of different heights.

Once the binding assistant determines that a volume is complete or decides to bind it incomplete, she ties the issues together and prepares a binding slip. The form that accompanies a serial to the bindery may be manually or computer produced, depending upon the binder's and library's capabilities. Any paper clips used on library serials should be vinyl covered.

In addition, the binding assistant needs to record at every appropriate location the titles and volumes that are at the bindery and the date they left the library. If there is a serials public service point, the record should be close by or available on a computer terminal, so patrons can learn the status of volumes. Some libraries elect to make this information part of the central circulation file. Whichever location is used, it is important that staff members know where to direct patrons to confirm that a specific volume is at the bindery. When this record resides within the serials department, it is possible also to record the date the piece returns from the bindery. This information can help locate a recently bound serial, which may travel through a number of checkpoints before it reaches its place in the stacks. A review of such records can also alert the staff to initiate an enquiry about serials that have been sent to the bindery but have not returned within a reasonable time.

Administrators of a library system must decide whether centralized or decentralized binding preparation is best. If there is a backlog in a library binding unit, it benefits patrons for individual issues to be available at their unbound location as close as possible to the time when they leave the building; this can be done best if binding is prepared at the location of the unbound issues. On the other hand, if there is not sufficient staff at these interim locations to prepare the volumes for commercial binding, centralized processing is efficient. In either case the library with several locations for unbound serials must have one place at which the binder's truck picks up and delivers the shipments. This station can have adequate staffing to give a final check to materials being sent and an initial review of volumes being returned.

Guidelines for Selecting a Commercial Binder

The first thing a library should require of its binder is that the company be a "certified library binder," a member of the Library Binding Institute. Without the assurance of this professional association and support, the librarian has no way of knowing that the binder's work will be satisfactory and no recourse if it is not. If a commercial binder is not a member of LBI, the library customer is taking an unnecessary risk with its materials requiring binding.

Even though they may be certified library binders, commercial binders are not equal. Prices, equipment, procedures, and services all vary among binders. There is general agreement in the literature that it is the responsibility of the librarian in charge of binding to select the binder; the decision should not be made by a state or an institutional purchasing agent or by a library bindery staff member. If the binder is selected on the basis of a bid, it is again the librarian and not someone outside the library who must have the knowledge to select from the competitors.

In comparing binders, each should be evaluated upon several points. Samples of their work will be available for examination and, if it is necessary, for evaluation by LBI. Visits to the binderies and observation of their procedures and equipment are also recommended. Other libraries using the binderies under consideration can advise as to reliability, treatment of the library materials, length of time volumes can be expected to be away from the library, flexibility in adapting to terms set by the library, and other aspects of service such as computerized binding slips and insertion of security system strips. The librarian must examine price quotations from competing binderies carefully, for there may be charges for lettering, collating, and so on, which one binder lists separately and another includes in the basic price. Not least, the library, and particularly the librarian in charge of binding, must be certain to take great care in writing the specifications for the binding of serial volumes. The instructions must be explicit and obvious. The binder cannot be expected to follow directions that are vague and fail to spell out the library's needs in detail.

The choice of a binder or the process of changing from one binder to another is an occasion when the binding librarian should communicate with colleagues and with the Library Binding Institute, if need be, for it is a crucial decision.

Changing from one binder to another is perhaps more disruptive of processes and more expensive to the library than changing subscription agents.

When there is no transferable automated record of binding specifications, one must give all of the relevant information about each title to the new binder. Also, all binders do not use the same automated system, and staff members may have to learn to use a new one, which may be better or worse than that of the previous binder. Both of these processes slow the rate of library binding and promote loss of serials waiting to be bound. If a federal, state or municipal library is compelled to accept the lowest competitive bid and must change binders, it may find that quality of binding deteriorates, and it will need to rebind materials sooner and more often than in the past.

Some libraries have all their binding done by a local bindery in the library or elsewhere on campus. This is an impractical course in most cases because, even if there is no question of quality, there is a loss of the economies of scale. Modern bindery equipment, particularly where some parts of the operation are automated, can be efficient only with high volume; the machines must be kept operating. Unless a local bindery can reach the volume of work that will make the equipment cost-effective, something few libraries can do alone, the cost of permanent binding done in-house will be significantly higher than work done by a commercial binder.

Standards and Quality Control

The Library Binding Institute is an association of commercial binders whose business is primarily with libraries, and of their suppliers. This institute was established in 1935, when binders who were specifically *library* binders left the Book Manufacturers' Institute to form their own group. Since that time LBI has worked to formulate, revise, and promote standards for various types of book and serial binding done for libraries. This group works closely with the American Library Association and its Library Technology Project and with the Special Libraries Association, to their mutual advantage.

As early as 1923 there were "specifications" for library binding. The specifications were based on materials and methods of manufacture of the binding and were widely adhered to in the industry. The 1933 Specifications and a 1939 document, "Standards for Reinforced (Pre-Library Bound) New Books," were the foundation for the "Library Binding Institute Standard for Library Binding" and the "Library Binding Institute Standard for Pre-Bound Books." These were issued in 1958 and revised several times, until they were combined into one standard, "The Library Binding Institute Standard for Library Binding," revised last in 1986. LBI publishes a periodical, *New Library Scene*, covering binding matters and the binding industry.

The following is a statement of the ways in which the Library Binding Institute members work to implement the Standard. The Institute:

A. Has established a certification system to inform librarians which binders can do work in accordance with the Standards, are reputable, have been recommended by librarians, and carry insurance to protect their customers' property.

B. Maintains a Free Examination Service for librarians to determine whether binding has been done in accordance with contractual requirements.

C. Sponsored the promulgation by the Federal Trade Commission of Trade Practice Rules to insure the highest possible standards of equitable and fair dealing in the industry and to protect librarians against deceit and misrepresentations.

D. Maintains a continuous program of research and education involving binders, their customers and suppliers.

E. Has established the use of a warranty on invoices of Certified Library Binders, stating that work complies with the LBI Standard for Library Binding unless otherwise stated thereon.

F. Established a Quality Control Program whereby the plant of each Certified Library Binder is periodically examined for adherence to a carefully planned quality control program.[4]

The work of the Library Binding Institute, the national library organizations, and the certified library binders has greatly benefitted libraries by virtually abolishing nonstandard commercial library binding that lacks the library's consent. However, the standard is only the minimum required for routine binding. Its value is, in part, as a means of communication between the librarian and the commercial binder. Both understand that binding will meet the printed standards unless some other arrangement is made; if the library requires a higher quality binding or a lower quality binding than the standard, it must work with the binder to determine mutually acceptable standards.

The librarian who works with the commercial binder to establish local standards has a responsibility to become knowledgeable about the binding process through visiting the binder and attending workshops and seminars on library binding and preservation. This person should examine the binder's work on a regular basis to be sure the binder understands the library's instructions. The librarian can flag certain volumes to examine when they return to the library.

Matt Roberts, writing in *Special Libraries*, supported the preceding suggestions by urging librarians not to let their concern with binding end with the completion of the binding slip, but to learn to recognize materials having special binding problems, and to evaluate the work of the bindery. While the owners and officers of the commercial bindery may be far more knowledgeable about their work than a librarian can expect to be, Roberts reminded his readers that these persons are not the ones who actually bind the library's serials. The persons who handle the material are likely to be employees who have less overall binding knowledge than the owner and less time to examine each volume than the librarian. And, Roberts wrote, the mechanization of the binding process makes this handling even more superficial, for the cost of the machinery requires that materials be processed as rapidly as possible. One cannot expect the binder to correct the library's mistakes.[5]

The most useful point this section can communicate is that the librarian responsible for binding serials has an obligation to (1) be knowledgeable about current binding and preservation standards, (2) be informed about the current binder's work, and (3) communicate with the binder about the library's particular preservation requirements.

MICROFORMS

Many libraries, particularly those that have developed during the past few decades, have chosen to retain some or most of their periodicals in microform, rather than bound or otherwise maintained in their original format. Some newer libraries have had no realistic alternative, for much retrospective material is available only in microform or expensive reprint. Established libraries, outgrowing their stack space and facing the problem of mutilation, have turned to microform as a solution. The companies producing the microfilm and microfiche, and equipment for using them, are convincing in their promotion of these products. They also keep the prices of current volumes of periodicals in microform at just about the cost of binding. Some libraries have the equipment to do their own filming of serials that are not available commercially. Selective local filming is valid as part of a larger preservation effort, but it is almost prohibitively expensive for a library to film its own serials individually, unless there is a market for the filmed product and the library promotes its availability.

At present there are three types of microform processes on the market: silver halide, diazo, and vesicular. Of these, diazo is clearly unacceptable for library preservation use because of its relatively short shelf life. The inexpensive diazo is adequate for short-term use in COM catalogs that are replaced periodically. Silver halide is the archival standard film, but it is expensive and subject to scratching with repeated use. The polyester vesicular process has been controversial but is apparently perfectly acceptable for copies of serials that will be used by patrons. Vesicular microforms are tough, inexpensive, and likely to last as long as silver halide in a library situation. For archival purposes silver halide is still the recommended medium, but few libraries will be concerned with archival microform serials, since most will purchase copies from commercial dealers who will maintain their own archives in the form of the master negative copies.

When a library develops a policy about serials retention in microform, it must proceed cautiously and not neglect the costs and space requirements of factors other than the microform itself: mechanical readers and copiers; service and replacement parts; staff to assist readers in locating, using, and copying the material and to reshelve it; and the attitude of the library's patrons. The physical characteristics of specific serials and their local use are so significant in this decision that each type of material needs individual consideration.

Daily newspapers are unquestionably best retained in microform because of the poor quality of their paper, the awkward size of bound newspaper volumes, and the amount of shelf space required. Binding newspapers is not a form of permanent retention. If a library decides to collect backfiles of newspapers, the cost of microform equipment and staff assistance has no alternative, and it must be calculated during the decision making process by library selectors. It remains to be seen whether compact discs will become the format of choice for newspapers.

On the other hand, most periodicals, particularly scholarly publications, will not fall to pieces after a few years of use. The library has more leeway in determining its treatment of them. Some periodicals use as poor quality paper as newspapers; if their content is of permanent value to the collection, the costs of microform are justified. Heavily used periodicals retained only in microform can create congestion in the area of mechanical readers, a situation which leads to frustration among users. At the same time, a patron who finds all the articles on a term paper topic cut or ripped from serials or who finds entire volumes missing will be at least as angry and frustrated as the one who has to wait for a reader.

A case can be made for the conversion of backfiles of little used journals to microform or for the original purchase of the title in this format. This policy will generate less use of equipment than would converting more heavily used titles, and it frees stack space for more often consulted material. When a library is able to have microform subscriptions to back up bound subscriptions to popular and heavily used periodicals, the cost may be justified by the elimination of the frustration caused by mutilation, assuming the microform copy is not lost or stolen. This duplication is a luxury most libraries have to use selectively, for ordinarily funds can be better spent on titles that are not available in the library in any other format.

It is possible to alleviate somewhat the congestion that occurs when many patrons want to use microform readers. Commercially produced readers for both microfilm and microfiche have become more reasonably priced and give better images than earlier models. Their presence can lead to a more positive attitude toward microform on the part of users who object to being restricted to a dark, crowded room. The alternative of taking the microform and a circulating compact reader to one's office or home and studying the material at leisure appeals to some patrons.

With all the benefits of microform, some types of serials are not suited to any format except the original paper. Journals which have long articles are more easily read in print, because most persons' eyes are bothered more by long hours of reading microform than by reading print on paper. Periodicals where colored illustrations are a significant part of the articles, such as those with color-keyed charts and maps, are not acceptable in microform, often not even in expensive colored microform. Reference tools, such as indexes and bibliographies, until recently were not successful in microform. However, the increasing dependence of librarians upon collections of, for instance, telephone directories and college catalogs on microfiche brought a change in the appearance of reference collections. Many more reference works are acceptable in microform than heretofore. Today, though, compact discs are replacing microform for reference works because of superior searching capabilities.

Traditionally, libraries subscribing to periodicals in microform have preferred reel film, the most popular reason being that microfiche is easily misfiled and, thus, lost. Microfiche has gained in popularity because of its ease of use, reproduction, and replacement. The mechanical equipment required to use microfiche is simpler, and therefore, easier to use and to repair, than that for microfilm. It is likely that the former wide use of computer output microfiche for libraries' public records of serials holdings and the experience of patrons in libraries that ventured to retain their periodicals on fiche outweighed the fears of confusion in refiling sheets of microfiche. Not least among the reasons for increased popularity of microfiche over microfilm is UMI's policy of distributing periodicals quarterly instead of annually, as had been the custom. Despite the general acceptance of microfiche, the misfiling problem remains and occasional single fiche continue to be lost.

Often there is a choice to make between positive and negative microform. For a patron reading a positive copy, the printing is dark on a light background, as is a printed work. When this positive microform is copied on a reader-printer, the reproduction usually comes out as a negative copy; that is, light printing on a dark background. With negative microform, the copy is positive. There are machines capable of printing a positive copy from a positive microform; however, a negative microform produces a noticeably better print than a positive one. Negative microforms, thus, are the preferred medium for copying and will also cause users of the original microform less eyestrain. Patron resistance to negative microforms, however, is higher than to positive, especially when photographs or illustrations appear in the articles reproduced.

Whatever the characteristics of the material that is copied, the print on paper is not yet as good quality as copies made from printed material on a coin paper copier. The quality of reader-printers is vastly better than it used to be, but there is still room for improvement. One must keep in mind also that certain illustrations such as plates and colored photographs do not show up well in microform and do not copy satisfactorily on reader-printers because of the chemical composition of film designed to achieve the sharpest contrast between print and paper. Maps and plans lose their calibrations when they are copied, because most photocopies are not exact size reproductions, and copies from microform are one more step away from the original. The amount and importance of illustrative matter is a definite consideration in the decision to bind or purchase microform.

ELECTRONIC TEXT

The evolving technology for the 1990s is electronic text, and this brings with it both advantages and hazards. The two forms of electronic text covered in this section are CD-ROM (compact disc, read-only memory) and online serials.

CD-ROM

The compact disc has been touted as the successor to microform for libraries, and it is widely used for serials, especially reference serials. Similar in appearance to the musical compact disc, CD-ROM can be accessed and searched via computer or terminal, but not altered. Its advantages are its small (compact) size and ease of storage and the sophisticated searching capability. For example, the Library of Congress produces a CD-ROM of the MARC-S file on a single disc that is searchable by sixteen data elements. Contrast this to *New Serial Titles*! The compact disc is especially appropriate for periodical indexes, telephone directories, and encyclopedias. Information can be downloaded and/or printed. The capabilities of compact discs are evolving, and they are becoming much more flexible in their uses.

Some publishers and vendors of secondary material offer the full text of journals on compact disc. Because of the large capacity of the disc, this format is not appropriate for a single title unless a long back file is provided—an expensive proposition! Already secondary producers have available systems containing many journals on one subject. These products, however, often employ a mechanism that charges for each copy made.

There is a downside to compact discs. Searching is only as good as the software adopted by the producer. The author's staff members have found, using Ulrich's Plus, that many title searches do not retrieve the serial. Only use of the ISSN or another data element will bring up the entry.

There are questions about the durability of the plastic discs themselves. Some reports project a life expectancy of only three to five years. This span is no problem for a work where the disc is replaced every quarter or every year, but on a long-term basis, preservation by means of compact disc may be a risky decision.

The life expectancy of compact discs may not be such a problem as it may seem, because in most instances the subscription to a CD version of a serial does not mean that the library has purchased the material, but has only leased it. When a new disc arrives, the old one often must be returned to the publisher. This policy causes much uneasiness among librarians, but it has not prevented them from subscribing. It has, however, made librarians reluctant to discontinue their subscriptions to the paper versions of these serials.

One must also consider equipment required by the compact disc. Access is through either stand-alone personal computers with compact disc drives or via a network of computers. CDs have such great capacity that most serials are contained on a single disc. This means that only one person can access the title at a time, unless the serial is on a network, in which case it is one person to one computer. Most networked compact discs have a higher license fee the more simultaneous users are accommodated. There is also the question of future compact disc technology requiring more and more computer capacity. It is not yet known how often the hardware used for compact discs will have to be upgraded.

Online Serials

Online serials, for the purposes of this chapter, are those available electronically through the Internet. They may be published only in this format, or they may be online versions of printed journals. At the present time electronic-only titles are generally labors of love and may be acquired at no charge through one's electronic mailbox. However, commercial publishers, university presses, and societies are launching new electronic journals, for which there is a subscription charge. Advantages of electronic serials are the speed with which they are published, the ease of searching them, and often the absence of a subscription charge. The limitations of the Internet have precluded its use for journals in disciplines where illustrations are necessary, but this format is excellent for newsletters and more substantial journals that do not need illustrations. The latest software, World Wide Web (WWW), eliminates problems with illustrations.

The library has several options for access or preservation of online serials. Those available through listserver software (i.e., using this means to distribute each issue to a mailing list of electronic mail subscribers) may have an archive at the Internet node from which the journal originates. One can send an electronic mail message to the listserver and receive an issue. If the archive is issue-by-issue, and if there are many issues, retrieving the entire file is time-consuming, for each issue must be requested separately. A second way of retrieving an issue of an online serial is by file transfer protocol (FTP). One sends a message to another computer, one that has made the title available, and retrieves a copy. A third means is by accessing from one's mailbox a remote "gopher" (a multi-level file of documents). Once an issue comes to the electronic mailbox, it is easily saved to an electronic file folder or downloaded and printed. It can also be forwarded to another address. The World Wide Web improves on searching and access capabilities of FTP and gopher.

Just as with compact disc serials, there are concerns about online serials. As yet, no standards exist for format, and the technology is still primitive. Librarians have expressed fears about losing the "official" version of an online journal, because it is easy to edit or damage the text. These fears are directly related to preservation.

There is also the question of what one does with the retrieved copy of the online journal. Some libraries have mounted the files on their online catalogs, on another library or campus-wide system, or the library's or the institution's own gopher or Web site. As in the case of compact discs, one must provide staff time and attention for maintenance. Some other libraries have cataloged online serials residing on a remote computer and have provided instructions (a URL, or Uniform Resource Locator, or a URN, Uniform Resource Name) so patrons can access the file themselves.

SECURITY

Security, another aspect of preservation, involves circulation, exit control, and the housing of paper serials and multi-media supplements to serials. Deciding whether to circulate serials for use outside the library is a public service question with broader implications than security alone, so it is discussed in Chapter 13. Restricted access to serials within the building is a preservation concern because of the serious problem of mutilation of journals. Too often librarians make the decision to restrict access to a specific periodical after much of it has been cut out and stolen, instead of at the time of purchase. Just as each serial should be evaluated for retention as a permanent part of the collection, so it should be examined for high risk of mutilation and theft. Some serials are subject to damage or loss: those treating current controversial topics in a popular way, education and particularly physical education journals, newsletters and journals devoted to a single author, and popular culture serials. Local additions to this list of categories become apparent to the staff member who must order replacement pages and issues, so that new titles fitting the high-risk profile can be restricted from the beginning. Unless the library's policy requires that all unbound journals be shelved in a closed storage area, the number of restricted titles should be kept to a reasonable minimum, because of both staff time required for paging and the reduction in number of periodicals available for browsing. It is not fair to the patron to take away all the journals attracting his or her attention, leaving only those which hold no interest. A reading room filled with grey journal covers in foreign languages is probably very secure and very little used. Each library will find a balance between security and accessibility.

Exit control, if it is done well, deters theft and stops inadvertent removal of library materials. A staff member who examines briefcases and armloads of books can be effective, but this job does not appeal to or challenge many persons. It pays little, it places one in unpleasant confrontations with patrons or fellow staff members who feel that they should be trusted, and often it exposes the checker to cold winds blowing through the door each time a patron leaves the building in winter. Most persons who can and will do this job conscientiously are able to handle a higher level position and are soon promoted. Unfortunately, many checkers prefer to read or talk with their friends instead of examining volumes leaving the library. Some libraries attempt to make unbound periodicals easier to spot by putting colored stripes on the edges of three sides of the issues, but this is effective only if the checker looks for it.

Many libraries have installed one of the electronic security systems available. Although they are expensive, their cost can probably be justified by savings in salary or wages of exit control personnel together with replacement cost of books and serials. Selective treatment of library materials combined with publicity directed toward patrons should be nearly as effective as preparing every volume to sound the system's alarm. Some library binders include this preparation in their operations. The wisdom of security stripping journal issues that will be bound together later has been questioned. It is one more task for busy staff members, and some bound volumes may have twelve strips, where one would do. However, the replacement costs of serials are so high that a few issues retained will pay for many issues to be treated. It would be unrealistically expensive to have an electronic security system for a periodicals reading room alone, so patrons will continue to take journals to the far reaches of the bookstack as they have always done, and others needing those materials will continue to have to wait until they have been discovered and retrieved.

Electronic security systems can stop inadvertent theft, but some persistent patrons will circumvent the best control. One university library staff queried students and identified and interviewed periodical mutilators, in an attempt to develop a program to combat destruction of materials. The investigators determined that their best recourse was a publicity campaign, combined with obvious penalty warning signs.[6] No library has yet found a total solution to the security problem. In addition to publicity and warnings of penalties, a periodicals reading room should have only one public exit, with unobtrusive observation, as a deterrent. This single exit, of course, can be a problem when the fire alarm goes off!

The availability of low cost, efficient coin or card photocopy machines probably reduces both mutilation and theft. At the same time, the presence of the self-service machine works against preservation efforts because of the chance of damage to the volume as it is held on the machine by a patron who is thinking only of getting every word copied. Even salaried operators of sophisticated copiers in a library photographic laboratory may not take time to handle volumes carefully. It is becoming increasingly difficult to copy without hurting the volume, because of narrow margins and poor quality paper; that is reason to educate both staff members and patrons in the proper way to treat a bound volume. Some brands of photocopy machine permit copying of volumes partially opened, saving wear on the binding. A new copier even turns pages!

The security problems just discussed—theft, mutilation, and inadvertent damage to volumes—can be nearly eliminated by retaining serials in microform. For some titles this policy would only exchange one set of problems for another, as noted earlier, but it may be a viable alternative for many serials if administered with care. Mutilation of microforms occurs only rarely and inadvertently in a well-run reading room; photocopying (printing) produces no more strain on the materials than does reading, and theft is almost nonexistent.

Every library needs to have a policy concerning disposition of multi-media supplemental materials received with printed serials. *National Geographic* publishes maps that accompany many monthly issues; other journals supply sound recordings, slides, charts, computer disks, games, and so forth, placed inside or attached to issues. Some of them require equipment for use, others do not. Libraries with closed serials stacks may elect to place this supplementary material in a pocket at the back of the volume. Otherwise, those parts which must be used with audiovisual and computer equipment may be kept with other recordings and disks in a supervised part of the library near machines for their use. Again, each library will determine the best policy for its patrons.

In open stack collections, leaving nonbook material with the bound volume or the unbound issue is asking for it to be misplaced or stolen. A map is more secure in a map collection than in the pocket of a book; the librarian needs to decide if it is worth the inconvenience to patrons. In general, if supplementary material is worth keeping, it is worth preserving in an appropriate manner, and the library has this obligation. For ease in locating supplements housed away from their parent volumes, a written or printed notice in the volume directs patrons to the material. Serials public service staff members must be aware of the policy too, because some readers will not see the notice. A library that has no map room and no audiovisual collection may prefer to store all serials supplementary material in a restricted area of the periodicals reading room or reference department, so patrons may charge it out as they would reserve materials. The essential point is that there must be a policy and procedure so these items will not have to be treated as problems. Lack of policy can easily lead to supplements being misplaced by staff members before patrons can have an opportunity to use them. Cataloging and acquisition records, in accordance with the policy, should clearly reflect the presence of this material and its exact location, if different from the parent title.

NOTES

1. *Library Binding Institute Standard for Library Binding*, edited by Paul A. Parisi and Jan Merrill-Oldham. 8th edition. (Austin, Texas: Library Binding Institute, 1986).

2. *Library Binding Institute Standard*, 3.

3. Merrill-Oldham, Jan, and Parisi, Paul, *Guide to the Library Binding Institute Standard for Library Binding*. (Chicago: American Library Association, 1990).

4. Library Binding Institute, *Library Binding Handbook* (Boston: Library Binding Institute, 1963), pp. 10-11.

5. Matt Roberts, "The Role of the Librarian in the Binding Process," *Special Libraries* 62 (1971): 413-420; reprinted in *Library Scene* 2 (1973): 26-30.

6. Clyde Hendrick and Marjorie E. Murfin, "Project Library Ripoff: A Study of Periodical Mutilation in a University Library," *College and Research Libraries* 35 (1974): 402-411.

Chapter 13

ACCESS TO SERIALS:
SERIALS PUBLIC SERVICE

This chapter considers the *reason* for selecting, acquiring, cataloging, and preserving serials. That reason is the *use* of serial publications. Specifically, the following sections treat the ways librarians (and increasingly, library users themselves) facilitate the uniting of the reader and the desired serially-produced information.

The chapter title uses the words "access" and "public service," not "reference." These words reflect the fact that much serials public service is not strictly reference, but is related to circulation. Reference is defined here as "What is it?" and circulation as "Where is it?"

This book divides access to serials and their contents into two chapters. The first one concentrates on locating information in journals and other serials within the library. Chapter 14 focuses on access to and acquisition of serial information from outside one's own library.

SERIALS PUBLIC SERVICE

"Has the fall issue of *Economic Geography* arrived?" "I can't find the 1990 volume of *Parks and Recreation*." "Where is *Asian Folklore Studies* indexed?" "What library has *Paris Match*?" "Is this citation for a book or a journal?"

Serials public service is the assistance given or made available by staff members to library patrons who want to identify, locate, and use journals and other serials. The process involves internal and public serial records, other bibliographic tools, and the serials themselves. Often today it involves resources not held by the library. Serials public service consists of circulation, reference and a variety of other functions, many of which are often not managed or performed by serials specialists. The library's reference department, circulation department, branch libraries, and other units routinely provide public service related to serials. Thus, the activities discussed in this chapter are not limited to staff members who work only with serials.

Most library service involving serials may be designated either circulation or reference, and it is often difficult to separate the two. However, this chapter attempts to distinguish between the handling function—circulation—and the investigating function—reference. In addition, two special types of service require treatment here: assistance for disabled patrons, and microform public service.

CIRCULATION

A major share of the public service work at a serials service desk is, broadly defined, circulation. This work includes handling, locating, and retrieving serials. The common conception of library circulation is charging materials for use outside the building and maintaining borrowers records. However, a great many libraries do not permit serials to be removed from the building, so serials circulation includes helping patrons locate volumes, interpreting library records, searching for missing serials, shelving, and recognizing volumes that need to be repaired or replaced.

Written Policy

One decision which every library must make concerns charging out serials to patrons—both removing bound volumes and unbound issues from one location in the library to another and taking these items outside the building. "Do serials circulate or not?" There is no way to avoid answering this question. Each library administration can make its serials staff members' jobs easier by having a written policy describing the circulation of each type of serial. This policy should be concise and easy to understand, it should be publicized, and it should be enforced. The policy should have few exceptions with specific exceptions stated in writing: "Current journals may be checked out for class use for one half hour longer than the class period." The availability of written circulation policy provides support to staff members when patrons ask about checkout rules and, especially, when users ask to circulate serials in ways contrary to policy. When these situations arise, a strong and immediate response based upon a written policy is more effective than hesitation, uncertainty, and consultation. At the same time, one or two senior staff members may be given authority to make occasional exceptions to the circulation policy.

The library's collection, its function, and its patrons all determine the specifications of a serials circulation policy. Which serials, if any, circulate depends on four conditions: (1) type of library (research, college, public); (2) type of serial (journal, monographic series, annual review); (3) cataloging and retention practice (analyzed issues bound together or retained separately; back volumes in microform); and (4) category of patron (faculty member, town official, student, research assistant). Any library can probably make a case for both circulation and noncirculation of periodicals and of nonperiodical serials. Consider the following:

1. Is it better for a scholar to have both monographs and serials together for research outside the library, or should serials remain in the building in case another patron needs them?
2. Should the library retain periodicals unbound so they can circulate without removing a year's worth of articles from the library? These issues may become worn through being transported outside the building, but they may not be exposed so often to the destruction of careless photocopying.
3. Does free circulation of journals deter mutilation?
4. Does the availability of inexpensive photocopy machines reduce the perceived need to use serials outside the building?
5. Should analyzed series be circulated differently from classed separately series?
6. Should journals be retained on microfiche so they can be reproduced inexpensively for patrons who have outside access to mechanical readers, thus bypassing the question of circulation?

The list of examples could go on; one must examine all of these aspects of the question and others which apply to the local library when formulating a written circulation policy for serials.

In current practice most research libraries do not circulate journals, while college and public libraries may permit all serials to be used outside the library. With a limited and highly focused clientele, special libraries, including university departmental libraries, often compromise by circulating journals and other serials in the immediate vicinity, such as in adjacent offices, where they can (at least in theory) be retrieved quickly if needed. In all types of libraries, nonperiodical serials—annuals, monographic series—can be circulated differently from and more liberally than periodicals. They are not usually collections of articles or essays; nor are they as apt to be covered in periodical indexes and abstract journals.

Whatever the library's decision about the circulation of serials, and in spite of the previous emphasis on a written policy with few exceptions, there should be limited flexibility in practice. At times noncirculating materials must be used outside the library, just as circulating serials must sometimes be immediately available on reserve. The exception to policy is most often determined by a special need, although a special person—a mayor or a chancellor—usually merits an exemption. When weighing a request for a circulation policy exception, try to determine the best course of action for the whole group of library patrons, as well as for political implications.

HOUSING

The library's policies about housing the serials collection constitute another aspect of circulation. Determining factors in arriving at the best treatment of serials include the configuration of the library building and the balance of accessibility and security considered appropriate for each library. Often the serials librarian has no choice in the location and arrangement of serials and must accept longstanding practice. Sometimes there is opportunity for evaluation and change, for example, when the library is planning a new building, when there is a major stack shift, or when a serials department or reading room is created. A discussion of the options in housing the serials collection must consider four factors: (1) Are the serials in question bound volumes or unbound issues? (2) Are they periodicals or nonperiodical serials? (3) Are the library stacks open to all patrons, or are they closed? and (4) Is the serials collection classified or alphabetized? This section does not cover housing of microforms; that comes later in the chapter.

Bound Volumes

Many libraries, particularly research libraries, treat bound serials and monographs alike with respect to housing. They catalog and classify each title and interfile all bound serials with monographs in a single stack arrangement. Other libraries place all serials except monographic series in alphabetical order, with or without a class number. Still others shelve all nonperiodical serials with monographs and alphabetize bound journals. A final option is to classify all serials, but segregate them from monographs.

Periodicals. The first decision to make about housing bound volumes is how to treat periodicals, because they comprise the largest number of serial volumes and are a high percentage of the total collection in special and academic departmental libraries. Because they are usually collections of articles, periodicals are used differently than monographs. More than other serials, they are accessible through indexes and abstract journals. On the other hand, periodicals contain information, just as the rest of the collection does; to some librarians and patrons, format is not valid justification for different shelving treatment.

The needs of patrons and staff members determine the appropriate means of housing bound periodicals. If the bookstack is closed to patrons, their need is only that staff members locate a volume quickly. In open stacks patrons can browse in their subjects of interest and have a larger base for examination when all volumes are together regardless of format. However, most periodicals cover a wider range of subjects than monographs and have general classification numbers, bringing a large group of periodicals together in those general numbers. For example, periodicals on American literature and twentieth-century fiction are likely to contain articles on Fitzgerald, but only a journal restricted to studies of this author is classified with monographs about his work.

New and infrequent library users may need guidance to the location of specific periodicals. It is often simpler to direct them to an alphabetical periodicals collection than to a classified bookstack where there is a possibility of the patron's not understanding the classification scheme. A segregated periodicals stack also permits fast reshelving of volumes which have been used, especially if there is a class number to eliminate the need for guesswork. This means of housing periodicals works best in a small library; the organization can get out of hand very quickly in a large collection.

Until two decades ago, the most obvious problem with an alphabetical arrangement of journals was generic titles having corporate authors. With AACR2, corporate authors have gradually decreased and the number of entries beginning "Journal" and "Bulletin" increased, relieving the corporate author problem but creating large groups of periodical titles beginning with the same generic word. One must decide how to file initials and prepositions. The library may elect the traditional word by word alphabetizing, or it can use "computer filing," in which prepositions and articles are ignored. After years of learning exact titles, such as *Journal of THE History of Ideas* and *Review of Economics AND Statistics,* some librarians have had to adapt gracefully to filing titles in a sequence designed for the way nonlibrarians think. Keyword searching and browsing in online catalogs have relieved the problem somewhat.

Bound periodicals housed separately from monographs and kept in alphabetical order may be easier for staff members to work with than a classified arrangement. There is no need to look up a call number to locate a journal. When a title changes, the new title, once cataloged, files under its own title, the name by which patrons will look for it. Circulation staff can project growth of the collection more easily if journals, which expand quickly and somewhat predictably, are segregated from the irregularly expanding monographs.

In a library having bound volumes shelved in closed stacks compact shelving can resolve a space problem. This shelving is suitable for open stacks if patrons are familiar with its operation, but it is more appropriate for closed areas because of the equipment movement involved. An additional benefit of closed stacks is the ease and increased validity of any use studies the staff conducts. With all serials use controlled through a checkout point, attendants can be sure of recording each consultation. Libraries with closed periodicals stacks also have the option of shelving by size, which conserves space. Here, especially, the use of a class number is essential. The serials public service staff that has a choice must weigh the pros and cons of each arrangement and determine the combination of options that will be most suitable to the local situation.

Nonperiodical Serials. The same options exist for housing nonperiodical serials, and the same factors are considered. When periodicals are interfiled with monographs, all nonperiodical serials are interfiled also; if periodicals are housed separately from monographs, one must consider each type of nonperiodical serial individually. Monographic series classified separately are not a concern for serials personnel after the volumes are received and cataloged; they belong with other monographs in a classified bookstack. Analyzed monographic series consist of volumes that can stand alone, but they receive the same call number because they are closely related in content. Since many libraries circulate volumes of analyzed series as if they were monographs, they fit well into a classified collection. In libraries where analyzed series do not circulate, the decision may be to house them with periodicals if there is a separate periodicals stack. Annual reviews, proceedings, and other nonperiodical serials that are collections of articles require more study before their shelving location is determined. In general, if they do not circulate, they may be treated as periodicals; if they circulate, they may be shelved with monographs.

Whatever one decides, there must be written procedures and guidelines so the library staff understands the arrangement and can explain it to patrons, direct them to journals they seek, or quickly retrieve a bound volume. An alphabetically arranged periodicals collection with public access benefits from cross references in the form of wooden or heavy cardboard "dummies" showing relationships between titles: "*Zetetic* changed title to *Skeptical Inquirer* with vol. 2, no. 3. For later volumes see that title." Many librarians consider this detail a luxury, since the public record of serial holdings makes the relationship clear, but not all patrons use the official record, and citations in journals do not give earlier and later titles. On the other hand, not all patrons need to know the journal's history. A library may choose to employ cross references only in collections of bound volumes shelved in a periodicals reading room, although in the long run, the use of dummies saves staff time.

Unbound Issues

This section covers only periodicals, because other serials either arrive hardbound and go directly to their permanent location, or staff members process individually as soon as they arrive. When a library displays unbound issues of periodicals, some of the same considerations apply as with bound volumes, for example, the question of whether the arrangement is to be classified or alphabetical. Arrangement also depends on whether the collection of unbound serials is on open or restricted shelves, because access determines whether the order is for the patron's or the staff's convenience. The question of "alphabetical or classified" crops up regularly in the online discussion group SERIALST, and feelings run strong on both sides.

The author is a confirmed alphabetizer, although she realizes that there is another point of view. Presumably every library user and staff member knows the ABCs; not everyone knows the Library of Congress Classification or the Dewey Decimal System. To be sure, numerous faculty members would prefer to have all the journals of interest to them gathered together, in an alcove perhaps. Pleasing these patrons requires more duplicate subscriptions than use can justify, given the interdisciplinary nature of so many heavily used periodicals. Unbound journals in an open shelf reading room should be arranged by title or other main entry. If the collection is too large for the prime space allotted, select titles which will not be heavily used and shelve them in a secondary location. Although this practice is not ideal, it is preferable to breaking up the collection by subject or to using a strict classified arrangement.

Some libraries have the latest issue of selected titles on a display rack, perhaps protected in plastic covers. Another practice is to shelve all unbound issues on bookcases. A third alternative is use of the type of shelving that displays a single issue and stores other recent issues beneath that one.

A library providing a reading room for patrons using current periodicals will probably have lounge furniture, especially if newspapers are part of the collection. There will also be tables and individual carrels for persons doing research. If space permits, there can be an area for conversation and communal use of periodicals, although the location of such a grouping must be one which will ensure that talking does not disturb other patrons. At least one photocopy machine in the room helps keep periodicals in the area.

The library may not opt to display unbound issues on open shelves; alternatives are storing in a closed area or shelving them with the bound volumes (if those are also in closed stacks). The latter arrangement works best with a small journal collection and helps to keep retrieval time brief. For the same reason one might decide to keep unbound issues of selected high use titles close to the service point. When volumes and individual issues are housed together a page needs to look in only one place to locate the material and does not have to check binding records first. Even where open stacks are used, volumes and issues can be shelved together, provided the serials public service staff and library administration are able to compensate for the consequences of the lack of security for recent issues. This arrangement is not recommended because, with the larger space involved, it is virtually impossible to ensure that much used periodicals will remain in the vicinity of their shelf location.

Public Service Records

Whatever decisions the library makes about housing and circulating serials, there are occasions when staff members must rely on records to determine the current location and, therefore, the availability, of an item. One of these is the check-in record. Another heavily used tool is the binding record. Both of these technical processing files, which may be part of the same database, are essential for serials public service, because from them one can quickly answer the questions: "Have we received it?" and "Where should it be?" These two questions and their answers constitute a large percentage of serials public service communications. Thus, the proximity of both of these records to the service point is desirable and is another strong reason to have an integrated serials department and an integrated online management system.

The circulation record reveals whether a specific item is in use and may tell what serials are overdue to return. Even when library policy is not to circulate serials outside the building, there is occasionally a need to charge out some serials. However, circulation of noncirculating serials does not always fit well into the library's automated system. In this case, the serial circulation file may be more effective as a manual file, with each issue having its own checkout card. Or, the system could use a paper transaction slip which requires the notation of title, date, and borrower's identification.

Inhouse circulation of serials from closed areas is even easier done manually. At the University of North Carolina at Chapel Hill staff members use a simple mimeographed form for inhouse circulation of material that usually does not circulate. The assistant writes title, volume or issue, current date and his/her initials. Attached to this form as a sort of deposit or hostage is the patron's library card, or drivers license. (No credit cards, checkbooks, or car keys are accepted!) When the material returns, the patron gets the ID back. The system is not without minor problems—some patrons forget to pick up their IDs, others invariably come to the library without identification—but it works better than any other circulation method yet tried. One disadvantage of using a manual system is the absence of automated recording of use statistics.

Reserve

Sometimes a separate serials reserve is necessary, in addition to and separate from the library's main reserve collection. Many journal articles are too long to copy for reserve, and occasionally an entire periodical issue is devoted to one relevant topic. A professor mentions an article in class and twenty-five students want to read it within an hour. These are examples of situations in which the person responsible for serials public service can retrieve a volume from the stacks (leaving a dummy is a good idea) and temporarily circulate it for short periods from the serials service desk. Despite the fact that patrons must make an extra effort to obtain the material, the security often means that all those who need to use it are able to do so. When only a short or medium length article is needed, it is best to include it as part of the regular reserve collection, provided it can be photocopied legally and without damaging the journal. The article is conveniently located with other class reading on reserve, and the bound volume is available to other patrons in its place in the stacks. Only when the photocopying cannot be done and a reprint is not available should a serial volume be removed from its usual place and put on reserve.

Maintenance

A final aspect of the circulation function of serials public service is maintenance of the collection. Little is challenging about keeping bookstacks and reading rooms orderly, but no library can function without this care. Someone must reshelve the items and retrieve volumes and issues from the far reaches of the library. As issues accumulate, someone must identify those ready to be bound or replaced by microform and send them to be processed or discarded. Periodicals, especially daily newspapers, get misshelved and scattered; someone must straighten them. Staff members must identify and acquire or replace lost, not-yet-received, and mutilated pieces. Stacks need shifting more often than anyone would think. This list of necessary tasks points out the labor intensive nature of serials circulation work. Some of the operations are done or assisted by computers, but it is not likely that the time will ever come when some maintenance will not be done by human beings. The persons who perform maintenance tasks and their supervisors are essential to the successful operation of the serials department.

Another facet of serials maintenance is providing directional and instructional signs. In addition, patrons appreciate handouts describing the serials collection and services and giving instructions in the use of the department and its resources. A typical brochure describes the arrangement of the public areas of the department, type of assistance available, circulation policy, and reference tools at hand for patron use. Many libraries have posted visual guides that are phrased in the negative: "Materials may not be removed from this room" and "No refunds. Use coin copiers at your own risk." It has been suggested that signs with messages stated positively, "Please use materials only in this room," may be more effective than those stated negatively. With the continuing increase in mutilation of library materials, it is often beneficial to display a sign giving the state law concerning destruction of property and the resulting penalty. The sign serves as a deterrent and as an aid to staff when a patron is observed tampering with library material.

REFERENCE

This chapter earlier defined serials reference as the investigating function of serials public service. The need for an intermediate finding tool to identify journal articles makes access to the library's serials one step more difficult than locating monographs. Some libraries make available periodical indexes, abstracting tools, and even full-text databases through their online public catalogs, but most have not yet reached this point.

This discussion of serials reference service considers three phases of the topic: (1) selecting, identifying, and using indexes and abstract journals; (2) sources used to verify bibliographic information and interpretation of abbreviations; and (3) locating serials within the library or library system. Chapter 14 discusses locating serials in other libraries, current awareness services, and acquiring articles from beyond the library. The arrangement of these subtopics is deliberate; the patron first identifies the article needed, then learns the title of the journal which contains the article. Next, in most cases, the patron locates the journal and volume within the library, then reads or photocopies the relevant article. Journals which are not available in the library are located elsewhere, and interlibrary loan or another service obtains a copy of the article.

Indexes, Abstract Journals, and Bibliographies

"Where can I find articles on the South African election?" "Does *The Journal of Marriage and the Family* have its own index? Well, then, where is it indexed?" A popular category of serials public service questions concerns the availability of indexing coverage for periodicals. Several standard printed and electronic serials directories include in their list of subjects a category for periodical indexes and abstracting journals.

Ulrich's International Periodicals Directory[1] or its compact disc counterpart *Ulrich's Plus* is a good place to begin to look for current coverage, because journal entries list the names of periodical indexes which include their articles. The *Serials Directory*,[2] either in paper or on compact disc, based on the CONSER files, also lists this information. *Magazines for Libraries*[3] contains indexing availability for the titles included. *Indexed Periodicals*, by Joseph V. Marconi,[4] is a source for retrospective index sources of domestic and foreign titles covered by thirty-three standard American indexes before 1973. A more recent reference source is *Books and Periodicals Online*,[5] which lists 60,000 publications indexed in over 1,800 online sources and gives the years of indexing (and often the scope of major articles). These data are also available for loading into libraries' online catalogs. Subscription agents' annual catalogs are another source for indexing information. This listing has long been a feature of The Faxon Company's *Librarians' Guide* and EBSCO's *Librarians' Handbook*. At least once a year, if not in each issue, the indexes themselves print a list of titles included, so a good guess as to which source will index a specific periodical can often provide the answer quickly.

Some journals list their index coverage on the contents page or elsewhere in the front matter of each issue, but not enough of them do so to make it practical to check there first. This situation should have changed several years ago, however, because one proposal for consideration by the subcommittee revising the ANSI standard on "Periodicals: Format and Arrangement" was "that information be provided on the abstract journals and the bibliographic databases carrying abstracts or references to articles in the publication."[6] Unfortunately, the proposal was not incorporated into a standard.

The librarian who selects periodical indexes and abstract sources for purchase needs to know what proportion of the titles included are currently received or are likely to be added to the collection. If the library's constituency is primarily undergraduate students or townspeople needing general information, the match should be high to avoid having patrons frustrated by not being able to examine articles they find cited. For example, serials public service staff members found that a popular undergraduate resource, the old Infotrac, which indexed numerous periodicals (many of them obscure) caused consternation for students when they learned that the library lacked a high proportion of articles listed on their printouts. However, when a significant proportion of use is by graduate students and faculty members, it is not necessary for the library to subscribe to all the titles indexed or abstracted. Their contents are available through interlibrary loan and other library cooperative programs, and some periodicals covered in the index may be only remotely related to the library's areas of interest. Scholars may use indexes to establish that a topic has not been covered in the literature and proceed with their research with greater assurance of breaking new ground.

In general, the scope of the index considered for purchase should match closely the curriculum of the institution or the interests of the community supporting the library. If the index is acquired, it should be used. It should be relatively easy to use and to show patrons how to use. The service being evaluated needs to be examined in relation to other resources in the library or in nearby libraries. Finally, unless the index is new, one should look at its track record. Is it up to date? Is the list of titles covered increasing or at least stable? Are reviews of the index available? Serials are expensive and place a continuing and increasing obligation on the library materials budget; periodical indexes, especially electronic indexes, are expensive serials and must be purchased with particular care.

Much of the information in this section applies to serially published bibliographies as well as to periodical indexes and abstract sources. Recently, all of these secondary serials have increased in number and in the diversity of their physical characteristics. Not long ago the majority of American periodical indexes, and certainly most of those found in public and college libraries, were published in paper format by the H.W. Wilson Company: *Readers' Guide to Periodical Literature, Education Index, Business Periodicals Index*, and so on. There were other publishers; *Music Index* and *Public Affairs Information Service Bulletin* are examples of standard non-Wilson periodical indexes. Research libraries also subscribed to appropriate paper abstract journals, serials indexes which give, in addition to bibliographic data, a summary of the content of the article. *Chemical Abstracts, Biological Abstracts*, and *Psychological Abstracts* are examples of established print titles. Many scholarly disciplines have national or international associations which sponsor an annual bibliography of articles in journals and Festschriften, such as the *MLA Bibliography, Writings in American History*, and *L'Annee Philologique.*

As serial literature increased in volume in the second half of the twentieth century, as scholars began to specialize in more specific areas than before, and as federal grants gave libraries additional purchasing power, a market evolved for indexes, abstract journals, and bibliographies of increasingly narrow scope, for example, *Deafness, Speech and Hearing Abstracts* and *Pollution Abstracts*. Wilson's *Social Sciences and Humanities Index* divided into *Social Sciences Index* and *Humanities Index.*

During the 1970s indexers increased their attention to material other than journals. The *New York Times Index* has been published in book form for many years, but except for the indexes to *The Times* [*London*], the *Wall Street Journal*, and the *Christian Science Monitor*, there was no other serially published commercial newspaper index. In 1972 the microform publisher Bell and Howell began a current paper index to four newspapers for which they sold the microfilm edition: the *Washington Post*, the *Chicago Tribune*, the *Los Angeles Times*, and the *New Orleans Times-Picayune*. The existence of the index made the newspaper film more attractive to libraries and provided access to columns, editorials, and news stories which had previously been lost. Bell and Howell indexed other newspapers as well, particularly those contained in their ethnic and cultural microfilm collections. Additional microfilming companies followed this lead. When Research Publications won the right to film the *Washington Post*, it began to publish a printed index to the newspaper which, apparently, was so successful that Bell and Howell gave up their index. An expansion of the practice of indexing newspapers was making available the contents of television news programs. For example, Microfilming Corporation of America published microform transcripts of CBS news broadcasts and special news programs and of the "MacNeil-Lehrer Report," with printed indexes to both series. Research Publications and UMI are among the companies now producing full-text, compact disc versions of news programs from the networks. The searching capability of the compact disc has obviated the need for printed or online indexes to these resources.

A trend begun in the mid-1960s led back toward resources with a broader scope, possibly because of the early automation of indexing and the practice of Key-Word-In-Context (KWIC) indexing. Institute for Scientific Information was a trailblazer of this period with, first *Science Citation Index*, then *Social Science Citation Index* and *Arts and Humanities Citation Index*, all of which employ the concept of citation analysis to evaluate journals. Several of the standard abstract journals became available on magnetic tape, and large libraries and consortia that could justify the high price purchased them in this format.

The next step was online bibliographic services, such as Knight-Ridder's DIALOG and Bibliographic Retrieval Services, Inc., through which subscribers could access several databases, one at a time, by the use of a search strategy. (Dialog later introduced OneSearch, that lets an individual search a number of databases at the same time.) Terms could be included and excluded, and a search could be made more specific by combining concepts (for example: advertising + children). A patron could see online a list of the articles that the search had identified—a bibliography tailor made to a person's research needs— and could obtain a printout of the references. These services charged for access, so patrons or the library paid a cost for each use. At additional cost the patron could often acquire copies of the articles cited. Thus, currency and speed were available to scholars and other researchers for a price. The online bibliographic services in academic libraries were used most often by graduate students who were beginning the literature search for their theses and dissertations.

It was assumed that online services would increase in popularity but would never totally replace the printed indexes and abstract journals, because the cost, even if it should drop sharply, could not always be justified. An undergraduate doing a class term paper seldom requires the speed that money can buy; the comparatively inexpensive *Readers' Guide* and similar printed indexes served well for that term paper. In addition, librarians recognized that the person who identified references and located articles manually was learning to do research. There would be time later for data to be provided by a machine, if that were necessary. Many libraries did not need to support the kind of research for which the online bibliographic services were designed, and they would waste funds that could be used to better advantage. But the online bibliographic services were irreplaceable for those whose need for current data could justify the cost.

Librarians believed that online databases would become crucial for them to access in their support of scholarly research. *Psychological Abstracts*, for instance, had more sources of data available online than were available in the printed index. In addition, online databases indexed newspapers such as the *New York Times* and the *Washington Post*. Some periodical indexes, such as *Magazine Index*, were available only online or on microfiche. The *Magazine Index* covered all periodicals included in the *Readers' Guide* and more, and a complete new cumulation of the microfiche edition was provided monthly.

During the 1980s secondary serials indexing the contents of journals began to appear in a format that resolved the problem of cost of access. The compact-disc-read-only-memory, or CD-ROM, seemed to be the near-perfect combination of currency and cost. Libraries subscribing to the usual periodical indexes and abstract journals on compact disc pay an annual subscription fee and have access without a per-use charge. The only equipment required is a compact disc drive attached to a personal computer. Many CD-ROM indexes can be marked to indicate which journals the library owns, and some can be edited to give the local call number. Likewise, some online databases that are loaded into library catalogs have this capability.

Access to the discs' contents is by means of several elements, for example, title, publisher, date, author. As with online services, terms can be combined, but in addition, many compact discs permit Boolean searching (i.e., the use of "or," and "not"), although CD indexes are still not as flexible as the online services. Indexes that had been published on microfilm or other technologies (e.g., *Infotrac, Magazine Index*) switched to compact disc and were infinitely more useful than they had been with only a single access point. The index is updated, usually quarterly, by receipt of a new cumulated disc. The success of a specific publication depends on the quality of its software, and some are more sophisticated than others. An index is not necessarily published by a single company. The H.W. Wilson indexes, for example, are available on compact discs from both that company and other publishers such as Silver-Platter.

In acquiring compact discs, librarians had to resolve a potential problem. One does not purchase the disc, but signs a lease agreement with the publisher to return the outdated disc upon receipt of a new one. If the library cancels its subscription to the index, it agrees to return the last disc. Institutional attorneys needed to examine the agreements and to approve their acceptance. Leasing rather than purchasing had an impact on library acquisition of indexing and abstracting serials. It would seem natural for the library to cancel its subscription to the paper edition of a publication for which it received the compact disc edition. However, the need to return the last disc in the event of cancellation means that if the library does cancel, it will be left with nothing for the years during which it received only the compact disc. This possibility has made many librarians refrain from cancelling paper subscriptions that they had perhaps considered giving up. In addition, some CD-ROM indexes have a lower price if the library subscribes to the paper version. Librarians must reevaluate this policy in times of fiscal crisis.

An even bigger problem in the beginning was getting companies to realize that librarians wanted to network CD-ROMs and that "networking" did not mean buying three discs to let three users have access. In other words, librarians did not want to pay three times the cost, although they recognized that they should pay more than for a single use service. The producers' responses have varied; some charge more, some do not care, and some are still trying to figure it out.

In the beginning, CD-ROM was touted as the format to end all formats; so was microfilm a few decades ago. There will always be a newer, better format, and librarians can expect something to eclipse compact discs in time. Another claim being questioned is the longevity of the discs. They were believed to be virtually indestructible when they appeared. Now, some tests project compact discs' lifespan to be no more than five or ten years. For a disc used no longer than three months, five years is no problem, but discs used for other purposes than cumulating indexes may force librarians to consider useful life of the disc and devise means of refreshing their data.

The indexes and abstract journals already discussed have been commercial publications. An index to a single journal, distributed as a part of the subscription, or a cumulative index to a journal, available from the publisher, is usually more a service and less for profit than the indexes noted above. To the patron looking for articles on a specific topic, indexes to individual journals are less useful than an index covering many periodicals. However, self-indexes can be valuable for serials which are not covered in commercial indexes in the library collection, for identification of an article when the source journal is known, and for a historical study or an analysis of the content of a single journal.

Indexes and abstract journals may be housed either with the periodical collection or in the reference department, in both places, or in some other location which suits the library's needs. Wherever these works are located, there should be staff assistance and adequate hardware. This guidance is particularly important for the basic indexes used by high school students or undergraduates, because training in the best use of a standard, general periodical index is the groundwork for later use of complex indexing and abstracting tools. The library's physical facilities and its patrons' level of sophistication in library use are both factors in determining the optimum location for indexes. Self-indexes are conveniently shelved with the journal, so the patron does not need to search elsewhere for the periodical after the locating the citation, as he or she must do when using commercial indexes and abstract journals or printed indexes to microform serials.

Sources Used for Verification of Bibliographic Information and Interpretation of Abbreviations

This chapter makes no effort to list comprehensively the tools one uses in answering identification questions about serials. The reference collection is not limited to works housed in a single department but extends to the entire range of library resources and gateways. Part of the satisfaction and joy of reference service is discovering (preferably with the patron along to share the excitement) that obscure work which answers exactly the question being asked.

Records assisting in the identification of serials and the verification of title, price, address, and other facts about a serial fall into several groups: directories (*Ulrich's International Periodicals Directory*), union lists (*Union List of Serials in Libraries of the United States and Canada*), subject guides (*Writings in American History*), catalogs (*National Union Catalog*), bibliographic utility databases, and a huge miscellaneous class. When using these tools, and especially when evaluating conflicting information, consider the authority of the person or organization responsible for the contents.

American librarians traditionally have accepted the work done by the staff members of the Library of Congress as the best authority in the area of cataloging and bibliographic control. Works or databases reproducing LC cataloging were taken as accurate unless there was reason to question the cataloging, such as an obvious typographical error or transposed letters in a call number.

The Library of Congress publishes works that reproduce the cataloging of a number of other research libraries, for example, *CONSER on CD* and *MARC on CD*. In the old *National Union Catalog* it was easy to recognize entries representing LC cataloging; those were the printed (not typed) cards with LC card numbers. In the CONSER file, however, only the notation of the Library of Congress as a holding library ensures that the cataloging was done by LC. There was no indication of the responsibility for cataloging the serials listed in the old *New Serial Titles*; only in the "Changes in Serials" section was the contributing institution named. For this reason NST (like ULS) did not have quite the authority of NUC. Beginning in 1981, NST was produced from CONSER tapes showing the complete bibliographic record in catalog card format entered into the database by LC, the National Library of Canada, the National Serials Data Program, and other CONSER participants. At the same time NST dropped its union catalog function, the "Changes in Serials" section, and the post-1949 starting date requirement. The first issues of NST in its new format contained only Library of Congress cataloging, much of which was partial (lacking call number and subject heading) or not according to AACR2. While the 1950 to 1980 volumes of NST are a valuable resource, the later issues are of little use to the serials public service librarian who has access to the OCLC or RLIN database or *CONSER on CD*. Because of the strict cataloging standards to which CONSER members are held, their cataloging is accepted today as authoritative by many librarians. Staff cuts have forced libraries to lessen their standards for economic reasons.

Reed Reference Publishing, formerly the R.R. Bowker Company, produces several directories and other serials reference sources which use the *Anglo-American Cataloguing Rules* in determining the main entry. The Reed publications also make liberal use of cross references from earlier and variant entries. In 1981 the Bowker database became available online. The fact that the Bowker serials database was selected to assign the first group of ISSN bestows further authority upon that company. The H.W. Wilson Company in the United States and certain publishers in other countries have a similar relationship to the library community.

For reference questions concerning subscriptions and other types of purchases, the date of information is a crucial consideration in determining authority. Serials occasionally change title and publisher, but price is the aspect of a periodical which changes most rapidly; today a printed source more than a year or two old cannot give a reliable approximation of price. The cutoff dates for printed listings in *Ulrich's, Standard Periodical Directory*, and similar works is a year or more before publication. Prices in *Ulrich's Plus* are probably more current. Additional help for this type of question comes in the form of subscription agents' databases, whose prices reflect very recent information, because the vendor has placed orders for the publications listed. In the United States both EBSCO Subscription Services and The Faxon Company have good, extensive databases. The agents' databases are available online to subscribing libraries, for up-to-the-minute information. Chapter 6 discusses these tools more fully.

Two kinds of sources of abbreviations aid the patron who needs to determine the full name of a serial: abbreviation dictionaries and lists of abbreviations used in specific publications. One of the most useful book collections of abbreviations, compiled from many periodical indexes and annual bibliographies, is *Periodical Title Abbreviations*.[7] It does not include chemical serial abbreviations, because this field has an excellent guide to its literature in *Chemical Abstracts Service Source Index* (CASSI). Deciphering abbreviations can be frustrating for both librarian and patron, because some authors devise their own journal abbreviations (which may not appear in any directory). Some patrons decide for themselves what an abbreviation stands for and may request help in locating a journal title that does not exist. The first step in resolving this problem is to verify the title in a serials directory.

Most periodical indexes, subject bibliographies, and similar works either contain a list of the serial title abbreviations they use or state that they follow standard abbreviations, such as those of the Modern Language Association. Most lists are not long and are usually included in each issue or at least in one issue a year. A librarian might assume that the patron would expect to find a list of abbreviations for *Education Index* serials in the publication itself and would locate and use it, but patrons do not always reason the way librarians hope they will. However, when a patron presents an abbreviation from one of the standard indexes and asks for help, there is a great opportunity to teach library use. One method is to have a photocopy of the list of abbreviations at hand and to explain; another is to accompany the patron to the index and assist him or her there. As a diehard "Teach-Them-To-Use-the-Library-for-Themselves" advocate, the author opposes simply answering the title identification question without showing the patron how to find the full title next time.

Location of Serials Within the Library or Library System

Location of serials is the aspect of reference that bears most resemblance to circulation. It is a function of reference service to enable the patron to determine where an article should be; if the volume is not there, the query becomes a circulation matter. In serials work the same library staff member often assists in both cases. Many patrons have not figured out that journals as well as books are in the online catalog. When they do discover this, the next problem may be determining which of the five or six listings for *Time,* for example, is the one they need.

The tool used to determine the permanent and, sometimes, temporary location of a serial is the library's serials holdings record. Many years ago, in most libraries this record was in card form, either interfiled with cards for monographs in the public catalog or segregated in a serials card catalog. When the library received a bound serial or when a collected volume returned from the bindery, part of the internal processing was changing the holdings record on the card, either by erasing the pencilled final volume number and date and supplying the new one, or by checking the next date or volume on a specially printed holdings card.

A few libraries may still use this card record as either the official record of holdings or a supplement to a COM catalog or automated system. In either case this method of noting serial holdings is expensive, a labor intensive luxury. Yet there are times when only this record will give the answer to a patron's question; there is something reassuring about a check mark made forty years ago. Or not made! It may be that this card record is the only one which provides complete bibliographic information about a title, for the early automated catalogs of serials often gave no more than title and, perhaps, place of publication and beginning date, along with summarized local holdings. There were no standards, no OCLC, no CONSER. Each library set up its own system and tried to produce a serials holdings list as inexpensively as possible. More recently the existence of the MARC format, the reduced costs of computer hardware and software, and the necessity and desirability of interlibrary cooperation have worked together to improve the quality and usefulness of many computerized serial holdings records. Increasingly, the official record of serial holdings is integrated into the online public catalog. Assistance is available in the form of a NISO standard: *Serial Holdings Statements* (Z39.44-1986). This standard is evidence of an increased awareness on the part of the library and scholarly world of serials' value to research and of problems in bibliographic control of serials. The impact of the standard depends upon its voluntary use by librarians, just as the impact of other standards such as the ISSN and ISBN have depended upon their use by publishers and others.

The serial acquisitions check-in record is also a reference tool, provided one asks the right questions. It is most reliable when consulted for recent information. The definition of "recent" depends upon several library policies: Are all received serials entered on the serial record? How long are these records retained? There are other questions that help to define the usefulness of the serial record as a reference source: Does this file include serials received for the entire library system? Are binding records kept in the check-in file? An earlier discussion of the serial record presents other factors to consider for reference use. But the simplest and probably most asked serials reference question is: "Has the library received the [latest] issue?" And that is what the serial record is all about!

SERVICES TO PEOPLE WITH DISABILITIES

by Naomi Kietzke
University of North Carolina at Chapel Hill

The library profession, along with other service occupations, has on its own and by necessity become more aware of the difficulties that persons with disabilities face in an environment designed for the majority. Statutes require that public institutions, and private institutions receiving public funds, be accessible for all persons. The best known of these, in the United States, is the federal Americans with Disabilities Act of 1991. Other jurisdictions have similar requirements. Many people have looked with alarm at the provisions of these laws, believing them to be an additional stress on overburdened agencies. Closer examination shows, however, that the library ethic of information access to all people (as well as the profession's skill at "providing more and more with less and less") means that librarians are ideally prepared in many ways to comply with the law's provisions.

One exception may be physical access to the collections. Unfortunately, the cost of compliance within existing buildings prohibits remodelling in most cases, and new construction is slow to replace the old. The library's overall policy on service to disabled patrons, as well as applicable national or local standards, determines such things as access to the building and facilities and the width of aisles in the stacks. While a library's ultimate plan for new construction must include plans for providing optimal access, creative use of the library's existing resources can be an excellent interim solution.

Serials public service staff members can do much to promote the use of serials resources by those who are mobility, sight, or hearing impaired, or otherwise restricted in their use of the library. The most significant step in expanding access is providing information about the availability of services. Like many "average" patrons, people with disabilities may not be aware of the range of services the library offers, or they may have exaggerated expectations. The key is reference interviewing; determining the patron's need and matching it to library resources. Your patrons will often be your best help in finding creative suggestions, once they know they are going to be heard respectfully. Many adaptations can be grouped under the policy of relaxing the rules: permitting serials to be checked out to areas where reading equipment is available; extending informal limits on the length of an interview to allow for the slower process of note writing or using an ASL interpreter; providing typing rooms and a Kurzweil Reader, if available; retrieving volumes from the stacks for those who cannot do so for themselves; arranging furnishings in the best way possible for patrons who use wheelchairs; offering a chair to a patron on crutches before beginning lengthy bibliographic instruction. Some institutions offer sign language courses for their employees; a staff member able to communicate in this way is a decided asset to the library and to the community.

Equally as important as written policies on service to disabled patrons is a good staff attitude, one characterized by a willingness to ease, with respect, the difficulty of using the library. This necessary flexibility does not differ for serials public service from any other area of the library; it is a consideration that must not be neglected or denied.

NONPRINT PUBLIC SERVICE

Both compact disc serials and microform serials present a different set of decisions regarding their treatment than paper serials. Perhaps in a few years CD-ROM materials will become as easy to use as printed resources, but for now many people need assistance in the use of the discs and the computers through which they are accessed. When a library has invested heavily in compact discs and the associated hardware, it is often practical to group them in a separate public service area, generally associated with a reference department, and to train certain staff members in the use of electronic resources. The housing of CD-ROMs depends on their use; heavily-used works may, if permitted by the license, be networked or offered as menu items through the online catalog. Other services may be restricted to registered users of the library and thus to specific computers. Circumstances may change, but for now there is need for centralized administration of CD-ROM serials and services.

Despite the fact that many reference serials are now produced on CD-ROM, libraries still receive a significant number of serials in microform. Besides having been available longer, microforms are simpler to use and are not restricted by licensing agreements.

Chapter 12 discusses the factors to consider in deciding whether to retain serials in microform. This section suggests ways of providing public service for whatever titles the library chooses to preserve in this format. Serials in microform, like bound volumes, can be housed in a number of ways. It is efficient to house all microforms together, whether serials or monographs, because of the mechanical readers and copiers necessary for patrons to use them. Much microform public service is instruction in use of the reader; operating the reader/printer, which may or may not be coin operated; and limited machine maintenance, such as replacing light bulbs and unjamming the focus. The library gives best service to the user by bringing together microforms and mechanical readers in the same unit. This arrangement promotes use of microforms, deters patrons from scattering microforms all over the library, and facilitates timely reshelving. A separate serials stack within a large microform area means that the serial microforms are concentrated in a smaller area, thus making use and service simpler. This concentration can be effected through the classification scheme.

If bound and microform serials are interfiled, either there must be readers throughout the stack without staff attention at hand, or microforms must be taken to the area of the library which contains the readers. Another possibility is circulating microforms and portable readers for use outside the building, provided the library is willing to maintain these readers.

Microforms can be placed on open shelves with printed serials, but this practice sacrifices both shelf space and the means of protection from climate, dirt, and loss. ANSI standards recommend a temperature of 60-70 degrees Fahrenheit, with humidity between 40 and 50 percent. These conditions are difficult to obtain in open stacks under the best conditions. In addition, the acid content of most nonarchival paper is even more destructive to film than it is to the paper itself.

There are many types of microform storage units, and special adaptations of regular shelving exist. Some libraries simply put the stack shelves five inches apart instead of twelve in areas where they have a large amount of reel microfilm, but if the library has made a commitment to preserve its resources in microform, then it should have invested in special cabinets. This equipment is expensive and is not used to best advantage if it is scattered, partially filled, through a library's bookstack. For the storage of microfiche there is no better method than special cabinets, but for microfilm, storage in cabinets may present problems for uninitiated patrons and can damage film containers. Special five by five inch shelving appears more inviting to the patron and can be easier on the film, but this form of storage needs to be braced across the top, since it is high and narrow.

For optimum use of space and equipment, all or most microforms the library owns should be kept in one location with machines and staff. This arrangement separates serial microforms from bound volumes, but the need for microform staff to be trained specifically in serials public service really does not exist. Once the patron identifies the article needed, he or she rarely requires assistance from serials staff. Thus, there is no need for microform service to be a part of the serials department. However, if microforms are part of the serials unit, serials public service staff members must be familiar with machine maintenance procedures, as well as with serials work. If there is a separate microform reading area, microform staff members need know little about serials, provided they are able to communicate quickly with serials personnel.

Microform serials that are collections of source material on a theme or transcripts of network news programming often create problems for users and require staff assistance. Some of these sets have indexes. For example, UMI's *American Periodicals Series* has a print index and a CD-ROM index that gets down to the article level. Many collections still have no index. The proper location for the indexes that do exist can be a controversial matter when microforms are segregated and housed away from professional public service staff. If there are two copies of the index, one can go with the microforms and one can be kept in reference; if there is only one index, the library needs a policy about location. Having the index in reference, away from the set, can lead to a feeling on the part of staff that the microform must be used with instruction and therefore must be moved out of the microform area into the reference department. This practice undermines the policy of grouping microforms for most efficient use of readers and space. When the lone copy of an index is located at any distance from the microform, patrons may need to travel back and forth and thus become disgruntled. The best policy is to order two copies of the index to a microform set. When there is an index housed with the microform collection, microform staff members can learn to use it.

CONCLUSION

Many aspects of the serials public service function of the library have developed in recent years—electronic bibliographic service, circulation of microforms with their readers. It is reasonable to expect that more and better ways of assisting patrons in the use of serials resources will be possible in years to come. There will begin to be less traditional public service as described in this chapter and more assistance tailored to the individual patron. Nonetheless, it will be many years before reference sources and human assistance are totally replaced by machines, if that time ever comes.

NOTES

1. *Ulrich's International Periodicals Directory*. (New Providence, NJ: Reed Reference Publishing).

2. *The Serials Directory*. (Birmingham, AL: EBSCO Publishing).

3. Katz, Bill, and Katz, Linda Sternberg, eds. *Magazines for Libraries*. 7th ed. (New Providence, NJ: Reed Reference Publishing, 1992).

4. Marconi, Joseph V. *Indexed Periodicals.* (Ann Arbor, MI: Pierian Press, 1976).

5. *Books and Periodicals Online.* 6th ed. (New York: Library Alliance, 1994).

6. *Voice of Z39.* 2 (1980): 23.

7. *Periodical Title Abbreviations*, 9th ed. (Detroit: Gale Research Company, 1992).

Chapter 14

ACCESS TO SERIALS:
SERIALS OUTSIDE THE LIBRARY

Library patrons need to use information in serials not held by their own library. That need is heightened by the "access versus ownership" issue discussed in Chapter 1. The purchasing power of library materials funds is in a steady downfall, and no library can subscribe to every serial one of its patrons may need. Again and again we hear that the days of "Just in Case" are gone; this is the era of "Just in Time," or acquisition of information at the point of need. Now, through increasingly sophisticated electronic technology, librarians and library users can retrieve articles easily and quickly from journals held elsewhere. The use of acquisitions monies is shifting from subscriptions and standing orders to document delivery services of various types. At the same time, individuals are spending more of their own funds for this information, which may actually cost less than using the interlibrary loan service.

This chapter defines "document delivery" very broadly. It covers traditional interlibrary loan, sharing of serial resources within a library consortium, and commercial article delivery services. Document delivery itself is nothing new, but rapid document delivery *is* new, as is the shift from the librarian serving as an intermediary to the user identifying and retrieving his or her own articles.

Because no library can or wants to own every existing serial, there are times when a patron or a staff member needs to know what other library holds a specific title and which volumes it has. Historically there were two serious obstacles to using serials in other libraries: bibliographic access and physical access.

Card catalogs and printed union lists of serials had limited use to researchers unable to consult them in person. Online bibliographic access has virtually eliminated this problem. Physical access has been more difficult to change, what with an overloaded interlibrary loan system, although the use of fax machines has helped. With commercial document delivery, physical access to serials not in one's own library has become quite easy, for a price. In most cases, the commercial services aim at least as much toward the individual consumer as toward the library. These new services have many implications for libraries and librarians.

LOCATING SERIALS IN OTHER LIBRARIES

In a startling departure from the access frustrations of two decades ago, the Internet has proved to be a most useful way to locate serials in other libraries. Increasing numbers of libraries provide World Wide Web or gopher access to their online catalogs. The researcher, however, must use these resources one by one; union lists of serials may be easier to use.

Union Lists of Serials

A union list of serials is a single source designed to answer questions about serial location and holdings in several libraries. The scope of contributors to the union list may be national, as was the *British Union-Catalogue of Periodicals*; international, as is OCLC's CONSER File; regional, as is the Minnesota Union List of Serials; or local, as is the catalog of the serial holdings of all libraries on a university campus or in a municipal library system.

With the economic necessity for cooperation among libraries beginning in the 1970s, union lists of serials proliferated and appeared in various formats: cards, printed books, microform, and automated. The ALA/ALCTS Serials Section formed a committee on union lists of serials; NISO Z39 created the serial holdings standard. Libraries sought and received federal and private grants to fund projects leading to union lists of serials. Subscription agents produced union lists for both customers and noncustomers, and the bibliographic utilities developed union listing capability, in addition to the entire utility database serving as a giant union list.

The value of union lists of serials, both for locating a specific title in a library and for purposes such as verification of bibliographic data varies widely. At one extreme is the uncomplicated finding list with title, location, and holdings; at the other is the online union list which attaches the issue-specific holdings record to a full, current cataloging record. Most union lists of serials fall somewhere in between and, used together, complement each other. When conflicting information appears, one may tentatively resolve the problem by considering the authority of the compiling institution, the purpose of the union list, and the currency of the data.

Union lists of serials began as manually compiled holdings lists for individual libraries; some were only abbreviated replicas of receipt file information that could be distributed to locations distant from the check-in center. In a library system with branches, the list probably originated as a combined list for all or part of the system. Universities belonging to a multi-campus system and public libraries belonging to a city or county system compiled union lists of the holdings of all member libraries. Later, groups of librarians began to work together, forming networks and consortia. Some of these cooperative groups formed primarily because of a desire to produce a union list of serial holdings.

The *Union List of Serials in Libraries of the United States and Canada* (*ULS*), originally published in 1927, was the first nationwide or international list of serial titles and holdings. The preface to the third edition, published in 1965, contains a fascinating account of the preparation of each edition; it is worth reading. Consider the labor intensiveness of the project and the increasing cost of producing each edition. Also impressive is the growth in number of serials listed, growth not primarily because the scope of the list was expanded, but because new serials appeared and more libraries contributed their titles and holdings. The first edition of *ULS* listed 75,000 titles, nearly twice as many as anticipated, and holdings for 225 libraries. When the second edition appeared in 1943, it had 115,000 titles from 650 libraries, and the third edition (with a cutoff date of 1949) contained over 156,000 titles and holdings from 956 libraries.[1]

By the time the third edition was underway, the cost of continuing *ULS* had become prohibitively expensive. Further, in 1951 the Library of Congress had begun to issue a list of its newly acquired serials. Beginning in 1953 LC expanded its list to include coverage of other American libraries and renamed it *New Serial Titles* (*NST*). The scope of *NST* was limited to serial titles first published after December 31, 1949, and received by LC and cooperating libraries. Unlike *ULS*, *NST* was able to report bibliographic and holdings data on a current basis, because it was issued monthly, with quarterly, annual, and multi-year cumulations. In 1973 the R.R. Bowker Company published a twenty-one year cumulation to *NST* for the years 1950 to 1970, enabling libraries to replace multiple alphabetical lists with one.

Beginning in 1981, *NST* dropped its union list function, along with its valuable "Changes in Serials" section. It now reproduces the CONSER bibliographic records created within the period of coverage. Each current issue is larger than in the early years because *NST* is no longer restricted to titles beginning publication after 1949. Today *NST* reproduces the entire catalog record in card format, similar to records formerly included in the *National Union Catalog*. For librarians and patrons with easy access to the OCLC database, *NST* is now redundant as a source of current information because each record appears online well before it is distributed in print. OCLC members also have access to the symbols of libraries holding newly cataloged serials and, for union list participants, to standardized holdings statements.

The value to American libraries of the *Union List of Serials* and *New Serial Titles* was immense. They provided in convenient format a guide to the location of serial literature throughout the continent. Local and regional union lists are more useful for popular titles such as *Cosmopolitan* and *American Historical Review*, because the expense of borrowing or obtaining photocopies of articles is likely to be lower from a nearby library. Institutions in the same geographical area often have reciprocal copying or borrowing agreements. For smaller circulation titles, however, the national union lists have served a need well. Librarians used them not only for interlibrary loan purposes, but also for verification, because their bibliographic information is among the most authoritative available. The third edition of *ULS* followed Library of Congress cataloging, but *NST* carries that authority only if LC is listed as a holding library. Other *NST* entries are those submitted by the library that cataloged the title, so their authority equals that of the contributing library's cataloging.

Editors of and contributors to local and regional union lists of serials face many of the same problems as compilers of the national lists. Both the absence of standards for reporting holdings statements and the differences in library cataloging policies and detail made centralized editing and quality control a thankless job in manually produced lists. With the growing number of online union lists possible on the local level and through the bibliographic utilities, editing is likely to be decentralized and quality control is even more difficult unless participants adhere to standards.

National Periodical System / National Periodical Center

In the past the research library attempted to supply from its own collection virtually all materials its patrons needed. Increasingly, librarians have turned to interlibrary loan to supplement their collections as the growing volume and cost of books and journals made it unrealistic for any library to be independent of other libraries. In recent years, photocopies of articles replaced the actual periodical requested on interlibrary loan. The "lending" library usually assesses a charge to cover copying, service, and postage charges. However, by the mid-1970s, the volume of serial requests, the cost of obtaining the photocopy and the time required for the transaction had all so increased that the traditional system was no longer considered satisfactory.

Great Britain has a very successful program for lending and photocopying articles administered by the British Library Document Supply Centre (BLDSC). This resource, originally the National Lending Library for Science and Technology and later the British Library Lending Division, is located near the city of York and subscribes to over 50,000 serials. It holds, in addition, technical reports, conference proceedings, and translations of foreign language articles. BLDSC lends volumes domestically and supplies photocopies for foreign requests, many of them through the Center for Research Libraries, UnCover, and other document suppliers. In 1994/95 BLDSC received 2,992,139 domestic and 920,076 foreign requests and supplied 89.3 percent from its own holdings. Use of other collections reduced the unfilled rate to 6.6 percent.[2]

In 1977 the Library of Congress, acting on a recommendation of the National Commission on Libraries and Information Science (NCLIS), asked the Council on Library Resources to devise a technical plan for a National Periodical Center (NPC, to be operated by the Library of Congress) to house certain journals and to provide libraries with copies of articles in lieu of interlibrary loan. Completed in August 1978 under the direction of C. Lee Jones, the *National Periodicals Center: Technical Development Plan* recommended a three-tier National Periodical System, of which NPC was the middle level. Tier one was the local and regional level and tier three was NPC referral to specified research and special libraries. NPC would be

> a centralized collection of periodical literature directly accessible to libraries throughout the nation. Initially projected at 36,000 titles...the collection would continue to grow prospectively (adding more titles) and retrospectively (acquiring back files) according to an established strategy and in as timely a fashion as possible....Eventually the collection may number in excess of 60,000 current titles, but it will never contain all of the estimated 200,000 currently published periodicals.[3]

Other details presented in the technical plan concerned (1) the existence of a "finding tool" organized by ISSN and key title, (2) establishment of a deposit account for each library or consortium having direct access to NPC, (3) provision for compliance with copyright legislation, (4) internal processing and transportation of requests, (5) funding, and (6) governance.

After reviewing the CLR technical plan, NCLIS encouraged reaction from all those concerned and held an open forum attended by 190 persons. The NCLIS 1978/79 Annual Report stated:

> The forum, as well as some of the letters and statements received in response to NCLIS' solicitation of comments, revealed that a certain amount of doubt and skepticism existed, primarily within the private sector, on such questions as: whether a national periodical center was, indeed, needed; whether it should be subsidized through federal funding; whether new technology would make outmoded a service based on physical collections; whether the present concept adequately exploits private sector capabilities; whether copyright liability was properly addressed; whether the proposed center's collections should duplicate commonly held titles and whether the center needed to develop new finding tools.[4]

One librarian's dilemma on the subject was revealed in the following statement:

> The Center...would eventually have any part of any journal on all subjects except clinical medicine available to any library, within a 24-hour period, with even copyright problems settled....With a program such as this one, along with the better coordination of the networks, where will the challenge come for that special breed of people called serials librarians?[5]

While the debate continued, NCLIS commissioned and received from Arthur D. Little, Inc., a report entitled *A Comparative Evaluation of Alternative Systems for the Provision of Effective Access to Periodical Literature*, which described three levels of access systems but did not make a firm recommendation. In the meantime a Periodicals Legislative Drafting Team of NCLIS had prepared a draft bill creating a federally subsidized National Periodical System, of which the Center was to be a part. NCLIS voted to support this draft plan.

Efforts continued to have legislation passed creating a National Periodical System and in late 1980 Congress approved the amendment and extension of the Higher Education Act of 1965. Part D of Title II provided for a

> National Periodical System Corporation, which shall not be considered an agency or establishment of the United States Government....The corporation shall assess the feasibility and advisability of a national system and, if feasible and advisable, design such a system to provide reliable and timely document delivery from a comprehensive collection of periodical literature.[6]

Unfortunately, funding of Part D depended upon full funding of Part A, Part B, and Part C, which did not occur, so there the matter ended. Other factors worked against the NPC, including the lack of wholehearted support from the library community, the opposition of publishers and the ambitions of other groups to fill this purpose.

It appears that today commercial document delivery services have filled the gap left by the rejection of the National Periodical Center. That "special breed of people called serials librarians" are, in many libraries, very much involved in document delivery.

Current Contents Services

In the future it is almost certain that there will be fewer journals issued in the print format we know now. Production and distribution costs have reached levels that prohibit libraries from continuing the most expensive and marginal subscriptions. There is a growing feeling that scholarly information will eventually be communicated routinely by the selective dissemination of information (SDI). That is, the scholar will rely primarily on a computer terminal display of bibliographic citations with either abstracts or complete articles and will order electronically produced and transmitted copies of the texts of relevant works. The proliferation of esoteric journals will diminish and cease; libraries will no longer subscribe to periodicals which are consulted by only one or two patrons.

Some libraries have a current awareness service for patrons through which they regularly send photocopies of title pages or abstracts from selected journals. In special libraries this service may be free of charge, but many other libraries impose a fee to cover at least the photocopying costs. SDI is an almost impossible activity for serials public service librarians in a general academic or public library to attempt for their patrons because of the subject knowledge required to select and abstract and the amount of time consumed by this service. It might be feasible to permit faculty members and graduate students to submit lists of journals for which they will purchase copies of contents pages, if the financing and staff time can be arranged. Patrons who enjoy browsing among recent journals might not find SDI attractive, but there is a market for this service when it is offered.

Alternatively, the library may prefer to subscribe to one or more subject sections of the weekly *Current Contents*, which reproduce journal contents pages. *Current Contents* may be held in the library or it may be circulated to faculty members or other researchers. The publication is also available on disc and online. Commercial article delivery services also offer SDI-type access to information through profiles created by librarians or individual patrons.

Journal editors have begun to submit their contents pages to online discussion groups, bulletin boards, and World Wide Web sites at the time of print publication. Some journal publishers offer electronic or faxed copies of the listed articles, for a fee. Some online article suppliers offer a customized table of contents service.

When this evolution has matured, the cost of electronic communication may be higher than that of today's interlibrary loan, but the delay in receipt of the information will be significantly shorter—no longer, perhaps, than the time required to locate a volume in its place on the shelf. Serials public service librarians will need to continue to adapt to the changing technology, however it develops, so they can meet the needs of their patrons with the best aids available.

ACQUIRING SERIAL INFORMATION FROM OUTSIDE THE LIBRARY

With the pricing crisis of the middle to late 1980s, the time was right for commercial services to supply copies of journal articles. This section reviews the interlibrary loan process then assesses the current document delivery situation and speculates about the future.

Interlibrary Loan

Years ago it was not uncommon for libraries to send serials, including bound periodicals, through the interlibrary loan system, usually the postal service. Most libraries changed their loan policies and made serials noncirculating, even to their local patrons. Their reasoning was that removing an entire volume from the library so one person could use a small portion of it was unfair to other patrons who might need to see other small portions. And if local patrons could not take a serial from the library, why should a patron of some other library be able to borrow it? There is risk involved in every circulation, especially interlibrary loan, and in general it is more difficult and more expensive to replace a serial volume than a monograph. Another factor in the decision not to lend serials to other libraries was probably the slowing of the service, both within the libraries and through the mail.

At the same time technological advances enabled manufacturers to produce better and less expensive photocopy machines. Healthy competition among these manufacturers helped bring prices down. Librarians preferred to substitute a photocopy of a periodical article for sending the actual volumes; the copy was either free of charge or cost ten to twenty-five cents a page. All was well for a while, until the cost of labor, paper, and postage forced libraries to increase their photocopy prices by adding handling charges and an increasing minimum amount to each order. The copyright section later in this chapter discusses the implications of the latest copyright law for interlibrary loan.

Interlibrary lending of serials, or substitution of photocopies, is primarily a circulation function, unless the bibliographic citation received from another library is incorrect. The routine transaction involves retrieving the serial from the stacks, copying the requested article, recording the action and mailing or, increasingly, faxing the photocopy to the borrowing library. Added to this procedure may be billing and receipt of payment. On the other hand, interlibrary borrowing of serials, or a patron's request for a photocopy, requires that a staff member verify the citation reported by the patron and determine which holding library is the best choice for the request. This procedure is serials reference work involving a variety of bibliographic tools and in some libraries is entrusted only to librarians.

One way to deter the effect of rising prices for interlibrary loan is to participate in cooperative and reciprocal agreements between and among libraries. The scope of the agreement may be determined by proximity (North Carolina's Triangle Research Libraries Network), subject (medical libraries), or nature of library (Research Libraries Group). The agreement usually is not limited to interlibrary loan but also involves cooperative collection development, joint use of computer facilities, or other expense-cutting projects. Research libraries need cooperative acquisition, cataloging, and reference for long-range survival as responsible institutions.

"Interlibrary loan" (i.e., the acquisition of photocopy in lieu of original) has increased so greatly in recent years, and the process has slowed so dramatically because of understaffing and detailed recordkeeping that a perception exists that the system is no longer effective. Certainly the internal and external costs have grown. While the fax machine has enabled photocopied articles to bypass the postal service, bottlenecks still exist in libraries at both ends of the transaction. In addition, journal publishers have never accepted library copyright policies, particularly the "fair use" concept. They blame patron photocopying and the supply of article copies to other libraries for "lost" subscriptions and declining orders. For example, to the dismay of British journal publishers, BLDSC for years furnished journal articles, either a copy or the original, to requesting libraries throughout the world, with no royalty payments to the publishers. This dispute has been settled, and BLDSC now charges its customers the royalty fee.

The fax machine has fast become the transmission method of choice for journal articles acquired from outside the library. Around 1990 the cost of the equipment fell to a level that libraries could afford to purchase a machine, and at the same time, the quality of fax reproduction improved noticeably. Plain paper fax machines are within reach of most libraries.

Thus, the time was right for the appearance of efficient and automated commercial document suppliers to ease the logjam of interlibrary loan requests.

RISE OF COMMERCIAL DOCUMENT DELIVERY

Electronic technology can provide relief from the photocopying issue in a business that would seem to benefit all parties: the commercial document delivery service. There is little doubt that librarians would prefer to have on-site every journal article that their patrons need, but this has never been a realistic goal. Interlibrary loan is not entirely satisfactory because of the cost and the time delay before one receives the desired article. Now companies such as UnCover, OCLC, UMI, and the Institute for Scientific Information offer article delivery within a day or two, sometimes in five minutes. Many libraries make this service available to patrons, either at no charge or at the user's expense. The transaction is conducted electronically, and the article is delivered by fax or another method of the purchaser's choosing. UnCover's per article charge for gateway libraries is only $6.50 (a fax charge is added for destinations outside the United States). A pass-through royalty fee set by the publisher is added to each copy. The royalty is then paid by UnCover either to the Copyright Clearance Center or directly to the publisher (or author, when the author holds the copyright).

Subscription agents, not wanting to be the losers in this arena, have developed their own document delivery services or have formed partnerships with UnCover (Blackwell and Readmore), the British Library Document Supply Centre (EBSCO), or another company.

Some considerations do exist with commercial document delivery. A few publishers will not permit UnCover and the other suppliers to sell copies of articles in their journals, for example, Haworth Press and Gordon and Breach.

One must order copies directly from these publishers or a designated supplier. Also, some librarians question the need to pay royalties for every article purchased, when they might be exempt by virtue of the fair use provision of the U.S. Copyright Law. These persons are likely to use the commercial services only when the article is not available on interlibrary loan or when the user needs the material immediately.

Librarians have seen the royalty fee for commercially-delivered articles rise noticeably in the few years since the commercial services began operation, and they worry about further increases. The rise in fee is the publisher's effort to compensate for actual and projected loss of subscriptions in favor of document delivery. A few publishers already have priced their articles out of the market, in the opinion of some. Nonetheless, it is tempting to cancel subscriptions to high-priced, low-use scientific journals and substitute library-funded article delivery from one or more of the services. It is the author's conviction that most libraries can cancel many more subscriptions, use some of the money saved to subsidize article delivery, and reallocate most of the savings. They should retain money saved from these cancellations in the materials budget and use it to purchase monographs and new subscriptions.

Librarians need to determine who pays the charge for document delivery. Some libraries have applied part of their former serials funds to document delivery, and patrons receive the articles free. In other cases the library provides the gateway to a service, perhaps costing several thousand dollars a year, and the user pays for each article. In some instances the user pays the entire cost. Many librarians are wondering if the real market for the commercial document delivery services is not the individual researcher instead of the library.

A final consideration in document delivery is administration. Who manages the services within the library? Is this just another form of interlibrary loan? Should ordering and billing not be handled through the acquisitions department? Could this function provide job security for that endangered species, the serials librarian? All of these questions will be answered eventually, and document delivery may become just another library service.

Commercial Article Supply Sources

Library patrons (and some librarians), finding that they were paying several dollars for copies of journal articles on interlibrary loan, were ready for a company that would sell them these copies, transmit them quickly, and take care of any copyright fee. The services are available to both libraries and individuals, so some researchers, who paid for their materials anyway, now bypass the library entirely and deal directly with the supplier. All of the standard commercial services pay a copyright fee (royalty) to the publisher. Fax is standard or available for quick delivery, although the time will come when articles are transmitted via the Internet or the National Information Infrastructure.

Commercial document delivery is not without problems, however. There have been instances of extra charges for verification, much time elapsing before delivery, and orders being filled with copies of articles acquired through interlibrary loan from a library.

Electronic mail is not generally used now for the delivery of articles because of its limitation to text files for most recipients. However, the time will come when sending articles with illustrations is feasible. Also, not all those who purchase documents use electronic mail yet, but the number of "connected" libraries, researchers, and others is growing rapidly. Publishers also have reservations about permitting their articles to be distributed electronically. Two concerns are central: the document can easily be redistributed to one or more other electronic mailboxes, depriving the publisher of royalties; and the integrity of the text is easily compromised through online editing by a recipient.

Because all of these document delivery services are developing rapidly and adding frequent enhancements, first one then another will appear to be the most sophisticated. UnCover, being the first electronic service, lacks some of the features of the later ones, but it is updating its capability. Librarians may want to make more than one service available to interlibrary loan personnel and patrons.[7]

Criteria for Choice of Document Delivery Services

In general, commercial document delivery services survive on their ability to fill a library's or an individual's information needs, fill these needs quickly, and supply articles at an acceptable price. These are three major criteria in evaluating a service, but there are others; and there are distinct differences in suppliers.

Before a library subscribes to any electronic document delivery service, it should arrange for a free, limited trial period in order to evaluate the service on the following criteria. If no such trial is available, the message is clear.

Coverage. One needs to know the scope of the document delivery service being considered: How many titles does it include? In what subject areas does the company specialize? What time frame does the database cover? From whom does the supplier get its articles?

As in selecting periodical indexes, the size and mission of the library determines how close a match in size and subject matter is best; if one needs articles from magazines, a service specializing in science journals would be a waste of funds.

Some document delivery services are general, broad in scope, among them UnCover, OCLC's First Search, and UMI. Others concentrate on science journals but are not limited to them, for example, ISI's The Genuine Article. In addition, some services supply documents in only one discipline, such as engineering, physics, or mathematics; others send articles from one or a few large publishers. With the variety of options, the library should be able to find a compatible document supplier.

A library that has cancelled a significant proportion of its journals collection recently will be well served by a database that does not have an extensive back file, while a library that has grown or added programs will need a back file to compensate for serials never acquired.

Companies supplying copies of journal articles get these articles from various sources. Some, such as the BLDSC and the Canada Institute for Scientific and Technical Information (CISTI) have a large collection of journals on site and have only to retrieve the volume and scan or photocopy the article. Other suppliers have entered into arrangements with libraries and get article copies from those collections. The latter practice can mean a delay in receipt of the article.

Method of Access. The service that has ideal coverage for one's library is a good choice only if it is accessible to librarians and/or patrons. Nearly all libraries are on the Internet now; this is a popular means of accessing the supplier's database and communicating with customer service staff members. However, there are times when only a conversation will resolve the problem. Will the service accept telephone calls and fax requests? Announced availability of e-mail addresses, toll-free telephone numbers, and fax machines is good, but can you get through to someone and get an immediate answer?

The Internet is not necessarily the best way to access a document delivery database because of traffic; inability to connect to the service may be very frustrating and delay the receipt of a needed article. In situations where assured access is essential or highly desired, the library or consortium may be a "gateway" to the company's files and have (for a price) a direct line to the database. There may be services where is it mandatory that the library serve as a gateway, and if the speed is not required and the cost not justified, perhaps another service would be a better fit.

Some suppliers require that one subscribe to (or become a member of) another service to get to the document supply module. This structure adds another level of cost, unless the library already subscribes to the broader service. A variation on this practice is two-tiered pricing, where subscribers to the parent system pay less than those who are not subscribers.

Costs. As noted above, the prices of a document delivery service can vary depending upon other conditions. Thus, the advertised price per article is not the entire story. One must determine whether there are separate fees for processing, delivery, and actual document cost and what these fees are. What form of delivery is the default and included in the base price? At the time of this writing fax transmittal is the fastest method. Some services charge for fax delivery and others do not. In some cases rush requests carry a premium fee; in other instances 24-hour service is the norm.

Another facet of costs is the means of payment. Some services require a library to establish a deposit account while others will bill. Credit card payment has become popular for some services, especially those catering to individual users as much as to libraries. It is no longer unheard of for a library to acquire a credit card for document delivery use, but most libraries find some other arrangement more convenient. However, the credit card account is ideal for individual purchasers.

Copyright. A detailed discussion of copyright and its application to commercial document delivery comes later in this chapter. Suffice it to say here that one needs to determine whether the company being considered provides copyright cleared services. In other words, does the library pay a royalty fee for each transaction? If so, is the copyright fee bundled with the service's document processing cost, or is it separate? Does the company reveal the amount of this fee before one has committed to ordering?

If the document supplier does not include the publisher's stated royalty fee in the cost of the article, the librarian should proceed carefully and should remit the correct amount to the Copyright Clearance Center or to the publisher—if the article is not within fair use guidelines and if the librarian can determine the amount of the fee.

Speed. The speed at which a person needs information varies with both the person and the specific instance. There are times, however, when the article should arrive rapidly. Services differ in the speed at which they can supply a document, in part because they differ in their hours of operation. Is the service available on weekends and holidays? Can requests be submitted in the early morning hours? Any company aiming to be an international supplier must have around the clock access and must account for the fact that holidays vary by country. Even services having no international aspirations need to remember that individual researchers keep different schedules.

Quality. Consider here both quality of service and quality of product. How often does the service get it right? If an incorrect article arrives, is it possible that the person ordering it inadvertently asked for the wrong thing? The system should have checks to ensure that the purchaser verifies the accuracy of the order.

Some photocopiers, scanners, and fax machines are better and in better repair than others, and differences in quality show up in the clarity of the product. Even careless maintenance of the company's equipment may reduce the legibility of an article copy. Will the service replace an illegible document?

Customer Service. Problems are bound to occur in any heavily-used system, and the supplier's customer service personnel and policies need to be evaluated. Is someone available when you call, fax, or e-mail? Can representatives answer your questions? Do they advise you of the status of your requests? As in any customer service operation, courtesy is essential and its absence is reason for complaint.

UnCover

The first company to take advantage of the market for commercially-supplied copies of journal articles was UnCover, Inc. (originally called CARL, Inc.), then the for-profit arm of the Colorado Alliance of Research Libraries (CARL), headquartered in Denver. Knight-Ridder, Inc. purchased UnCover in mid-1995. In late 1988 CARL began centralized check-in of its members' journals, in order to create a database of tables of contents (a current awareness service) and bibliographic citations to articles (an index). Boolean searches are possible. When the database had grown to a sufficient size, CARL, Inc. announced the UnCover program, whereby a library or an individual can request online a copy of an article included in the database and have it delivered to a fax machine in a very short time. Individuals (and libraries if they are able) can charge the cost of the article to a credit card. A library can also create a deposit account for article purchase or arrange for monthly billings. UnCover is now available via the Internet to anyone who wants it, but association with a subscribing library gets a better price for the articles. One can also order articles from BLDSC through the UnCover menu.

CARL officers entered into agreements with journal publishers regarding royalty payments, so there would be no question of violating the copyright law. To the UnCover fee for an article is added the royalty fee set by the publisher. The total of these two prices is the cost of the article. In many cases UnCover sells articles at less cost than the charges of the lending library in the interlibrary loan system.

In late 1995 the UnCover database promises 24-hour service for articles from 17,000 journals. The file grows at approximately 5,000 citations daily. Because data are entered at the time of check-in, UnCover is always current in its citations. Over the years since 1988 UnCover has enhanced its database by adding titles from the collections of several research and special libraries outside of Colorado, including the University of Maryland, University of Hawaii, Linda Hall Library and the National Library of Australia. The special collections in these libraries have enhanced the scope of the UnCover database. The list of titles should grow to around 20,000.

When they receive a request for an article, UnCover staff in participating libraries retrieve the issue and scan the article. The text, in turn, goes to a bank of fax servers and on to the fax number listed on the request. The final copy at the purchaser's machine is the only paper copy of the article. The copyright fee imposed by the publisher is paid by UnCover to the Copyright Clearance Center or the publisher or other copyright holder directly. In the future UnCover hopes to be able to send articles to computer workstations as well, but first the copyright implications must be resolved.

Certain publishers have agreed to permit UnCover to retain articles on an optical storage device after the first request. For these articles, so noted in the database, the purchaser receives one-hour service at worst; often the copy arrives in a very few minutes.

UnCover continues to grow and to add new services. One of these, called UnCover Complete, makes available articles published before 1988 or items not indexed, such as book reviews and letters to the editor. REVEAL is a popular alerting service whereby an individual or a library requests that tables of contents for one or more journals be sent to an electronic mail box as each issue arrives. The recipient may then order copies of articles using the contents list and the mailbox.

A recent enhancement to UnCover is called SUMO, SUbsidized Unmediated Ordering. This feature permits library patrons to place orders for articles that the library pays for, while the library sets dollar limits for individual articles. Also, the library can block subsidized orders for articles from titles held in its collection.

Because UnCover is aging and lacks some of the most user-friendly features of other services, it has introduced Personal UnCover Navigator (PUN), a graphical user interface that provides easier searching and ordering than the original system. PUN is intended to facilitate individuals' access to UnCover's services, as well as to add new features.

The CARL home page on the World Wide Web enables interested persons to view a list of journals in the UnCover system and to keep current with enhancements. The URL is: http://www.carl.org.

OCLC ContentsFirst and ArticleFirst

Through its FirstSearch service OCLC offers librarians and library users a table of contents database, ContentsFirst, and an article delivery capability, ArticleFirst. In late 1995 the services provide access to nearly 11,000 journals, indexing not only articles, but also news stories, editorials, technical communications, proceedings, and letters to the editor. The indexed journals are primarily in English, with some multilingual publications. The databases include more than 1,000,000 articles in a variety of subjects dating from January 1990. They are updated daily and claim a growth rate of approximately 1,000,000 new articles each year. Of benefit to interlibrary loan personnel is the inclusion of OCLC holdings symbols and the ability for PRISM users to generate loan requests electronically from ArticleFirst.

OCLC does not provide article copies itself, but acts as vendor for several document suppliers such as UMI InfoStore, ISI's "The Genuine Article," EBSCODoc, and BLDSC. Its objective is to offer at least two sources for each article. Prices for a single document vary according to supplier and method of delivery (fax, rush mail, and regular mail). Royalty fee is not listed separately from the supplier's handling charge.

ContentsFirst will deliver journal tables of contents automatically, either to an individual electronic mailbox or to a library mailbox for distribution (either electronically or in print) to multiple persons. OCLC charges the library a one-time fee to set up an account and an annual subscription fee for each journal. The rate varies according to whether the address is domestic or international and whether the contents go to one person or several.

Further features of FirstSearch (and separate from ArticleFirst and ContentsFirst) are PapersFirst and ProceedingsFirst. Through the databases at BLDSC, users can locate and order papers presented at conferences, symposia, and other meetings worldwide.

Most of the information in this section about the OCLC services came from the organization's World Wide Web site, and that is the best place to learn of changes and enhancements. The URL is: http://www.oclc.org.

UMI InfoStore

Long a supplier of microform and paper copies of dissertations and journals, UMI recently began to promote its article delivery services. The company purchased The Information Store, a San Francisco document delivery company in 1994 and merged its resources with those of UMI. Now, the UMI InfoStore supplies documents both from the UMI collection of 15,000 titles and from beyond this collection. The subject scope of the collection is general, with specialties in science and the social sciences.

The internal collection includes not only journal articles, but magazines, conference proceedings, newspapers, and government documents. The level of the source publications ranges from popular to highly technical. For documents not on hand, one can send a complete bibliographic citation for searching and retrieval of the material. Even if the complete citation is missing, for a finder's fee, the company will do the necessary research to identify the article, report, or other document. All in all, UMI promises to deliver material of a vast number of types, including standards, government documents, patents, AV material, maps, press releases, training materials, advertisements, and manuscripts, among others. The UMI InfoStore offers, in addition to features already mentioned, status reports, customized monthly billing and usage reports for libraries.

Twenty-four hour delivery is standard for documents from inside the collection, via first class mail, fax, overnight courier, or Ariel electronic delivery, with price determined by delivery method. Four-hour rush delivery is also an option by fax or Ariel. Standard delivery for documents from outside the collection is by first class mail within two to five days. Rush delivery, same-day or next day rush service or overnight courier, costs more.

One may order articles directly from the UMI InfoStore by telephone or fax during US east coast working hours (until 9:30 p.m.), or one may access UMI's Periodical Abstracts database through OCLC's FirstSearch. Others of the company's ProQuest databases will be added to the FirstSearch link. Some articles may be ordered through OCLC's FastDoc for one-hour delivery. Payment may be made by credit card or deposit account. As of August 1995, UMI promised that soon their home page on the World Wide Web will contain the full catalog of their titles and the ability to place document orders through the home page. The URL for the UMI InfoStore is http://www.umi.com.

The Genuine Article

This service of the Institute for Scientific Information has been supplying tear sheets of journal articles for many years. Now it can accept electronic orders over the Internet to an electronic mail address and through several sources including OCLC's ArticleFirst, Dialog, STN, and others. Postal service is the standard delivery method, although rush mail, courier, and fax are more expensive options. ISI offers 24-hour turnaround on all orders. Purchasers have the option of using their credit cards for payment, as well as deposit accounts, prepayment, and monthly billing. The Genuine Article supplies copies from about 7,000 research journals from 1989 to date. There is also an "Extended Service" that includes an additional 6,000 journals and other publications dating back as far as the 1800s. Although it is primarily a supplier of scientific articles, The Genuine Article collection includes social sciences and the humanities.

In 1995 ISI announced the ISI Electronic Library pilot project, designed to permit both publishers and users to test the variables associated with electronic journal distribution. The prototype, in partnership with IBM and 350 STM publishers, will offer libraries site licenses for electronic access to journals listed in *Current Contents: Life Sciences* to which the library has a paper subscription.

Subscription Agents' Services

Some years ago subscription agents saw document delivery as a new service to libraries that would compensate them for the loss of revenue resulting from library journal cancellations and reduced discounts from publishers. Many agents began to develop their own document delivery services, but the challenge apparently proved too expensive. None of the original vendor projects has survived. Instead, the agents formed partnerships with other services or purchased existing companies. This section discusses the document delivery efforts of two large American subscription agents.

Faxon Finder. Faxon's document delivery service received perhaps the most publicity of any of the early projects, and it is taking a long time to become reality. Early reports indicated that Faxon was targeting the end-user as its market, but it now appears that the company is directing its efforts toward libraries and is concentrating on delivering table-of-contents information and facilitating actual delivery of articles from other companies.

According to a recent announcement, Faxon has established document delivery relationships with two document delivery companies: the Institute for Scientific Information (ISI) and Information Express. Faxon's partners will supply articles at a discount off their regular prices in conjunction with Faxon's table-of-contents database, Faxon Finder. Users will have the option of choosing 24-hour fax, courier, or U.S. mail delivery, and document delivery payment options will include credit card, deposit account, or invoice. The companies will provide documents for all titles found in Finder unless the article is copyright restricted.

As described in promotional material from the agent's World Wide Web site (http://www.faxon.com), the Faxon Finder database contains the tables of contents of more than 12,000 journals and other serials (in late 1995), dating from January 1990. Entries include not only articles, but also letters to the editor, book reviews, obituaries, and all other citable references from the contents pages. The system supports Boolean searching for both journal title and article title, as well as wildcard searches and proximity searches. The ISSN is another means of access to the journals. Unlike other services, Faxon Finder lists up to ten authors of an article.

The three licensing options are Faxon Finder Online, Faxon Finder on CD-ROM, and Faxon Finder Onsite (database site license). The library purchases online access on a subscription basis for Internet, dial-up, dedicated line, or X.25 communications protocol connection. Faxon Finder Onsite allows libraries the flexibility to set up the Finder database on their own networks. Charges for a Faxon Finder site license depend on hardware, software and telecommunication requirements and duration of the license. The Windows-based CD-ROM version of the service comes with a built-in document ordering feature for use with a fax machine. An additional feature is the option to link and display the library's local serial title holdings data in Finder on CD-ROM.

Faxon updates the online database daily, and the CD-ROM monthly. Faxon Finder data appear 7-10 days after Faxon's supplier libraries receive the table of contents.

The newest enhancement to Faxon Finder is Faxon Flash Search Profiling, by which one may receive a weekly delivery of specific tables of contents or article citation lists by e-mail or fax. The company offers the WWW version of Faxon Flash; Faxon FlashTOC is offered through its home page, where users can search the Faxon Finder title list and select and order tables of contents. Faxon Flash is also available through subscription to Finder or by sending a request to Finder@Faxon.com. ISI and Information Express supply articles listed on Flash tables of contents, where permitted by the publisher.

EBSCODoc. EBSCO is heavily involved in document delivery, primarily to libraries, through a number of services. The company's World Wide Web site (http://vax.ebsco com) describes EBSCODoc as "a full service document delivery company offering fast and efficient document delivery from an electronically linked network of inhouse and world wide library sources....We also offer several databases for searching, browsing, document ordering and Current Awareness."

In 1994 EBSCO bought Dynamic Information Corporation of Burlingame CA, a document delivery company built on partnerships with owners of intellectual property. The company, now EBSCODoc, has employees in ten or more sites for document retrieval and transmission, as well as deciphering problem citations. The standard service level is shipment of a document 24 hours after receipt of the request. There are a number of shipping options, but first class or international air mail are standard.

EBSCO also offers its Current Citations Journal Coverage, which includes BLDSC's Inside Information, tables of contents for its 10,000 most requested journals, and the ADONIS database of more than 500 biomedical journals. Current Citations, heavily scientific, technical, and medical, is available by online subscription (via the Internet, PC/modem, or dedicated terminal), by CD-ROM subscription, and by license on magnetic tape. Search options include keyword, author, article title, journal title, volume/issue, ISSN and SICI (Serials Item Contribution Identifier). OCLC's ArticleFirst also lists EBSCO availability and pricing information.

According to information on the WWW site, the company offers "a keyword searchable database of citations to all of the articles found within ADONIS." One can order an article on the Web or by other methods and receive a fax copy within 30 minutes.

In addition to document delivery, EBSCO makes tables of contents available to libraries and individuals through its EBSCODoc ALERT. One may order copies of articles from the alerting capability. The scope of this service is currently 29,000 titles, including the BLDSC Inside Information and its contents from 15,000 currently-received conferences and ADONIS. There is an extensive array of access methods and delivery formats, including licensing for redistribution of the contents within the same institution.

For all of EBSCO's document delivery services the librarian may take advantage of quantity discounts, some of which are as much as 50 percent lower than the standard price. Some services also offer discounts for ordering through the World Wide Web. Most prices are listed on the EBSCO Web site.

EBSCO has always been known for its willingness to customize invoices and reports to meet librarians' needs. This policy holds true for document delivery services; data are included and arranged according to the customer's wishes.

SwetScan. Swets Subscription Services, based in The Netherlands, offers SwetScan, containing tables of contents from 13,000 scholarly journals and supported by a "rapid document delivery service." This subscription agent conducts a very active consolidation service and thus receives a large number of journals in its offices. Personnel scan and edit these journals' contents pages for SwetScan, which supports Boolean searching at author, keyword, subject, and journal title level. Swets is negotiating with publishers to receive prepublication contents data in order to provide faster information.

A library or a consortium may subscribe to the entire database or receive a subset based on areas of interest. Subsets are charged by title. Subscribers have a large number of access options: diskette, magnetic tape, ftp (file transfer protocol), electronic mail, via DataSwets (the company's online bibliographic and subscription service), and paper. In the United States and Canada SwetScan is available online from CISTI. The actual ordering of documents occurs through DataSwets. The company provides 24 to 48 hour air mail service (fax is extra) and gets the documents from BLDSC. Further information may be found at Swets' World Wide Web site, http://www.swets.nl.

FROM ARTICLE COPIES TO FULL TEXT

Accustomed now to the ease of acquiring journal articles electronically, library patrons of all types have expressed a desire for full-text articles to be available at or near their workstations. Whether full text will replace most of the commercial tables of contents services or exist alongside them remains to be seen. This section discusses two types of full-text journal articles: those from a supplier of journals from multiple publishers and those from an individual publisher.

Full Text from Multiple Publishers

Undergraduate and high school students are very fond of viewing and copying online or CD-ROM collections of the complete text of journal articles. Now that electronic technology can transmit and printers can reproduce illustrations, this means of access to periodicals is increasingly attractive. This section discusses examples of such resources, but it must begin with a system that is not intended for students.

The earliest experiment in distributing full text of separate journal articles was ADONIS, originally containing in machine-readable form the contents of 219 biomedical journals from four scientific and medical publishers. The ADONIS project's objective was to test the idea "that publishers can gain copyright revenue by supplying their journals in machine-readable form for document delivery centers to print out individual journal articles on demand at lower cost than was photocopying from back runs stored on shelves."[8] Planning for ADONIS began in 1979, but it was not until appropriate technology became available in the late 1980s that national libraries and commercial document suppliers began to receive article texts on compact disc. The composition of ADONIS is broader now than in the beginning, with more than 500 journals included, although the vast file is still not intended for most local libraries. Some pharmaceutical librarians can justify the expense of purchasing ADONIS, but most librarians cannot.

The longtime microfilm supplier UMI produces a number of full-text periodicals databases on compact disc, for example, Business Dateline and CBS News Transcripts. Annual subscriptions include monthly updates, ProQuest search and retrieval software, documentation, and toll-free technical support. In most cases additional backfile coverage is available.

UMI also markets full-image databases, including Business Periodicals and Magazine Express. Each product consists of an index database for complete bibliographic citations and abstracts and a full-image database containing scanned images of articles. The company promises "laser-quality reprints." The library can also lease or purchase a workstation from UMI that is appropriate for these databases.

Information Access Company (IAC), (WWW address: http://www.iacnet.com) publisher of the extremely popular Infotrac periodical index, now markets on a subscription basis several online products that contain many journals in full text. Other types of materials included in these databases are newspapers, news wires, and research reports. Examples of IAC full-text databases are *Magazine Index Select/ASAP*, 2-year coverage of 230 titles for small public libraries; *Academic Index/ASAP* coverage of 550 journals for 3 years and suited to smaller academic libraries; *Business and Company ProFile*; and *Expanded Academic Index/ASAP*. IAC offers backfiles for many of the databases. Libraries subscribe to as many of these services as they wish and receive state-of-the-art monitors and printers. The remotely-located services may be accessed through the library's online catalog menu inhouse or through password by members of the institution community. Where there is full text of an article, the user may elect to print the article, either on a printer attached to the computer or terminal being used or on the publisher-supplied printer, which gives an excellent reproduction of the original article. There is no per-use or per-print charge.

EBSCO Publishing produces several abstracting resources on CD-ROM which have full text for fifteen to thirty percent of the journals or magazines included. Among these is *Academic Abstracts FullTEXT* with text for 125 of its 800 abstracted journals and "thousands of *Magill Book Reviews.*" Another product, *MAS FullTEXT Elite*, gives abstracting coverage for about 400 general interest magazines and searchable full text for 125 of them, plus the Magill book reviews. *Public Library FullTEXT* provides abstracts and indexing for 850 magazines and full text for 125 of them. Several other compact disc abstracting resources include a smaller number of full-text journals.

Publishers as Article Brokers

Not being willing to lose control of articles in their journals, several large publishers launched experimental document delivery projects, some in cooperation with libraries. The earliest efforts involved delivery of articles, but later publishers began to concentrate on transmission of entire issues of journals. People wondered whether these projects would be the first of many or only a transitional stage on the way to true electronic publishing. What is significant is the partnership between publishers and librarians in an effort to provide access to journal contents in ways that are fair to both library and publisher.

In 1991 Elsevier Science Publishers and a number of American research libraries initiated the experimental TULIP Project (The University Library Information Project), in which every library received bitmapped images of the text of Elsevier's journals in materials science. Each library took responsibility for developing software to make the journals accessible on its campus. The experiment was to last for three years, at which time it was to be evaluated and any future course determined. In 1995 Elsevier announced that it was following other courses; many of its journals are available online in full text through OCLC and will later become accessible in various other ways.

Springer Verlag New York, in 1992, in cooperation with Bell Labs and the University of California at San Francisco, created Red Sage, an experiment using Bell Labs' Right Pages software. This project, using medical journals, came close to replicating the experience of handling a journal issue, with virtual pageturning. Other publishers became participants in the effort, but Red Sage quietly went underground as changes were made. The future of Red Sage appears to be uncertain.

More recently, Johns Hopkins University Press, in cooperation with the university library, has begun to mount all of its journals on the World Wide Web. Also, MIT Press, working with the MIT Library as archive site, is publishing *The Chicago Journal of Theoretical Computer Science.*

These examples are only the beginning of projects on which publishers and librarians will work together to bring electronic full-text information to scholars and other library patrons.

COPYRIGHT

The United States Constitution in Article 1, section 8, clause 8, defines the purpose of copyright as "to promote the Progress of Science and useful Arts by securing for limited Times to Authors and Inventors the exclusive Right to their respective Writings and Discoveries." The intent of this clause is to balance public and private interests in intellectual property, to protect the author's rights and to promote access to the author's ideas. This section does not attempt to discuss copyright issues broadly or in depth, but focuses on the perceived questions and problems of the mid-1990s. The literature contains excellent articles by such persons as Scott Bennett[9] and Laura Gasaway,[10] from the librarian's perspective and Janet Fisher[11] and Carol Risher[12] from the publisher's perspective.

In 1976 the United States Congress passed a copyright law to replace both the 1908 law and the "Gentlemen's Agreement" of 1935, which defined the concept of "fair use" regarding reproduction of materials under copyright. The development of rapid, inexpensive copy machines has created a volume of library photocopying which could not have been imagined in 1935. Congress, assisted by librarians, authors, and publishers, worked for nearly twenty years to write a law that would be fair to all parties. The result was somewhat ambiguous and provided an opportunity for the scholarly and artistic communities to work with it, interpret it, and test it. Since 1976, developments in facsimile and computer technology have complicated the situation even more.

At the implementation of the new U.S. Copyright Law (PL-553) in 1978, librarians did not know whether their continued adherence to the principle of fair use—one copy for scholarly purposes—would be in jeopardy. The law required librarians to post warning signs at public copy machines. These statements of copyright restriction transferred the responsibility for compliance to the patrons using the unsupervised copiers. Thus, the library has no responsibility for personal copying made on its machines, so long as the copyright notice is displayed. Interlibrary loan librarians had to keep records of the number of copies made from each journal published within the previous five years. The law required library photocopy centers to post a warning notice/disclaimer and to have the patron sign a statement that the material was to be used for scholarly purposes and would not be resold. Otherwise, librarians could only begin to work under their interpretation of the provisions of the law and, on the basis of their experience, assess the effect it had on their photocopying of library materials. One early review of the copyright law indicated that it had not had any great effect on copying practices of either libraries or their patrons.[13] Continued observation of the law appears to support this hypothesis; it is not library photocopying which has changed, only recordkeeping.

Journal publishers were not happy with the fair use provision of the 1976 law and claimed that it led to lost revenue from subscription cancellations and, thus, higher prices. Their response was to expand their practice of charging libraries a subscription rate significantly higher than that for individuals. Dual pricing became the norm for scholarly journals, and librarians complained by means of articles, letters to publishers, and face-to-face discussions in professional meetings. However, the dual pricing structure continued. Many publishers now list a subscription price, then offer a greatly reduced rate for individuals who state that the journal is for their own use. This practice is just a public relations gesture to avoid the label "Institutional Rate." Often the statement of the price that libraries must pay is followed by an explanation that this rate includes the right to make either unrestricted or limited photocopies of the contents, without permission of the publisher or payment of a fee. Sometimes this offer carries meaning, but often it adds no privilege beyond that already granted by the copyright law. At the bottom of the first page of each article, many scholarly journals print a coded line that identifies the article and gives the price to be paid for photocopying it. This should not intimidate librarians who are exercising their legal rights, but it should be observed when it applies.

Certain commercial journal publishers have attempted to convince serials librarians to subscribe to contracts which claim to permit unlimited copying and to free library staff members from the necessity of recording and paying for each reproduction of the publisher's serials. The librarian must examine carefully each of these "offers" from publishers to determine whether it is either necessary or a bargain. Librarians have a responsibility to observe the copyright law, but they must not hesitate to reject expensive ploys that attempt to charge libraries for photocopying that should be free of royalty fees. The librarian who feels that he or she cannot interpret adequately these communications from publishers, should seek advice from the institution's legal counsel.

There is restlessness among some librarians and authors about the practice of an author's transferring copyright to the journal publisher, specifically their belief that it leads to runaway subscription price increases. One response was the "Model University Policy Regarding Faculty Publication in Scientific and Technical Scholarly Journals," developed by a joint committee of faculty, librarians, and university press editors from the Triangle Research Libraries Network (Duke University, North Carolina State University, and the University of North Carolina at Chapel Hill). The document is prefaced by a background paper and a review of the issues, including response to criticisms of an earlier draft. The policy itself is:

> As a non-profit institution which relies heavily on government and foundation grants to support its research activities, this university asks its faculty to publish their scientific and technical research results in journals supported by universities, scholarly associations, or

other organizations sharing the mission to promote widespread, reasonable-cost access to research information. Where this is not possible, faculty should use the model "Authorization to Publish" form...to ensure that control of copyright in the published results of their university research remains within the academic research community.

Where publishers' pricing practices would restrict widespread access to research results, individual retention of copyright to scientific and technical journal articles will help to ensure that faculty maintain their rights individually or collectively to disseminate this information, as appropriate, to colleagues, students and the public at large using existing and emerging print and electronic technologies. Current copyright law specifically gives the owner the right to reproduce, distribute, prepare derivative versions, and to perform or display articles or other works.

The model "Authorization to Publish" form stipulates that the article will be published with a statement on the first page notifying readers that copyright remains with the author(s) and giving permission for the noncommercial reproduction of the article for educational or research purposes. Thus, only commercial reproduction beyond initial publication in the journal would require that the author(s) be contacted directly for permission. Faculty may also want to consider negotiating a contract which gives the publisher a nonexclusive right to sell licenses to reproduce the article at agreed-upon reasonable rates (for instance, to commercial copy services which reproduce articles for use in university "course packs").[14]

Not all librarians are convinced that the TRLN policy is the best course, and it would not be successful unless it were widely adopted by universities and other nonprofit institutions. Publishers, quite naturally, have nothing good to say about the concept. Nevertheless, it is a first step toward discussion and resolution of what librarians perceive as a serious problem.

With the appearance of commercial document delivery services, the traditional copyright controversy may be quieting. By using UnCover or another supplier, the library and the individual purchaser forego the fair use right and pay a copyright fee on every article purchased. At the same time, the library does not need to count articles and keep records. The journal publisher receives a royalty fee for every copy made by a commercial supplier; the fee is set by the publisher. With the growth in popularity of the commercial services, publishers have begun to increase their royalty fees as they increase subscription prices. What has been traditionally a low revenue generator— royalty payments—is becoming a source of significant revenue to compensate for the loss of prepaid subscriptions to the entire journals.

At the same time, the development of electronic publishing brings other concerns. The ease of altering the text of an article and of retransmitting an electronic document cause publishers to fear further serious loss of revenue. Librarians (and patrons who are aware of the controversy) insist on their fair use rights and are forming consortia to provide electronic document delivery to their constituents. Representatives of six library associations developed a Working Document dated January 18, 1995 that spells out these rights in the electronic environment, as they understand them. The document follows in its entirety:

FAIR USE IN THE ELECTRONIC AGE:
SERVING THE PUBLIC INTEREST

The genius of United States copyright law is that, in conformance with its Constitutional foundation, it balances the intellectual property interests of authors, publishers, and copyright owners with society's need for the free exchange of ideas. Taken together, fair use and other public rights to utilize copyrighted works, as confirmed in the Copyright Act of 1976, constitute indispensable legal doctrines for promoting the dissemination of knowledge, while ensuring authors, publishers, and copyright owners appropriate protection of their creative works and economic investments.

The fair use provision of the Copyright Act allows reproduction and other uses of copyrighted works under certain conditions for purposes such as criticism, comment, news reporting, teaching (including multiple copies for classroom use), scholarship, and research. Additional provisions of the law allow uses specifically permitted by Congress to further educational and library activities. The preservation and continuation of these balanced rights in an electronic environment, as well as in traditional formats, are essential to the free flow of information and to the development of an information infrastructure that serves the public interest.

It follows that the benefits of new technologies should flow to the public as well as to copyright proprietors. As more information becomes available only in electronic formats, the public's legitimate right to use copyrighted material must be protected. In order for copyright to truly serve its purpose of "promoting progress," the public's right of fair use must continue in the electronic era, and these lawful uses of copyrighted works must be allowed without individual transaction fees.

Without infringing copyright, the public has a right to expect:
- to read, listen to, or view publicly marketed copyrighted material privately, on site, or remotely;
- to browse through publicly marketed copyrighted material;
- to experiment with variations of copyrighted material for fair use purposes, while preserving the integrity of the original;
- to make or have made a first generation copy, for personal use, of an article or other small part of a publicly marketed copyrighted work, or a work in a library's collection, for such purpose as study, scholarship, or research; and
- to make transitory copies if ephemeral or incidental to a lawful use and if retained only temporarily.

Without infringing copyright, nonprofit libraries and other Section 108 libraries, on behalf of their clientele, should be able:
- to use electronic technologies to preserve copyrighted materials in their collections;
- to provide copyrighted materials as part of electronic reserve room service;
- to provide copyrighted materials as part of electronic interlibrary loan service; and
- to avoid liability, after posting appropriate copyright notices, for the unsupervised actions of their users.

Users, libraries, and educational institutions have a right to expect:
- that the terms of licenses will not restrict fair use or other lawful library or educational uses;
- that U.S. government works and other public domain materials will be readily available without restriction and at a government price not exceeding the marginal cost of dissemination; and

- that rights of use for nonprofit education apply in face-to-face teaching, and in transmittal or broadcast to remote locations, where educational institutions of the future must increasingly reach their students.

Carefully constructed copyright guidelines and practices have emerged for the print environment to ensure that there is a balance between the rights of users and those of authors, publishers, and copyright owners. New understandings, developed by all stakeholders, will help to ensure that this balance is retained in a rapidly changing electronic environment. This working statement addresses lawful uses of copyrighted works in both the print and electronic environments.[15]

If it took twenty years for Congress to write and pass the 1976 U.S. Copyright Law, one wonders about the next revision. The parties involved cannot agree at this time about whether the country needs a new law to account for electronic publication and transmission of intellectual property, much less the provisions of such a law. Questions abound on this emotional issue, and there is promise of exciting times ahead.

NOTES

1. *Union List of Serials in Libraries of the United States and Canada*, 3rd ed. (New York: H.W. Wilson Company, 1965), pp. [iii]-[iv].

2. *The British Library Document Supply Centre Facts & Figures*. (Boston Spa, England: British Library Document Supply Centre, April 1995).

3. Council on Library Resources, *A National Periodicals Center: Technical Development Plan* (Washington DC: 1978). The Plan's "Summary" is reprinted in *Serials Librarian* 3 (1979): 338-342. The quotation is from page xi of the *Technical Development Plan*.

4. National Commission on Library and Information Science, *Annual Report, 1978/79* (Washington DC: 1980), p. 22.

5. Clara D. Brown and Lynn S. Smith, *Serials: Past, Present and Future* (Birmingham AL: EBSCO Industries, 1980), p. 315.

6. Public Law 96-374-Oct. 3, 1980: *An Act to Amend and Extend the Higher Education Act of 1965*, 94 Stat. 1387.

7. Janifer Holt and Karen A. Schmidt, "CARL UnCover2 or Faxon Finder? A Comparison of Articles and Journals in CARL UnCover2 and Faxon Finder." *Library Resources and Technical Services* 39 (1995): 221-228.

8. Barrie T. Stern and Robert M. Campbell, "ADONIS: Publishing Journal Articles in CD-ROM." *Advances in Serials Management* 3 (1989): 2.

9. Scott Bennett, "The Copyright Challenge: Strengthening the Public Interest in the Digital Age." *Library Journal* 119:9 (November 15, 1994): 34-37.

10. Laura N. Gasaway, "Scholarly Publication and Copyright in Networked Electronic Publishing." *Library Trends* 43 (Spring 1995): 679-700. See also note 12.

11. Janet Fisher, "Intellectual Property Issues and Licensing: Enhancing Dissemination of Scholarly Research." *Scholarly Publishing Today* 3, no. 5/6 (September/December 1994): 3-6.

12. Carol A. Risher and Laura Gasaway, "The Great Copyright Debate: Two Experts Face Off on How to Deal with Intellectual Property in the Digital Age." *Library Journal* 119:15 (September 15, 1994): 34-37.

13. John Steuben, "Interlibrary Loan of Photocopies of Articles Under the New Copyright Law," *Special Libraries* 70 (1979): 227-232.

14. Copyright Policy Task Force of the Triangle Research Libraries Network. "Model University Policy Regarding Faculty Publication in Scientific and Technical Scholarly Journals: A Background Paper and Review of the Issues," Durham, Raleigh and Chapel Hill, North Carolina (July 1993): 1-2.

15. The document was published in *ARL* 179 (March 1995): 5.

INDEX